The Centrality
of Jesus Christ To
Calvary

W9-CZZ-112

Merla Hughe

WWW. Seekovex. Com

Where there is no
Vision the People will
Certainly go to pieces!

Vision Comes — By way of Revelation
of the Spirit of God as we pray &
meditate on God's Word — (Rev. - Spirit).
will live in every world that God has given us
much of God!

The
Writings
of
T. Austin-Sparks

Volume II

A limited edition

The
HOUSE
of
GOD

The House of God
All *new* material in this edition
copyrighted by SeedSowers Publishing House
Printed in the United States of America
All rights reserved

Published by The SeedSowers
        P.O.Box 285, Sargent, GA 30275
        1-800-827 9825

Cover design by Jenny Jeffries

Library of Congress Cataloging-in-Publication Data

Sparks, T. Austin
        The House of God / T. Austin-Sparks
        ISBN 0-940232-63-4
        1. Spiritual Life.   1. Title

Times New Roman 12pt

The
HOUSE
of
GOD

by
T. Austin-Sparks

This volume contains
eleven of T. Austin-Sparks' books,
all on the subject of
The House of God.

Preface

T. Austin-Sparks is one of the great figures of the twentieth century who ministered outside of the organized church. For over forty years he held forth at Honor Oak in London, England. The conferences he spoke at, both in Europe and America, have had a profound influence on our time.

Brother Sparks published over one hundred books and pamphlets. The majority of them have ceased to be available to the Christian family. This has been a great loss, as the content of his message has placed him in the category of only a few men of the last one hundred years.

T. Austin-Sparks and Watchman Nee, more than any other men, have influenced the lives of believers who are outside traditional churches. We have felt very strongly that all of brother Sparks' books and pamphlets should be brought back into print if at all possible.

This is the second volume of a series that will ultimately contain all of his ministry that found its way into books.

Read T. Austin-Sparks. It is our hope that in republishing his works, his ministry will take wings again, and the influence of his word will spread across the English-speaking world. Hopefully this will give his message a greater influence than ever before.

We send these volumes forth with a prayer that what he ministered will become realities in the 21st century.

The SeedSowers

The Church
Which is
His Body

THE BODY OF CHRIST:
ITS HEAVENLY ASPECT.

CHAPTER ONE.

We are going, as the Lord enables us, to meditate afresh on the Body of Christ. We know, when we want to have the larger unfoldings of this "Mystery" where to turn ; we instinctively turn to the Ephesian letter. In this letter we note, first of all, the simple preliminary fact, that the Church is designated "The Body of Christ," it is "the Church which is His Body." That distinguishes the Church in this letter from other designations which we find elsewhere. There is the Temple, there is the House of God, and other such-like designations, but in this letter it is particularly The Body of Christ that is basic to all that the letter unfolds, and what is contained in the letter is in line with the conception of a body.* Now the word which seems to predominate through this letter in connection with that designation is the word translated "Together." It is impressive to note how frequently that word occurs. Here we are said to have been "quickened together" in Him. That does not only mean that our together-ness individually was with the Lord Jesus in His rising, but it means that we corporately were quickened, we were together quickened in Him, not only with Him but in Him corporately quickened.

The Eternal Oneness of the Body.

In the resurrection of the Lord Jesus the whole Church was included together. And then in the same verse, ii. 6, we are said to be "raised together" in Him.

---

* We remember that the "Body" is spoken of in I. Corinthians, but there it is not the main theme of the letter, nor the sole object in view.

Further, in the same place, we are said to be "seated together" in Him. Coming back a step into i. 10, we are "gathered together into one" and then on again to ii. 21, we are "framed together." In verse 22 we are "builded together." So this word "together" brings into view in a very simple way the fact of the corporate nature of the Church, the Body of Christ. We want to get the full force of that as far as it is possible, because this letter undoubtedly emphasizes the fact that the Church is a corporate Body; not that it one day will be when the work of grace is completed; not that it is merely that in the mind and thought of God, the will of God, the intention of God; not that it was intended to be when the Lord started it; but that it IS; that in spite of what is seen here on the earth; in spite of the ever-increasing number of divisions and separations, all the unhappy schisms which have entered into the fellowships of God's people on the earth, in spite of everything that ever has been and ever is or will be along that line, the Church is still a corporate whole. It is that, not as to the people as on the earth, but it is true as to the essential nature of the Church, the Body of Christ, and the sooner we get that rooted and settled in our spiritual acceptance and consciousness the better. No schism, beloved, that is incidental to the relationships of Christian people on the earth can alter that fact. The differences which exist or which come about by the different mentalities, choices and preferences, likes and dislikes, intellectual acceptances or rejections; all those differences do not touch this ultimate fact that there is a realm in which there is a togetherness, a oneness, a corporateness which is unaffected by anything that is of man in himself religiously or theologically. There is a realm of course in which there may be a breach of fellowship, that is where it enters into the realm of the spirit and where the spirit is affected. There you may very definitely strike a blow at the Body of

Christ, but ultimately this Body is one; which, of course, clearly indicates that this is something other than an earthly thing and that it is a heavenly Body, unaffected and untouched by earth.

We are inclined to accept what we see, to be affected by the divisions that are here, and are almost in despair because of what we see. The sooner we sweep that whole thing aside the better, and let there be fifty thousand earthly departments of Christian people, the Body of Christ remains one. It is a seamless robe, it is a Body which cannot be divided, it remains one. That is the basic fact to which we must come back, that is where we begin. This letter, in which there is the unveiling of the mystery of Christ and His members, the Church, the one Body, states most emphatically the fact of the corporate nature of the Body. It does not argue about it, or discuss it, it takes it for granted, it is a settled thing. Of course there are degrees of enjoyment of it, and there are degrees of the fruitfulness of it as here, but there are no degrees of the fact of it. The fact remains as solid and settled. Our business is to enter into the settled fact and come into the meaning of it : but our not having come into the full meaning of it does not mean that it does not exist. The trouble is that we do not come into what God has established from the beginning ; that is, we have to know what it is that makes the Body one, and that is our business. The unity exists ; our business is to apprehend it, not make it. We go on to that almost immediately, but note, the letter to the Ephesians is still alive, it is still applicable, it is still true for to-day. After all these centuries when we have all that we have on the earth, the departments and divisions of Christian people, all of whom may be members of the Body of Christ, still after all these centuries the Ephesian letter remains where it was at the beginning, and it represents the Body as a solid whole, a corporate unity.

A Heavenly Position Necessary to Apprehending the Oneness.

It is only as we get up into the heavenlies and away from the earthlies that we begin to enter into that fact and realise what that fact means to God, to the heavenlies, to hell, and to this world. So, in order that we should enter into the fact with all that that fact contains of effective vocation and life, we have to introduce the whole matter by our position in Christ in the heavenlies, and see exactly where we are placed spiritually : for not until we come to recognise that and to enter into our heavenly position in Christ can we see, appreciate, or come into the meaning of this heavenly reality the Church, which is His Body. We cannot see the Church from the earthlies, we can only see it from the heavenlies.

Our Attitude Towards Differences.

I do not want to pass away from that as having merely stated something. I do want that we should get the benefit

of it. You and I may have a disagree-
ment, but it makes no difference to our
relationship in the Lord Jesus. The
fact that you and I fall out or disagree
does not tear us as limbs out of the Body
of Christ. No, that is *our* loss, that is
our shame, that is incidental in our
Christian life, that is a breakdown somewhere in grace in us, but we shall
recover ourselves from that if we yield
to the movements of the Spirit in us,
and come back to find that we have not
to be rejoined in Christ in His Body,
that fact remains. You see the working
principle is this : that there may be
much amongst believers on this earth of
division, but we have not to accept that
as ultimate, we have not to take that as
meaning that some are in Christ and
some are out of Christ, that we are in
Christ and others are not, and that the
Body has altogether collapsed and disintegrated. The only hope of enjoying
the fact is that we repudiate what looks
like another fact, and we seek to get
above that which, being earthly, brings

these things about, and discover we are in the heavenlies, and fellowship abides. That is a working principle and we should recognise that is the meaning of the fact. We have got to accept the fact, and we have to seek to overcome or repudiate the other things which come in against the ultimate fact.

CHAPTER TWO.

The Basis of Oneness.

Now, seeing that it is set forth as being so, that we are together, we want to see something more of the ground of this oneness. I think perhaps we could be helped most by reminding ourselves of the 23rd chapter of Leviticus, the chapter which contains the establishing of the Feasts of the Lord. Now the main feature, the dominating feature of these feasts is that they represent the corporate life of the people of God, the corporate life of the Church. You see they are the gatherings together of all the Lord's people. These feasts are called holy convocations. The people are convoked, their oneness is revealed on these occasions and by these occasions, so that the primary element is the corporate life of the people of God as expressed at these times. That is what is in view. That at these times people cease to live private lives, cease to live detached individual lives, even their own domestic lives or their own social lives within their own circle. All that which is departmental is abandoned at these times and the people are found as one. That being the case you proceed to take account of what it is that makes their oneness, and you see it is the feasts. Yes, but then it is the different kinds of feasts all put together making one whole which is the foundation of the corporate life and fellowship of the Lord's people. So you go through the feasts. (I am not going to deal with them at large or in detail, I simply mention them and perhaps the outstanding feature of them.) You begin with

The Feast of the Passover.

A great many Divine principles are gathered up in the Feast of the Passover, but there is one thing which embraces all the others and becomes that for which the Passover stands, that which it represents, that is, A COVENANT IN LIFE BY BLOOD. Everything is gathered up into that. God makes a covenant.

He makes that covenant by blood; that blood of the covenant is deliverance from judgment and death, a holding in life when death is abroad in judgment, the destroyer rendered inoperative. Well, that is life triumphant in the presence of death, over the Devil, in the power of shed and sprinkled blood, and there is a covenant between God and His own. That is the first step, the first thing which brings into being the corporate life of God's people. Now I want to discriminate. A great many people of to-day have tried, and are trying to realise the oneness of the Church upon the basis of the doctrine of the virtue and efficacy of the Blood of the Lord Jesus, the doctrine of the Blood; if you like—the atonement, the value of the Blood, the whole teaching of the Blood of the Lord Jesus from whatsoever angle it may be preached, in whatsoever direction it may be applied; they are trying to realise the oneness of the Church by establishing that as an essential doctrine, and if you accept that as one of the doctrines of the faith, then you come into the oneness of the Church. But never yet has doctrine been able to realise oneness. It is not sufficient that you have fundamentalism, which after all may only be the gathering together of certain recognised fundamental doctrines; it is not enough to have that as the basis of unity. It does not work, you cannot get it on the basis of doctrine, on the basis of creed, you have got to have it on the basis of experience, on the basis of power, of something wrought, something brought about. We know that there are plenty of people who believe in all the eternal and infinite virtue and value of the Blood of the Lord Jesus who know very little experimentally about the power of His Blood in their lives as a mighty force working against the power of death within and without. That is a heavenly thing, but creed can be quite an earthly thing, perfectly sound and true, but quite an earthly thing for an earthly society, not efficacious in the spiritual realm.

It is the spiritual power of the Blood
as registered in the spiritual universe
that is the true value of the Blood, and
it is when you come into that that you
come into the true oneness of the Church
—spiritual, not credal. It is experimental, not doctrinal. It is life as an
active, energetic, mighty thing. It is
not our loyalty to sound doctrine. It is
very important to notice that distinction.
The maintenance of the oneness of the
Body of Christ, beloved, requires something infinitely more than a sound creed
and true doctrine; it needs a power, a
terrific power, a force mightier than any
other force in this universe, and the
Blood is that. It is on the ground of
that Blood that the Church has been
brought into being. Christ now lives in
virtue of His own Blood, and He, living
in virtue of that has brought all His
members into heavenly fellowship with
Him by the same virtue of His Blood.
It is a living, working, operating thing
is this, and the Passover is just that we
have come into an experimental, living,

active union with one another in Christ in the power of His Blood in that covenant. That is the oneness of the Church, the Body of Christ. Until something of that operates we have not come into the active operation of the Church's life as a heavenly body. If the Church is going to count, fulfil her vocation, register her impact upon the principalities and powers and world rulers of this darkness, hosts of wickedness, and accomplish her universal mission, her pre-destined purpose, it can only be on the basis of this tremendous power that is in the precious Blood of the Lord Jesus. That being true, the Church has no existence apart from that Blood, and therefore no vocation apart from the Blood.

We have said we have got to come into an appreciation of it, to approximate to what is already true; but in the mind of God no one is a member of Christ's Body who does not stand right in all the virtue of His precious Blood. I do not mean that they intelligently apprehend all the meaning of that Blood, that they have come into the full revelation of what that Blood is, but that their relationship to the Lord Jesus is brought about in virtue of that Blood, and that in heaven it is the Blood that has joined them to Him and one another. It is in the power of that that the Church is going to be ultimately triumphant. "They overcame because of the blood of the Lamb." That is just the beginning, you see. So if we are going to know, appreciate, enjoy and profit by the corporate truth of the Body of Christ, we have got to learn what the power of the Blood is, and that Blood has got to become a recognised force in our lives against the things which the Devil seeks to use for breaking up fellowship. Oh, how much less there might have been of Satanic success along the line of schism and division if only the Lord's people had recognised the power and virtue of the Blood against all such Satanic activity! If you and I came into a state of strain in our relationships as the result of some work of the enemy, beloved, the only thing that will bring us back into fellowship is the pleading of the power of the Blood against all that the enemy has done. That itself is full proof of the fact that the Body is one in virtue of the Blood initially, continually and finally.

The Passover yields that primary truth, so the coming together of the Lord's people in the Old Testament, their corporate life, their fellowship, was in the first place upon a basis of a covenant in the blood as triumphant over death and the destroyer, the first phase of their fellowship. The second of these feasts was

The Feast of Unleavened Bread.

The Feast of Unleavened Bread was to be continued for seven whole days, representing a perfect period, a perfect spiritual period—(seven is the number of spiritual perfection)—that is a perfect spiritual period throughout which all that is of the flesh is eliminated and ruled out, for the leaven is the ferment of the flesh, is the work of the flesh, the potent element of the flesh which is corrupt, and we know that it is the leaven which is the basis of corruption. The flesh is corrupt, the flesh has got to be eliminated, ruled out throughout the whole period of spiritual life. We have to come to Romans vi. and see in the Cross of the Lord Jesus the body of the flesh put out of operation, where we recognise that this flesh is by God ruled out. The Lord demands that it shall be set aside, we must repudiate it, we must accept God's position about this, that the flesh must not have a place. It does not mean that we shall never be tempted along the line of the flesh, nor that we shall never be conscious that the flesh is there, but it does mean that we have to repudiate the flesh even though we might be touched by it; we have to take back that ground and repudiate it and say, "I repent, I put that back, I recognise that is corruption and that will corrupt everything, and I put it down, I put it out. I reckon myself dead to it.'' Just as on the eve of the Passover the father of the Jewish household would light his lamp and go through the house room by room, searching in every corner, every cupboard, every out of the way place to find any leaven if he could, and having swept his house clean of leaven so far as he knew by the most thorough search, even then before God he was not satisfied, he would make the declaration, ''I have searched my house, I have purged it of the leaven which I know, but if there should yet be some leaven which has eluded my utmost search and scrutiny, I repudiate it also.''

The thoroughness of the repudiation of the flesh as the corrupting element, that is the feast of unleavened bread. The Oneness of the Church the Body of Christ demands that not only our sins should have been put away, but that we should have been put away in the flesh. The natural man corrupts things, spoils things, divides. We know it is the ferment of the flesh that works against the unity of the Body, brings about schisms, upsets the positive spiritual functioning of the Lord's people in spiritual oneness.   It is the flesh that does it all; so that when all the people are going to express their oneness of life in God it is necessary for them to repudiate the flesh, to get rid of the leaven. Any slight uprising of jealousy, or envy, or personal feeling, or heat of myself, or provocation which is personal provocation, not on a basis of principle, righteousness, but personal provocation which casts a shadow between me and another, I have got to go back on that at once and with all my heart I have got to say, "That was wrong and I repent of it and seek to have that leaven extracted, put aside." We have all got to do that. We are still in this natural life susceptible to being upset and offended, we are still very touchy. Oh, yes, we know it quite well! Whether we feel we have a right to be upset or not, that is not the question, the thing is has our flesh come into the situation?

If it has it has put up a barrier between us and others, and we must go and confess the fault of which we were guilty. Not all the time excusing ourselves because we were more wronged than wrong, nor hiding our own wrong because they were wrong. We must go back and say, "I ought not to have reacted as I did to it, I ought to have sought grace to return good for evil." We do not always do that, not any of us; but unless we do that, unless we keep short accounts there is going to rise up a barrier between us.

The Body of Christ in its corporate oneness is based upon the working fact of Romans vi. and Colossians ii. 11, 12, the whole body of the flesh circumcised put away. You see again how necessary it is to have something more than the principle of our identification with Christ in death; it has got to be, not the principle, but the active working of the principle. The principle probably does not do anything other than put us into a false position, and it will do so if it is not applied. We can be just as deluded by truth as we can be by error. Quite a lot of people are deluded by truth. They have the principle, they have the doctrine, and for them that is the end of everything; they do not see that what is necessary is that the principle should operate and that it should be life. You see that the corporate life of Israel was based upon this second thing the putting away of the flesh.

The third of the feasts was

The Feast of the First-fruits.

Now that embraces many aspects of truth and leads on to much more than at present we have it in mind to mention. We just take the primary thing, the initial thing, the outstanding thing which governs everything else in these feasts. When you come to the Feast of the First-fruits you are simply coming to the great truth of the resurrection of the Lord Jesus as representative. The first ripe fruits represent all the other to follow, the first-fruits are taken in representation of the whole. The Jew takes those first ripe ears of corn to the Lord and thanks the Lord for the whole harvest. These are the earnest of the harvest, and we know from "Corinthians" what the Apostle says about this, that the Lord Jesus is a First-fruits, so that He is in His own Person representatively the Church in resurrection. "We are risen together with Him," says "Ephesians." We have been buried with Him, that is the old man put away, now we are risen with Him, and the real oneness of the members of Christ, the oneness of the Body of Christ is found in its living testimony to resurrection union with the Lord Jesus. We know how He established that principle in His simple and well-known little parable of the grain of wheat. "Except a corn of wheat fall into the ground and die it abideth alone, but if it die it bringeth forth much fruit." You see there is a multiplication, a hundred-fold. One corn dying issues in a hundred corns living. It is resurrection corporeity in

Christ through His death. Oh that we should enter into the working force of that as the Body of Christ; and you know when we really do begin to enter experimentally and livingly into the fact that we were planted together with Him in the likeness of His resurrection, and the power of His resurrection is operative in us, what a sense of fellowship that brings to us, what a difference in our relationships. If we are knowing the power of resurrection life at work in us, what fellowship we have. If we know something mutually of life triumphant over death, a working thing in us, a mutuality in experience, that mutuality is going to count, and it already is a testimony in the heavenlies, it is working against the forces of death and darkness.

That thing wrought into the Body of Christ is the testimony to the fact that the power of the Devil is broken, and a testimony to the fact that Christ has overcome death and has swallowed up death in victory. Unless we know that experimentally in the spiritual realm we shall not know it in the physical. The physical always follows the spiritual in the Divine order. We will never know resurrection of the body unto eternal life unless we know already resurrection in the spirit. It is a working force that constitutes the very basis of the existence of the Church's activity and function. To enter into the fact of the oneness of the Body we have got to enter into the experience of the power of resurrection. The fourth is

The Day of Atonement.

As in all the others, there are many principles included, but one thing predominates. The Lord says, "It is a Sabbath of rest unto you, ye shall do no work." This is a feast of gathering together of the Lord's people into rest, the Day of Atonement. Now, leaving all the other elements, let us notice the significance of the Sabbath rest coming in at this point. The feasts have been already introduced with the establishment of the Sabbath; here the Sabbath rest comes in in a special, peculiar, particular place in connection with the Day of Atonement, and it says this to us; that on the basis of our covenant union with God in life triumphant over death by the Blood shed and sprinkled, on the basis of our old man having been crucified with Christ, the body of the flesh put away, on the basis of our having come into the knowledge of union with Christ risen, the power of His resurrection, we enter into rest. We enter into rest; we come to an end of our works and enter into God's Sabbath, God's rest; we come to the place where we no longer strive after an end but where we have reached the end, where struggling to satisfy God ceases, and God is satisfied. He looks upon His works perfectly satisfied, we come into God's satisfaction. In this Day of Atonement, in the atoning work of the Lord Jesus and the atoning value of His Blood sprinkled on the mercy seat right in the presence of God, God has found

an answer to all His desires and require-
ments and has come to His rest, full
satisfaction in His Son. That Blood is
taken into the presence of God as a
testimony to the fact that all is done and
finished and God rests in the full accomplishment of the Lord Jesus, through
His Blood, and there is no more striving.
When we come there, to the apprehension of the perfect work of the Lord
Jesus in His atonement we ought to
come to rest. All fretful care to satisfy
God ought to be put aside and we ought
to find Christ meeting all our need for
us before the Father. What about our
progressive sanctification? Is there
nothing to be done of that *in* us? Yes,
but you will never progressively move
into perfection, holiness, until that basis
is fully settled, the Lord Jesus has
presented everything for you for the
satisfaction of the Father. We grow in
grace on the basis that already Christ
has accomplished the whole work for us
and we have nothing that we can do to
add to His work for our sanctification.

Jesus is our sanctification — Jesus is our life.
I Cor. 1:30. *Col. 3:3-4*

Luther was sent to Rome with a commission and he was very anxious to visit the City and that special place of penance that he might get special privileges and indulgences and so on by climbing those stairs on his hands and knees. He thought by imposing upon himself that terrible suffering he would find the rest of justification. He started, the thing became laborious and something said, "The just shall live by faith," and on he went again; the voice said again, "The just shall live by faith," and he tried more steps; the emphasis came back again upon one word, "The just shall LIVE by faith," and that was what led to his conversion and his abandonment of the whole Romish system of justification by works. The just shall LIVE by faith. It is not our faith as something in itself, it is the Object of our faith, the work of the Lord Jesus. We make far too much of the measure of our faith, it is the Object of our faith. It is when we get our faith fastened upon the Object,

Christ and His perfect work for us, that
we enter into rest. We climb no more
stone steps on hands and knees. This
is a basic thing to the corporate life of
the Lord's people. The element of
unrest, ferment, dissatisfaction goes
out, and we have peace with God, we
have got harmony, for that is only
another word for peace. That is rest.
Peace in the Bible is not some sort of
atmosphere, but a right adjustment of
all elements to one another in a perfect
harmony. The last of these feasts is

The Feast of Tabernacles,

and how proper is their order. You see
how their sequence is just right when
you come to the Feast of Tabernacles.
You notice that the people during their
time of convocation are called upon to
leave their houses and come out and go
and cut down boughs of trees and build
themselves booths and dwell in these
booths outside their houses throughout
the whole of the time of the feasts. It is
a corporate action, and if you will just

follow through the Feast of Tabernacles
in the Old Testament into the Book of
Nehemiah you will find that it points
backward, and in the case of the remnant
where the Feast of Tabernacles was
reinstated there is a distinct link made
between that reinstating and Israel's
coming out of Egypt. (Lev. xxiii. 42.)

It is said that this Feast of Tabernacles is meant to perpetuate the
memory of Israel's coming out of
Egypt, and yet when they came out
of Egypt there was no Feast of Tabernacles established. The Feast of
Tabernacles is the means of perpetua-
ting the memory of Exodus. They
came out of stone houses, directly
related to the earth, they came out
into a wilderness where everything was
not earthly, everything was heavenly.
Heavenly symbols—the blue robe of the
High Priest and the bit of the same blue
on the border of the garment of every
man, woman and child throughout all
their generations. So heavenliness was
the character of these people, they were

not of this earth, but out for God unto the heavenlies, and the Feast of Tabernacles speaks of the heavenliness of the people of God. Beloved, that is an important basic factor of the Church which is His Body. We were saying that God in this dispensation is doing nothing whatever publicly to constitute something on this earth, and yet men are striving as hard as they can to set up something on this earth for God. *Note*

There at the end of the second century of this Christian era, perhaps before that, this thing came in, and there were means and methods adopted to make the Church something on this earth, to organise it as a world force, to put it into such form that it would appeal to men and impress men of this world, so that the world would take account of it, and say it was a great force, and something that cannot be ignored. That has developed and has ever been an absolute violation of the principle of God for this *Note* whole dispensation. What God is doing is building a heavenly Church, a Body in the heavens, and the Church of God is not a thing seen, it is a thing unseen, a secret people, spiritual, by the world unknown—it knew Him not. That is basic to our oneness. Immediately there is a tendency to set up something here on the earth you will get divisions; it does not matter how spiritual it is, immediately it touches the earth you will get divisions. Some of the most beautiful movements of God, really God's movement from heaven, immediately they get into the hands of men and become something on the earth, division comes in and you get more sects. The only safety is to keep off the earth, the only safety is to recognise what God is doing. There will be a testimony here in the world, but there is a difference between there being a testimony in the world and there being an organisation in the world.

The Lord is out of sympathy with every movement to set up something here on the earth. He will do that in a coming age, but not in this. If we do things by way of setting up something here on the earth, even for God, it is not long before the Lord leaves us to take the responsibility for it, the Lord will not take the responsibility for that. He will take responsibility for all that is according to His own mind in this age, that which is absolutely heavenly.

CHAPTER THREE.

The Nature of the Body of Christ.

We now proceed to consider the nature of the corporate life of the Church, and we want to note first of all one or two quite elementary facts which, nevertheless, always carry a freshness of meaning to those who are spiritually alive to the Lord, and the first simple truth is this, that the term, the designation "The Body of Christ," is peculiar to the Apostle Paul. Other designations of the Church are found before Paul's day and in other parts of the Scriptures outside of the writings of Paul, but the title, "The Body of Christ," "the Body," "The Church which is His Body," is peculiar to Paul. The Church was not a new idea at all. The Lord's people were familiar with that title. The Lord Jesus had spoken of His Church to the Apostles. There was nothing new in that, but when you come to speak of that Church as "The Body of Christ," it is an entirely new idea, a

new thought, a new conception bringing
with it an entirely new presentation of
the nature of this thing. It says very
emphatically and forcefully and clearly
that the Church, as regarded by God, is
not just a community; it is not a
congregation, it is not something
denominational, or interdenominational,
or even undenominational.

And yet you may use the term
"Church" and have a mentality
encircling that term which conceives of
the Church as a community of Christian
people, a Christian society, a company
of people on the earth of mutual interest
in the things of Christ. But this
designation carries things into an altogether different realm. It is a body.
Not a body of people, but that which
is represented and illustrated by the
physical body of a man. I do not mean
that the Church is the physical body of
Christ, do not misunderstand, but that
the physical body of a man is taken as
an illustration of what the Church is.
(Christ still has His own personal and

separate being and spiritual body in glory.)

No Such Thing as a Local "Body."

Now another factor in the truth of the Body of Christ is that there is no such thing as a local body. There are local churches, or local assemblies, but there is no such thing as a local Body. That is made clear in one passage at least when rightly translated—I. Cor. xii. 27—where the unfortunate translation of some of our versions is "Ye are the body of Christ." In the Greek there is no article there, it does not say, "Ye are the body of Christ," but "Ye are Christ's body." That gives an entirely different complexion to the local assembly. This word spoken to a local company of believers at Corinth most clearly implies that the part is the whole in implication, that the local body is the whole in representation, the whole body is represented by that local company. Now that need not be so in the case of local assemblies or local Churches, but

you cannot localise the Body of Christ
in that way.   That is, you cannot cut
off so many members of a physical frame
and put them in one corner and call that
the body.   Wherever members of Christ
are, there in implication and representation the whole Body of Christ is, and the
Lord's mind is that every local company
shall be a living representation of the
whole Body, a microcosm of the whole
Body of Christ.   What is true of the
whole Body has got to be true there,
because they are not a detached company, not an isolated or separated assembly, there by implication the whole
Body is.   That embraces—whether you
are able to grasp it or not—all the great
elements and factors of the Body of
Christ.   It says quite clearly that nothing in the thought of God is local,
departmental, separate or independent.
In the thought of God everything to do
with His Church is universal, relative,
interdependent ; the Church is one.   It
is saying that you are so vitally related
to other believers that you are the Body

of Christ in implication, in effect, in
nature. It declares most emphatically
that the part is the whole in the thought
of God, and is to be regarded as the
whole. Let us put it this way.

Here are we in this place in this part
of this city, a company of the Lord's
people, and vitally related to this company here is the whole Body of Christ.
We are not a detached or separate
company, an independent assembly, we
are in a living, functioning spiritual
union with every other member of the
Body of Christ in this whole world
wherever they may be. France, Switzer-
land, Germany, Poland, America,
Africa, China, India, etc., they are all
here in the relativity of the Body of
Christ, and all involved in our gathering
together. We have to see that more
fully presently, but when once that
principle is spiritually apprehended
then we have got our feet on the way
of our universal ministry. Whenever we
gather together, even as two or three,
the whole Body is gathered with us in

the heavenlies and is affected by our gathering together. It is tremendous to think that two or three of the children of God gathered in one place anywhere, in living touch with the Head, are affecting and can affect, the whole Body of Christ; every member, however many millions there may be, so that they are in effect the Body of Christ. Now how does that come to you? Does it reach you, or is it so familiar that you say that you know all about that? It is necessary to place fresh emphasis upon it from time to time.

The Body—Christ's Complement.

Now further, the Church as the Body is the complement and fulness of Christ, associated with Him as Head over all things, the complement of Christ, completion of Christ, the fulness of Christ. We are in Ephesians, you know, and here the Church, the Body is "the fulness of Him that filleth all in all," the Church is said to be the fulness of Him. Associated with Him as Head over all things. To illustrate : while unrevealed, while still a mystery held from the ages and generations, the Body truth in principle is contained in the Word right from the beginning. It had never been specifically unveiled or mentioned but it is there. Truths are eternal, and from the very beginning you have a principle of the Body represented and illustrated in the case of Adam and Eve. The woman was taken out of the man and then brought to the man to complete him, and that is the Church, that is the Body of Christ ; taken out of Christ and then brought to Christ to complete Him. His completion, His complement unto His fulness, associated with Him as Head. "As the man is the head of the woman so Christ is the Head of the Church," associated with Him as Head over all things. We will take that up again presently for its practical outworking. Let us note still further, the Word of the Lord reveals the Church as complete in the mind of God at any given time. This is never

dealt with in tenses in the Word of God,
that is, past, present and future. It is
always complete in the present tense, in
the mind of God. The Lord never talks
about the Church when it will be complete; the Lord never talks about the
completing of the Church in a future
time. You have such phrases as these,
"The whole Body," that is a declaration
now, as though in Paul's day, when
he wrote that phrase, the Body was
complete; he is speaking *now* about
the whole Body. "All the Body fitly
framed," speaking in his own day.
You have either got to decide that it was
only the saints in Paul's day who made
up the Body of Christ, or ruling that
out and admitting believers after Paul's
day, you have to come to this conclusion
that in the thought of God as expressed
by the Holy Spirit in these words the
Body is complete in any given time.
That takes you back to the Ephesian
word to the "before times eternal" when
God completed the Body in His own
mind, "whom he foreknew He pre-

destinated.'' Back there in eternity the thing was complete, and that completeness *in the mind* of God exists at any time and every time. Then we go on to note that the Body is for the display of Christ. Just as a man expresses himself through his body, so Christ expresses Himself through His Body, and the Body's supreme and all inclusive function is for the display of Christ.

The Holy Spirit the Unifying Factor in the Body.

Now as to the great unifying factor in the Body of Christ. What is the unifying factor in the Body of Christ? It is not a mutual acceptance of certain truths presented. That does not constitute the Body of Christ. It is not that we all agree to believe certain doctrines. The unifying factor of the Body of Christ is the Holy Spirit. ''We were all baptized in one Spirit into one Body'' (I. Cor. xii. 13). ''There is one Body and one Spirit'' (Eph. iv. 4). Individually we have each a spirit, a separate spirit.

The Body of Christ has only one Spirit and that is the factor which makes the Body one. Now you can clearly and immediately see how, out of that, many practical issues proceed. The necessity, for instance, for receiving the Holy Spirit. You cannot be a member of the Church which is His Body unless you have received the Holy Spirit.

That is very elementary, I know, but it is a foundational fact. Our "Churchmanship" is tested on that truth. Have we received the Holy Spirit? If not, we have no claim whatever to be a member of Christ, His Body the Church. That is where it begins. But then the fact is not enough, the function is necessary; and for the Body to function, it is not only necessary that the members should receive the Holy Spirit, but that the Holy Spirit should have His full place in every member. His full place! The Body can only function when the Spirit has His full place, His complete place given Him in each member. Now the order of things, not chronologically but

spiritually, is very clear in the arrange-
ment of the New Testament. Romans
precedes Corinthians, and Corinthians
precedes Ephesians, and necessarily so.
Romans brings in the Cross specifically
for the setting aside of the natural man.
Corinthians has as its objective, its stress,
its note, the place of Christ in absolute
Lordship. All the trouble at Corinth
was because the Lord Jesus was not in
His place as Sovereign Head, as Lord;
and the word of the Apostle is "We
proclaim Christ Jesus as Lord." They
were making men lords—Paul, Apollos,
Peter; they were putting men in the
place of the Lord Jesus. They were
putting things in the place of the Lord
Jesus, even the spirituals, they were not
giving Him His right place as absolute
Sovereign Head, and the letter was
brought in for that purpose. Romans
to set aside the natural man, Corinthians
to bring Christ into His place as Lord;
then Ephesians can come in and you
have, as constructed upon those two
principles—the natural man set aside,

the Lord Jesus established as Lord—the
Body presented and functioning upon
that two-fold basis. You cannot have an
expression of the Body of Christ until
the natural man has been set aside. The
uprising of the natural man in any way
or measure violates the whole Body of
Christ, and is a positive antagonism to
the Sovereignty of the Holy Spirit. The
flesh cannot have a place in the Body of
Christ if the Body of Christ is to be
what the Lord conceives it should be. If
it is to function, the Lord Jesus must be
absolutely Lord in the case of every
believer.

So that is the order, and then,
beloved, the Spirit's method is again
revealed in His wisdom in following
that up by Colossians. Chronologically
Colossians comes before, spiritually
after, Ephesians. Colossians is the full
inheritance in Christ, the fulness of
God is vested in Christ, He is the
sum total of all the Divine fulness.
Colossians is the New Testament
counterpart of the Book of Joshua.

Christ is the inheritance. He is the land of promise flowing with milk and honey, the land of riches and wealth. He is all that, and you come into the fulness of Christ as the Body on the ground of His having become Lord, and the flesh, the natural man having been set aside. That is the Body of Christ in its nature. Apply those laws to-day and you will get a living expression of what is in Ephesians. The reason why we have no, or such little, expression of what is in Ephesians to-day, the Body mightily functioning in the heavenlies, is because the natural man has not been ruled out, because Christ is not in His place as absolute Lord. Therefore, what is basic in the first instance to the Church, the Body of Christ, and to the revelation of the Body of Christ, is the practical outworking of the Cross. We shall never, by the Lord, be led to see the Body of Christ until we have been led to see Romans, especially Romans vi., until there has been a revelation to us of the Cross. I do not mean a presentation of the principle of the Cross, but a revelation of the Cross. Now probably in quite a number of cases that has been borne out.

Speaking for one's self, one preached Romans vi. for years, one preached the message of the Cross in fulness for years, as truth, as Scripture, and you could never find a flaw with the doctrine of the Cross as then preached. But then the practical application of it had not come about, and the time came when the Lord confronted one with the implications of Romans vi., and it was as though one knew nothing of Romans vi. when confronted with the real meaning of it, for the thing was so drastic, so terrific that it nearly knocked one off one's feet, and slew one. Such a difference between the doctrine of the Cross and the applying of it. When that was got through and worked in we came to see that the Lord had included us in the death of Christ, not only as sinners, but as men with every bit of our natural equipment, our natural facility, even to preach the Gospel (which was a natural facility to preach), and all those things which were employed in Christian service as our resources, the whole range, intellectual and every other realm. The Lord brought us to see that all was included in the death of Christ and that all things have to be out from Himself in the new creation (that is the law of the servant of the Lord, as the Lord Jesus Himself said, "I do nothing of myself," everything now out from God, a life of total dependence upon Him for everything) when that was applied in a practical way it meant a tremendous upheaval and for a time it was death to everything, it was the end. Now that is true to our experience, but when that was got through, when that in principle was established—not that there has been no more of the Cross applied since, for it is always being applied—when the Lord had the thing so registered that for evermore we recognized the necessity for the natural man to be kept out, then after a while the Lord began to reveal the great truth of the Body. We had preached on the Church which is His Body for years, had been of an interdenominational spirit and frame of mind where we regarded all believers as members of the one Church, the one great spiritual community, had studied Ephesians most thoroughly. But when the thing began to break as a revelation from heaven it was as though we knew nothing about it at all, and the practical outworking was tremendous as to cause again another revolution, for the teaching which before never raised practical issues in certain realms now began to raise these.

For instance, with the teaching apart from the revelation, the denominational issue was never raised at all; when the revelation came it was found impossible to be a denominationalist. It was not a mental attitude taken, but one had come into a spiritual position where one was out of the whole thing and it was a contradiction to go on in that thing when one was out of it. I am illustrating, not applying this to you as teaching and saying that the teaching of the Body of Christ demands that you shall leave a denomination. The revelation may put you into another position, but don't you move out on mere doctrine, or because of what I say. Stay where you are until you get a revelation which makes it impossible for you to remain. Revelation raises practical issues while doctrine may not do so in the same way. We need more than the apprehension of Bible truth with our natural minds, for many minds have many different apprehensions.

We were saying what is foundational to the Body of Christ is a revelation and application of the Cross, for when the natural man of the flesh is ruled out, put aside, smitten, then you see the way is paved for true spiritual apprehension of the Body of Christ because the Body of Christ cannot exist and function with any natural man about. That is the nature of the Body of Christ. The natural man is put out altogether, so again let us resay that the revelation of the Body is based upon a revelation and an application of the Cross. Then the Body becomes the sphere of the Holy Spirit's activity. The little phrase is in I. Cor. xii., "As He wills," He appoints, He gives gifts, He equips, as He wills, implying the complete liberty, the unrestricted liberty of the Holy Spirit. If the Holy Spirit is restricted, in that measure the Body is limited in its realisation of the Divine calling and the fulfilment of the Divine purpose of its existence. Only the unrestricted liberty of the Holy Spirit can produce a right representation and a right functioning and activity of the Body because the Body is the sphere of the Holy Spirit's activity.

We have seen that Christ is the Head of the Body, and that the Holy Spirit has His sphere of activity in the Body. Now taking the familiar illustration from the physical body, we know that every member and ever faculty of this physical body is related vitally to the head, and functions in relation to the head, if the body, of course, is in right order. Throughout the whole of this complex physical system there is the network of nerves; a tremendously comprehensive system, linking every needle-point of our physical frame to the farthest extremities with the head, so that you register pain from your finger or toe in your head. Cut your head off and you can injure as many fingers and toes as you like and you will not feel it! Everything has its location in the head, all the sensibilities of the members are registered in the head. It is possible to take a needle and, if the whole brain system is understood, to apply the needle-point to any given part of the brain and put out of action any member of the body, and leave the others untouched. By an understanding of that system a needle can be applied to a certain point in the brain and put the hand, or the foot, out of operation and leave the other members operating, this whole thing is so wonderfully gathered up in the head. Christ is the Head of the Body, all the members are joined to the Head, all the members are consciously registered in the Head, have their consciousness by reason of their relationship to the Head, their consciousness spiritally, which Paul means when he says, "We have the mind of Christ."

But what is that nerve system? It is the Holy Spirit. He is the spiritual nerve system of the whole Body, linking all with the Head, He is the consciousness of the Body, He is the One who brings from the Head those reactions of the judgments and decisions of the Head. He is the One who brings to the Head everything concerning every member, and so makes the Body and the Head one complete whole. The Holy Spirit is that nerve system throughout the whole Body. Now if the Holy Spirit is arrested, checked, injured in any one member the completeness of the Body's functioning is at once hindered, interfered with. That is why I said at the beginning that any local company is the whole in effect, that if we, beloved, here, for instance, check the Holy Spirit, or He is arrested, or if here this member is injured in relation to the Holy Spirit the whole Body is affected by that. If the Holy Spirit is checked here, for instance, in the matter of prayer, the whole Body suffers in that, not the local company merely; the whole Body. If the Holy Spirit, on the other hand, has His full way here the whole Body will reap the benefit. This Body is a universal thing and its universality is centred in any local company, the whole is there. How in these bodies of ours, when they are in proper order, one member affects the rest! Have the toothache and every bit of your body suffers with it, it is not long before that abscess in the tooth has you universally involved! It is true. You suddenly burn a bit of your body, a small bit, and your whole body goes through with a shudder.

How true this presentation of the Body is in the Word of God. "If one member suffer all the members suffer with it.'' But that is not on the earth. I may be going through a very great deal of suffering without you knowing anything about it so far as the natural life is concerned, you are not affected by it, but beloved, there is a realm where if one member spiritually suffers the whole Body is involved in that suffering, which shows this Body is a heavenly thing and its relationships are not natural, they are spiritual, and that the unifying factor of the Holy Spirit operates apart from the natural consciousness. Have you got that? If we neglect our private prayer the Lord is losing something in His Body far away—His children the other side of the world are affected by our behaviour. To the natural consciousness it is not so, but the Holy Spirit knows it. But why always take the negative side, why not the positive, that the maintenance of a true Holy Spirit life is always, whether we are conscious of it or not, to the good of the whole Body of Christ. We do not live to ourselves or die to ourselves, but the maintenance of a true testimony even where other believers know nothing of the conflict, it may be in a home or business place, where we are physically out of touch with all other believers, members of Christ, yet the maintenance of the testimony there in faithfulness is in that realm of the Body, the heavenlies, a great service to the whole Body. That is why the enemy likes if he can to smash a testimony in a home or in a business, because it is not merely the local situation which is affected but because of the universal blow that he can strike at the very Head, Christ, and we should see to it that the testimony is not something we try to keep up in public gatherings, it is involved in our domestic life, our business life.

Heavenly Relationships Reflected in the "Body."

This brings us back to the Ephesian letter again. All the relationships of the believers are to be on the principle of the one Body. It is not a sweep down from the heavenlies to the earthlies to bring in "Husbands love your wives," etc. That is not coming down to the earthlies, that is saying that relationships of believers are to be on the principle of the one Body. Am I a husband, then my attitude, relationship, conduct to my wife must not be on a human basis but as a fellow member of the Body of Christ, realising that not merely natural interests are involved but universal interests. In our relationships the whole Body is bound up. You know quite well that is true. If husbands and wives become spiritually dislocated as children of the Lord, there is something in that which does great harm to the testimony of the Lord, and great harm to the Lord Himself and is used by the enemy to become a great adverse spiritual factor over and beyond that local domestic situation, it registers something in the spiritual realm which is harmful. And so in all other relationships; servants to masters, a maid to her mistress. Not just good Christians as on the earth doing their service in a good Christian way—earning wages; not just as an earthly thing, but to regard that master, that mistress, as a fellow-member of Christ. Not unto them as men and women but to recognise that bound up with our service to them is the whole universality of the Body of Christ. Paul includes the whole Body in the relationships of master and servant, mistress and maid, in principle. That is, I think, most obvious in its outworking. You get believers who are in these relationships of masters and mistresses and servants, and you get some strain between them; beloved, that reaches far beyond the mere location of it, it reaches out and affects the Lord's interests in a much wider range than that.

If only we recognised this as a declared law of the Body of Christ! It is not a matter of whether we see it doing the mischief or not, it is whether the Lord says it is so. The Lord says here

as clearly as anything can be said, that
these relationships are not locked up
within the compass of their own operation, but they do reach out into a great
universal expanse of the heavenly Body
and the whole Body of Christ is spiritually affected by these strains which
come into these relationships. You see
what is involved, you see what a motive
we have in our relationships for keeping
them on a high level. If there comes
between those in these relationships,
these strains, these cross-purposes,
these cross-currents, this being offended
and upset, this breach of true love, our
attitude must be, not just that this is
a miserable unhappy thing, and the
sooner we make it up the better; our
attitude must be, this thing out in the
realm of spiritual intelligences is working against the glory of Christ, this is
working against Him as the Head
because all these relationships are joined
so vitally to the Head; this is working
against the Holy Spirit as the unifying
power of the whole Body, this is doing

damage, and therefore, inasmuch as we are so minutely related to all the members by the Holy Spirit, what one does must somehow, all beyond our realisation or consciousness, touch Christ, touch the Holy Spirit, and therefore, all other members. It is doing that. That is the revelation here, that is the nature of the Body. You see why we should see to these relationships and lift them up out of the earthlies. I think that is something to think more about.

Relativity is the law of the Body of Christ. Relativity is holding fast the Head; and let us beware of trying to maintain the Body in its oneness along the horizontal line. You cannot do it. It is a hopeless thing, and we shall always be running round and making apologies. On the horizontal we cannot do it, but if we hold fast the Head, we shall find our gravitation is together. We cannot give Christ His place fully and absolutely and be at cross-purposes with another believer. Christ must have His place so that we do everything unto Him, all for Him, all for His sake. We cannot have an attitude like that and maintain a grievance with another believer. Holding fast the Head and everything being unto Him would demand an adjustment in our relationships and bring it about. *We cannot love the Lord with all our hearts and not love one of His;* that is a contradiction. So that the oneness of the Body first of all demands that we hold fast the Head.

The Liberty of the Spirit.

There must be the liberty of the Spirit in us in order to realise the Body and its ministry. I am coming down to practical questions. There must be absolute freedom from human organisation, ecclesiastical government, man's control *as such* if there is going to be a full functioning of the Holy Spirit. To get into a hide-bound religious system, ecclesiastical control, a human organisation of the Church where you have to

preach every so often whether you have
anything to say or not because you are
paid to do it is absolutely against the
Holy Spirit. That is not the principle
of the Holy Spirit, and we must be
absolutely free from all such things if
the Spirit is going to function freely
and we are going to have ministry in
the Holy Ghost. That is the principle
of the Spirit. It was that that the Jews,
the Jewish leaders, were so set against
in the case of the Apostle Paul. He
said, "certain came in to spy out our
liberty." What was it? That he had
thrown off the yoke of the law and the
Jewish system and now he was exercis-
ing himself in the universal realm of
the Body of Christ, Gentiles and Jews,
just as much the one as the other, liberty
in Christ. He was free from all yokes
of tradition, system, and organisation
religiously on the earth, in order to
fulfil his ministry of revelation as the
Holy Spirit led him. That is essential
to the Body of Christ. By which I mean
that to try to organise the Body of

Christ, the Church, and to try to set a programme for it and hand it to the Holy Spirit and say, "will you kindly take the chair and carry out our programme" (that may seem irreverent, I know, but it is not meant to be so) is so utterly contrary to the principle here revealed. The Body of Christ is a thing emancipated from the earthly systems; it must be to function. It is not our forsaking the earthly system because we have taken hold of certain truths, but our being emancipated. There is a right place for spiritual government and subjection in the Church, and the "free lance" principle is just as wrong as officialism.

But I must come to a close. We will close on that point. We cannot take up Church membership, and we cannot take up Church work in the Body of Christ. We have heard people say they are going to take up Church work. Those ideas are utterly foreign to the truth of the Body of Christ. We cannot join the Body of Christ. Take the physical illustration again, and see how ludicrous it is for someone else's hand or arm to say that it is coming to join my body! It is absurd. This is a Church which we cannot enter into horizontally, we have got to come into it from heaven, we have to come into it by birth, not by adhering or accretion. That is the law of the Body's growth. It is by birth, out from the heavenlies, and what is true of the relationship, the membership of the Body of Christ, is true of the ministry, the work. We cannot take up work or ministry in the Body of Christ. When we get a true spiritual thing representing adequately the Lord's mind people from the outside cannot come into that and begin to minister. They have to come into the revelation that is there by the Holy Ghost and come into that on an experimental basis. You cannot invite preachers to come and preach. The fellowship in that ministry is the fellowship of revelation : that you have come into it on the same ground, by the same

Note

way, you have been born into it from
above, the only basis of Body ministry.
The organised Church can do anything
it likes, but in the Body of Christ, no!
In its ministry the thing is essentially
coming in from above and not joining
from the outside. So we cannot join the
Church in the New Testament sense,
we cannot take up Church work in the
New Testament sense, we have to be an
organic part of it, and the revelation of
the truth of the Body has no place for
that system which appoints officers and
workers in a kind of mechanical, official
way. (You cannot take hold of a brother
and make him an official in the Body of
Christ, you can in an earthly system,
but not here. Such must grow up by a
spiritual process, and the ministry is
expressed, grows up, out of the inner
life, it is not official, it is organic.

That opens up a whole realm of truth
that would be· profitable, but we will
stop there just now, and ask the Lord
to give us the revelation, if we have not
got it, for however much more we may

say about it, after all it will become to us only as teaching, truth, doctrine, unless the Lord makes it live, gives us the revelation. But oh, there is such a vast difference between what is called the Church here, its system, its methods, its relationships, and this truth that the Body of Christ is a spiritual, heavenly thing : such a great difference! This heavenly thing is universal in its range and in its ministry even though it may be but represented by a handful in a location; a universal ministry, something that does not belong to time or space; it is essentially spiritual and that is heavenly, illimitable.

The City
Which Hath
Foundations

SYNOPSIS.

The City which hath Foundations.

Meditations on the Spiritual Background of Jerusalem.

CHAPTER I.

An Introductory Review.

READING : Hebrew xi. 10; Ezekiel v. 5.

Our object is to see that because Jerusalem is so closely related to God, indeed has been brought into being by Him, her values must be pre-eminently spiritual and divine. Back of her history there lie those elements which are not of this world, nor are they merely of time, but are heavenly and eternal.

The Land of Syria.

Before we can consider the city particularly we must view the land as a whole, because very largely the city is the concentration of the features of the land. We note that in Hebrews xi. the city which hath foundations is closely related to the heavenly country (verses 10, 16), so that the city is but the concentration of the country. That is an important thing to bear in mind as we go on.

We will note several of the relationships of the land.

Firstly, *the relationship of the land to the rest of the world.* Syria has been of greater significance to mankind, both spiritually and materially, than any other single country in the world.

We observe at once its centrality. It stands between Asia and Africa, between the two primeval homes of man, the valleys of the Euphrates and the Nile; also between the two great centres of empire, Western Asia and Egypt. One side represents the eastern and ancient world, the other side the Mediterranean as the gateway to the western and modern world.

Secondly, we note *the connection between Syria and Arabia.* Syria is at the northern end of the Arabian world. Arabia was the cradle of the Semites. The Semites went out in four directions : (1) to Ethiopia (2) to Egypt via the isthmus of Suez (3) to Mesopotamia through the Arabian Desert (4) to Western Syria via the Jordan. More than in any other direction these Semites have gravitated toward Syria, and we know of their coming into that land in two special ways, in the case of Abraham from Mesopotamia, and Israel (the Hebrews) from Egypt.

Thirdly, *the relationship of the land to Asia, Africa and Europe.* We note that the oldest road in the world, from the Euphrates to the Nile, which is still used (although the old camel caravan has given place to motor transport) runs through Damascus, through Galilee, the Plain of Esdraelon, down the maritime Plain of Palestine, through Gaza to Egypt.

Fourthly, *the nations and peoples of the earth who have had to do with Syria.* There is a tremendous catalogue of these. This land has been either the objective, or the actual dwelling-place, or the battle-field, of all these nations; mostly the dwelling-place. The Hittites came South from Asia Minor, and the Ethiopians came North from the conquest of the Nile. Here is the list of invaders: the Hittites, the Ethiopians, the Scythians, the Babylonians, the Persians, the Moslem invasion, the Turks, the Mongols, the Greeks, the Romans, the Arabs, the Crusaders, Napoleon, and finally the Allies of the Great War. All these have had special interest in this little country, so that it is quite clear that Syria has occupied a very important place in the history of this world.

Then we note one or two details as to the land itself. The length of the land is about four hundred miles in all, with a width varying from eighty to one hundred miles, bounded by the sea on the West, Mount Taurus on the North, and by the desert on the East and South. The name "Syria" is short for "Assyria." The name was originally applied by the Greeks to the whole of the Assyrian Empire from the Caucasus to the Levant. Then that Empire shrank to this side of the Euphrates, and finally to the present limits which we have noted. Palestine is only a part of Syria, defined by the Greeks the Southern part of Syria, including Judea.

The country is broken by mountain ranges, so much so as never to have been brought together under one government. There is the triple barrier against the desert; firstly the Jordan Valley, secondly the Western Range, and thirdly the Eastern Range; and four lines can be drawn down the land marking distinct features; firstly there is the sea plain, secondly the Western Range, thirdly the Jordan and the Jordan Valley, fourthly the Eastern Range.

We now turn to note the spiritual instruction which comes to us from the historic.

I. The Centrality of Jerusalem.

That which we have just noted shows how central that land, and Jerusalem the city, are geographically, historically, and—as we shall yet see more fully—spiritually. If you want to be impressed with the centrality of the land and of the city geographically, all you have to do is to take a map of the world, and put your pencil upon Syria (Mercator's projection).

The centrality of this country is tremendously impressive, and when you add to the geographical centrality the historic centrality, and see how all the way through history the nations of the world have been attracted toward that point, have been interested in it, have in some way or other been related to Syria, that again is an impressive thing. But when you add to the geographical and the historical the religious, or rather, the spiritual, and see that, in the main, it is because God in some way is related to that central point, then the significance goes much further, and becomes very much more impressive. Surely this is not just a natural thing; this is not normal; there is something about this which speaks of wider issues than merely a few miles of Syrian soil, a fragment of this earth as something in itself! It is like the arena of a great amphitheatre where God has been working out in history a

drama with spiritual significance, showing to
the world things which are not merely of time
nor of the earth, but of eternity and of heaven.
So that Jerusalem, in the very first place,
speaks of centrality.

The Anti-Type—The New Jerusalem.

Turning from the historic Jerusalem, the
type, to the anti-type, the spiritual Jerusalem
of the Book of the Revelation and elsewhere, we
know that feature is revealed to be the first
thing about the heavenly Jerusalem, which
is the Church.   Take two things, for instance,
which are said about the New Jerusalem.

Firstly, that the nations shall walk in the
light thereof, and shall bring their glory into it
(Revelation xxi. 24 and 26).   If we bear in
mind that the New Jerusalem is not a mere
geographical thing, but the Church, then the
Church is seen ultimately to be in a central
place to all the rest of the world.   It occupies
that point with all the nations round about
related thereto.   Just as the historic Jerusalem
occupies that central place geographically and
historically, so in a spiritual way the Church
ultimately will be at the centre of God's
universe, and everything will be toward it and
as from it.   It will be central, the nations and

the kings all moving to and from it, all the kingdoms of this world recognising the Church as the universal metropolis.

Secondly, it is said that the New Jerusalem has on its four sides three gates (Revelation xxi. 13), and "the city lieth foursquare" (verse 16). "Four" is the number of creation, the whole creation. The whole creation is represented by the City. On each of the four sides of the City there are three gates. That means there is equality in all directions. If the City were represented as being to one side of the world, it would not need three gates on the back side. Its gates would be in the other three directions, but if three gates are equally on every side it surely means that what lies before those gates is equal. Everything speaks of centrality in the Church.

All that means has yet to be seen and worked out, but we want in the first place to get the City set, we want to see what the place and position of the Church is intended to be, and when that is recognised we can understand the many-sided activity of the enemy to destroy the Church, we can understand that aspect of Jerusalem's history which is so fraught with contest, conflict, dispute, siege, assault. What a tremendous history Jerusalem has had ! Well might the Psalmist urge that we should pray for the peace of Jerusalem. There has been

good reason to pray thus for Jerusalem, for
she has known tribulation beyond any other
on this earth.

That is suggestive and significant, and
carries its own spiritual meaning. What a
history the Church has! What a history of
conflict the true spiritual people of God have!
Well might the Lord have said to His own true
ones : "In the world ye shall have tribulation
. . . ." (John xvi. 33). To come really into a
living relationship with Christ as a vital part
of His Church means to come into the conflict
of all the ages, to the realm of ceaseless conflict.
But there is a reason, and the best of reasons,
for when once Jerusalem is set, comes down
from God out of heaven, and is set in her place
at the centre of the universe, no other power
will be able to lift itself against her. That
Church is destined to occupy the place of
centrality and supremacy in Christ throughout
all the ages yet to be. Not least of the many-
sided activities of the enemy has been his effort
to set up a false church, an imitation church,
a counterfeit church.

More will be said about that as we go on,
but we have laid down our first principle and
seen the first feature of the "Jerusalem which
is above" as to God's thought for her.

We pass to the second feature :

II. The Heavenliness of Jerusalem.

We go back to the first movements of which we know in the relationship of God to Jerusalem. These movements began with Abraham. There is a sense in which we could say that Abraham was the father of the City of God. The Word says of him that "he looked for a city." Somehow (it is not recorded how) he came to look for a city related to God. There is nothing which tells us that God spoke to him about the city, but here is the statement clearly made that "he looked for a city . . . . whose builder and maker is God" (Hebrews xi. 10). Somehow he came into the quest for a city related to God, of which God was the Architect (for that is the literal word) and Maker. That surely means that the City would take its form and character from God. If God is the Architect and Maker, then the thing made, designed, would take its character from Him. Thus Abraham looked for something which was an expression of the thought and will of God, which was the result of Divine activity, a City.

What was the first step toward that City? We are told by a man who is said to have been full of the Holy Ghost, Stephen : "The God of glory appeared unto our father Abraham" (Acts vii. 2). That was the first step in relation

to the City which was to be the expression of
God's thought. From that point the Divine
association with Jerusalem has always been as
with what is in the world, and yet outside of it.
The God of glory has not attached Himself)
wholly to anything of this earth since the fall.)
He took up something and made it an illustration of something else which was not of this
earth at all, and from the point when the God
of glory appeared unto Abraham God's association with Jerusalem was always, has always
been, as with that which, while being in the
world is yet outside of it. We emphasise this,
that *God's association* with it has been on that
wise. We mean that God associated Himself
with Jerusalem only so long as she stood true
to His thought of something in the world and
yet outside of it. When Jerusalem failed to
maintain that principle and became associated
with the world God forsook it. God's association was only on the ground that it was outside
of the world while in it. This is made very
clear, both positively and negatively ; positively,
as Jerusalem expressed the Divine thought
of a Heavenly City and maintained separation
from the world, God associated Himself with
Jerusalem ; negatively, whenever Jerusalem
failed or ceased to express that Divine thought,
God withdrew. So that we have it, by contrast,
showing what God's mind was, that the dark

history of Jerusalem, destruction, suffering, and being forsaken, is a very strong proof and evidence that God will not associate Himself with anything which does not express His thought as being entirely heavenly although here on this earth; such a thing He will not uphold nor maintain. That is a very important thing in our consideration.

Features in the Life of Abraham.

Turning again to Abraham we shall see that *Abraham was the inclusive type of the City*. In order to follow that out we take this principle of heavenliness and trace the heavenly features in the life of Abraham. If Abraham is being spiritually constituted according to God's thought for the City because he is the father of the City, then you expect to see the features of the City running right through Abraham's life, and this feature of heavenliness is not difficult to trace in the life of Abraham. We will trace it in eight respects.

I. Heavenly Vision.

"The God of glory appeared unto our father Abraham" (Acts vii. 2). That is heavenly vision. In the New Testament we should call it Divine revelation, God revealing Himself.

Note

What is the Church? It is the place in which God is revealed, the place of heavenly vision. The Church is the embodiment of the revelation of God in Christ. The Church has to be the sphere in which men and women come to a knowledge of God, an ever-growing knowledge of God. The Church is not just something to carry out a set order of things, maintain a form. The Church is the place in which there abides the living unveiling of God, and just as soon as something claiming to be the Church ceases to be the place in which there is any living unveiling of God it ceases to be what God calls "the Church," and when it fails in these Divine features God withdraws. It may go on, but God withdraws. When Jerusalem ceased to be the place of the revelation of God to the nations then God withdrew. The purpose of the Church in God's mind is that it should be the sphere of the abiding and continuous unveiling of God, the God of glory appearing. (See the first three chapters of Revelation.)

It is a grand thing to belong to that Church, and to know that Church. Do we know what it is to be where God is showing Himself, making Himself known, where constantly, again and again, the God of glory is appearing? Are you able to say that from week to week in the local assembly to which you belong the

God of glory is appearing? So often our hearts have warmed in the realisation that the Lord is showing Himself to us. That feature which was foundational to the life of Abraham is also foundational to Jerusalem, both earthly and heavenly. It is a governing law of the Church.

II. Separation from Earth.

Because of the revelation from heaven there is the consequent and essential separation from earth. "The God of glory appeared to Abraham when he was in Ur of the Chaldees." What was the result? "Get thee out of thy country, and from thy kindred . . ." (Genesis xii. 1). And he went *out*. Whence? From his world, his native world, his old world, all the world of nature, the world of natural birth, the world of natural relationship, the world of natural interests. He went *out*, and everything had to be new. It was *separation*.

That was hammered out through long centuries for Jerusalem. Go through the Word with "Jerusalem" again, and see how God continuously appeals for Jerusalem to be clean, to be separate, to be holy, to have no relationships with the countries round about, to stand as for God in the midst of the nations; and Jerusalem's terrible tragedy—the tragedy

B

which is told in the sobs of one prophet after another—is the tragedy of lost separation.

That is the tragedy of the Church. We see God's thought by the very tragedy of the Church's history. You cannot violate God's thoughts for His people and have anything but a tragic history. What the Church needs to realise so much is its heavenly relationship, calling for an *utter* separation from the world, in order that God may wholeheartedly associate Himself with it.

III. Heavenly Citizenship.

"For he looked for the city which hath the foundations, whose builder (Architect) and maker is God" (Hebrews xi. 10). Where did he find it? He never found it on this earth at all! When we turn to Hebrews xi. we find that Abraham did see something a long, long way off, and hailed it. The Lord Jesus said : ". . . Abraham rejoiced to see my day . . ." (John viii. 56). He saw by faith. "By faith Abraham, when he was called, obeyed . . . and he went out . . ." (Hebrews xi. 8). "These all died in faith, not having received . . ." (verse 13). His citizenship was not a citizenship of this earth at all, it was a heavenly citizenship. The New Testament makes that perfectly clear. The true seed of Abraham are the believers (not the Jewish nation) who are linked with the Jerusalem which is above, "which is the mother of us all" (Galatians iv. 26). That is how Paul puts it. So the Apostle also says : "For our citizenship is in heaven ; from whence also we wait for a Saviour . . ." (Philippians iii. 20).

IV. A Pilgrim and a Stranger.

As running closely with that, and corresponding with it, we are told that Abraham in the land was as a pilgrim and a stranger, dwelling in tents, having no part in the land, being in the land a stranger. Is not that a feature of heavenliness? Pilgrims and strangers here. But where, then, do we belong? Peter in writing his letter says : "Beloved, I beseech you as strangers and pilgrims . . ." (1 Peter ii. 11), belonging to the heavenly country, with the heavenly citizenship.

V. No Earthly Patronage or Rewards.

No patronage or rewards from this world were for Abraham. Though he may have done service in the interests of certain righteous principles, and in so doing his service may have been of value to those in this world (and who shall say that the spiritual service of the Lord's people on this earth has not meant some value to this world, even to this ungodly world? the Lord alone knows what the world would be without His people in it), Abraham said, No, to those of this world, of the cities of Sodom and Gomorrah, who had derived some benefit from his activity, when they would offer him some reward and would patronise him. Abraham still stands outside.

That has been one of those deeply laid snares of the Devil, to make something of the service of the people of God on this earth, to confer upon them recognition, titles, position, to make them something here on this earth amongst men. You will notice that so often when these preferments take place, and these gifts are made, and this recognition is granted, and these positions are given, there is a farewell to the deep spiritual note, there is an end of the real spiritual value of that life. The tragedy of many a really valuable servant of God, who was used mightily of God in a spiritual way and finished up life without that note, having lost that spiritual value, was upon this very thing, that in some way they became recognised and accepted, they received recognition, preference, awards from this world. To maintain heavenliness, separation is essential to the maintenance of spiritual value.

VI. No Natural Resources or Energies.

Abraham had to learn that lesson in a very hard school. His life was marred by a terrible mark and scar, when he broke down and tried by natural means and methods and courses to realise Divine ends. The world to-day holds that scar in a most terrible way. Look at Islam, look at Ishmael, and you have the full growth of that fatal mistake of Abraham when he tried to realise a Divine purpose along natural lines. Heavenly people may not do that. A heavenly Church may not do that. The Church has tried to do that. It has tried to accomplish its Divine mission by worldly means, by natural resources and energies. Its tragedy is clear. Its weakness is manifest to all. For the heavenly thing no resources or energies of nature are permissible.

VII. No merely Earthly Fruit for God.

I am thinking of Isaac. Isaac came eventually, and came through Sarah. There is an earthly link in Isaac, though he be born by Divine intervention, through heavenly power. But God will sever that earthly link, God will cut clean in between what is of heaven and of earth, and take Isaac to death. And who can raise the dead but God? Seeing then that only God can raise the dead, what is raised from the dead is *all of God*. So God will have no link with earth, even in what may be for Him.

Very often God causes some of His heavenly purpose to be born in a human heart, a purpose of God born in the heart of a man or a woman. In the course of time that man or woman takes that heavenly vision and in some way it becomes *their* vision : for God, yes, but theirs ! It is a terrible thing to interfere with somebody who has a heavenly vision from the Lord which *they* hold. So often they become the most spiky people that you have to deal with. Yes, they have a vision from the Lord, they have a sense of call from the Lord, and they are holding that thing for the Lord. That is quite good, but *they* are holding it, and *they* have got it, and it is *theirs,* and God often has to take that thing which had its origin in Himself clean away to death ; it has to go, and it is as though they never had a vision. Worse than that, they are in confusion, utterly confounded. God gave a vision, and now it has all been smashed and broken. God gave a call and a purpose, and now everything contradicts that, it has all gone. God will not have even that which is of Himself held by man, laid hold of by man.

Perhaps Abraham's peril was, even though

he had got Isaac by a miracle, to make Isaac his, dear to his own heart, to make Isaac his own; and God said, in effect, No, Abraham, no earth ties, even in Divine things! This thing is utterly of Me, and not of you! It is so easy to bring God's great purpose within the compass of some human instrumentality, to be very concerned maybe for world evangelisation, but it must be through our Mission! That is taking hold of God's purposes and making them private property. God will not have that if the thing is going to realise His full end, if He is wholly to commit Himself to it.

VIII. No Place in the Heavenly for the Hand of Man.

Nothing of man must have any place, hold or prerogative in that which is of heaven. I am thinking of the tomb at Machpelah. You remember that Sarah died, and Abraham, who had good standing in the country, sought a place of burial for his wife, for himself and his seed, and the cave of Machpelah was proved to be the very place. He offered to buy it, but the men who owned it offered it to him free, they well nigh besought him to accept it as a present. But he would not have it cheaply, he would have the full price weighed and purchase it outright, so that no one should be able to say : You got it cheaply, you really owe us something, you really are in our debt, we really have a claim over you ! No ! to the last farthing he will buy it outright. No hand of man shall be able to have a claim, never shall it be possible for anybody of this world to suggest that Abraham and his descendents are under an obligation to them.

Do you see the working of the principle? No hand of man, no rights as of this world in the Church ! Jerusalem which is above is free, is *free* ! This world has no claims there. There is no other power which has any rights there. The Church stands free in God ; but, oh, look at the complications to-day, look at the obligations, look how the Church has sold itself to the world, and how the world has a hold upon it. It is saying, and has a perfect right to say : You are under obligations to us ! That is not the Church according to His thought.

All these are aspects of the one great truth of heavenliness.

The necessity for our time is for the Lord's people to come to a spiritual understanding of what heavenliness means. Only so can the Church, the Lord's people, know power. I am certain that the whole question of spiritual power is bound up with heavenliness. The Lord Jesus, Who is the land and Who is to be, in all the essential elements of His being, gathered up in the Church represented by the City, said : "The prince of this world cometh, and hath nothing in me" (John xiv. 30). What a place of power! What a place of victory! What a place of ascendency! Imagine it! "The prince of this world"—with all that he has (and he has a tremendous amount in his hands, tremendous power),—"cometh, and hath nothing in Me" (John xiv. 30). "Now shall the prince of this world be cast out" (John xii. 31). Those two things go together, and it is because the Lord's people do not stand in that position that *they cannot* cast out the prince of this world, *they cannot* overcome him. He has so much power in the midst of the Lord's people because he has ground, and the ground is this world. No ground, therefore no rights! That is tremendous. Oh, that God might get a people there.

Listen to this. "The Jerusalem that is above is *free,* which is the mother of us all" (Galatians iv. 26). "And there appeared a great wonder in heaven; a woman clothed with the sun, and the moon under her feet . . . and behold a great red dragon . . . and the dragon stood before the woman . . . to devour her child . . ." (Revelation xii. 1-4). Jerusalem is our mother. The Church above is our mother. But there is a man-child being born out from the Church, out from the mother, a man-child, and a great red dragon waiting to devour, and that man-child is caught up to the Throne. What is that? That is something *out of* the general Church which is specific in its overcoming power. That goes to the Throne.

The Lord is seeking to have at least out from the whole Church a company of an entirely and utterly heavenly nature, to govern, to rule, so that the enemy is cast down and has no more place in heaven.

Let us ask the Lord to teach us the meaning of heavenliness. It is a tremendous thing in the realisation of His end.

Lord teach me what it means to be , seated with you in the heavenly realm. !

CHAPTER II.

Heavenly Features in the Heavenly Jerusalem, the Church.

Rev. xxi. 9-11. In this passage we see the Apostle was carried away in the Spirit into a mountain great and high, and shown the New Jerusalem *"coming down out of heaven. . . ."*

Rev. iii. 12. "I will write upon him the name of my God, and the name of the city of my God, the new Jerusalem, which *cometh down out of heaven* from my God. . . ."

Heb. xi. 16. ". . . he hath prepared for them a city."

You will recognise the tense and the position of that last statement. While it is referring to those martyrs of the faith of the old dispensation of Old Testament times, the word here "he *hath* prepared for them a city" —not, He prepared for them a city, as though they inherited it in Jerusalem on this earth, but He *hath* prepared for them a city—shows that they have not yet entered into it. It awaits their entrance. I believe that the city there, referring as it does to the Church, would be very closely touched upon by that inclusive declaration of the Apostle in that same chapter, that "These all died in faith, not having received the promises . . . God having provided some better thing concerning *us,* that apart from us they should not be made perfect'' (Heb. xi. 13, 39, 40). So that the words *"hath* prepared for them a city'' really mean that they are coming into this heavenly Jerusalem, the Church.

In chapter xii. of the Hebrew letter, verse 22, there is this word : ''. . . ye are come . . . unto the city of the living God, the heavenly Jerusalem. . . .'' In chapter xiii., verse 14, there is this word : ''. . . we seek after the city *which is to come.''* Then back in the letter to the Galatians, chapter iv., verses 25 and 26, we have these words : ''the Jerusalem that is above is free, which is our mother.'' The letter to the Galatians stands over against the Jewish order of things, was intended so to do, and Jerusalem was always regarded by Israel as their mother. She was looked upon as the mother of all the Israelites. Now over against the earthly Jerusalem, and that earthly conception of Jerusalem, the Apostle here says : ''the Jerusalem which is above is free, which is our mother'' : and in Philippians iii. 20 we find these words : ''our *citizenship* is in heaven.''

You can see from these various passages that the thought of heavenliness is very strongly related to the Church, which is the heavenly Jerusalem, of which God is the Builder and Maker. God is building His heavenly Jerusalem now, and He is building it with heavenly material, that is, the constitution and the construction of the Church must all be heavenly, and that which is employed (or, to put it another way, the saints) must partake of a heavenly nature, in order to become the heavenly City. The Great Architect and Builder is, therefore, engaged with the saints in seeking to make them heavenly in their whole constitution.

We have to see a little further what heavenliness means, and we can do this by way of illustration from the Old Testament again, by turning to Psalm lxxxvii. The first thing which comes out in that Psalm is the jealousy of God over Jerusalem. "The Lord loveth the gates of Zion more than all the dwellings of Jacob." "Zion" is a word which came to embrace the whole city. It was not always so, but it came in the course of time to represent Jerusalem, and is very often, in the prophecies especially, synonymous with Jerusalem. "The Lord loveth the gates of Zion more than all the dwellings of Jacob." There is a partiality of God, a jealousy of God for Jerusalem. When you ask why the Lord is jealous in this way, as to what is behind this Divine partiality, the answer can be given in the word which we are

using, "heavenliness." The Divine thought
about Jerusalem concerns her heavenliness,
and that feature comes out, as you notice, with
the very first sentence : "His foundation is in
the holy mountains." Mountains are always
features or types of spiritual elevation, and if
you want that borne out, you can turn to
another Psalm and read this literal translation : "Great is the Lord and greatly to be
praised, in the city of our God, in his holy
mountain. Beautiful in elevation, the joy of
the whole earth, is mount Zion" (Psalm xlviii.
1). Beautiful in elevation, the joy of the whole
earth ! You see this is a matter of elevation.
It is a matter of a high position, a conspicuous
place. It is heavenliness, spiritual ascendency.

We will speak about that more from the
spiritual standpoint presently, but we will just
go through this Psalm lxxxvii. step by step
to see that there is bound up with that initial
statement about the Lord's jealousy and
partiality a contrast between Zion and other
cities, and the contrast is based upon the
spiritual features which they represent.

The Contrast between Zion and Egypt.

First of all you have Egypt. "Rahab" is
the word used here, but you may know that
"Rahab" refers to Egypt. We remember that
when Abraham, the father of the city, entered

into the land of Canaan, the land of promise,
his faith was instantly met with a very severe
test, for he found the whole country given up
to idolatry. He also found a state of severe
famine in the land, His faith wavered, and
some kind of question evidently crept into his
heart, which led him eventually to conclude
either that he had made a mistake, had been
misled, or else he was altogether out of his
time. So turning from the land he went down
to Egypt, and Egypt, therefore, became the
place that typifies the opposite of faith. What
is the opposite of faith? If God, and God
alone, is the object of faith, then if faith breaks
down it means that God is set aside, and you
look for something else to take the place of God.
So that Egypt is clearly seen to represent
resources of the earth, natural resources, to
which men turn when they lose faith in God.
We know what happened to Abraham, that his
lapse of faith and his turning to Egypt led to
disaster, brought him into compromise, into
entanglement, into shame; and that is ever the
result of turning from God, as our one and only
resource, to other resources which are of men.
Very early, you see, in the history of the
Church you have those elements which have
repeatedly all the way through been its danger,
and too often those to which it has succumbed.
The history of the Church is one sad story of

repeated lapses from God to human resources, natural means, natural methods, the results of which have always been the same—compromise, entanglement, shame.

What Abraham did as the father of the race, Israel also did in the days of spiritual declension; for when Israel's spiritual life waned, and God therefore became distant and remote to faith, Israel turned to Egypt for help in the day of trouble. Egypt, therefore, always stands to represent those resources which men employ when God appears distant from them owing to the weakness of their own faith. You can see how clearly this is a coming down to earth, and therein is the contrast: "The Lord loveth the gates of Zion," "His foundation is in the holy mountains" (Psa. lxxxvii.), "the city of our God," "in his holy mountain," "beautiful in elevation," "the joy of the whole earth . . ." (Psa. xlviii. 1). There is a great contrast to Egypt. Egypt is down below, Zion up above, which is why the Lord loves Zion. The Lord has a special partiality for heavenliness about His people.

The Contrast between Zion and Babylon.

Passing that point of contrast, we come to Babylon. We know what Babylon represents. Babylon was the product of human effort and human glory. The city was built not far from the Tower of Babel, and the Tower of Babel was built with the object of making a name for man. It was human effort for human glory. That tower for ever speaks of the super-man, the glory of fallen man, and the Devil's object has always been to try to get fallen man to reach unto heaven. Just as they sought to make that tower to reach unto heaven, so Satan has always sought to make man a super-man by his own effort, and in his own glory. Babylon always speaks of that, "Let us build us a city, and a tower . . . and let us make us a name . . ." (Gen. xi. 4). Many years afterward the great king of Babylon, Nebuchadnezzar, uttered these words : "Is not this great Babylon, that I have builded . . ." (Dan. iv. 30).

How clearly, then, Babylon speaks of man's power, man's effort, man's glory, seeking to reach unto the very clouds. Babylon stands for the glory of human power, but, of course, in a religious way; for Babylon was very religious, strongly religious. The idea here is of something glorious in this world, with man's name upon it. When we recognise that, how impressive are the words : "I will write upon him the name of my God, and the name of the city of my God——" (Rev. iii. 12). Man's design is to have something glorious in the way of a city with his own name upon it. God's thought is to have a glorious thing of a heavenly order, with *His* Name upon it, and this He will have. The Church has God's Name on it, because it will be an expression of God's glory and God's power and God's effort, and it will be glorious indeed. But here is the difference between Zion, spiritual elevation in heavenliness, and Babylon, that which stands in the glory of man. No wonder God is jealous over Zion.

The Contrast between Zion and Philistia.

Next we come to the contrast between Zion and Philistia. Philistia, we are well aware, speaks of the natural mind intruding into Divine things. We know the Philistines were always impinging upon Divine things. Closely associated all the time geographically with Israel, they were a most persistent foe, yet repeatedly seen as peering into the things of God, as, for example, into the Ark. Here then is uncircumcised, or if you like, uncrucified flesh taking hold of Divine things, and manipulating them. It is, in a sense, the rationalistic line of things, which does not recognise that the things of the Spirit of God are only known by the spiritual, and will seek by purely human means of intellect and

reason to arrive at Divine ends. That cannot
be done. Philistia represents that. Babylon
is natural effort, Philistia is natural reason,
and all is down there on the earth still, standing in contrast to Zion, because Zion is the
expression, not of any kind of human effort of
mind or body, but of the revelation of the Spirit
of God.

The Contrast between Zion and Tyre.

Tyre stands for the business or commercial
world. There were tremendous activities in
Tyre as a sea port. The one thing which Tyre
represented, and which the whole atmosphere
of Tyre expressed, was commerce, expansion,
business, the affairs of this world. We hardly
need dwell upon that as over against Zion. We
know this, at any rate, that the enemy is all
too eager to get people so tied up in business
affairs as to have no time or strength for
contemplating heavenly things. Any business
man will tell you that, and I suppose anybody,
except those people who really have nothing
whatever to do in business of any kind, will
tell you that responsibilities are so pressed
home, that it is a matter of supreme effort to
get time for heavenly things. Tyre is always
a challenge to Zion. In spiritual principle we
are up against Tyre every day. Oh, how the

enemy through this world's affairs seeks to make inroads upon our time for the things of the Lord. The Lord is very jealous for the heavenly side of things, and His partiality is to the detriment of Tyre.

The Contrast between Zion and Ethiopia.

Finally, Ethiopia. Let us recall the incident in chapter viii. of the book of the Acts, of an Ethiopian who had been up to Jerusalem at the time of the Feast, and was evidently deeply exercised about spiritual matters, being in a state of inquiry, yet not having found an answer to his question, and his heart need. He was still in the shadows, still in the dark, and the Lord recognised that need, that search, not satisfied in the place where it ought to have been satisfied, the official headquarters, and sent Philip from Samaria to join his chariot in the wilderness, to open his eyes, to lead him out of his darkness. So that Ethiopia becomes there, and elsewhere in the Scriptures, a type of the darkened understanding, the understanding needing enlightenment, natural darkness; a type also of that which is true of us all. The word of Philip to the eunuch was: "Understandest thou?" and his answer: "How can I . . ." How true that is of all men by nature.

The Ethiopian here in Psalm lxxxvii. is taken as an expression of the state of all men by nature, having the understanding darkened, and needing someone to teach. Over against that, Zion speaks of the eyes of the heart being enlightened, the Spirit of wisdom and revelation in the knowledge of Him. It says the citizens of Zion are those who have had their eyes opened, and the Lord loves that which expresses His mighty eye-opening work, His work of illumination, of enlightenment, of quickened understanding. The Lord delights in the light, and in that which walks in the light, while He does not delight in darkness.

So we see in this five-fold contrast Zion is supreme, because of this main feature of heavenliness. Jerusalem is the concentration of the features of the whole land of Syria. In the same way the Church is the concentration of the features of Christ. Christ is our land of promise. The Church is a concentrated expression of Christ, or is intended to be, and it is not difficult to see that this feature of Christ—heavenliness—is a very marked one. You touch it wherever you touch the Lord Jesus. How constantly He speaks of Himself as having come out from heaven, of being in heaven, and of everything in His life being heavenly. The great governing feature of Christ is heavenliness, and you see from the

Revelation that the New Jerusalem, the Church which is the concentrated expression of Christ, can be seen only from the vantage ground of elevation : "And he carried me away in the Spirit to a mountain great and high, and showed me the holy city Jerusalem . . ." (Rev. xxi. 10). If you look into the context you will see that Babylon was also shown, but no mountain was needed to view Babylon ; Babylon could be seen in the plain. If you are going to see heavenly things you need to be in the heavenlies. "He carried me away in the Spirit to a mountain great and high, and showed me the holy city Jerusalem . . ." To see Christ, and to express Christ, necessitates a heavenly union with Christ in the Spirit.

The Constituents of Heavenliness.

We will break up this feature into its constituents. What are the constituents of heavenliness?

I. Spirituality.

The first is spirituality. You cannot understand or enjoy heavenly things unless you are a spiritual man or a spiritual woman. A spiritual state is necessary for comprehending spiritual things. Paul declared that when he said : "Eye hath not seen, nor ear heard, neither hath entered into the heart of man, the things which God hath prepared for them that love him. But God hath revealed them unto us by his Spirit . . .'' (1 Cor. ii. 9). The natural man cannot receive the things of the Spirit of God, he cannot know them, the spiritual judge all things. A spiritual state is, of course, in the first instance by new birth—born of the Spirit; and then there is a progressive spiritual life. Spiritual growth is the only way, but it is the sure way of grasping, knowing, understanding, comprehending heavenly things. John's Gospel is the Gospel of spirituality, and everything in ''John'' is heavenly. You find it full of people in difficulties. Nicodemus is in difficulty, he cannot understand spiritual things at all and there is one great question mark which holds him in complete bondage : *How?* The Lord makes perfectly clear to him that he has to become a spiritual man, to be spiritually born, before he can understand spiritual things. The woman of Sychar is in just the same case, in as big a fog as was Nicodemus. The Lord makes it clear to her that what she needs is the Spirit dwelling within, when she will understand the meaning of life. And so you go through that Gospel, finding a large number of people in the dark, and the Lord in relation to every one of them touches upon the one principle. What is necessary is spiritual illumination? The man born blind needs the Lord to open his eyes, and on their being opened, he sees better than all the religious authorities around him, who are then quite manifestly in the dark. It is the Gospel of spirituality, which means that to comprehend heavenly things you must be spiritual in your essential being, born of the Spirit, indwelt and governed by the Spirit.

II. Elevation.

That is spiritual ascendency. Anyone who really does seek to walk with the Lord, to have his life maintained in the Spirit, understands quite well, apart from the technical words used, what spiritual elevation or ascendency means. You know what it is to have to battle constantly to maintain your position spiritually above. You know what it is to have almost everything brought upon you to press you down and to get you under. Once your spirit is under, to circumstances, to feelings, to appearances, to sensations, or to anything else, you are beaten, you are broken, you are useless, your testimony has gone. That the Church is called to be in the heavenlies in Christ Jesus is only another way of saying that this life must be in spiritual elevation, spiritual ascendency. The Lord, the Architect, is seeking to teach us every day how to take and maintain ascendency. Many opportunities are afforded each day of learning that lesson. Many times in a day you and I could go under to something if we let go. It is very easy to drop down, but the Lord calls upon us day by day, again and again, to refuse to go under. He urges us to take a strong hold upon Him, upon His Spirit, to be strengthened with might into the inward man, that we may not go under, but maintain our spiritual ascendency. That is the elevation of Zion, that is the elevation of the Church in all its members.

III. Faith.

That is made very clear by the father of the city, Abraham. If that city is eventually to be reached, then Abraham must, as its father (so to speak), be essentially a man of faith, and we know that to be the particular factor for which Abraham has stood all through history. "By faith Abraham . . ." And when all has been said about faith that can be said, it comes at last to this, believing in God's faithfulness. It is standing solidly with God on His faithfulness. Sometimes you can do no more than that. All the other aspects of faith, or faith's expression, may be impossible, and you simply have to stand back on that one final thing, Well, God is faithful! Eventually it will be

proved! Once through the present perplexity,
problem, and we shall find that God is faithful.
It may look now as though He has let us go,
as though He has failed us, as though He has
not answered, as though our expectation is disappointed; but when we get through we shall
find that God had not forsaken, God had not
abandoned us, and God had not contradicted,
but has been faithful. You and I will steadily
learn that. We do not learn that lesson all at
once. We are not incapable of asking questions
as to the Lord, and we sometimes have to put
up a fight against the suggestion of a doubt as
to the Lord's faithfulness; but God is faithful.
That is the final refuge of faith : but it is a
mighty thing to stand there, and Abraham
came to that position.

Heavenliness is a tremendous factor in the
life of the Lord's people. Heavenliness, which
is spirituality, which is ascendency, or elevation, and which is faith, is a tremendous factor.
All that is gathered up in Jerusalem. It means
being on other ground than on the ground of
this world, the ground of the natural man. Oh,
that the Church had maintained that position
all the way through! What terrible tragedies
have resulted from coming down to lower
ground!

We said that we would give an illustration
of the tragedy of coming down from a heavenly

position on the part of the Church. I found this, written by Sir George Adam Smith. Speaking of the Moslem invasion of Syria, by which Syria became swept and dominated by Islam, he writes—

"The Christianity of Syria fell before Islam because it was corrupt, and it deserved to fall."

And again :

"In attempting by purely human means to regain her birthplace, the Church was beaten back by Islam because she was selfish and worldly."

"In neither of these cases was it a true Christianity that was overthrown, though the true Christianity bears to this day the reproach, and the burden of the results. The irony of the Divine judgment is clearly seen in this, that it was on the very land where a spiritual monotheism first appeared that the Church was first punished for idolatry and materialism; that it was in sight of the scenes where Christ taught ar 1 healed, and went about doing good with His band of pure devoted disciples, that the envious, treacherous, truculent hosts of the Cross were put to sword and fire. They who in His Name sought a kingdom of this world by worldly means could not hope to succeed on the very fields where He had put such a temptation from Him. The victory of Islam over Christianity is no more a problem than the victory of Babylon over Israel."

That is a tremendous statement. What history there is in a statement like that ! Perhaps the greatest problem to-day of Christianity, of the mission field, is Islam. I do not think there is a greater problem than Islam for

the Church. Why? Well, Sir George Adam
Smith puts his finger right on the cause when
he says the power of Islam is due to the
corruption of the Church at a given point in
history; divided, selfish, and worldly. Islam
gained the mastery because of that.

How, then, would Islam be overthrown?
How would the mischief be undone? Surely
by a *heavenly* Church, by that which has been
wholly separated from this world in all means
and methods, and united in one spirit as a great
spiritual force, under the government of the
Holy Spirit. That, and that alone, will overthrow the forces which have gained their
position by reason of the unspirituality and
unheavenliness of the Church.

If that applies to the whole, it applies to us
individually, that spiritual power over any
ground of the enemy demands detachment
spiritually from the world, a close walk with
God, and a heavenly life, a life which is above
with Christ. The Lord lay upon our hearts
the tremendous importance of this heavenly
fellowship with Him from day to day, for the
sake of spiritual power and His glory.

CHAPTER III.

The Outcome of Departure from Heavenly Vision.

We have been seeking to bring into view that essential heavenliness of the Church which is a basic and governing law of God's purpose for her. This we have seen to be a factor of tremendous importance in God's dealings with Jerusalem. The more we read and meditate upon the matter, the more we see that this lies behind Jerusalem's history. Jerusalem and Palestine present for us a solid block of evidence on this matter. When we pass our eye over the Old Testament, we see that Jerusalem's coming into position, her ascendency or her revival, always related to those elements which speak of heavenliness, just as, on the contrary, her loss of place, of power, of glory, was due to earthly and worldly elements getting the upper hand.

Jerusalem reached her supreme crisis, when the Lord Jesus came into her midst. It was then that two things in an outstanding way marked the crisis of her history; the first, the heavenliness of His Own Person and life, ministry and mission; the second, the earthliness of Judea's vision, interests, and associations. This contrast is one of the most

45

outstanding elements of the Gospels. Never was Jerusalem's earthliness, earthboundness, more apparent, more conspicuous, than when the Lord was in her midst. He brought heaven in His Own Person. He was the embodiment of everything heavenly, and by reason of His presence the opposite state was dragged out into the light and made unmistakably clear.

The Heavenliness of Christ and His Own.

As to the first of these two things, the heavenliness of His Person, life, ministry and mission, John's Gospel more than any other brings it into view. We know that the Gospel by John is mainly concerned with matters within the compass of Judaism, and we know that in that Gospel Jerusalem figures very largely, and in a special, intensive way. Against that fact we see in this Gospel the heavenliness of Christ, as that which represents Him more particularly than anything else. Then, so far as His Own people are concerned, that Gospel makes the spiritual life of the believer a heavenly thing at every point. That is to say, the spiritual life of the believer is seen there to have its beginning in heaven ; he is born anew, or from above. That life is seen to be sustained from heaven. All the relationships of that life are seen to be heavenly. In that Gospel the Lord takes pains to woo His own from this world, and allows the shadow, if it must be so termed, of His going, to fall very heavily upon them, until their hearts are much troubled and distressed by what He says about His leaving them and going to the Father within a little while. All this, however, is with the definite and deliberate purpose of showing, firstly, that their life is to be a heavenly life, their hope a heavenly hope, not an earthly one—for their trouble of heart was largely due to disappointment as to their worldly expectations in relation to Himself— and He carries them away from the world, from the earth, and fastens their hope upon Himself in glory. That is to say, their's becomes a heavenly hope and not an earthly one. Their service is also set forth as a heavenly service. "As the Father hath sent me, even so send I you" (John xx. 21), making their commission a heavenly one upon a heavenly basis, and settling it for all time that the nature of His Own mission here was equally the nature of theirs, a heavenly mission.

We know how all that is gathered up into one heart cry in chapter xvii., and how repeatedly in that prayer the statements are positively made concerning both Himself and

them, that they are not of this world. His
prayer moreover was that they should be kept,
while in the world, from the world, and from
the Evil One, as the one who governs the evil
world. The heavenliness of Christ and His
own is brought very clearly into view right in
the midst of Judaism at its official headquarters
in Jerusalem, and it was on that ground that
the earthly Jerusalem reached its supreme
crisis.

The Earthboundness of Judaism.

As to the second thing, that is, the earthboundness of Judaism in all its aspects, there is
no doubt that this was the background and the
cause of its rejection of Christ, and John's
Gospel brings that also very clearly before us.
That earthboundness of theirs, the grip of
historic tradition upon their minds, resulted in
spiritual blindness to all that was heavenly.
This became manifest, as blindness always is
manifested, in various ways. The Gospel by
John gives us a clear unveiling of the outworking of that spiritual blindness in jealousy,
envy, prejudice, hatred, smallness and pettiness, suspicion, passion. These all run riot in
the Gospel by John, and the Jews are seen in a
very bad light there. And when you reflect
upon that in connection with this dominating

feature, the heavenliness of everything in relation to Christ, you see how utterly blind they were to all that was really heavenly. That blindness, working out in all these ways, led that nation to a full and final rejection of Him, and Jerusalem became the centre, and the seat, and the focal point of that intensified religious earthliness in its out-working.

It may be well for us to remind ourselves at this point, that we are having to do with the Church. You and I are supremely interested in the Church. Our great concern is the Church, which is His Body. And that being so, you and I are very deeply exercised, or should be, to know the nature of the Church, what it is that spiritually constitutes the true Church. If these things are true about the earthly Jerusalem, and stand at length in such vivid contrast to the heavenly Christ and the heavenly Church, they lead us to see quite clearly that jealousy, envy, prejudice, pettiness, suspicion, passion, hatred, and such like things, are marks of spiritual blindness. At very best they are marks of spiritual short-sightedness. Conversely, that means that spiritual vision and spiritual revelation should always work out to the absence of such things as jealousy, and envy, suspicion, and prejudice. It is a contradiction to say that we have heavenly light, revelation, that the heavenly Christ has broken upon our hearts, and to have any of these things. That in which they are found is not the heavenly Church.

The state to which we have just referred, obtaining in the earthly Jerusalem in the days of Christ, has been the state of that Jerusalem and of Judaism ever since, and is their state to-day. In Christ risen from the dead two things can be noted : (1) He did not again appear to Jerusalem nor to official Judaism; (2) He took the Church away from the earth spiritually, and centred it in Himself in heaven. But then history began to develop upon two planes, and along two lines, a true and a false; firstly, the Church as a spiritual and heavenly thing, developing under the direct government and control of the heavenly Holy Spirit; that is, its entire management became a thing as out from heaven; secondly, a false expression of Christianity as an earthly and man-governed system. Along these two lines history moved after the resurrection of Christ. Very soon in the Apostolic age this point of departure could be recognised.

The Jerusalem beneath has from very early in this dispensation become the seat of the most intensified expression of this false idea, this false conception of the Church. Palestine itself

has since Christ's day seen the greatest out-
rages on the heavenly conception of the Church.
We concluded our last section of this meditation
with a citation from the history of Islam's
conquest of Christianity, with this focal point
in Palestine, and we saw then how that Islam
triumphed over Christianity because of the
corruption of Christianity, evidenced by these
very things of which we have spoken ; divisions,
warrings, jealousies, factions amongst Christians.　And Islam as a solid body, presenting
a solid front, knowing nothing of such factions
and divisions, was able to overwhelm that
divided thing, that schismatic thing, that
internally disintegrated thing ; and that overwhelming had its seat in this very country,
around this very city of which we are speaking.
That in itself is a very forceful lesson ; that the
subjugation of the earthly Jerusalem, being the
result of weakness produced by spiritual
division, points to the absolute necessity for the
Church's oneness in spirit as the heavenly
Jerusalem, if she is really to rise to her place
of universal supremacy.　We know how very
much is connected in the New Testament with
that truth.　Oh, if it is true that the Lord Jesus
was moving out of this world, and taking His
Church spiritually with Him, recognising that
Jerusalem's undoing was coming because of
these unhappy and unholy conditions, how

essential it was that He should pray, "that they may all be one" (John xvii. 21). Error, whether it be Islam or any other error, ancient or modern, known or something quite new, will always gain its advantage by the spiritual weakness produced by division amongst the Lord's people. Such things are only kept at bay as the people of God stand together in spiritual oneness.

We said earlier that the history of Jerusalem presents to us a solid block of evidence, that the governing law of God's Jerusalem is heavenliness, and heavenliness is most certainly spiritual oneness, and spiritual oneness is heavenliness. To put that in another way, immediately you and I come down to earthly considerations, earthly levels of things, our oneness is bound to be assailed, to be broken, and therefore God's Own thought for His people is set on one side.

The Earthboundness of Christendom.

Not only is this seen so clearly in the triumph of Islam over Christianity, but one other page of history affords very strong evidence and very clear illustration. We refer to the history of the Crusades. Lasting a hundred years, they are really the story of one of the most disgraceful happenings in the history of Christianity, destined, of course, to fail, as indeed they did. As children we were primed with the heroics and the romance of the Crusades, of Richard Cœur de Lion, and such like. But since we have grown up, we have read the story for ourselves, and all our childish glamour has disappeared, and the more we come to understand things from God's standpoint, the more we blush with shame as we look back upon that page in the history of Christianity, when mighty armies were gathered and lives slaughtered wholesale, desolation and carnage brought about in the name of the Church, to try to re-capture Palestine for Christianity. No! That is not the heavenly way of doing things. Our warfare is *not with flesh and blood,* and the weapons of our warfare *are not carnal* but spiritual. "My kingdom is not of this world : if my kingdom were of this world, then would my servants fight . . ." (John xviii. 36). These are bed-rock laws of the heavenly Jerusalem. Palestine to-day is a nauseating spectacle. Every place connected in any special way with Christ's earthly life is marked by something which is more than a tragic misrepresentation of Christianity, a shameful misrepresentation is nearer the truth, something called a church in which rivalries run so high that even soldiers have to be kept, either on the premises or in the vicinity, for safety's sake amongst the Christians.

I expect many of you have been reading Morton's book, *In the steps of the Master*. I will give you one or two fragments from it, to illustrate what I mean. He is speaking here of his visit to Jerusalem, to the Church of the Holy Sepulchre. This is what he says :—

"The church gives one an overwhelming impression of darkness and decay. There were passages so dark that I had to strike matches to find my way. And the decay everywhere of stone, of wood, and of iron was fantastic. I saw pictures that were rotting on their canvases, and I even saw canvases still framed, that were bleached white : the last fragments of paint had peeled off, but they were still in position. There were ominous cracks and fissures in stone and marble. I thought how odd it is that extreme devotion can have exactly the same effect as extreme neglect. The Church of the Holy Sepulchre wears its air of shabby decay for the simple reason that the re-hanging of a picture, the repair of a stone, and even the mending of a window, assume such gigantic importance in the eyes of the communities, that they provoke a situation capable of indefinite postponement. . . . Art and vulgarity stand side by side. A priceless chalice, the gift of an emperor, stands next to something tawdry and tinsely that might have been pulled from a Christmas tree. And hundreds of ikons, glimmering in old gold, receive candle drippings on the stiff Byzantine figures of saint and king.

"The Greek monks swing their censers towards the blaze of candle-light, and the blue clouds of their incense spurt out to hang about the ikons and the gilded screens. The worshippers, kneeling on the marble floors, seem to be prostrate before a series of exotic jewellers' shops. . . . .

"This was the hill of the Crucifixion : Calvary, the holiest place on earth. I looked round, hoping to be able to detect some sign of its former aspect, but that has been obliterated for ever beneath the suffocating trappings of piety. The chapel before which I was kneeling was the Chapel of the Raising of the Cross, the chapel next to it was the Chapel of the Nailing to the Cross."

Turning to his visit to Bethlehem he speaks of his entering the Church of the Nativity, and of this he says :

"The church is built above a cave which was recognised as the birthplace of Jesus Christ. . . .

"Fifty-three silver lamps lighten the gloom of the underground cavern. It is a small cave about fourteen yards long and four yards wide. Its walls are covered with tapestry that reeks of stale incense. If you draw this tapestry aside, you see that the walls are the rough, smoke-blackened walls of a cave. Gold, silver, and tinsel ornaments gleam in the pale glow of the fifty-three lamps. . . .

"This church, like the Church of the Holy Sepulchre, suffers from divided ownership. It is in the hands of the Latins, the Greeks, and the Armenians.

"So jealous are the various churches of their rights, that even the sweeping of the dust is sometimes a dangerous task, and there is a column in which are three nails, one on which the Latins may hang a picture, one on which the Greeks may do so, and a neutral nail on which no sect may hang anything.

"In the floor there is a star, and round it a Latin inscription which says : 'Here Jesus Christ was born of the Virgin Mary.' The removal of this star years ago led to a quarrel between France and Russia which blazed into the Crimean War."

My point is this, that that place which rejected the heavenly Christ has become the scene of the expression, the most intensive expression, of the false Church, the false conception of what that Church is. We have said that in Jerusalem the delusion of Christendom has its intense expression, but it is only an explanation of how far a failure to represent God's thought really can go. The degree may vary ; the principle remains the same. If man, apart from the dominion of the Holy Spirit in any measure however minute, intrudes into the things of God, be it in thought, intellect, reason or feeling, desire, emotion or will, determination, possession, the effect will be a proportionate measure of death, division, confusion and contradiction.

I have carefully written that statement, so that it should be precisely presented. I am going to repeat it, because upon that everything hangs. The degree may vary ; the principle is the same. If man, apart from the dominion of the Holy Spirit in any measure however minute, intrudes into the things of God, the effect will be a proportionate measure of death, division, confusion and contradiction !

Therefore, man must go out as man : Christ, the heavenly Man, must be the Son over God's House, must be the Head of the Church, and His Headship must be administered only by the heavenly Holy Spirit. Herein, also, lies the necessity for the Cross as a constantly working and active reality by which that whole realm, and range, and tissue of carnal man is ruled out, and kept out. Herein, then, is the necessity for the fulness of the Holy Spirit, if the Church is to come to that place seen for her, as coming down from out of heaven, to be the centre of God's universe, God's government of this universe.

There is no middle ground: If it is not By The spirit of God : it is Death.

CHAPTER IV.

Features of the Overcomer.

READING : Rev. iii. 7-13 ; xxi. 1-4.

You will notice in the passage in chapter iii. of the Revelation, that the overcomer is to have the name of the City of God written upon him. "He that overcometh . . . I will write upon him the name of my God, and the name of the city of my God, the new Jerusalem. . . ." That is a somewhat remarkable statement, and full of interest ; and certainly the more you think about it, the more you wonder what it means that the overcomer is to have the name of the New Jerusalem written upon him. We want to understand, therefore, a little more of what that name signifies, and how it is associated with overcoming.

As has been our custom so far, so again, we go back to the earliest touches upon Jerusalem which we have in the Scripture, and there we shall get our key.

The first reference to Jerusalem in the Bible comes in with Melchizedek in Genesis xiv. 18-19. There we find the first mention of it by its abbreviated title of Salem. "Jerusalem" means "the City of Peace." A very great deal more has been made of it, and there are volumes written upon the name of Jerusalem, and many

58

very wonderful ideas have been associated with the name, but it is quite simply expressed as "the City of Peace." There may be a root in the word which means safety by reason of its position, its strength and elevation, and in that sense it may be termed the City of Peace, as being a city exceedingly difficult to upset, to destroy. But we can be content for our purpose with the simplest of definitions. Apparently, Melchizedek was king of this city, as well as priest of "God Most High."

We see from this chapter that Melchizedek first comes into view with Abram's return from the defeat of the kings. If you read the whole chapter, you will see that a number of kings made a league, and they brought the rulers of Sodom and other local cities under their power. These served them and paid tribute to them for a number of years. Then they revolted against these allied kings, with the result that the allied kings made this assault upon them to bring them to heel again. They overpowered them, robbed them, and carried away spoil and many prisoners, including Lot and his wife. Abram was informed of what had happened, and with some three hundred and eighteen men, trained in his own household, he pursued after the kings, and by a night manoeuvre gained an advantage, overpowered them, recovered all that had been taken, including Lot, and brought them back. On his return from this successful and victorious expedition, the king of Salem as well as the king of Sodom met him, and Melchizedek blessed him, and Abram gave him a tenth of all.

Here, then, is Abram in the capacity of an overcomer, and you recognise, as we pointed out in our last meditation, that Abram's strength— a strength which in a spiritual sense he passed on to the City of which he was, in a sense, the father, for which he looked—was largely due to his own spiritual detachment from this world. He refused all gifts from the king of Sodom, refused this world's honours and favours, and in various other ways kept himself free, while in some cases the Lord, on His part, very strongly broke him free from earthly elements and relationships, and so maintained him in a position of spiritual strength. Now we find that spiritual strength, by reason of his detachment from things earthly and attachment to things heavenly, expressing itself in this victorious warfare, and in the position of an overcomer he comes into touch with Melchizedek, and Melchizedek with him, and certain pre-eminent spiritual elements and features are introduced. It is interesting to notice that all the associations of Melchizedek are spiritual and not temporal. Wherever you touch Melchizedek in the Scriptures, you touch some abiding spiritual principle, something which is not temporal, not passing, and not merely of this earth; not even related to this earth when what is touched is of God, but something higher than that. The bringing of Melchizedek and Abram together in this way brings out this series of spiritual elements, which run right on and become the governing features of the New Jerusalem.

If you look at some of these elements, you will see that they are impressive, but you will, in the first place, be impressed with the uniqueness of the person of Melchizedek. How strangely he comes on the scene. He is never heard of before, and nothing is known about him, beyond what is said here in a couple of sentences, and yet here he is, a king, and priest of God Most High, in a land full of iniquity. He suddenly comes into full view like that, king of Salem, priest of God Most High, blessing Abram in the Name of the Lord: a remarkable personality, and quite fitted by these very features, by the uniqueness of his person, to occupy some very important place in the spiritual history of Jerusalem. He seems, so to speak, to have come out of the unknown, to have suddenly dropped out of heaven, in immediate maturity. There is no immaturity here: you do not begin in infancy, you find this man right in the fulness of things, the fulness which is to take centuries to develop in the history of the Lord's work. A tremendous amount of history will come before there is realised on this earth what is represented by Melchizedek. He enters in this full way, this mature way, and it seems as though he immediately sets up the whole thought of God. The whole mind of God is represented in one man, who comes we know not whence. It is as though God puts the fulness of His thought in a man at the beginning of things, and then develops history according to that pattern. That is how God does things. So Melchizedek becomes a most impressive person, and we know from the New Testament, especially the letter to the Hebrews, that he was intended by God to be a type of something very full. He introduces an order of things which is super-earthly, super-Aaronic—without genealogy, without father, without mother, without beginning of days or end of life. There you have eternity, universality, all gathered up in this one man.

Typical Relationships of Melchizedek with Christ.

Note his typical relationships with Christ, as he introduces these pre-eminent spiritual elements. I think we can say that they are, in the main, five.

1. Kingship.

The first is kingship among the Lord's Own people in relation to the elect : kingship in contact with the overcomer, and the overcomer brought into touch with the throne. That is the first full thought of God, represented in Melchizedek. As we have just mentioned, a tremendous amount of history will develop before that is fully realised, but God is going to work from this point toward something which we shall note in a moment.

2. Priesthood.

Not an earthly, but a heavenly priesthood : not after the order of Aaron, but after the order of Melchizedek—a heavenly priesthood, an abiding priesthood is what is set forth ; in a word, priesthood in God's full thought.

3. Righteousness.

The principle of righteousness comes in with Melchizedek in a special way. It is no new principle. Righteousness is as old as God. It comes in in a special way with Melchizedek, as he becomes king of righteousness. We mention it now, and will speak more fully of it later.

4. Peace.

Righteousness leading to peace ; peace and righteousness in relation to kingship and priesthood is what is brought before us. When you put those things together, you cover an immense range of the work and Person of the Lord Jesus. Work backwards—peace, because of righteousness, because of heavenly priesthood, because of absolute sovereignty.

5. The Endless Life.

". . . like unto the Son of God . . . after the power of an endless life" (Heb. vii. 3, 16). That is the designation given by the New Testament to Melchizedek.

Let us sum those up again both ways—kingship, priesthood of a heavenly order, righteousness, peace and endless life : endless life, because of peace being given, on the ground of righteousness, through the heavenly priesthood, with the throne of universal sovereignty upholding it all. That is an outstanding vision and setting forth in one man of those typical elements of the Person and work of the Lord Jesus.

Think a moment or two longer of kingship as introduced by Melchizedek in relation to Christ. The remarkable thing is that Christ came out of Judah, the tribe of government, the tribe of monarchy. But no priest came out of Judah : there was no priesthood there. The Apostle argues that if Christ had been on earth—a striking phrase—He would not have been a priest, because there are no priests out of Judah. That carries His priesthood away from earth at once and brings in a heavenly order of priesthood. So that Christ's priesthood arises on another ground from that of Aaron. He is Priest established in relation to resurrection. The one hundred and tenth Psalm makes it very clear that His priesthood does not belong to that side of the grave which relates wholly to this earth. The grave breaks fully and finally our contact with this earth. That is the meaning of baptism. Baptism is intended to be a declaration of the fact that in our death-union with Christ all relationship of a spiritual kind with this earth has been brought to an end. Mark you, we only come into the values of Christ's heavenly priesthood in so far as that is true, because His priesthood is not of the Aaronic order, applying to people on the earth living earth-bound lives. Christ's priesthood is founded upon the fact that He is in heaven, and that at once speaks of resurrection. So that His priesthood is in the virtue and the good of resurrection.

Come back to Abram, and you will see that, with regard to the City, Abram had to come in a typical way right on to this ground, the ground of resurrection, with even Isaac broken away from this earth as holding any kind of relationship with it still, and that right out on resurrection ground in relation to heaven the purpose of God as to the City is fulfilled. So Christ's Priesthood is established as related to resurrection. "Thou art my Son, this day have I begotten thee" (Heb. i. 5) touches His resurrection, and this priesthood of Melchizedek is typically after the power of an endless life.

Why did Christ's Priesthood become dependent entirely upon His resurrection? For the simple reason that God was awaiting kingship; that there can be no true priesthood apart from kingship in the thought of God. Lay hold of that, and dwell upon it. There is no full priesthood in God's mind apart from kingship. Kingship is essential to priesthood, if priesthood is to have its fullest expression.

The Aaronic priesthood broke down in Eli. Samuel was then brought in, and what happened? Samuel was not brought in to introduce a new order of priesthood. Samuel was brought in to introduce the king; and from that time the king always took precedence over the priest. David, himself king, wore the linen ephod, combined the two in his own person. But the priesthood in David was subservient to his kingship. All the meaning and value of the order of Aaron, of course, is gathered up and included in Christ, but it is transcended by the order of Melchizedek.

Kingship is the supreme, the dominating note. That is the first and highest position. Then what comes next? Righteousness! But that introduces the priesthood. The question of righteousness is dealt with by priesthood; but it is a righteousness which can only be established by a throne of supreme authority. It is the throne, the kingship, which gives the power to the priesthood. The Old Testament makes that perfectly clear. The priesthood afterward derived its power and its appointment from the throne. Notice how David dealt with the priests. He dismissed high priests and brought in others. When high priests failed God, David put them out of office. That was a momentous thing to do. Go back to the days before there were kings in Israel, and let anybody touch the priest! But here is a man who has taken a position above the priests. With David it was a question of the throne governing in the matter of righteousness. If the high priests failed God, broke down on the question of righteousness, then the throne intervened, and that priesthood could no longer stand.

These two things are found together in Christ, and you see that He is King and Priest, and by His very throne He upholds righteous-

ness and His priestly work. We have a *great*
High Priest, Who is King, Who is Sovereign.

When you have the throne established,
righteousness upheld by supreme authority,
then you can know peace. All these are operating in the power of resurrection. He is King,
He is Priest, and He has established peace in
virtue of His resurrection.

Thus sovereignty comes in, and sovereignty
is seen to be not a matter of a realm only, but
rather a matter of moral and spiritual glory.
His Kingship is that. It is the sovereignty of
peace.

There is a great value about this, if we could
grasp it. These moral and spiritual elements,
such as peace and righteousness, are things
which have behind them all the tremendous
power of supreme lordship. You and I know
quite well that our righteousness cannot
support us : and neither can it support anyone
else. Our righteousness will break down. It
is a poor thing, a puny thing. We know quite
well that our peace will not support very much.
What is the strength of our own peace? Well,
it is as the strength of a very weak assault upon
it. It does not take much to upset *our* peace.
Then take any other moral and spiritual virtue
you may think of, and see just how far man's
own virtue will carry him ; man's own moral
and spiritual features. Not very far ! But

then think of the Lord having righteousness and peace and all the other virtues, and by His Spirit imparting those, and putting all the strength of His *throne* behind them, all that that throne means of victory. It is righteousness triumphant, because of One Who is absolute Sovereign in this universe. The sovereignty of the Lord Jesus is the sovereignty of righteousness. If you can upset His throne, you upset His righteousness. If you can upset His righteousness, you upset His throne. If you can destroy His peace, you destroy His sovereignty. These things go together. What we need is that the Lord should be enthroned at the centre of our being with all the sovereign power of His mighty righteousness, all His glorious peace, all His deep imperturbable joy. It is not an abstract element. The throne, and all that it means, is with and behind all.

That is surely what was intended to be the embodiment of those spiritual and moral truths and realities. When Jerusalem was supported by righteousness, then Jerusalem was unshakable. When Jerusalem forsook righteousness, then the very support of Jerusalem was withdrawn, and Jerusalem collapsed.

"Pray for the peace of Jerusalem" (Psalm cxxii. 6). Jerusalem lost its peace, when it lost its righteousness, because it lost its sovereign upholding. These things go together. You cannot have the Lord supporting you in His sovereignty, in His kingship, if you are violating righteousness.

Abraham was made to know God on this matter in connection with the cities of the plain. "Shall I hide from Abraham that which I do?" (Gen. xviii. 17). The Lord told Abraham that he was going to destroy the cities, and Abraham went in search of righteousness. "Wilt thou consume the righteous with the wicked?" God said in effect, Try it! That is not My way! I never destroy righteousness! If you find righteousness, I cannot destroy; I am bound to uphold righteousness! So Abraham made his exhaustive search, and found none. He had to say, You are perfectly justified in doing this thing! God could not have done it if Abraham had found righteousness. Righteousness and the protection of the throne go together. The lack of righteousness means that the throne cannot function to protect. The New Jerusalem, which came into view through Abraham, was to take its character from him, was to be the embodiment of all these things. And when you carry the matter beyond the historic Jerusalem, you find the next focal point is Christ Himself, and then the Church, which is His Body—the New Jerusalem, which is to express all that God had in His mind as spiritual thought concerning His Own people.

CHAPTER V.

Features of the Overcomer—*continued.*

We follow on where we broke off the last meditation, and complete what was not completed then.

From Genesis xxii. (Mt. Moriah) Jerusalem does not come into view again until the book of Judges is reached. Immediately after the death of Joshua, Judah and Simeon attempted to take the City, which at that time was called Jebus. Josephus tells us that only the lower part of the City was captured. The Benjamites followed Judah in the attempt, but had no better success, and the City remained in the hands of the Jebusites during the whole period of the Judges, throughout the reign of Saul, and through the reign of David at Hebron.

Jerusalem in the Days of the Judges.

If you look at that period, you will recognise that it was one of spiritual weakness, and therefore of failure. We are familiar with the conditions that obtained through the period of the Judges. We have only to read the book to recognise that it covers several hundreds of years, and we are sadly impressed with the low spiritual state of the Lord's people, and the great weakness which characterised them

during that time. We reach the close of the
period, and Samuel comes on the scene, to find
a very sorry state of things indeed. Saul is
brought in through Samuel, and still the condition is one of spiritual weakness, and therefore the City is not in possession, and is not
occupying its place in the purpose of God.

The point is this, that for Jerusalem to
express the mind of God, the very highest and
fullest spiritual life is demanded of the Lord's
people. The obverse fact is equally true, that
whenever the spritual life of the Lord's people
is lower than it should be, the glory of
Jerusalem is veiled, the City is not in the
ascendant, and the Name of the Lord is not
being honoured in it.

We gather from this extensive survey that,
so far as time is concerned, Jerusalem represents the spiritual state of the Lord's people.
That truth runs throughout the Old Testament
by way of illustration, and is carried over in
its spiritual meaning to the Church. That is
why we speak of Jerusalem and the features
of the overcomer. Eventually the heavenly
Jerusalem, the Church, will come into view in
heavenly glory, on the ground of spiritual
maturity, spiritual fulness. It will be an
expression of the very highest life to which
the Lord's people can ever come, and that
expression will be the power of the overcomer.

We know, in reading backward from the end, that Jerusalem does finally represent a very high standard of spiritual life, and that the overcomer company, as presented to us in the book of the Revelation, is a company which has reached the very highest point of spiritual attainment.

It is important for us to recognise that while the Jerusalem of the Old Testament, the earthly Jerusalem, is historical in a literal way, Jerusalem which is above has its history upon a purely spiritual basis. Its rise and fall, if we may speak of it in that way, is a matter of the rise and fall of spiritual life, and the Lord while now in heaven, having in His Own mind a perfect City, is seeking to bring His people, His Church, to that state of spiritual perfection which, when accomplished, will display His glory and bring with it the realisation of that vision which was seen of the Apostle : ''And he carried me away in the Spirit to a mountain great and high, and showed the holy city of Jerusalem, coming down out of heaven from God, having the glory of God : her light was like unto a stone most precious . . .'' (Rev. xxi. 10-11). That is a spiritual state that the Lord is seeking to realise in His Church. It will eventually be realised in those who truly constitute that Church, that City.

We see, then, that through the long period of which we spoke Jerusalem does not come into its place, and is not seen as expressing Divine thoughts, because of the spiritual weakness and failure of the Lord's people.

David and the Capture of Jerusalem.

At length we come to the time when David goes up to Jerusalem and issues a challenge to his mighty men, who accept the challenge and attempt the taking of the stronghold of the Jebusites, and wherein Joab succeeds. Joab is an interesting character. He does not always shine in the best way, but the noteworthy thing about Joab, the thing that determines what Joab is, is *his relationship with David the king.* If Joab were in pursuit of personal interests, or if his interests were diverted from David to other considerations, he did not show up very well. But you find that whenever Joab was selflessly attached to David, and had David's interest and glory wholly at heart, he is always seen to advantage. Now here in the taking of the stronghold Joab excels, because of his unreserved devotion to David, and because of that he becomes yet another type of the overcomer who takes the stronghold.

There a new feature is introduced as to the City, and the overcomers in relation to the

City, namely, that the overcomers will be those whose hearts are unreservedly devoted to the King, their Lord, and who, because of their abandonment to Him, will come to the place of supremacy. If we have personal interests, or if our interests are in any way diverted from the Lord, we shall not be overcomers, and we shall not stand very well in the main issue. In this connection we recall the passage in Revelation iii. 7-12. David is mentioned there, and the temple is mentioned, and you have the City, and association with what is represented by those three is seen to be the portion of the overcomer.

Surveying once more, we note that Abraham, Melchizedek, and David, represent the power of that which is *wholly* of God in a spiritual way. Two things have come clearly before us. (1) The *heavenly* Kingship. (2) The *heavenly* Priesthood. We see that these are realised in Christ. Then they are shared by a heavenly people, and they are related throughout to the heavenly Jerusalem.

Now the Lord made a covenant with David that he should never want for a man to sit upon his throne, as is recorded for us in the first book of Kings, chapter viii. Then you find that David and Israel have been without a king, without a temple, and without a priest for long centuries. There are only two ways, as far as

I can see, of explaining the apparent contradiction. The one is the way of "British Israel," the other is the way of seeing that all is transferred to the Lord Jesus; that the covenant with David has been fulfilled in David's greater Son, and that He is on the throne, the government upon His shoulders, and the key of David in His possession.*

In the first place, then, all is taken up in Christ in a heavenly position, but in a secondary sense it is transferred to and taken up in the heavenly Jerusalem, which is now regarded as being in existence. Paul says : "But the Jerusalem that *is* above (not which is going to be) is free, which is our mother" (Gal. iv. 26). Just as the Church in Paul's letters is always seen as already complete and perfect, though we know it is not so literally, so Jerusalem is looked upon as now above in existence, and all that is said about it carries that feature. Thus the heavenly Jerusalem, of which we are now a part, seeing that we are seated together with Christ in the heavenlies, takes up and embodies this heavenly kingship and kingdom, and this heavenly priesthood. We are brought into that, and that is transferred to us. If Scripture is necessary to bear

---

* From such passages as Acts ii., 30, this is surely the only true interpretation.

that out, we have very precise statements on the matter. To the Jews the Lord Jesus said, as recorded in Matt. xxi. 43 : "The kingdom of God shall be taken away from you, and shall be given to a nation bringing forth the fruits thereof." Alongside of that you place Luke xii. 32 : "Fear not, little flock ; for it is your Father's good pleasure to give you the kingdom." Then the words of Peter in his first Letter, chapter ii., verse 9 : "But ye are an elect race, a royal priesthood, a holy nation." So that the Church as the heavenly Jerusalem takes up the kingdom, the kingdom is transferred to the Church, and the Church takes up the priesthood. "Our citizenship is in heaven." That is present tense. That at once links up with the heavenly Jerusalem as now existent. The kingdom at this time is, of course, so far as we are concerned, a spiritual one. The kingship and the kingdom at present are in spiritual expression. Later it will be literally expressed ; that is, the Church will literally take the place of governing this world in the coming age.

The priesthood is also spiritual at present. We are *now* priests. We shall be priests then. We see how the book of the Revelation presents a very full thought of what already obtains, as well as of what awaits consummation. In two places, both at the beginning of the book and a little further, in chapter i., verse 6, and in chapter v., verse 10, we have the statement that He has made us a kingdom and priests unto our God.

The vital point, upon which everything that we have said, or can say, hangs, is that *all is bound up with and inseparable from resurrection.* Resurrection is a far greater, deeper, more significant thing than any of us have yet recognised. Resurrection is the key to everything, and you will notice that everything which relates to God's heavenly purpose is bound up with resurrection. Indeed resurrection, if in Christ, implies and involves that the thing is heavenly.

The City, as we have seen, comes into view in the first instance with Abraham, and we know that the central thing of the life of Abraham is the great power and fact of resurrection; that when Abraham had come to the altar, and had definitely quitted all that was of the earth, even though of Godly origin, then it was that Abraham moved out into what was something more than an earthly vision and purpose of God, into what was the heavenly and the universal purpose of God. It was resurrection that became the basis of what was and is heavenly in the covenant with Abraham.

It was the earthliness of things during the time of the Judges, and during Saul's life, which kept the City in a place of eclipse, out of sight, and out of function. And when you come to the reign of David, you notice it is as the threshing floor of Ornan is secured for the temple that the City comes into its full place. It was then that God secured His habitation there in a typical way, and it is by the habitation of God that the City is what it is. It always has been, it always will be. It is the presence of God that makes anything Divine and heavenly. Now the securing of the threshing floor of Ornan was in the day when the angel put up his sword; when death raging throughout the land was arrested; when the sacrifice was slain on that threshing floor, and an end to a curse was brought about. Thereafter you have a new beginning on resurrection ground. Resurrection always occupies the central place in relation to heavenly purposes.

Resurrection is a Separating thing.

Resurrection is the key to everything. It is the key to every fresh movement of God in the securing of His fullest intention and thought, and it is always a separating or a dividing thing.

Take a chapter like John v. In that chapter the Lord Jesus is found speaking about resurrection. "The hour cometh, and now is, when the dead shall hear the voice of the Son of God ; and they that hear shall live" (verse 25). That, of course, must be taken spiritually. Who hear the voice ? Not all. It is those who hear that live, but all do not live. That is to say, the power of resurrection in the Word of the Lord divides spiritually between those who live and those who remain dead. Resurrection is a dividing thing. It cleaves the company in two, as it were. Some hear the spoken Word and live. They are raised from spiritual death. Others do not hear. You know that later the Lord Jesus said : "My sheep hear my voice. . . ." There we have the first form of resurrection. It is spiritual. It is a raising from spiritual death, or from among the spiritually dead, and in a spiritual way men become two companies, the living and the dead.

In the same chapter the Lord Jesus projects things further into the future. "The hour cometh (He does not say 'and now is'), in which all that are in the tombs shall hear his voice (not the spoken Word)." That links us with 1 Thess. iv. 16. "The hour cometh, in which all that are in the tombs shall hear his *voice.*" That must be taken literally, not spiritually. What happens in that resurrection ? "And shall come forth ; they that have done good, unto the resurrection of life ; and they that have done ill, unto the resurrection of judgement'' (verse 29). Again resurrection divides.

There are other resurrections in the Word, and you find that every one of them divides. There is the general resurrection of believers mentioned in 1 Thessalonians, and there is a specific resurrection of believers spoken of in Philippians iii., the out-resurrection from among the dead. Paul was quite sure of his position in 1 Thessalonians. He had no doubt whatever of his being in that resurrection, no question at all. But of the resurrection mentioned in Philippians iii. he is not so sure, not at all sure. Of that his own words are: ''If by any means I may attain unto the out-resurrection''; ''Not that I have already obtained''; ''I count not myself yet to have apprehended.'' Here is another dividing in resurrection.

We are bound to come to this conclusion, I feel, that at the same time that resurrection divides, it also puts in a position, and that the resurrection of Philippians iii. is not the resurrection of 1 Thessalonians iv. 1 Thessalonians iv. is a far more general thing than Philippians iii. Philippians iii. applies to a much higher position in the expression of the Divine thought than does 1 Thessalonians iv.

F

When you come to the Revelation, you find the statement that the rest of the dead lived not for a thousand years. Well, there has been a resurrection, the first resurrection, and it has wrought a division. "Blessed and holy is he that hath part in the first resurrection . . ." (Rev. xx. 6); but a good many have been left out of that. Resurrection has divided again, you see : it has taken some, and left others.

But again at the end of the thousand years there is yet another resurrection, and again a dividing. There is a resurrection, and in connection with this resurrection we read : "And if any was not found written in the book of life, he was cast into the lake of fire" (Rev. xx. 15). Why state that, if at that time, at that point in the course of things, all whose names were in the book of life had been raised a thousand years before? Do you mark the significance, that even after the thousand years there will be some raised whose names are in the book, who missed something for a thousand years? Thus after a thousand years there takes place a resurrection, which divides between those whose names are in the book, and those whose names are not found in the book. If that were not so, surely a divinely inspired Word would say that at the end of the thousand years the rest of the dead were raised and straightway cast into the lake of fire.

Why say : ". . . if any was not found written in the book of life"? Resurrection has come, even at that late date, to divide.

What does all this mean? It means that there are resurrections (not one resurrection, not two resurrections), and every resurrection represents some stage, some position, some bound of advancement in the Divine purpose; and you can come quickly to this conclusion that the first, the out-resurrection, is of a company which reaches the highest position. Every subsequent resurrection represents something less than that. We can be Christians and lose the thousand years. If that is true, there may be other things that we can lose.

That is the significance of the overcomer in relation to Jerusalem. The overcomer, as seen in Revelation iii., comes to the throne, but that overcomer company of Philadelphia and Laodicea is the overcomer company of chapter xii., of the man-child. It is a special out-resurrection company; and surely it is with that in view that the Lord has brought into our consideration the urgency of our being a people who are not in any degree earth-bound, world-tied, but utterly out, so that we might form a part of that company which shall express the fullest thought of God, and know the out-resurrection from among the dead.

If you have any doubt as to whether there is more than one resurrection, read the New Testament along that one line only. Unfortunately the Authorised Version in this case does not bring the fact out clearly, but the Revised Version will help you a great deal more. You will find that two words are used in relation to resurrection in the New Testament. Those words are the resurrection of the dead, and the resurrection *from* the dead. The Revised Version makes that distinction. Resurrection *of the dead* is one thing. There is to be a resurrection of the dead that is going to include everybody, but there is a resurrection *from the dead,* that is, from among the dead, which does not include everybody. The Bethany sister beautifully stumbled upon that truth for our good : "I know that he shall rise again in the resurrection at the last day" (John xi. 24). She is speaking of the resurrection *of the dead,* when everybody should be raised. Jesus drew her up and said : "I am the resurrection" (verse 25). Now note : John xii. which immediately follows (it is the continuation of the narrative) says : "Jesus therefore six days before the passover came to Bethany, where Lazarus was, whom Jesus raised from the dead." The word is "ek," out from among. "I am the resurrection"—"Whom Jesus raised from the dead."

In relation to Christ there is something more than general resurrection from the dead, there is an out-resurrection. The fuller the relationship to Christ the more God secures by resurrection.

So that Jerusalem has as its highest feature the overcomer, on the ground of a resurrection which, as we see, is of those who have gone *all* the way in their relationship to the Lord, or, in keeping with our general thought, of those who have not in any way been earth-bound, world-related.

Resurrection is separation, but resurrection as separation is simply following out the principle of spiritual separation now. If you and I are truly separated unto God *now,* so that Colossians iii. 1 is true of us : "If then ye were raised together with Christ, seek the things that are above, where Christ is, seated on the right hand of God," we are on the way to the following out of that spiritual separation in an out-resurrection from the dead. I am not of those who believe that all who have been saved, who are living semi or partially worldly lives, are going to know the out-resurrection. They are going to lose something, and it is going to be possible for people to have their names in the book of life and miss the thousand years, if the Word means anything at all. I ask you to look at the Word. Does it say that ? "The rest of the dead lived not until the thousand years should be finished" (Rev. xx. 5). Then there is a resurrection, the books are opened, and those whose names are not in the book of life are cast into the lake of fire.

Now we understand those tremendous warnings in the letter to the Hebrews, for instance, about failing of the inheritance, failing of God's purpose, and losing the birthright, the intention of God. There is that tremendous statement made about Esau, that he sold his birthright for a mess of pottage. And then what? He sought with tears, but found no place of repentance. Then the letter to the Hebrews says : ". . . it is impossible to renew them again unto repentance . . ." (Heb. vi. 6). Does that mean that they are eternally lost? No! They have lost their birthright, they have lost their inheritance, not necessarily their eternal life. They may at the end of the thousand years still be in the book of life, but lose their inheritance.

Now you understand why it is that there is such stress laid on utterness for God : perhaps you understand a little better the nature of what we call the Testimony, and why it is necessary for us to come out in a spiritual way from everything, even religiously, as of this world, and stand apart for God. Why all that ? Why not succour the more generally accepted thing? For this reason, that God has shown a more utter thing of His will, which makes a more utter demand, and represents a more utter cost. It brings into a realm of a more utter conflict and anguish. But what can we do, when we have seen the heavenly vision, but go on? "To him that overcometh will I grant to sit with me in my throne . . ." There is kingship.

Resurrection is the key to everything in the purpose of God. It is the basis of everything. And resurrection is always a dividing thing. You can come to one resurrection and miss another. It depends on how far you have gone on with the Lord. This is not a question of salvation, this is subsequent to salvation. Paul had no doubt about his salvation, and no doubt about that which was bound up with salvation unto life. But there is another resurrection inside of that, and of that he was not so sure. For that he had to strain every nerve spiritually: "If by *any* means I may attain." That resurrection is not the resurrection which goes along with eternal life, that resurrection is the prize of the upward calling. It is for the overcomer.

CHAPTER VI.

The City, the Seat of Heavenly Government.

Thus saith the Lord God : This is Jerusalem : I have set her in the midst of the nations, and countries are round about her" (Ezekiel v. 5).

We have traced Jerusalem from Melchizedek, king of Salem, to David, the great king, and then on to the Book of the Revelation, to the New Jerusalem. The government is always in the heavens. That fact is set forth in types and symbols, and in many other ways, and is also directly declared to be the case.

The Word of God also teaches that there is a place in that government reserved for certain saints. It is clear that the Throne of God can be shared, and the first sharer of that throne is the Lord Jesus. But He offers the same privilege to certain saints, telling them that on certain conditions—the same conditions as those upon which He shares His Father's throne—they shall share His throne. Thus a place is reserved in the ultimate government of this world for certain saints.

The figure used in connection with government is the figure of a city, out from which the government goes forth, and we know that city to be a people, not merely a place. Everything by which that city or people is constituted is heavenly. It is the nature which gives the place and the power. The nature is the heavenliness of everything.

In the Book of the Revelation we have a certain city spoken of as MYSTERY BABYLON. That means, of course, that it is not the literal historic Babylon of this world, the city built by men in a literal way, but MYSTERY BABYLON is a spiritual Babylon, a people whose characteristics are moral and spiritual elements of Babylon. Knowing as we do what came in a moral and a spiritual way from the literal Babylon, we have very little difficulty in identifying MYSTERY BABYLON. The point is this, that this is Satan's counterfeit of God's city, the MYSTERY JERUSALEM. The word "mystery" used in this connection means something which does not appear on the surface. There is an expression seen, but the real thing is behind, and can only be discerned by spiritual intelligence. It is true of MYSTERY BABYLON. It is true of MYSTERY JERUSALEM. MYSTERY BABYLON is the great snare, deception, and trap of religious history, and all who get into the toils of MYSTERY BABYLON are deceived and blinded in a most terrible way. They can even resort to the most ghastly things known in history and think they do God service. We need not mention the name by which MYSTERY BABYLON is known to us.

What is true of MYSTERY BABYLON on the side of Satan, is true of MYSTERY JERUSALEM on the side of God, in the heavenly and glorious sense that therein are gathered up all those things which are hidden from the wise and the prudent, things hidden from the world and open only to those who have a spirit of wisdom and revelation in the knowledge of Him.

In the letter to the Ephesians, which, as we know, has the Church wholly in view, there are, at least by inference, all the metaphors which are used of the Church in the Word of God. The main metaphor in this letter, as we know, is

1. The Body.

Then we further have

2. The House.
3. The Temple.
4. The City.
5. The Ecclesia, or Called-out Company.
6. The Family.
7. The One New Man.
8. The Bride.

All these metaphors are in Ephesians. They are the various aspects of the one Church.

THE BODY :   chapter i. verse 23.
                    ,, iii.   ,,   6.
                    the whole of chapter iv.

THE HOUSE :   chapter ii. verse 19.
                    (In that connection I would
                    suggest you follow through
                    the words " Father " and
                    " child " in this letter).

THE TEMPLE :   chapter ii. verse 22.

THE CITY :   chapter ii. verse 19.
                        ,, iii.   ,,   18.   (That
                    carries your thought forward
                    to the Book of the Revelation,
                    the city which lieth four-
                    square; the breadth, the
                    height, and the length thereof
                    are equal.)

THE ECCLESIA :   Take every reference to the
                    "Church."

THE FAMILY :   chapter iii. verse 15.

THE ONE NEW
    MAN :   chapter ii. 15; iv. 13, 24.

THE BRIDE :   chapter v. 25-28, 31-32.

So you see there are eight metaphors of the
Church in this letter, and there are other
inferences in the letter which you might do well
to trace out.

The point to which we come is that there are three things which stand out in this inclusive presentation of the Church.

I. The Mystery.

The first is the mystery. That word, as you know, is peculiarly characteristic of the letter to the Ephesians. Paul writes about the mystery of His will; ". . . made known unto us the mystery of his will . . ." ". . . made known unto me the mystery . . ." ". . . the fellowship of the mystery . . ." "This is a great mystery . . ."; and finally, ". . . the mystery of the gospel. . . ."

While the phrase MYSTERY JERUSA-LEM does not occur in the Scriptures, it is clear that Jerusalem is the Church, and that the Church coming so fully into view in this letter to the Ephesians is related immediately and intimately to the mystery. So that the Church as the City, and the City as the Church, is the mystery, and, as we have just pointed out, the significance of the word "mystery" is that it is something which can only be known by revelation. It cannot be apprehended by any natural faculties whatsoever—the mystery, something to be revealed. *It has always existed.* Let us be clear about that. The Church, the MYSTERY JERUSALEM, can only be known by revelation of the Holy Spirit. It exists now. But the Church is still a hidden thing to this world. That is said deliberately, in spite of all the publicity, all the demonstration, all the effort that is made to impress the world with its existence. In spite of that the true Church is still hidden from the eyes of the world. The City is not seen by this world. The revelation, the unveiling of the mystery, has come only to the saints, not to the world, and has come by revelation of the Holy Ghost. The remarkable thing is this, that you can still hold the New Testament in your hand, that you can hold this very letter to the Ephesians in your hand, and be able to recite it from the first to the last verse, and know all its terms, and all that it says, and still have the veil over the eyes of your hearts as to what the Church is. It needs a revelation by the Holy Spirit for one to see it.

II. The Heavenliness of Everything.

The second thing, which is clearly here alongside of the mystery, is the heavenliness of everything. Just as ''mystery'' is found these six or seven times in the letter to the Ephesians, so the ''heavenlies'' are the outstanding feature of the letter. That points plainly to the heavenly nature of the City, the Church. We merely state that once more, without dwelling upon it, as that is what is especially before us in our meditation, and we come back to it again and again.

III. The Governmental Feature.

The third thing which is here in this letter in relation to the Church, and for our present purposes the Church as "the City which hath foundations," is the governmental feature. In this letter you have those things which clearly indicate that, by reason of the heavenliness and spirituality of this people who constitute this City, this Church, there is a strong governmental factor. Look at one or two passages in this connection.

Ephesians i. 21-22 : "Far above all rule, and authority and power, and dominion, and every name that is named, not only in this world, but also in that which is to come : And he put all things in subjection under his feet, and gave him to be head over all things to the church. . . ." That is where you begin, with the Lord Himself, and in His capacity as Sovereign Head of the Church.

Chapter ii. 6 : "And raised us up with him, and made us to sit with him in the heavenly places, in Christ Jesus." So that in what He is, as well as where He is, is our privileged union. We are seen to be in spiritual union with Him, not only where He is in the heavenlies, but in what He is as in the heavenlies, far above all rule and authority, power and dominion, and so on. The Church is linked with Him in that position.

Chapter iii. 10 : "To the intent that now unto the principalities and the powers in the heavenly places might be made known through the church the manifold wisdom of God." That is a governmental element, is it not? It is quite clear that, by the Church, God is governing the intelligence of principalities and powers, impressing the intelligence, instructing them, making known His many-sided wisdom.

Chapter vi. from verse 12. Here in the heavenlies, while the Church is seen in conflict, in wrestling, it is also seen in power. This is not a conflict to get advantage, to get ascendency, but rather, to express ascendency, to express the fact that these principalities and powers have been defeated and are subject to Christ and to His Church as in the heavenlies.

We need to make a comparison at this point between Ephesians vi. and Revelation xii. In Ephesians vi. the Church is seen to be in conflict with the principalities and powers in the heavenlies. In Revelation xii. the case is that of a company being met by a mighty onslaught

of the evil one, the forces of darkness, and then
hurling those forces down out of the heavenlies,
and assuming fully and finally the place of
government in the sphere where those forces
have been in action. It is the end of the
conflict, the great final battle with the enemy,
in which he is hurled from his place in the air,
or in the heavenlies. It is good to pass the
eye on from Ephesians vi. to Revelation xii. In
Ephesians vi. you see the conflict going on, the
age-long conflict. In Revelation xii. you see
that conflict reaching its climax, and the issue
is that those forces which in Ephesians vi. are
still in the heavenlies are cast out of the
heavenlies and no more place is found for them,
and the Church is left in the heavenlies, in full
occupation, in a governmental position in the
throne.

The Factor of Election.

There is one other factor which is clearly
seen in this letter to the Ephesians. It is the
factor of election, and it is characteristic of both
Jerusalems, the earthly and the heavenly.
"This is Jerusalem : I have set her in the midst
of the nations . . ." (Ezek. v. 5). That speaks
of Divine appointment, and we know from very
much in the Old Testament that Jerusalem was
Divinely chosen, an elect city, an elect vessel,
that under the sovereignty of God Jerusalem

was picked out, appointed, and held for Divine purposes, though transient. Lifted into the realm of the great anti-type, that of which the earthly Jerusalem is but a faint picture, how very much more true that becomes. In the letter to the Ephesians, speaking of the Church in its full presentation, there are these tremendously strong notes upon election : "Chosen in Him," "Elect," and "Chosen according to the purpose of His will." God has determined from eternity that this heavenly Jerusalem shall occupy the place of government and supremacy.

Ruling in the Heavens now.

That which is of supreme importance and value, and which arises out of all that, is this, there is a link now between the Church and the heavenly government of this world in relation to the purpose of God in this dispensation. That sums up everything. That is clearly what comes out of a right reading of the letter to the Ephesians alone, but there is a very great deal more besides that letter to substantiate the statement.

Firstly, the government of this world is set in the heavens, and is functioning now. In spite of all that seems to the contrary it is functioning now. The Church is seen in a spiritual relationship with the heavenlies, and is said spiritually to be seated there now. The Church is therefore in vital link and association with the governing of this world now in a spiritual way, unto the purpose of God for this dispensation. The Church is not linked with the governing of this world for general purposes, but only in relation to God's purpose, and we must remember that its functioning in this governmental union is spiritual, and is secret. It is not manifest. The Church is not governing this world manifestly, but there is a government of it with which the Church is associated now in secret.

Heavenly Government as seen in Elisha and Daniel.

The Old Testament is full of this in illustration. One of the outstanding, if not the most outstanding, personal types of the Church in the Old Testament is Elisha, the only prophet who was ever anointed; the successor of Elijah, receiving the double portion of the Spirit, and doing the greater works. He is conspicuously the type of the Church as the successor of Christ, so to speak, on this earth. Look at the life of Elisha and see the marvellous expression of this feature of government; secret, hidden, spiritual government. There was a league of certain kings. They came together for purposes of warfare, moved out against their enemies, and found themselves in difficulty because there was no water. The story is one which has often brought its own message of encouragement and inspiration to our own hearts. "Thus saith the Lord, Make this valley full of ditches" (II Kings iii. 16). And in the morning the waters filled all the ditches; it was like a sea. You know the sequel. The story affords a notable instance of the heavenly government of a situation. Here are men who, in spite of faults, were men who represented God, one of them at least. The situation was critical. But for some supernatural heavenly ruling, intervention, there would be an ignominious end. By silent, secret government of the heavens, brought in through a vessel, in this instance Elisha, the whole course of things is changed from tragedy and disaster to glory. No sound, nothing to see, nothing to hear, but the heavens rule.

Again, the Syrians would make war. Elisha is sitting in his home, in the secret place, and sends a message to the king of Israel : "Beware that thou pass not such a place ; for thither the Syrians are coming down" (II Kings vi. 9). And so the king of Israel saved himself there, not once nor twice. The king of Syria said to his war lords : "Will ye not show me which of us is for the king of Israel?'' (verse 11). The reply, with an intelligence for which I cannot account, was : "Nay, my lord, O king, but Elisha, the prophet that is in Israel, telleth the king of Israel the words that thou speakest in thy bedchamber.'' You see the secret, silent government, the undercutting of the enemy, the defeating of him without the drawing of a sword. This is heavenly government. The Old Testament is full of that sort of thing.

The city where the prophet dwelt is besieged. The prophet and his servant are in the city, and the servant sees the besieging army and cries : "Alas, my master ! how shall we do?'' Elisha prays : "Lord . . . open his eyes, that he may see. And the Lord opened the eyes of the young man ; and he saw : and, behold the mountain was full of horses and chariots of fire round about Elisha.'' That is heavenly government. You know the sequel to that.

We pass to the book of Daniel, and here we should have more than enough to occupy us, for the whole story is very true to the fact that the heavens do rule, that God ruleth in the kingdom of men. Think of Nebuchadnezzar, of his attempts against the Testimony, and the vessel of the Testimony, and mark the ruling of the heavens against those attempts of the mightiest of the kings, this head of gold, the highest of them all. It is a great thing to think that Nebuchadnezzar's was the greatest kingdom that this world has known. All those succeeding empires were of inferior cast. And yet the heavens ruled in that greatest of the empires. That rule was being expressed through a little handful of men right in the midst of the strength of this opposition to God. Right in the heart of that violent antagonism to God these few were set; the heavens expressed their government through an instrument which in itself was not much. How mighty was that rule! But it was secret. Where did Daniel rule? In the place of prayer! Where did Elisha rule? In his own house! There is a secret, spiritual going forth of heavenly power, heavenly government, which cannot be explained. There are none of the outward features of a great empire ruling. It is all spiritual; it is all hidden. To the natural eye there is no tracing it. Men only know it as they come into the sphere of its effect. Rulers and governments set against the purpose of God : that is one thing. Rulers, governments, empires, nations set with all their might, backed up by the powers of darkness, against the purpose of God, yet the purpose of God being fulfilled, and that through an instrument which in itself is worth practically nothing : that is the story. glory

What is that instrument? What about its nature, its position? Everything hangs upon that. It is essentially spiritual. It is heavenly, in its life, its relationships and all its resources. That is the city which rules, which governs, and is destined to govern for eternity. It is a spiritual people, a heavenly people, with all that word "heavenly" means.

That implies on the one hand, that a lack of spirituality, a lack of heavenliness of life, is the sure way to defeat. We may move out into this world and find ourselves up against the governments of this world, up against the rulers of this world, up against the laws which men have made, and these things may be dead set against the realisation of God's purpose in this dispensation. Governments may close and lock doors, rulers may withstand, decrees may be formed, nations, countries, may be closed, yet the heavens continue to rule, and all God's purpose is still possible. A people in heavenly union with the Lord, by the exercise of that heavenly function can still be the instrument of fulfilling God's purpose.

For example, I do not believe for a moment that the present régime in Russia is defeating

God's end for this dispensation. If the truth were known, as it will be known one day, probably it is facilitating God's end. Though terrible may be the way, and costly, God's end is not being defeated. The heavens still rule.

Mark you, the heavens demand an instrument in this world through which to exercise their rule, and you and I, by absolute separation from the realm of Satanic power and authority in a spiritual way, and in complete fellowship and harmony with the Lord in heaven, can still be instrumental in fulfilling God's purpose, in spite of every bit of opposition. Man, as we have said, may close doors, but God can say: "I have set before thee an opened door, which no man can shut." Men may forbid this and that. They may forbid preaching; they may forbid the printing; they may forbid all sorts of things, and still things be done. God has secret ways of doing things, through prayer and real spiritual fellowship with Him, which are after the character of this Elisha work in the secret place, without going in person to the scene at all. But, oh, the importance of being in the place where, when everything closes along the natural line, the work is not finished, is not closed! I can believe that countries will close, and governments will prohibit, and perhaps missionaries will have to quit. I can believe that all kinds of things are going to happen as the result of Satan's last effort to quench the purpose of God, as he uses man, governments, and peoples against the Gospel, against the Lord. But I do not believe that God's purpose will be curtailed thereby, nor do I believe that the purpose of God is just going to be effected in a sovereign way direct from heaven. I believe that it is still to be concluded through those who are in spiritual union with Him. We may not go into the places, but it will be done. God has His ways. But even if we do go in, what can we hope for of real eternal effectiveness, unless we are in utter union and league with heaven, unless we have made a complete break with all that is earthly, though "Christian" in name? Oh, the tremendous power of heavenliness and spirituality!

All this is what is meant by the City, which is a heavenly City, and that City is called to govern now in a spiritual way, even as it will function in government in a literal way in the ages to come. You and I are fellow-citizens. We may be the weak things, the foolish things, the things which are despised, and the things which are not, but God has linked tremendous possibilities with such, provided they are under the anointing of the Holy Ghost; which is only another way of saying, provided they are in league with heaven, joined with the reigning Lord. Mighty things can be done in the secret place. The government of the heavens is to come in through the weak saints by prayer. There may be times when no more than living in touch with the Lord will be possible. Words may be finished, all outward forms of expression may have to be suspended. Living in touch with God is a mighty thing. For myself I covet that more than anything, far, far more than public ministry. All forms of public expression are secondary compared with a life of secret fellowship with God, and any kind of public ministry which does not come out of that is of comparatively little value. There is a mighty thing to come out of our hidden life with God, more than we know. There may be no sight and no sound, but something will happen. The Lord make us true citizens of the City which hath foundations.

Col 3:3
For you have died and your life is hidden with Christ in God.

First minist To The Lord
II Chron 29:11

CHAPTER VII.

Jerusalem in Relation to Universality.

READING : Isa. lii. 1, 7-8, 14-15 ;

Acts ii. 5, 7-11 ; x. 11-16, 34-35.

Let us remind ourselves that Jerusalem, in the Word of God, especially stands for the Church. It is an inclusive and comprehensive representation of the Church ; and what we are seeking to see is the spiritual constitution of the Church, what the Church really is according to the Word of God, and what the Church's vocation is.

It does not require very much profound or energetic thinking to recognise that universality runs in very close relationship to spirituality and heavenliness. The heavens are always the symbol of universality. That is very clear. When you get into the heavens you get away from the narrow limitations of life, all the geographical confinement, and you are out in what is absolutely universal. The same is true in the matter of spirituality. When you get into the realm of things spiritual, there again you have left behind all that is small, and limited, and restricted ; you have broken all ties.

So that heavenliness and spirituality lead

us very definitely and distinctly into the universal, and one thing which is of the greatest importance for the Lord's people to be sure about is the universality of the Church. It is necessary to define that. It is necessary to have a very clear apprehension of it. Such as are really concerned with that great Divine object, that which has been in the mind of God before the world was, that which is the pre-eminent object of God in this dispensation, need to have a clear and definite grasp of its nature ; and when we speak of its universality we want to be careful, to be quite sure, as to what we mean by that.

The Exclusiveness and Universality of the Church as typified in Jerusalem.

When you come to the Word of God and study Jerusalem you find two things which seem, on the surface, to be mutually exclusive ; that is, these two things are difficult of reconciliation ; they appear to be contradictory.

On the one hand, *Jerusalem is a clearly defined and distinctly bounded city.* Jerusalem has a wall, and that wall goes right round : and Jerusalem has gates ; and the purpose of walls and gates is to exclude and admit, to govern, therefore, in the matter of who shall be in the city and who shall not. So that Jerusalem is very strictly defined, and, in a sense, appears to be both inclusive and exclusive; that is, it says to a certain company, You are of the city! and it says to another company, You are not of the city, and have no place in it!

On the other hand, there is the fact that *Jerusalem is represented as being universal.* You touch many universal elements when you read the history of Jerusalem. You find that all nations are touched by Jerusalem, and touch Jerusalem, that its relationships are comprehensive, extensive. The only word which adequately expresses it is "universal." It is set down in the midst of a country which can never be said for a moment to be of one fixed and exclusive aspect. Palestine is marked by two extremes, with every shade between them. At a certain time of the year you can sit at a particular point in Palestine and boil in a temperature of a hundred, and from where you sit thus perspiring with intense heat you view the snows of Hermon. You can stand upon a point and at one time see palm trees and pine trees, speaking of two extremes. At the southern part of the Jordan valley you have a sub-tropical climate; in the northern part of the Jordan valley you have a sub-Alpine climate; and there is every phase, and every degree, between these two extremes in the land. In some parts you find the shepherds wearing sheepskin cloaks, which speaks of cold; in other parts you find them doing everything to keep out the heat. These are geographical and climatic features which are illustrative and typical of the universality of the land. Jerusalem is set down in the midst of that land. Hardly a nation on this earth has failed at some time or other to have some kind of relationship with Jerusalem, and with Palestine, and we know that there is yet to be history in which all nations are gathered into that land, and will be met by the Lord Himself in battle.

What is true historically of the earthly Jerusalem is made clear as being true spiritually of the heavenly Jerusalem. All the nations are going to be related to it. The kings of the earth will bring their glory into it, the leaves of its tree will be for the health of the nations, and it will occupy a governmental position in relation to the rest of the universe. The universality of the heavenly Jerusalem is made perfectly clear in the Word of God with a very great deal of evidence.

All this points to the Church, and says quite simply and definitely that the Church partakes of these features in a spiritual way. On the one hand, there is the distinctiveness and definiteness which amounts to exclusiveness, and, on the other hand, there is the universality which brings into relation with the whole world, with all the nations. As we have said, we must get a matter like that quite clear in our hearts and minds. How do you reconcile the two seemingly opposing factors? We shall seek to do so as we go along.

This Two-fold Character of the Church seen in and derived from:—(a) The Head.

What is it that makes the Church on the one hand exclusive, and on the other hand universal? The answer is : That which makes it universal makes it exclusive, and that which makes its exclusive makes it universal. To begin with, that which gives it its universal nature and character is the Person Who is supreme in it, and in the heavenly Jerusalem, the Church, the Lord Jesus is the central and supreme Person, and His Person is a universal Person ; that is, having become Son of Man, He has come in a living way into touch with man as a race. It is not said that He is Son of Englishman, or Chinaman. He is Son of Man ; and that is all-embracing, that touches man of every nation, and clime, and kindred, and tongue. So that the contact with man in any part of the world, no matter what his make-up may be, what his history may be, what his language may be, what his outlook may be, the contact of the Lord Jesus with man, of whatever stock he be, has a living appeal, a living meaning. He is different altogether from any other man who has ever been. One of the marvels of the Lord Jesus is that He has a living appeal to man, no matter how you find man, or where you find him. He is the Saviour of all men. His salvation applies to every race, and every tongue, and every make-up. That cannot be true of any other man. When we go with the Gospel to other countries, very often what is met with is this : Oh, you are English (if it be an Englishman), and your way of thinking, your outlook, is altogether different from ours, and you cannot expect to put us into an English mould of thought, and disposition, and outlook. The door is closed, if the Gospel be presented on that level. Such a procedure affords no hope. It has proved to be disastrous again and again, when the Church has been brought out of its heavenly realm down on to an earthly level, and people of other nations have been striven with to take that mould of the Church that has been brought to them from another country. It cannot be done.

The Lord Jesus can constitute in any place on this earth a company of those who take their character from Him, and in so doing form what is universal. That is to say, He supersedes all national distinctions, and all differences of temperament and constitution, so that there comes about, by reason of a vital union with a central Person, a universal, spiritual Church which is above the nations, and so heavenly, spiritual, and universal. It is the Person with Whom the relationship is brought about Who occasions the universality of the Church. But unless Christ is kept in the central and the supreme place, and the one object of pursuit is conformity to Christ, you can never realise the Church of the Word of God. But with Christ given His place, and His getting really into the life and into the heart, all the other problems solve themselves, and the Church comes into being. Put anything in the place of Christ, even the Church itself, or what may be called the Church, and you destroy its universality and make it something local, something national, something earthly, and therefore something limited in its spiritual value.

The universality of the Church, as brought about by the Person, and living relationship to Him, creates the exclusiveness. That is not a contradictory but a complementary statement, for no one can enter into the Church except by coming into a living relationship with the central Person, the Lord Jesus Christ, and immediately, Christ is found to be a boundary as well as a universal centre. This fact will further be seen to affect not only the matter of entrance into the Church but also that of spiritual development in the Church. We can only grow as we are members of the spiritual Church, the Body of Christ, and the Church itself as a whole can only grow and develop in a spiritual way in so far as Christ becomes its life. Our difficulty is that we get mental pictures of a certain defined circle, when we really ought to be seeing that this is a spiritual matter, and that the Church is not only an area marked off, and you may be in it or outside of it, but that the Church is a spiritual state rather than a place, and that "state" determines how far we are livingly in the Church, and the measure of our conformity to Christ.

For my part, I believe that is why we have the distinction in the Word of God between Zion and Jerusalem. While the words are interchangeable, and are very often used of the same place, nevertheless there is a distinction between them. Zion is Jerusalem ideally, as God thinks of Jerusalem. Zion is the word used when God's full Church is in view. Jerusalem may fall short of Zion, may be less than Zion. Jerusalem may represent things as you find them; Zion represents things as God would have them. That difference is very marked in the Word. So that if Zion represents the full thought of God, God's desire is that Jerusalem should take its character from Zion. Bringing that into our own lives, it means that we are partakers in God's thought for Jerusalem just in so far as we are conformed to God's ideal as represented in His Son, the Lord Jesus. Churchmanship is not a matter of coming within a certain defined limit; Churchmanship is a matter of relationship with the Lord Jesus, and of spiritual condition. Failure to have come to that relationship and spiritual condition means exclusion from the Church. You see how destitute of truth the common idea of the Church is, the idea that you can belong to the Church if only you give assent to certain doctrinal propositions, and go through certain rites or ordinances. It is a completely false conception of the Church. The Church is Christ in corporate expression, and membership of the Church is membership of Christ, and our value as members of the Church is determined by the measure of Christ to which we have come. Christ is universal in His Person, and therefore the Church, related to Him, becomes universal, in the sense that it touches life at every point, and in every condition, in a living way; not in a formal way, but in a living way; as an application, an appeal, and a living touch, by reason of Christ being expressed in and through it. _wherever Christ is expressed there the Church is._

(b) The Cross.

Another thing which constitutes its universality, and at the same time its exclusiveness, is the Cross of Christ. The Cross of the Lord Jesus was a universal thing. No realm has been untouched by that Cross. Is sin proved to be a universal thing? Then the Cross is universal; it touches sin universally. Is man's fallen condition universal? Then the Cross is vitally related to that. All that the Cross stands for is found, and proved, to be of universal application, universal meaning. The only way into the City is by way of the Cross. That means that the Church is universal in its value, in its testimony, in its appeal, in its call, in its invitation; none need be excluded, though at the same time it is impossible to be in it except by way of the Cross. It is universal, and at the same time exclusive.

(c) The Life.

The third thing which bears the same feature is the life which Christ gives to His own. That is a universal life. It is not like other kinds of life. There are other kinds of life, which are limited in their range. Human life is limited. It belongs to man. No one else has human life but man. There is animal life in the lower sense. Life which animals have is a lower order of life; it belongs to animals. There is vegetable life, a still lower order of life; it belongs to that kingdom. These are watertight kingdoms, and the vegetable cannot pass through into the animal, and the animal cannot pass through into the human. So far as the life is concerned, they are exclusive, self-contained. Divine life is another kind of life. When it is given, and becomes the basis of man's life, there is something which he has in common with all children of God, whatever the differences are. He has a common foundation. It is that common foundation which makes fellowship possible, and makes everything real in relation to the Lord; that mighty, working, Divine life, energising, springing up within, gravitating backward to its source in God; and as it gravitates backward to its source it takes its object with it. It is the working of Divine life that brings men out of all nations, and all tongues, and all kindreds, and all temperaments, into a oneness, a universal Church. It is the Divine life in every member, making one Body.

(d) The Holy Spirit.

What is true of the Head, and the Cross, and the life, is true, in the fourth place, of the Holy Spirit. The Holy Spirit, Himself indwelling all who are in Christ through the

Cross, constitutes a universal Church. The universality of that Church is only maintained in its expression as the Holy Spirit is allowed to govern and dominate. Immediately man begins to rule in the Church its universality is upset, and it becomes something legal, a divided thing. But while the Holy Spirit has free course, and absolute dominion, He maintains that principle of the universality of Christ, and preserves the Church as a thing without barriers, without those hindrances to full fellowship which come about when man takes the place of the Holy Spirit.

These things, as you see, bring the balance, the harmony, of the two factors, universality on the one hand and exclusiveness on the other hand, because none can ever enter into the Church, into the heavenly City, save as he comes under the government of the Holy Spirit.

The Counterfeit of the Truth.

This great fact of the universality of the Church is so tremendously important as to have provoked every kind of effort on the part of the enemy to destroy it, and he has moved mainly along two lines. Firstly, he has wrought along the line of counterfeit universality, and then along the line of earthliness, resulting in divisions, and a false kind of exclusiveness.

As to counterfeit universality, this operates in every realm. It is seen in the social realm under the name of the brotherhood of all men. Behind that there is this subtle, evil work of the enemy to bring about a false universality. You can see it in Babylon. When they went to work to build Babylon it was in that manner : "Let us build us a city, and a tower, whose top may reach unto heaven, and let us make us a name; lest we be scattered abroad upon the face of the whole earth" (Gen. xi. 4). What was the object? It was a universal brotherhood, to maintain the power of dominion by unity. That is Babylon : and Babylon is an evil thing.

The same thing works in the industrial world. It works, or seeks to work, in the political world, the confederation of nations. It also seeks to work in the religious world, in the great union of the Churches. But it is a counterfeit and false universality. It is not the oneness of Christ and of the Holy Ghost.

Then there is not only the counterfeit side, but there is that earthly side, where spiritual things, the things of God, are dragged down to an earthly level; handled, gripped, manipulated by man, with the result that you get divisions. All the divisions amongst the Lord's people are the result in some way or other of man's interference in the things of God. Then you get an exclusiveness amongst these divisions, which is a false exclusiveness, and not the exclusiveness of the Cross.

These are Satan's oppositions, activities, against the great universality of the spiritual and heavenly Church of Christ. We shall only know and maintain that universality as we keep away from the earth in a spiritual way; as we allow the Holy Ghost to do the governing; as our teaching is not the teaching of man, but the teaching of the Spirit; as the Cross continually operates to keep out all that which is not of God. The heavenly City is universal, but it is exclusive. That then is the Church, but for its real value it must remain heavenly and spiritual in a practical way.

Lord guide us into the truth — (But) don't do it in ways we have already made up our minds as being wrong!

In order to be guided into all the truth we will have to take some "risks" and go in directions + follow "revelation" that may be different to what we have preconceived were right!

God's ways will not always be logical to us. His ways are not our ways nor His thoughts our thoughts.

CHAPTER VIII.

The Light of the City.

Clearness of Life and Testimony.

READING : Rev. xxi. 10-11, 18, 21; xxii. 1; Gal. iv. 25-26.

The word "clear" occurs on more than one occasion in those passages, and synonymous words are there, such as "pure gold," "as transparent glass." These words suggest the idea of light. They are associated with that light which is spoken of in connection with the heavenly Jerusalem coming down from God out of heaven, her light like unto a stone most precious, a jasper stone.

In speaking of the light of the Lord's heavenly people we are touching again a very solemn, and serious, and important feature, something which has a tremendous history associated with it. The entire history of the Lord's people, and of the spiritual life, is one of light and darkness, of truth and falsehood, of purity and adulteration or mixture, of clearness and cloudiness, of openness and secretiveness. And many other words can be used to express this long history, so long and so chequered all because of this persistent,

continuous effort to bring what is of God into
a place of doubtfulness, of uncertainty, to rob
it of the tremendous power of absolute truth,
absolute purity, absolute clearness.

Long before Christ came Satan had spread
abroad in this earth those Babylonish elements
which only waited for an hour when the Church
should fall into a state of spiritual declension or
weakness to seize the opportunity to pounce
upon this spiritual Body and become the
parasites which sapped and destroyed its life.
So that we find, even before we move out of the
New Testament, that where there was a state
of spiritual declension there was a condition of
Babylonish features, priestcraft, ecclesiasticism, formalism, ritualism, and a host of other
things which came from Babylon and are seen
in the occult, the mystic, the æsthetic, those
ideas which are now the very sum and substance
of the whole Romish system.   These all came
from Babylon, and were in the world waiting
for the Church to decline, and immediately
that decline took place they took hold, impinged
upon the Church.   You find them all there in
the first chapters of the book of the Revelation,
and in other places also, elements of this
religiousness of Mystery Babylon.   Their
object was not to blot out Christianity in a
direct and immediate way, not to wipe the
Church out of existence, but so to mix things

as to bring her into an uncertain place before God, that He could no longer recognise her as His pure Bride.

You notice the call in some of Paul's letters, as well as in those letters to the seven Churches, is to purge out these pagan elements. There is a tremendous amount of paganism represented in the conditions of those to whom he wrote. Take the letter to the Colossians. What was the object of the writing of that letter? Well, the whole spiritual hierarchy, the realm of spiritual beings, angels and archangels, had been, by paganism, so marvellously organised that even Jesus Christ had been placed as but a super-archangel. All the other angels, it is true, had been set under Him in different ranks, but He was given no more than the position of a super-archangel; one of them, though of much higher rank. And the Colossian letter was written, as you will see from the content, on the one hand, as denunciatory of this whole false system of teaching; to destroy it by pointing out how evil the whole thing was, and, on the other hand, to give Christ His rightful place. The first chapter of that letter is the classic as to the Person of the Lord Jesus and His eternal relationship with the Father. He was before all things; all things were made by Him; He is the Head.

But all that mischief had been done by mixture, that is, the destroying of the utter purity of truth, the truth which is only in Jesus.

This is but a very small and inadequate illustration of how the enemy has all the way through sought to destroy real spiritual power by introducing elements which would take from the utterness of the truth, destroy the Church's clearness, and work against this ultimate revelation in which she is seen with "her light like unto a stone most precious . . . a jasper stone. . . ." Pure gold, transparent glass, clear as crystal—that is the characteristic of Zion, the characteristic of the Lord's people; and against that the enemy has worked continuously, in order to compromise the Church's position, the position of the Lord's people, by getting them into an uncertain state in themselves and before God.

Dimming the Fine Gold.

This has been done in the first place, as we have seen, by doctrine. If the enemy can introduce any suggestion of false doctrine, if he can but insinuate the slightest degree of error, he will cause it to work like an evil leaven till a development of that kind has become the occasion for the Holy Spirit's drawing back, the Lord being unable to go on where that is, and a state of compromise, and paralysis, and weakness obtains. The pure gold, the fine gold, has become dimmed.

Not only along the line of doctrine has this been done, but along the line of life. The same method, and the same object, governs the enemy's activities. It is possible to stand very strongly upon what is absolutely orthodox as to doctrine, and to be in a very doubtful state in your own life, your own spiritual life, your own moral life; to be very faithful to the letter of the Word of God, and yet to be compromised in your own spiritual life and testimony. This may be in business dealings, in other relationships, or in your own life before God; something not clear, something not pure, something not clean, something not straight, something doubtful, maybe a secret habit. Oh, it may be one of a multitude of things which takes out of the life that certainty, that definiteness, that positiveness, that clearness, and creates, sometimes almost unconsciously in the one concerned, a fear of being confronted with something, of having to own up to being found out. There is something in the background of the life which is causing an arrest. It is taking the real drive out of testimony, the real impact out of life, and the real fruitfulness and value out of fellowship. There is something there, though very often intangible. You cannot put your hand upon it, but you know there is something there in that life which is not right, which is not clear; and then there develops a secretiveness, an evasiveness, a detachment, or many other kinds of evil symptoms may develop. It is all because there is something there which is not absolutely clear before God. The enemy has got in an element which has destroyed the pure light, and there is a shadow, a film about that life. The enemy's purpose is to destroy that perfect crystal clearness of a life in God, and so paralyse the whole life. The outward form may still be the same, the profession may be just as ever it was, but there is a check.

This is said, not by way of accusation, but by way of indicating one of the favourite lines along which the enemy works to destroy what God has in view for His people, for Jerusalem; namely, that she should eventually come out of heaven having the glory of God, her light like unto a stone most precious, as a jasper stone, and that everything about her should be pure gold, as transparent glass, clear as crystal. Oh, the spiritual value and weight of words and phrases like those!

All this is indisputable and patent. We have to recognise this, that the enemy is continuously seeking to get us into some place where, in spite of ourselves, we feel that we are under a cloud. Sometimes he sets up a false position, and makes us feel that we are false. We may not be false, but he seeks to make us feel that we are false, to get us into that realm where we have lost our confidence, our assurance, our certainty, our standing, our position, where we are weakened by some element which has crept in. The enemy is out to bring God's people under clouds, under suspicion, and to bring them in their own hearts under doubts and questions, so that the clearness, the certainty, the strength is destroyed and they are a big question to everyone, even to themselves.

Poison Gas from the Enemy.

Not only as to individuals, but as to collective instrumentalities of God, this is true. Whenever God raises up an instrument by which He intends to bring His Testimony into greater clearness and greater fullness, the object of which in His desire and thought is to reveal the nature of His Son more clearly, more perfectly, then the concentrated attention of all the powers of evil is to bring that thing under suspicion, and to put over it a great question mark in the eyes and minds of everybody.

Why are not the Lord's people alive to that fact? For a fact which runs parallel with that, and which is just as mighty a fact itself, is that when you really investigate that thing you find you have no reason for question at all. It was all an unfounded suspicion. This is clearly the Devil's work, to cast over something which the Lord would use for a fuller revelation of His Son, and of what He desires for His people, this film of questioning, suspicions, doubts, so that it is forced into a realm where it is regarded as dangerous, suspicious. Would to God that the Lord's people would obey the injunction to "prove all things"!

You see what the enemy is after, and how he goes to work. It is helpful to know sometimes what the enemy is after, and how he does operate. We may be saved from much if only we are aware of it.

This is a message to our hearts, not only of helpfulness in an objective direction through our being informed as to the danger, the peril, the devices of the enemy, but it sheds light upon the inward experience, and shows that all the Lord's dealings with us are intended to bring us to this state of crystal clearness. "Behold, thou desirest truth in the inward parts" (Psa. li. 6) : and what the Lord desires He will get. The dealings of the Lord with His own are purifying dealings, in order to have this crystal clearness, this pure gold, this stone most precious. They are for the getting rid of the dross, getting rid of the film, getting rid of all those secret and secretive elements which work in the direction of deception. Those are like unto a lie, a falsehood. The Lord wants to root all that out of us. He is against everything that is shadowy. He is for everything that is perfectly clear, and so to get rid of the dark substances He puts His fires to work in our lives to purify them. In our individual lives, and in the case of such collective instrumentalities as we have mentioned, He does this. He does not allow such to be out of the fire for long. He is after this state of utter purity.

You see what is involved. In the coming generations all the nations have to walk in that light; that is, they are going to have their knowledge of the Lord through the Church's instrumentality. They are going to be governed by the Church. The nations shall walk in the light thereof. What light is this? This is no mere external aurora. This is the out-shining of a spiritual and moral condition of glory. This is something out from the very nature of the thing—"having the glory of God." It is from the centre, and works as an expression of a spiritual and moral condition. God is not cleansing, purging, chastening you and me, and causing His fires to work to our purifying, just for the sake of doing it, and He is not doing it just for our own sakes inasmuch as He wants us individually to be good and not bad. I suppose He wants that, but that is not all. God has a mighty, universal purpose in view, an eternal vocation, and that is what He is after, and it requires a condition. That is one of the governing conditions of Zion, namely, the full expression of the Lord's mind. The Lord is always motived by things so much greater and vaster than we understand in the day when we are passing through the trial. We bring it down to a personal matter, and ask questions : Why should the Lord deal with *me* like this? We narrow down the range of His thought, His purpose, His intention. Because we make it so local we lose the strength and helpfulness which would come to us if we could see the great eternal vocation for which we were being prepared.

" The Wiles of the Devil."

If we had time to note all the secretive things of which the Word of God tells us concerning the earthly Jerusalem, we should find that it was the purposes of God that were so often threatened by those secretive elements. Think, by way of illustration, of Nehemiah's day, when the wall was being built, and how the enemy got one of his own representatives hidden right in the temple itself, and so sought to compromise everything, to weaken the whole work and position, by having a representative occuping a chamber in the temple itself. Then in Ezra's time the adversary said : We serve the same God as you do, let us come and work alongside of you ! Subtle ! But thank God the man of God was a man of such transparency himself that he could see through things, and he was not deceived. He saw quite clearly that in these people there was darkness. Their condition was not one of clearness, nor of light. There was duplicity, and he shut them out ; and immediately he did that they showed quite well where they were. In these and numerous other ways you can mark the enemy trying all the time to get that which was not suitable to God right into the heart of things, in order to destroy the effectiveness, the positiveness of testimony, and Jerusalem's history is a long history of these subtle elements working in the midst.

We come to the day of our Lord Himself. What a mass of this sort of thing he encountered in Jerusalem ! They tried to catch Him in His words. They were all the time laying traps for Him. They were working furtively, secretively, by deceptions, by snares, trying to take Him. The whole situation, the whole condition of Jerusalem was like that in His day, and clearness, transparency, was destroyed. Yet the temple worship was going on. Outwardly the whole of the religious system was proceeding as it had been wont to do, yet here was this dark interior. God forsakes it, because of the lie. The Lord put His finger upon that so often in very straight and terse language. "You make clean the outside of the platter . . . "! "Whited sepulchres"! What a picture! See them going round with their whitewash, making white their sepulchres; and within, He says, they are "full of dead men's bones." They were making the thing to appear something other than it was. Such is the lie, which is the Devil's work, leading to rejection. The Lord's desire toward us is that we should know that state of light, of clearness, of which we have spoken.

The next thing is love. What is the character of New Testament love? Love unfeigned! What a word! Fancy using that word to Christians—love unfeigned! Does that mean that some would love feignedly, feign to love, pretend to love, while really they do not love at all? That which the Lord seeks in every virtue, in every element, is something that is true.

That is what we mean by light in the sense of clearness. It is the purity and inwardness of things. Truth may be in word, in doctrine, but there has to be a corresponding truth in heart, truth in life. Light may be a matter of doctrine, but there has to be a corresponding state of light in the heart. The enemy will not object to us having plenty of the former kind of light and truth, but, if he can, he will seek to destroy its real value by introducing a lie over against it, a contradiction.

This may sound rather strong. Well, it is strong! It must be strong! It has not been put in this way to lay charges against anyone, but by way of warning. It will perhaps explain some things, but we must take it to our hearts as a word of exhortation or admonition. Remember that God never builds in the dark; that is, there can be no constructiveness where there is not light. Before ever God would bring this world back into order and fruitfulness He said : "Let there be light." God is out for the *manifestation* of the truth. God's works are never darkness, and we can never know constructiveness and progress unless there is absolute light. You know quite well that you cannot go on with people who are not straight, people who are crooked, people who are all the time furtive, not open, not frank, who have somewhere in the background a secretiveness. You have to say, I cannot go on with that one. God is like that. He would say to any one of us who might be there, I cannot go on with you until you are absolutely out in the open, until you have come to a place where you are going to be perfectly honest. Reality is God's demand for any kind of work that He will do. There may be many weaknesses, many imperfections, but if there is genuineness, reality, openness before God, where the spirit is clear and pure, God can go on with His work. But immediately we begin to lock something up inside, hold something back, cease to be perfectly open before God, the work stops. Light in the sense of clearness is an essential for the building of the city of God, because the ultimate purpose for that city is to shine forth with that glory of God in character. With Him there is no variableness, neither shadow cast by turning. That means that God can be relied upon.

The Lord make us like that.

Some Principles
of the
House of God

SOME PRINCIPLES OF THE HOUSE OF GOD

Reading : Psalm cxxxii.

" Then Solomon began to build the house of the Lord at Jerusalem on mount Moriah, where the Lord appeared unto David his father, which he made ready in the place that David had appointed, in the threshing-floor of Ornan the Jebusite " (II Chron. iii. 1).

THERE is much related Scripture which we ought to read, but must only refer to as we proceed, because of our limited space.

It needs no arguing amongst us, I think, that the centre of God's presence among men, namely, the house of God, is a matter of first importance. I have said the centre of God's presence, for the house of God embraces and relates to everything else which is of concern or interest to the Lord. The

1

house of God is within a wider range of God's interests and concerns. Ultimately there will be wide ranges to which it ministers, to which God manifests Himself through it. It is the centre of His presence.

From a consideration of its great type here in the Old Testament, the temple, we are able to learn something of the principles which constitute the foundation and basis of that central dwelling place of God.

THE TRIUMPH OF FAITH AND OBEDIENCE

The passage which we have just read is a key to so much, both historically and spiritually. I begin by pointing out again that the first principle of the house of God, the dwelling place of the Lord, is the triumph of faith and obedience when all else has been brought down to the dust. All Abraham's hopes and expectations, and the promises of God and the covenant of God with him, centred in Isaac. Beyond and apart from Isaac, Abraham had nothing. And then God said, " *Take now thy son . . . Isaac . . . and offer him . . . for a burnt offering* " *(Gen xxii. 2).* In the words from Job: " *Lay thou thy treasure in the dust* " *(Job xxii. 24).* And the

2

writer to the Hebrews makes a point of that—that he in whom all the covenant and promises were centred was being offered up by Abraham (Heb. xi. 17, 18). Looked at from one side only, Abraham was severing the very arteries of life, parting with everything of hope, prospect, possibility; all was, from that standpoint, brought to ashes. But for the intervention of God, Isaac would very soon have been reduced to ashes. In effect he was. So far as Abraham's heart attitude and obedience were concerned, Isaac was already in ashes. The wood was there for kindling, the altar and the knife were ready. But faith triumphed through obedience, and that very mount Moriah subsequently became the site of the temple, the house of God. The house of God is built on that sort of thing.

This foreshadows Calvary. From purely earthly standpoints Calvary was the end of all hope. It was a laying of treasure in the dust; it was ashes; it was an end. We know how it was for those around that Cross: it seemed the end of everything. But on the part of the one central figure of that great universal drama it was faith's obedience unto death, yea, the death of the Cross; and the house of God was and is built upon that. It is

3

a principle. It is the great reality, the great doctrine of Christ. But it is of practical application, namely, that the house of God can only be grounded and founded and built as that sort of thing goes on.

THE LAYING DOWN OF LIFE

A related principle is the continuous laying down of its own soul by the Church, letting go of its own life in obedience and in faith, when all is dark, when all seems hopeless beyond. Some course of obedience is required, calling for us to do that which seems to be without prospect or hope, and which involves, therefore, the laying down of our lives, of our souls. It is the way of building. It has ever been like that. When young men and women have given up all the prospects of this world and laid their treasures in the dust and gone forth at the command of the Lord, they have laid everything in ashes so far as this world's hopes and prospects are concerned. The Church has been built in that way. Even when it is not like that in great acts of life's vocation, it is a daily thing, a letting go of our own interests in obedience to the Lord, in faith in the Lord. It is thus the building goes

4

on. I could work that down to very fine points and show how often the house of God is delayed and arrested in its progress by the withholding of something on which the Lord has laid His finger and said, ' I want that '. However, there is the general principle, the triumph of faith through obedience when all is in the dust. Abraham believed God, and that great triumph provided God with the site for His temple, the great example and type of that spiritual house which is central to the fulfilment of all His purposes. God dwells in that sort of thing. But that central thing has to go through the depths. That which is the very heart of God's presence, to which He commits Himself, has to know stripping more than others. This involves a deep work where faith is brought to perfection through very deep testing.

FELLOWSHIP WITH GOD
IN HIS SACRIFICIAL LOVE

Alongside of that there is that factor of perfect fellowship with God in His sacrificial love. We have often made that point ·when speaking of Abraham's great step into the heart of the One who withheld not His Son, His Well-beloved, but

5

freely gave Him up for us all. It was indeed a movement right into fellowship with the sacrificial nature, the giving unto cost, of the love of God. That is the only way in which the house of God is established. There has to be a giving unto cost because of love. It is quite evident that Abraham loved God more than he loved Isaac, dear and important though Isaac was. Abraham saw that to obey was of greater importance than even to keep this tremendous treasure ; and that is love. That is what the Bible calls the fear of the Lord —that element of fear in love. I am sure you know what that means. If there is someone of great account to you, and whose love you esteem very highly, you are always very sensitive about causing that one disappointment. That is the nature of the fear of the Lord. Abraham feared God. The house of God is built upon that kind of fear. It is of very practical and everyday meaning—the love of God in our hearts leading to costliness in our sacrifice, our giving.

THE GLORY OF MAN ABASED

Then passing from Abraham to David ; this threshing floor of Ornan, the site of the temple, re-

6

The amount of our obedience & giving is in direct proportion to the love of God in our hearts. When we love little we give little.

presented and stood for the undercutting of Satan's man-glorifying work and the deep abasement of man himself. You remember that Satan incited David to number Israel—a thing which even a carnal man like Joab could see through, for he said, " *The Lord make his people a hundred times as many as they are : but, my lord the king, are they not all my lord's servants ? why doth my lord require this thing ? why will he be a cause of guilt unto Israel?* " *(I Chron. xxi. 3).* ' The Lord has done very much, and will do more, but do not begin to count heads, to take account of how big your resources are and to glory in the greatness of your kingdom '. Joab was a carnal man, but it seems that some carnal men sometimes see more than Christians do as to principles. But David set aside Divine wisdom and good human wisdom, and insisted on the numbering of Israel. You know the result. All came from Satan's prompting of David to do something which would glorify man and make much of his resources and achievements. The Lord came out and smote it hip and thigh, and that Satanic work of glorifying man was undercut and man was deeply abased. David was a sorry picture when he came to the threshing floor of Ornan. Oh, that man is now humbled to the dust !

This has to be done before there can be any building of God's house. Satan's work to make much of man has to be completely undercut. The glory of man, and man's desire for any kind of glory for himself, have to be abased. This is a house for the name of the Lord and for no other name in heaven, in earth, or in hell. " *My glory* ", says the Lord, " *will I not give to another* " *(Isa. xlii. 8)*. The Lord does that all the time. Oh, the horrible display of human flesh in the realm of Divine things ! Oh, the reputations made in the realm of what is of God ! Oh, the delight to have a place in the Church ! Oh, how often this flesh is active for its own pleasure and gratification ! The Lord is hitting it hard all the time, driving hard blows to ensure that His house is on the right foundation, not on anything that is of ourselves. It does come home to us.

" *Lord, remember for David all his humiliations* " *(Ps. cxxxii. 1)*. That last word is more accurate than the one used in our translation. " Afflictions " is the word in the text, but that does not convey the true meaning unless you add other words and say, ' The afflictions with which he afflicted himself '. He is saying, ' How I humiliated myself ! I would not allow my eyes to have sleep,

I would not allow my bed to entice me, I would not enjoy my own house ; I humiliated myself, deprived myself, in order to find a place for the Lord '. And the Lord does require that humiliation. He brings about this breaking down of man in order that the house should be rightly based. That explains His dealings with us. He will not let us be anything. If we are really to be the dwelling-place of God, then we are to be nothing in ourselves. Do not look for reputation, do not try to make an impression, do not stand on your own dignity, do not do any of those things in any way whatever which will give you prominence with people and make them think something of you. It will not pass with the Lord. So let us get rid of it, every bit of it, and recognize what we are in God's sight. He is going to bring that about ; so if we try to make people think we are other than we are in order to get an advantage, we are contradicting the principle of the house of God. All self-importance must go, and all desire for recognition. All that sort of thing has to be wiped out. The house of God is not founded on that. God will not have it. Man is abased, and all the other is the devil's work. It comes from him in whose heart pride was found.

9

THE MEETING OF MERCY AND JUDGMENT

Then, let me remind you that the threshing floor of Ornan, the site of the temple, was the place where judgment and mercy met. We sing

> ' With mercy and with judgment
> My web of time He wove '.

There must be judgment. It was so in the case of David. But judgment is only one side. Judgment and mercy met on that threshing floor that day and kissed each other, and the temple resulted. Judgment has to begin at the house of God, but, thank God, it is not judgment unto utter destruction. It is mercy mingled with judgment, and the end is the triumph of mercy over judgment. That is Calvary, that is the house of God. We shall find it like that all the time. There will be judgment ; it has to be ; we know it quite well. The Lord does not let pass things that are contrary to the principles of His house. If we only knew it, as Paul tried to make the Corinthians know it, many are suffering to-day in numerous ways because they are not observing the principles of the house of

10

God (I Cor. xi. 30). There is that side ; it goes on.
But oh, God only does that in order to have mercy.
It is mercy that is His end. So He founds and so
He builds His house.

GOD UNDER NO DEBT TO MAN

No indebtedness to man is allowed to be represented by God's house. How insistent David was,
how alive now to Divine principles ! The refining
fires wake us up to principles. It was so with David
on another occasion. You remember how the ark
was put on the cart. David had forgotten the
Scripture. He went through a time of suffering
until at last he came to see the Divine principle
in the Word of God and put things right (I Chron.
xiii, xv). Here he is alive to principles again. When
Ornan wanted to give David the threshing floor,
David said, ' No, I will pay you in full. No man
shall ever say that the house of God is in debt to
men ; no other shall ever be able to say afterward,
" Yes, I gave God that ; the site of that temple is
my gift " '. No, Ornan is bought out of all holding.
Man has no place as a creditor in the house of God;
there is no debt to man, he is bought right out.
You can apply that.

11

THE THRESHING OF THE CORN

This was a threshing-floor, the place where all is threshed out before the Lord. No chaff here ; nothing that is not real, genuine, true, solid ; nothing that will not contribute to building up. It must be the true corn. God is always seeking to do this. The house of God is a threshing floor. All our chaff, our vanity, our emptiness, is being got rid of, all that really does not count. God is after that which builds His house, or, to change the metaphor, the Body. He is after the corn. The chaff must go. In our very relationship to the Lord amongst His people, as forming His house, we find He is winnowing, threshing, getting rid of our vanity, our unreality, our chaff. But in so doing He is getting reality, He is getting what is solid, what will stand, what will feed. This is the basis of His building.

All that we have said should work out in very practical ways. The figures employed are but types and symbols, but the realities are in the hands of the Holy Spirit, and He will unceasingly press for their fulfilment in the lives of God's people. Let us see to it that as He works in our case He has our full co-operation.   T. Austin-Sparks

God's
Spiritual
House

CONTENTS.

GOD'S SPIRITUAL HOUSE

CHAPTER 1.

The Exaltation of God's Son

READING: I Chron. xxii. 1-19 ; xxviii. 5-7 ; xxix. 20, 22-25 ; Acts ii. 30-36 ; vii. 47-49 ; I Pet. ii. 4-5 ; Heb. iii. 6 ; ɪⱽ xii. 5, 9 ; Eph. i. 20-23.

I have been very much occupied of late with this matter of sonship in the House of God, and am led to the conclusion that something of this is to be the Lord's message at this time. There are many aspects of this spiritual house. How many of them we shall be able to consider must remain to be seen.

It is quite certain that this matter is very relevant to what is happening at this present time on the earth. In particular, there is a very real and living message in it for the Lord's people, and I trust that we shall seek to adjust ourselves to that fact and not regard this as just some further measure of Bible teaching which may be more or less familiar.

Christ Exalted on High—the Keystone of Testimony

We shall begin with what the Scriptures so clearly indicate as the point of commencement of the House of God, namely, the exaltation of the Son to the place of supreme authority and glory. The spiritual house, (which house are we,) prospectively exists for this very purpose of proclaiming and rejoicing in the fact of the exaltation of God's Son. The passages which we read from the Old Testament, which are prophetic, pointing on to the spiritual house, all bear out this fact and show it in type in a very wonderful and clear way. David's greatest son—for God had given him many sons—was brought out into clear view as the one chosen of God to be exalted to a place of glory and power above that which had been given to any before him; and it is interesting to note that, while Solomon was ordained and chosen of God for that position, he did not come out as distinguished for it until

5

someone else made a bid for that position. You will remember the little incident of Adonijah, who subtly worked to get the throne, to get what God had appointed for Solomon. By that subtle movement to usurp the throne appointed for another, Solomon was distinguished at once, brought out and proclaimed as the one chosen by God. That is only in passing; but it is interesting to notice that it was when God's Son and God's appointment concerning His Son was assailed, and His place sought after in a conspiracy, that the Lord Jesus was marked out, brought out into the light as the One whom God had chosen. That is something which recurs. There it was in the case of Solomon. It was so in the case of the Lord Jesus at the beginning of this dispensation. That will happen again at the end when Antichrist makes his bid for world domination, and then God will bring out His Son as the One chosen and anointed for that position, and all will then be manifestly put in subjection under His feet, as they are now spiritually and potentially.

The house which was brought into being through and by Solomon, came in specifically on the basis of Solomon's exaltation, on the ground that he was the appointed one and that God had summed up all things in him. When Solomon was brought into his place, then the house came into being; and all the things that are said about Solomon are very wonderful things. They all speak of his glory, of his power, of his wealth, God's thought for the one who shall have the throne, and the house becomes the very symbol of the glory of the Lord, the exaltation of the king. The house which is to be built for the Lord is to be exceeding magnificent. That house reflects the king, the one who is the son over the house in type.

We foresee by these Old Testament scriptures just what we have in the New Testament, and so we can come at once to this first and primary thing about the spiritual house of which we are called to be living stones, that our very existence is for the proclamation—in what we are as well as in our testimony—of the exaltation of God's Son.

Now, everything begins there, with the exaltation of Christ, and that firstly in heaven. It was when He was at the right hand of God exalted that the Church had its beginning. Everything came out from that, and in the beginning things in the Church spiritually were very glorious and very wonderful. I

have no doubt but that angels took account of what was then
going on to the glory and praise of God, and we have also
reason to believe that demons were tremendously impressed.
Everything took its rise from the exaltation of God's Son, this
even "greater than Solomon."

The Essential Counterpart of the Heavenly Exaltation

But for us, while that remains true, and has many blessings
associated with it, to have practical beginnings the exaltation
of the Lord Jesus has to be an inward thing, and the beginning
of everything for us necessitates there being a counterpart of
that Son's exaltation in heaven in our hearts; that what God
means by His having glorified His Son is a thing of spiritual
reality within us. He comes to absolute enthronement with
all things in subjection to Him. You notice how the account
of Solomon's enthronement concludes. "And all the princes,
and the mighty men, and all the sons likewise of king David,
submitted themselves unto Solomon the king" (I Chron. xxix.
24). He was doubly enthroned—"They made Solomon king
the second time." Now you have your ground, if there is one,
for a "second blessing"! You talk about second blessings.
Here you are, this is what it is, the second thing. What God
has done in heaven is done in our hearts. We have reason to
rejoice and feel greatly blessed that God has raised Jesus from
the dead and set Him at His own right hand. Tremendous
things are bound up with that for us. But the " second
blessing " is that this becomes something of reality in us, and
that what is true in heaven as to all things put under his feet,
submitting themselves to Him, is true within the kingdom of
our lives. That is the way of the fulness of the blessing.

All things, as I have said, spring from that, begin there.
Life itself begins in reality when Jesus is absolute Lord within.
We do not come into the fulness of blessing when Jesus is not
more than Saviour. The fulness of the blessing is known when
He is Lord and has everything within us under His feet, submitting to Him. It is the way of blessing. You see, all the
blessing that God meant for man, the fulness that was to be
man's inheritance, was lost because Satan, seeking to usurp
the place of God's Son as Lord, by his propaganda worked
subtly and made man believe that he would lose everything
by remaining in subjection to God. ' Why not be as God
yourself? ' said he. In other words, Why have a life limited

by being subject to God and dependent upon Him! Along that line, man lost all the fulness, and now all the fulness comes back by being absolutely subject to God's Son, and submitting to Him in all things. That was the great lie of Satan, and this is why Satan does not like Jesus Christ being Lord, and why he so strongly contends against any ministry that has in view that object, of bringing the Lord Jesus into His rightful place as supreme Lord in God's house. It is because by that his lie is exposed and the work which he achieved through his lie undone.

The whole question is that of the universal Lordship of Jesus Christ, and it is that which is coming out to-day as never before in the history of this world as the supreme issue. Who is going to be Lord in God's universe? Who is going to have world dominion? The enemy is still seeking to reach that end through man along the line of the lie, and we have never before known of his method being so tremendously, so universally and so insidiously employed—the lie! So much so, that for months past, this world has rocked on this question. Who can be trusted? Who can be believed? Who is speaking the truth? What man can you have confidence in? There has spread over the earth such an atmosphere of discrediting by lies that men almost look at those of their own household and wonder whether they can be trusted. That is a terrible reality in many lands. They dare not open their lips within the most limited circle, because truth faileth, trust-worthiness has been smitten almost to the ground. The lie, the propaganda of lies: and all, mark you, with this one end in view, namely, to get a grip on the dominion of this world. That is Satan's work behind what we see going on, and when Jesus Christ comes into His place as absolute Lord in you and in me, something results which declares that Satan has been defeated; the lie is exposed. The truth is that subjection to Jesus Christ is not a miserable life as a vassal. It is a life of triumph, a life of victory, a life of glory, a life of fulness. It is the blinding work of the enemy with men, to make them think that to belong to the Lord, to have the Lord in their lives, means they are going to lose all that is worth while, and be shut down, and all the time be poor cringing creatures, hardly able to lift their heads up, going about as beggars. That is Satan's lie. The Old Testament brings it out here so clearly that, when all things were subject to, submitting themselves to, God's appointed king, it was a time of fulness such as the people had never known: and so it is when Jesus is Lord within as in heaven.

In those days, following that great day of Pentecost, the Church knew something of liberation, enlargement, enrichment, glory, power and fulness, and it all sprang from the fact that Jesus was Lord. They lived upon that ground and in the appreciation of that great fact. Life commenced there, testimony commenced there and commences there, and all our service for the Lord should spring out of this. There is no true service which does not spring out from this fact of the Lordship of Jesus Christ. You see, every revival or great spiritual renewal has been by the Lord coming back into His place. Go again over the Old Testament, and you have instance after instance when the Lord was brought back into His place—it was a wonderful time. Think, for instance, of the days of Hezekiah, of Josiah, when the Lord was given His place anew in a wonderful way. They came back to re-enthrone the Lord as Lord in their midst in an utter and full way, and they were great days. If you pass your eye over history, you see that all real spiritual awakenings—call them revivals or renewals—have circled round this one thing, that the Lord was brought back into His place. He was given His place as absolute Lord, and people went down before Him. That was the secret of it, and it is like that.

What is true in history, true in the wider way, is true in the individual life. So much of our trouble, our declension, our spiritual weakness and failure, is because He is not Lord. We are thankful to know Him as Saviour, we believe that He is in heaven glorified, but there is a good deal of controversy within us on points. It all amounts to this one issue, namely, the utterness of His Lordship within, and, when those matters and controversies are settled, we find a new uprising of life. You can always have a little revival in your own heart on any one point where the Lord has a controversy with you. Test it. It may be only one point, but you know that one thing is holding you up. You have to get clear on that one thing, and when at last you go down with that thing under the Lord and put it under His feet, you have a little revival in your own heart and you come out with new life, new testimony, new release. Spread that over all things, and the kingdom has come. It is just like that.

B

The Cross and the Lordship of Christ

Well, this, His spiritual house, has been brought into being for no other purpose or no greater purpose than that—just to stand entirely in the enjoyment of the proclamation of the exaltation of the Lord Jesus. When you come to think of it, is not that the primary and deepest meaning and purpose of the Cross? The Cross may do many things, touch many questions and many issues, but when you get down to the meaning of the Cross at its deepest, it relates to the deposing of other gods. That was the great issue in the twenty-fourth chapter of Joshua, you remember. In reviewing the whole situation, Joshua has all Israel before him, and he begins with the history of Israel right back in the time of Abraham's father. 'Abraham's father lived in Ur of the Chaldees and served other gods. Then Abraham came out from the serving of his father's gods and crossed over the river and came into the land. After this your fathers came into Egypt and there they worshipped the gods of the Egyptians ; but at length they also came out over the river to serve the Lord.' The whole issue was other gods and the river between the other gods and the Lord every time. Now then, what about you? says Joshua. Are you going to allow the river really to stand effectively for what it means? Are you going to allow that river really to stand between you and the other gods which you worshipped and served in Egypt? "As for me and my house, we will serve the Lord." What about you? So the river was always related to other gods. The Cross, in its deepest meaning, touches other gods, other lords, other objects of worship receiving the good of our lives, and deposes them all, and brings the Lord into His place, so that we say, "As for me and my house, we will serve the Lord." That is the meaning of the Cross. It touches everything that stands in the way of the absolute Lordship of Jesus Christ. It gets right down there.

The Lord Jesus Exalted as our Kinsman

But then there is this other or further very blessed fact about the exaltation of the Lord Jesus. He is exalted as our Kinsman. The exaltation of Christ is the exaltation of our Brother. That comes out, you see, in the record. David said, "Of all my sons, (for Jehovah hath given me many sons), he hath chosen Solomon my son to sit upon the throne of the kingdom of Jehovah over Israel" (I Chron. xxviii. 5). Then later, when speaking of Solomon's enthronement, the record says, "And all the sons of David bowed down and did obeisance to Solomon and submitted themselves unto him." A great thing—his brethren all looking up to him as on the throne and acknowledging him as king. That is a permanent factor in all the types about the exaltation of the Lord Jesus.

In the book of Samuel, again, you have that time when Absalom had usurped the throne and brought a great deal of misery and suffering upon the people to whom he had promised so much ; and then Absalom was slain and the people were stranded. For some time everything was in a state of suspense, until there arose a questioning among the people, and someone said, "Why speak ye not a word of bringing the king back?" That became a rumour, and it got out over to where David was. David heard what was being said, and he took hold of it and sent a message to Zadok and Abiathar for the people, expressing himself thus: I am your flesh and your bone ; ye are my brethren: why speak ye not a word of bringing the king back? His appeal for his place was on the basis of his kinship and they brought him back on the basis of that appeal.

Now, what is the meaning and value of that? Well, God has exalted our Brother, God has exalted our Kinsman, and that Kinsman is God's Son, and He, as the Apostle puts it, is going to bring many sons to glory because He is the first-born among many brethren. The exaltation of our Kinsman means that the family is coming to exaltation. His enthronement is the earnest of ours ; and, beloved, we are never sure of coming to our exaltation, our fulness, until we recognize the Lord Jesus in His place as our Kinsman-representative. It is an exalted family, it is a household, you see : God's house for the Son, and then sons. But the Son must have His place before the sons can have theirs ; but, having His place, the sons have theirs guaranteed to them. Our Kinsman is exalted, and that says a great deal ; because He is not exalted just as a despot, just as an officially appointed monarch whether we like it or not—God has chosen Him, selected Him, put Him in that position: now then, Bow the knee! Oh no : He is our Brother, our Kinsman, and there is such a tie, such a link, such a oneness of life, that He cannot be there apart from us. There is an inward spiritual oneness with Him in His exaltation which spells something very big.

12

Perhaps I can illustrate it best by reminding you of Mordecai. You remember Haman again, in the train of these many usurpers, and Haman's devilish device to destroy all the Jews. Mordecai is in the place of rejection, ruled out. Then, by one of those marvellous acts of Divine sovereignty which make even a sleepless night of the most tremendous value in history, the king could not sleep one night. Would that all our sleepless nights were as profitable to the Lord as his was! He commanded to bring the book of records of the chronicles, and they were read before the king ; and he read something about Mordecai. Someone had lifted up his hand against the throne and a certain man, a Jew, had brought the thing to light and saved the king's life. Then the king said, "What honour and dignity hath been bestowed on Mordecai for this?" Then the story develops and it comes to the point where Haman goes home one day to his wife and all his friends and tells them of what had happened. He, who thought the king was going to honour him, has been made to honour Mordecai, and as he tells them this, the discerning answer made to Haman was this: "If Mordecai before whom thou hast begun to fall be of the seed of the Jews, thou shalt not prevail against him, but shalt surely fall before him." If he is of the seed of the Jews, you cannot prevail, your days are numbered! There is something about that, you see. It is this kinship with the Jews on the part of the exalted one which secures both their deliverance and the enemy's undoing.

Oh yes, this kinship with the Exalted One means for us deliverance and the overthrow of the enemy. There is a very great deal bound up with the exaltation of the Lord Jesus, and Satan knows it. He knows that his days are numbered when Christ is exalted in any life. When we come to that exaltation-union with the Lord Jesus in our own hearts, Satan is in despair. It is like that.

The Need for Diligence and Discipline in the Light of a Day to Come

Well now, we must stop somewhere, and I think we might just stay here by pointing out that this house, with all the significance of sonship, the Son and the sons in God's House, has a present spiritual meaning. It is something which has to be realised in a spiritual way now. It indeed is the great spiritual matter for all the children of God. If we ask, What is the issue in this dispensation where God and His people are concerned, the answer surely is this, that there shall be a house, a spiritual house, which stands in the good of the exaltation of the Lord Jesus. That is the issue, and that is to be a spiritual thing now.

But I also want you to remember that, so far as manifestation is concerned, this lies in the future ; and upon that hangs this wonderful and terrible little word ' if.' " Christ as a son, over God's house ; whose house are we, if..." Hebrews xii. which treats of God's dealings with us as with sons, has a big "if" there also. "If ye endure chastening, God dealeth with you as with sons." It is rather a strange way of putting things. It almost looks as though you are not a son if you do not endure chastening. Well, that is what it means. The "if" is in view of the fact that you and I have not yet come to the fulness of sonship. It will be the fulness of sonship in manifestation which brings in the House of God in all its glory. It is something future, it is prospective. If...if...

You notice, in that connection, how Israel in the wilderness is so often called up as a warning. They did not become, in God's intended sense, His house. They have perished in the wilderness. They did not suffer chastening. They would not let God deal with them as with sons along the line of child-training. They did not come to their adoption as sons. They fell short of the glory of the inheritance of the full purpose of God ; and that is brought over to Corinthians and to Hebrews as the warning. We are His house if...if...if...

Now, what is the significance of this? Oh, it is this, that what God's Son is in glory, He becomes in us now progressively ; that Christ is being more and more enlarged in us as the Son over God's house. I think it is so patent, as hardly to need pointing out, that the course of our spiritual experience under the hand of God is always with this one thing in view. All our difficulties with the Lord, all our bad times, are on the principle of submission to the Lord, with a view to the Lord having His place. Is it not like that? The Lord is finding us out by child-training. Take up the child and put the child under training, and you will discover what is in the child, whether the child is going to be compliant or not, whether the child is going on with you or not. Put the child under discipline, and you will find out all the revolt that is in the child's nature. That is how the Lord is dealing with us.

This word "chastening" is unfortunate, because it is confused in our minds with punishing. It means nothing of the kind. God is not punishing His children at all. The true meaning is child-training, and Satan always turns God's dealings with us into punishment in our minds. It is not that. What He is working at with us is to bring us to the place where He is utterly Lord and can do as He likes with us, and we have no question at all. None of us has reached that point yet, but that is what the Lord is doing, and there is a big "if," you see. We can say we are not going to have any more of this discipline, we are not going on with it. Well the throne is in view, not only for Him but for us. The Lord has a great purpose for His sons in union with the Son as joint-heirs and as fellow-rulers in His universe. It all springs out of the fact that Jesus Christ is Lord in heaven and in us, and then that this Lordship is wrought into us in a perfect way. All our training is in that direction. So it is prospective, it is future, and the "if" is there. We are God's house if... May the Lord so triumph in us that the "if" greatly loses weight and power and place, and eventually ceases to be at all, and we are His house.

CHAPTER 2.

Assurance as to God's Rest and Satisfaction in Christ

"... having foreordained us unto adoption as sons through Jesus Christ unto himself, according to the good pleasure of his will, to the praise of the glory of his grace, which he freely bestowed on us in the Beloved...to the end that we should be unto the praise of his glory, we who had before hoped in Christ" (Eph. i. 5-6, 12).

"For we are his workmanship, created in Christ Jesus for good works, which God afore prepared that we should walk in them" (Eph. ii. 10).

"And now, O Father, glorify thou me with thine own self with the glory which I had with thee before the world was" (John xvii. 5).

We are at this time being directed to take account of God's spiritual house, and in our previous meditation we were thinking of the first and pre-eminent feature of this spiritual house, in which we, in Christ, are living stones, as being the proclamation or setting forth of the exaltation of God's Son. We noticed that everything, so far as God's house is concerned, takes its rise from that exaltation. What happened on the day of Pentecost was the spontaneous outflow of that exaltation of God's Son to the right hand of the Majesty on high, and the secret of life, of power, of victory, in those first days of the Church's life and history was this very fact. Its life flowed out from this ; its testimony was this, that Jesus as God's Son was exalted to the throne on high. You know that was the testimony of Peter on the day of Pentecost. You know that was the note of Stephen. You know the Apostles continually testified to that great fact, that God had made Him Lord and Christ, that He was exalted. I repeat, everything came out of that, and it resolves itself into the great element of assurance, something which is always very necessary ; and never was there a time when it was more necessary than now.

The Assault upon Assurance

In our previous meditation, we referred to the fact that the great spiritual enemy has pursued his ambition for world

15

dominion along the line of the propagation of a lie, his great "fifth column" propaganda, and he has made great headway by the campaign of lies to the undermining of assurance and confidence.

There is another thing which he has done and is doing in a spiritual way, which is so clearly seen at present working out along temporal lines, and is indeed the confessed and published strategy of those who are now being driven and used and governed by Satan toward world domination by the elimination of Christ. They have put it on record that their strategy is to work secretly within the national life of their enemies steadily through the years, with a view to bringing about internal disintegration by the breakdown of confidence: and how they have done it and are doing it! I do not want to dwell on the earthly, temporal and political side of things, but it does disclose the principles of Satanic activity, this working subtly and secretly behind the scenes within the life of their enemies with a view to destroying confidence, and so bringing about collapse from the inside. Indeed, the phrase which is in print in that connection is, We will make our enemies defeat themselves! Well, they have done it in many countries.

Now, take it as a clue to what is happening spiritually. Oh, how Satan has pursued that course right through history, to destroy confidence; for confidence is a tremendous factor. You see how nations seek to bolster up and stimulate assurance within their own borders in order to secure strength against their enemies. What will they not do to reassure people, to put confidence into people? Satan knows that an assured people set him the biggest problem and represent the most impossible situation for him. Now, if you look at those first days of the Church's life, one outstanding feature was this assurance. They were men without questions, people without doubts. They could speak with authority because their hearts were settled; they were not divided inwardly. There were none of the seeds of internal disintegration. The basis of that assurance and settled position was just this, that the Holy Spirit had come and in them had mightily registered the fact that Jesus was on the throne. "Jesus...by the right hand of God exalted." They had no question about that, and therefore all doubts were set at rest. (The exaltation of the Lord Jesus, when it becomes something settled in our own hearts, is a

mighty factor in testimony, in life, in service, and unless we
have it we are altogether at a discount.

Now, in days such as these in which we are living, the
strategy of the enemy is to undermine assurance. I am not
speaking about world things now, but spiritual assurance. The
House of God is therefore built by this means, the assurance
that Jesus Christ is exalted, and you cannot build without it.
In the case of David and Solomon, we noted how the bringing
in of that house for the Lord God which was to be exceeding
magnificent, all sprang from the fact that God had secured
both His king and the throne for His king. God made a
covenant with David. God took an oath with David that of
the fruit of his loins should one sit upon his throne, and his
throne should be established for ever. Now, that is transferred, as you know, to the Lord Jesus. It only had a merely
figurative and very imperfect fulfilment in Solomon. Solomon
came to a shameful end, but in the days of his glory he was a
figure of another. Thus in the book of the Acts we have those
words quoted from the Psalm:

> "The Lord said unto my Lord, Sit thou on my right hand,
> Till I make thine enemies the footstool of thy feet"
> (Acts ii. 34-35).

The Apostle uses those words in connection with this other
word to David:

> "David...being therefore a prophet, and knowing that God
> had sworn with an oath to him, that of the fruit of his
> loins he would set one upon his throne; he foreseeing
> this spake of...the Christ,"

spake of this One; and God has fulfilled His word, not in a
shadow, not in a type, but right up to the hilt in this greater
Son of David. David's greater Son is on the throne of thrones,
and out of God's securing of His King in glory and exaltation,
the history of the Church begins, and the supreme note by
which the Church is built is the note of absolute assurance
which comes from what God has secured in glory in His Son.

Father God's sure promise (Word)

God's Rest in His Son

Assurance comes from heart rest. Here again let us mark
and how full of truth, exactitude, the Scriptures are everywhere
—that it was no accident or chance or hap that Solomon, the

Father is at Rest in Jesus Christ.
We are at Rest in John Christ.

Jesus Christ the God-Man.

18

man who was chosen for this position, had the name of
Solomon. Solomon means "rest." Now you notice Stephen,
referring to Solomon, says a rather interesting thing in
Acts vii. 47-49.

> "But Solomon built him a house. Howbeit the Most High
> dwelleth not in houses made with hands ; as saith the
> prophet :
> The heaven is my throne,
> And the earth the footstool of my feet :
> What manner of house will ye build me? saith the
> Lord :
> Or what is the place of my rest?"

Then Solomon had another name—Jedidiah, "Beloved of
God." That is what we read in Ephesians—"hath made us
accepted in the Beloved." You see, the Lord Jesus takes up
Solomon on both his names. He is God's rest, "the place of
my rest" ; and He is the Beloved of God, the Beloved of the
Father. So that, in the very first place, God gets all that His
heart is set upon, with regard to what His house is to be, in
the Person of His Son, and it is out of this that the house
corporately, of which we are parts, takes its rise. It is built
upon that heart rest which God has in His Son.

Now, you and I have to come to the same place as God
in regard to the Lord Jesus before we can really be an
expression of His house. We are His spiritual house : "Whose
house are we." But that does not mean that God just puts us
together as bricks. He must have living stones, and that
phrase "living stones" implies, as the context shows in
I Peter ii. 5, that it is by a living relation with the chief Corner
Stone that the house is built : "unto whom coming, a living
stone...ye also, as living stones, are built up a spiritual house."
The parts are one with the Corner Stone, all of a piece, so far
as their nature is concerned, one with Him in what He is. As
the building, we have to take our character from that chief
Corner Stone which God has chosen. "I lay in Zion a chief
corner stone, elect, precious." God works to Him and from
Him. You and I work to Him and from Him. But what is
this that gives the House its character? It is God's full and
perfect satisfaction in His Son which gives Him rest. God
rested from all His works on the seventh day, and God
beheld all things which He had made, and they were very
good. Now, carry that right through in this spiritual con-

nection with God's house, and long, long after you hear this word: "that he might present it (the church) to himself a glorious church, not having spot or wrinkle or any such thing." That is only saying, It is very good! The thing which first of all satisfies God's heart is that His Son has answered to all that He has ever required in a spiritual and a moral way. That is God's rest, and the exaltation of the Lord Jesus is God's seal to the fact. God is satisfied, God is at rest. Thus it is that, as the Lord Jesus is just about to step out on that last bit of the journey which is to see Him crucified, He says, "Father, glorify thou me with thine own self with the glory which I had with thee before the world was" (John xvii. 5). Glorify thou Me! Yes, that is coming almost at once by the darkest part of the road. It is the way to the glory. This last step, the Cross, is the final stage and summing up of all that has been in the satisfaction of God's heart.

The Value of the Blood of Jesus

What I am coming to in all that I have said is this, that it is by His precious Blood that God's absolute rest in the Lord Jesus is secured. Oh, beloved, you and I need ever more and more to apprehend the supreme value of the Blood of Jesus! The value of the Blood of Jesus is the great factor at the end time. It is the supreme factor in heart rest, and heart rest is the only ground of victory; and therefore Satan is always seeking to rob the children of God of heart rest on spiritual matters. I am going to make this appeal to you all at this time, although something more will have to be said at some other time about it; but I do want to make this appeal to you, that we ought to be at the place where the matter of our relationship with God in acceptance, in peace, in rest, in fellowship, is an absolute thing now. We must not allow the other side of our spiritual experience to cross that dividing line and come into the realm of our assurance. I mean, there is that other side where the Lord is conforming us to the image of His Son. He has a great work on hand in us, and, as He takes it in hand, we discover as never before what a work it is. We discover ourselves, discover the depths of iniquity that are to be found in our fallen nature. It becomes a terrible thing to us. But never allow that which comes to light by God's handling of us to cross over into that other place of our acceptance, our standing, our peace with God.

So many people fail to keep that line clearly defined and they accept all kinds of accusations from the enemy because the Lord is dealing with them in this way. They feel so bad, so worthless, so useless, so utterly impotent and evil, and suppose therefore that their relationship with the Lord is interrupted, and the Lord is not pleased with them, and all that sort of thing, and they lose their rest. I believe that is why a lot of people have turned strongly against the subjective side of God's working, because they have seen many Christians altogether breakdown in their assurance under it. You come to a place where you know the Lord has accepted you and that you have peace with God ; your sins are forgiven, and you are blessedly at peace, enjoying the Lord. Well, you are there for a time, and then you come into touch with something that has to do with spiritual progress and fuller life in Christ, and all that is bound up with that. Now many, as soon as they begin to touch that, lose their old basic assurance and joy, and because of that, there are those who have turned, not only against simple salvation and rejoicing in the Lord as Saviour, but all that is beyond besides. They will not have any more. They will not have what is subjective. That does not justify their position, but it does say that we have to be very careful about this matter: and we have to stand up to this thing. We have to take this position, and no doubt some of you have taken this position—Well, I know I am beginning to know something of the depths of evil in my own nature; I am coming to see what I never would have believed to be true of myself. I have never had worse times about myself, the hopelessness of myself, than I am having now. I am seeing more and more that in me, that is in my flesh, dwelleth no good thing! and so on, but...but that is the Lord's matter. That is for the Lord to deal with. I am not going to allow that to encroach upon my absolute acceptance with God, my basic standing before God. I am not going to allow all the problems of sanctification to come over and destroy the great assurance of justification! You must be very careful to keep that line clearly defined, because, if I am not mistaken, that is just the work of the devil to destroy the power of the Church and I believe that that is the heart of Rev. xii.—"They overcame him because of the blood of the Lamb"—and who is it they are overcoming? The accuser of the brethren. He is seeking to cast them down by accusation, and their answer to his accusation is the Blood of the Lamb. What is that? God

The church can only grow when it is at rest, in the finished work of Lord Jesus. When the church becomes it is one with Christ or Christ victory is its victory Christ exaltation is its Exaltation Christ Resurrection is its Ress. Christ seating in Heaven is its seating.

satisfied, God at rest, and I at rest on the basis of the Blood. They overcame him and he is cast down. They are not cast down when they maintain their position there. The Blood is not something just for initial salvation: it is something for final triumph ; it is the final thing. The value of the Blood is a tremendous thing to keep the Lord's people strong and assured, confident, and with the ringing note of authority ; God's basis of satisfaction, the Blood of His Son making possible His exaltation.

Well, this is all to do with that necessary, indispensable element of assurance by which the Church is built. The spiritual house goes forward on that line. I believe that that is the secret of the remarkable progress at the beginning. "The Lord added to them daily those who were being saved." The Church grew in a way in which it has never grown since, and the great factor in the building of the house then, in the growth of the Church, was that there was this note of absolute assurance and confidence. They were a people who had heart rest, and who knew that Jesus Christ was enthroned. For them that settled matters in their hearts between themselves and God. That is all going back to our previous meditation, but it leads us right on to this further thing which the passages we have read bring specially before us. It is that the spiritual house has its existence for the very purpose of answering to God's own desire, ministering to God's own pleasure and glory. There are these phrases in Ephesians : "That we should be to the praise of the glory of his grace" ; "to the praise of his glory," should exist to satisfy God's heart, to minister to His glory, to His pleasure. In this way, the spiritual house is to be God's answer to all that has happened in history.

God's New Creation

In the first creation gathered up into the first Adam, we have seen God surveying His working and saying, It is very good! Then followed breakdown, chaos, ruin in the creation. Out of a ruined creation, God lifted a nation, and the greatest thing that was ever said of Israel, I think, is in that little phrase, "Israel my glory." What a thing to say! Israel My glory! And in the early days of Solomon, Israel was God's glory. Again come breakdown, failure, ruin. Finally we see God coming back again, coming back on Israel, coming back on creation with a new creation in Christ Jesus. Firstly, as to

Christ Himself personally, and being able to say, as we have seen, "My beloved, in whom I am well pleased," I am fully satisfied. In other words, it is the new creation seen in Christ, and God saying, It is very good, I am well pleased.

But then there comes in the Church, the Church which is His Body, which is an extension of the new creation from Christ personal to Christ corporate, and the last thing in view about this Church is its coming down from heaven having the glory of God, or, to use the other words, "presented unto him a glorious church," or again, "when he shall come to be glorified in his saints, and to be marvelled at in all them that believed" (II Thess. i. 10). That is the end. So that this is God's final answer. There is not going to be another chaos and ruin in the creation. This is God's last answer to all that has gone before of ruin and breakdown. It is the Church, this spiritual house, a new creation.

What the Church Is

What, then, is this spiritual house? What is this Church? Let us not have an objective mentality about this, thinking of it as something somewhere outside of and apart from ourselves. What is it? The answer is a very simple one. The spiritual house of God is Christ Himself. Yes, but not Christ personally alone, but Christ in you, in me, the hope of glory. Oh, it is just here that all the mistakes have been made about the Church, with such disastrous results. The Church, the House of God, is simply Christ Himself in undivided oneness found in all those in whom He really dwells. That is all. That is the Church. Seek to root out of your mentality any and every other idea of the Church. It is not Christ divided into a thousand or a million fragments amongst so many believers. It is still one Christ. You and I are not the Church. It is Christ in you and in me that is the Church. We still remain what we are outside of the Church still on our natural ground, but it is the measure of Christ in us that constitutes the Church, a spiritual Church, a spiritual house, the one Christ by the one Spirit in all those in whom He dwells. That is the Church. God has never seen in that Church, in that Temple, anything but His Son. He is the Temple of God and you and I can never belong to the Church save as Christ is in us. I know that is a simple thing to say, but if we would just fasten on that and see what that means; it is one of the great factors of unspeakably great power against the enemy, if only we would live on that basis, if only we would abide there.

There are two ways of approaching the matter, and I see again the great success of Satanic propaganda in this matter. I do not know what you older Christians think about it. We can only speak of what we have recognized in our lifetime, but we have lived long enough to recognize the course of things, and to me it does seem, and it more than seems, that, in the last few years, the last few decades, there has been a far greater development and growth of suspicion amongst Christians than there used to be, so that to-day it is almost impossible to speak anywhere without people wondering if you are quite sound. It is in the atmosphere. It seems to me that there is a constant alertness to scent something that is not quite sound, and anything that is of God is prejudiced by that attitude, that state of things. The real truth of God is not getting a chance because this suspicion has spread over all the world, among all Christians. Is this quite right? Is this quite sound? Is this quite true? What is the snag here? What is the error in this? It is like that. That is the positive line, that has become the positive line, and, beloved, I believe that this is one of the marks of this Satanic propaganda to bring about collapse from the inside, because it means that there is internal disintegration, there is no cohesion, the people of God are broken up into thousands of fragments by this very spirit and atmosphere of suspicion bringing about pre-judice, and the Church cannot move together as a solid whole. There are very few Christians indeed who can move a hundred per cent. together, as one, simply because of this. Satan brings it into the most intimate circles of Christian life and fellow-ship, all the time bringing up this horrible element of uncertainty, question. Yes, he has got into the inside, and he is bringing about internal disintegration and collapse in a very quiet way, but subtly working through the years, and he can win many bloodless battles along that line. He can take territory very easily along that line and hold it and gain his end of dominion.

Take another earthly expression of this spiritual back-ground of things. Do you not see, beloved, that over there there is no room whatever for a second thought or a second mind? Anybody through the last seven years who has had another thought, another mind, a second idea, has been eliminated. You may not there have two minds. You have got to subjugate your mind to this other mind, this dominating mind. You must not have an opinion, you must not reason, you must not speak in any way that cuts across the prevailing mind, the mind of the dictator. There is no room for anything that is second. It is one. Satan knows the almost infinite value of oneness, and that is a secret of progress, of success ; a ruthless, murderous elimination of every second voice, to have only one voice, one mind, one will, dominating all others. Dare you think otherwise? Dare you have a mind of your own? Well, have it, but make very sure that you never let it be known. That is the regime, and what power there is for the object in view!

Well now, that is an earthly expression of a spiritual system. Bring that into the realm of the Church. Why is the Church paralysed, weakened, held up? Why can it not go forward terrible as an army with banners? Because there has been this disintegrating work secretly going on within its borders, so that suspicion is the order of the day. I suggest to you that, for the sake of the overthrow of the Satanic kingdom which is to be brought about by and through the Church in union with its Head, its Lord, in glory, for the sake of that and unto that end, you and I should make the opposite our positive course. Let us not be for ever suspiciously asking, what is wrong? What is doubtful? What is unsafe here? but positively, What is there of Christ in this? On that I fasten! What do I see or sense of the Lord Jesus in this matter? With that I engage, I co-operate. Oh, if we would only take that as our positive course, Satan would soon be losing ground, the Church would soon be coming up a glorious Church. One thing which characterised the Church at its beginning was oneness. They spoke the same things, they were all of one mind and one heart, and what ground the enemy lost! But, as soon as the enemy began his secret 'fifth column' work of propagating internal doubts, suspicions, prejudices, he very soon brought the Church down out of that realm of reigning life and scattered its power. Oh, we must pray the Lord that the one Christ, the one Spirit, shall be in the ascendant in us! We shall not be living either upon the ground of what we are naturally—for we shall always be affected by what we are naturally, but upon the ground of what there is of Christ in one another ; neither let us be dwelling upon the ground of possible error, possible false teaching, and possibility of it being there all the time and almost looking for that more than anything else. Oh, we must trust the Lord about this matter! I do believe, beloved, that the safest way, the way of our protection from error, is to go on with the Lord. Our position must be—I am going on with the Lord where I find the Lord, and I am going to trust the Lord in the matter of error, and, as we walk with the Lord, we shall sense, without looking for it, where the error is, and we shall be warned by the Spirit, we shall know. We must move on the positive basis, that of the Lord Himself, and that is glory in the Church, when it is the Lord. "Christ in you, the hope of glory."

We know quite well, in simple ways, that this is true. We meet one another, we have never met before. We discover very quickly by our spiritual sense that we belong to the Lord, and then we have a very blessed time simply on that ground. We flow together because we are the Lord's, and, if only we stood there, we would go on having a blessed time, but presently we begin to discuss some doctrine and find we do not agree. All the glory goes out, the fellowship breaks down. Oh, the Lord hold us into Himself!

Now, I am saying this spiritual house is Christ, and all that is not Christ has got to be kept in its own place, and we have got to seek to remain on the basis of Christ as in us and as in one another, and this is the glory of God, that we should be to the glory of His grace. That is where it begins—His grace. It seems to me, it has seemed to me through the years, (I do not know whether I am right in doctrine now or not, it is a forgivable mistake if it is error), but it has seemed to me through the years very often, that the Lord Himself has taken pains to keep me on the basis of grace, and by that I mean He has so often let me know in experience that, but for His grace, I am a lost man in experience, not a doctrine, not as truth. Oh, to-day, it would be a bad thing for me if it were not for the grace of God! Yes, to appeal even to-day to the Blood, to the grace of God, because of that precious Blood, to-day, after so many years of knowing the Lord! Yes, it is grace to-day, and it is that that brings glory to God, allowing us to know how base, how foul, we are, and letting us know that that makes no difference to Him because of the Blood. That is glory to God. I do not know what the deepest note in your heart is to-day, but that is the deepest note in my own heart after these years. Ah, it is the grace of God that is the glory of my heart, the glory of His grace. He is glorified by our recognition of His grace and our abiding on the basis of His grace. The glory is soon taken away from the Lord when we get on to any other ground ; what we are and can do and what we are doing. The Lord will very soon put a stake in our flesh when we begin to get exalted like that. He is being robbed of glory. He is glorified by our transfiguration, our conformity to the image of His Son. Paul says, "We... beholding as in a mirror the glory of the Lord, are transformed into the same image" (II Cor. iii. 18). The glory is connected with the change, transformed into the same image. He is glorified as we are changed into the image of His Son. He is glorified when our lives are becoming fruitful. "Herein is my Father glorified that ye bear much fruit" (John xv. 8). And the fruit, in the first place, is the fruit of the nature of the Lord Jesus, the fruit of the Spirit, love, joy, peace, long-suffering, kindness, goodness, faith, meekness, self-control. "Herein is my Father glorified." Fruit in service, of course, but fruit in life, and He is glorified by the endurance of the saints.

Ah, yes, let us lay this to heart as our final word. If only we recognised it. There is a great deal of glory brought to the Lord simply along the line of endurance. At times we can do no more. The only thing to do is to give up or to hold on ; to let go, or to endure. Peter has a lot to say about that. "This is grace, if a man endure," and just to endure brings glory to God. It will be a great story, it will be one of the large and glorious volumes in the library of heaven, the story of the endurance of the saints, how much glory it brought to God. Oh, the story will be a romance! How many people were influenced by it, how many unbelievers came to believe because of the endurance of some saint in the time of suffering! How many other saints were mightily supported as they saw the steadfast endurance of another under fiercest trial! How much the Lord got out of just sheer endurance! Yes, this is to the glory of God, if we endure. The Lord get glory in the Church by Christ Jesus unto all ages for ever and ever, and may we indeed be a house for His glory in these various ways.

CHAPTER 3.

Ministering to the Deliverance and Life of the Elect

"...unto whom coming, a living stone, rejected indeed of men, but with God elect, precious, ye also, as living stones, are built up a spiritual house, to be a holy priesthood, to offer up spiritual sacrifices, acceptable to God through Jesus Christ" (I Pet. ii. 4-5).

"But the priests the Levites, the sons of Zadok, that kept the charge of my sanctuary when the children of Israel went astray from me, they shall come near to me to minister unto me ; and they shall stand before me to offer unto me the fat and the blood, saith the Lord Jehovah: they shall enter into my sanctuary, and they shall come near to my table, to minister unto me, and they shall keep my charge. And it shall be that, when they enter in at the gates of the inner court, they shall be clothed with linen garments ; and no wool shall come upon them, while they minister in the gates of the inner court, and within. They shall have linen tires upon their heads, and shall have linen breeches upon their loins ; they shall not gird themselves with anything that causeth sweat." (Ezekiel xliv. 15-18).

We have been seeking to see some of the major features of this spiritual house, remembering the words of the Apostle, "Christ as a son, over God's house ; whose house are we" (Heb. iii. 6). Those features which we have already contemplated are that this spiritual house has as its object, in the first place, the setting forth of the exaltation of the Lord Jesus; in the second place, to be the vehicle through which the glory and pleasure of God are ministered to.

The Presence of a Spiritual House the Signal for Satanic Antagonism

Now for a little while we will dwell upon the third of those major features, which is that, in the purpose of God, this spiritual house is here to minister for the deliverance and life of the elect. We shall not dwell very much upon that last word, "the elect." We need not be particularly taken up with

27

it. It is the people of God who are in view ; the Church which is foreknown, elect according to the foreknowledge of God the Father, chosen in Christ before the world was, and the spiritual house exists to minister for the deliverance, and to the life, of that people. This is the great vocation of the people of God, or a part of that great vocation. So great, so vital is it, that immediately upon the bringing in of the Church, all hell was moved from beneath against it. The very bringing in of the Church was the signal and the occasion for a mighty move on the part of the enemy, a move along many lines and by many means, two of which can be clearly discerned, and indeed are being forced upon our attention in these days, if we recognize the fact that behind all that is taking place on the earth at this time there is a spiritual system of things. That twofold move on the part of the enemy from the beginning has been, firstly, by subtle working on the inside to bring the Church to a collapse inwardly ; and secondly to overwhelm it by sheer force. I think we need say no more by way of indicating the nature of things. That is indeed Satanic and a Satanic method.

The first indication in the Church's history that Satan was at work was by that secret, inward, subtle movement of the enemy through Ananias and Sapphira, and it was pronounced immediately to be Satanic. "Why hath Satan filled thy heart..." It was something right from the inside and a subtle movement of Satan to bring about internal collapse. But for the swift judgment of God upon that thing, it would have spread like a canker. It would have worked subtly until the Church was seething with that sort of thing. Then, not long after, the other form of Satanic activity became manifest, namely open, direct, aggressive force to try by direct means to crush and trample under foot this instrument of God which had been brought into being; and all that which has been pursued relentlessly and on an ever-growing scale down the ages is itself significant as to the greatness of the vocation of the Church. It is indicative that Satan recognizes the issue to be himself or the Church : these two cannot proceed together. Let me say again that we are not without ample evidence that the present world happenings are not merely political and temporal, but are spiritual in their nature and essence, and, as even men of the world recognize and pronounce, they are Satanic in their background. If that is true, we may come to one conclusion, namely, that it is not just the suppression of certain peoples on the earth which is in view with Satan. It is to get at something within or among the peoples which is a menace to that world domination of Satan through his Antichrist. If that really came home to our hearts as it ought to and as it may yet be brought home more forcibly by sheer force of circumstances, we should recognize that not only is our existence as the Church at stake, but that we are up against the great test, perhaps the final test, of whether we are fulfilling our heavenly calling.

The Assault of Satan Against Christ in His House

You see, the whole effort of Satan from the beginning has been to destroy the life of God's people here on the earth. Christ's life in the Church is the objective of Satan in this dispensation, and, inasmuch as the Church is called into relationship with the working out of God's eternal purpose— for the Church is not only called according to that purpose, but is the elect instrument for the working out of that purpose —that very fact must involve the manifestation of the most terrible power that this universe contains against God's purpose.

The Greatness of God's Christ

What is God's purpose? Well, it has to do with the first thing with which we were occupied in relation to this House of God, namely, the exaltation of God's Son to the throne of the universe. That is God's purpose comprehensively, inclusively, and the Church is called in, not only to share that exaltation, but to be instrumental in the working out of that purpose. If that be true, then, we repeat, that involves the manifestation of this terrible power of Satan; because the exaltation of the Lord Jesus to the supreme place is not a mechanical nor automatic thing. It is a spiritual thing, and it is accomplished by spiritual power. That is why we are designated "living stones." We are not just bricks being put together: we are part and parcel of the very life of Christ and of God's purpose concerning Christ, and it is that life of His in a final, full manifestation in the Church which will be the display of the glory of the Lord Jesus. The Lord Jesus cannot be manifested in glory as supreme Lord in God's universe until the elect come through to that place of absolute triumph over all the power of death, and thus it is by the

Church's triumph that the glory of Christ is displayed. It becomes therefore a living matter, a spiritual matter, and not just a cold, lifeless, mechanical thing. We are in something very real. We are going to know that, to reach God's end, the instrument by which that purpose is worked out to its completion has to come up against the last fragment and ounce of Satanic power. It involves the drawing out of Satan's power to the full in order that God may display how great His Christ is.

That is the principle which has run right through the Word of God. You can see it standing out again and again in conspicuous instances, one of which is contained in the word addressed to Pharaoh: "For this purpose have I raised thee up that I might display in thee my power." Pharaoh therefore was allowed very much liberty. When Pharaoh in the very first test refused God, God could have come in and crushed him and destroyed him out of hand, and that would have been the end of Pharaoh. But God drew him on, drew him out, once, twice, thrice, on to ten times, the full measure of Pharaoh's resource ; drew him out and all that was instigating him, in order that, showing how much power there was against God, God could come in at last and show how much greater He was than the greatest that was against Him. It is only a foreshadowing, a type. But, you see, it is not with mere Pharaohs or dictators that we have to do. We are up against the full power of Satan himself. I say the Church is up against that, and the Church, as being the instrument of reaching God's end and fulfilling or working out God's purpose, has therefore to be proved absolutely superior to Satan. Where the Lord gets His life into His people, the one certain thing which will happen to that people is that they will be instrumental in drawing out death against themselves. It is true. It is remarkable, is it not? You wonder why it is that, the more closely you walk with the Lord and the more you are set upon God's full thought, the more you seem to be drawing death upon yourself. One thing with which you are always in conflict is this death-working activity of Satan. That is a part of our vocation. We do not like the idea, we inwardly shrink, and all that is natural about us feels very bad at the thought ; but we just have to put all that on one side and trust the Lord in facing facts. We have to face spiritual facts. Therefore we take note of this, that, if it is true that this spiritual House, this Church, this

Body of Christ is in existence as the instrument by which God is going to fulfil His purpose concerning His Son, then that can only be as all Satan's power is drawn out and exhausted, to the end that, in that Church, the life whereby Jesus conquered death should be manifested as greater than all the power of death itself.

You see, then, the steps. The first is that the presence of a spiritual House here is the signal for Satanic action. The second is that the whole effort of Satan is set against Christ's life in that House, that Church, that Body. The third is that the very working out of God's purpose through the Church, the House, necessitates the drawing out of Satan's power and the Church's experience of something very terrible, in respect of what Satan's power is, all to one end, namely, the bringing out, not of the greatness of Satan's power, but the greatness of God's Christ. That is the goal.

The Course of the Conflict

It is quite clear that, through history, Satan has had a Satanic succession of instruments on the earth. He started with Cain. "Cain was of the evil one," the Scripture says, "and slew his brother." Right down through history as disclosed in the Old Testament, you have Satan's unholy succession of instruments. Again and again you come upon them. There they are lying in wait right to his hand for death purposes. There is Doeg the Edomite to hand, subtly to hand, watching for his advantage, with his eye upon God's king. There is Haman, the Agagite, scheming and planning for the death of all the Jews. So Satan has had his succession of instruments for the death of God's people right up to to-day. They are at work to-day and we know their names. But God has had His line of succession all the way through from Abel onward. Now these, every one of them, drew out the power of the adversary. Abel drew out the power of death through Cain. It seems as though he went down under it, but it is not so. In the long run we know otherwise, and he, being dead, yet speaketh. His testimony remains. Thus everyone of these links in the chain of God's successors has drawn out the adversary to display his power, and then eventually, although in their lives here on the earth they may have gone down under that power, the triumph is with that life which was in them, with the Lord whom they served. That is how it is now.

We must be very careful of our deductions, and in one connection especially, namely, with regard to the fact that the Lord gives the enemy a good deal of rope, and the enemy gains many advantages and has a large measure of success. But, remember, Satan's power and Satan's success are not in spite of God but because of God. If you can draw that distinction, you will be greatly helped. Satan's power is not in spite of God, but because of God. God is allowing it. It is under the sovereignty of God. God is simply drawing it out, extending it, and when the cup of iniquity is full, then God will come in and show how overwhelming He is. That is the end. Beware of your deductions when you see evil having a great measure of success. Understand what God is doing. He is not going to show His power against the thing in its infancy. What power of God would that be? No, God displays His power when a thing is fullgrown.

Now, while I must not diverge and get on to another very important aspect of what we are considering, I would here point out a very startling fact with reference to the matter of sonship. While sonship, which is full-grown manhood, is a Divine end, and with sonship comes the manifestation of glory, (that is, when things have become full, then glory is manifested—" waiting for the manifestation of the sons of God,") sonship is also a principle operating on the side of Satan. The Lord Jesus said to those Jewish rulers, "You compass sea and land to make one proselyte ; and when he is become so, ye make him twofold more a *son* of hell than yourselves" (Matt. xxiii. 15). He chooses His word—full-grown expression of hell. A terrible thing! But, you see, all that happens on that side under the sovereignty of God is bringing things to maturity before judgement comes in. The sovereignty of God requires that iniquity must come to the full, and its coming to the full is not because God is impotent or unable to cope with the thing. It is not in spite of God but because of God ; and God is going to answer the sum of Satan's power through the Church. Thus, in the end, it will be "unto him be the glory in the church and in Christ Jesus unto all ages for ever and ever."

The Church's Vocation

Now then, what is the vocation of the Church in relation to all this? We are here, as we said at the outset, for the

purpose of ministering to the deliverance and life of the elect.
The real ministry arises in a day like this. It is the ministry of
intercession, priestly intercession: "a spiritual house, a holy
priesthood, to offer up spiritual sacrifices." We are being
launched into our vocation now perhaps as never before as we
see the enemy coming out more fiercely and terribly against
the life of Christ in the Church. We are here to stand in God
for that life, and we have to be very careful in this matter
that we are not put off our ministry by any subtle, secret
working of the enemy. We cannot say too much about this
secret internal activity, this propaganda of the spiritual powers
to put the people of God out of action by breakdown and
collapse from within, and it is in this very connection that we
have those assurances and exhortations with regard to our
access unto God. Let us remember that these comforting
words about access, of being allowed even boldness to draw
nigh, are not just for our own comfort and satisfaction. It is
this vocation that is in view, and I believe that is proved again
by the action of the enemy. Is he not continually trying to
get the people off their ministry of prayer by throwing some
doubt upon their acceptance, their access, bringing them under
accusation and raising up the sense of some kind of spiritual
barrier between them and the Lord so that the very heart is
taken out of prayer. "What is the good of praying? There is
that and there is that and the other thing about me ; my very
state keeps me from prayer." Ah, yes, and if we act upon that
accusation, on the one hand it is a sheer denial of the value of
the Blood, setting it aside, which is what Satan wants, and on
the other hand it is playing into his hands and giving him the
advantage over the people of God. Remember, all interference with our prayer life is a strategic movement on the
enemy's part to destroy our vocation and to gain the advantage
over the people of God. We are here for the deliverance and
life of God's people. That is the very purpose of the Church's
existence.

Now, will you take that as more than something just said?
Will you listen to that from within? If you truly are a child
of God, will you pray at this time that you may both see and
accept all the meaning of the fact that you are a part of
Christ's Body, a living stone in the spiritual house, and that
your very existence as such is in relation to the life and
deliverance of God's people everywhere. You are not an

E

individual, ~~you are a part of~~ a house, and that house is God's ~~means of deliverance and life for~~ His people everywhere in ~~this in intensifying conflict with the power of death and dark-ness.~~ We exist for that, and if we are not ministering to that, we are denying the very object of our existence. Do take that to heart, because there is no option about this. It is not an ~~optional matter whether we~~ fulfil an intercessory ministry or ~~not, and pray for all saints at all seasons.~~ You are not invited + to come and do that *if you like.* That is not the House of God. We have to see that the House of God is not some inanimate lifeless thing. It is living, and the very marks of its life are that it is active, energetic, in a spiritual way ; and it is ~~characterized by the spirit of intercession.~~ The position is not that you have prayer meetings at different times and people pray or do not pray according as they feel like it. The House ~~is characterised~~ by intercession, and it is that which deter-~~mines whether~~ we are corresponding to the very nature of our ~~life as~~ God's children. If we were really living up to what we are in Christ, ~~whenever there is~~ an opportunity to pray, we ~~would be on the mark.~~ At the least we should be alive to it, ~~and, whether we~~ prayed audibly or not, we would be in it ; it ~~would be spontaneous.~~ Life is spontaneous : and so inter-~~cession is a part of life, which is spontaneous.~~ If the Spirit of ~~the Lord~~ really has His way in us, we will be people of inter-~~cession. We cannot~~ help it, it will be so.

But unto that, we have to watch these points where our intercession is assailed, and the points at which intercession or prayer is assailed are numerous. Remember, a basic point is this matter of access. ~~We have to be sure of our access unto God, and to be sure about it,~~ we have to know the infinite ~~value of that precious Blood, and we~~ must not to be deterred ~~by anything, for the Blood forbids us to be deterred.~~ That Blood exists to deal with anything that would deter us. Yes, ~~we may fail, we may blunder, we may breakdown ;~~ there may ~~be those things which grieve us and grieve the Lord,~~ but oh, ~~let us recognize that the precious Blood makes possible~~ the ~~keeping of the shortest accounts with those things,~~ so that ~~instantly, right now, and not waiting until we have got~~ over ~~the violent reaction and sting of our mistake and~~ feel a bit ~~better, that precious Blood must~~ be appropriated to deal with ~~that. Let us remember that all this persistence of the enemy to lay us low has something more in view than~~ just laying us low. It is to destroy our spiritual vocation in pray thereby to give him opportunity for assaulting and oppressing the saints. We are responsible for the life and deliverance of the Lord's people. That is what we are here for.

The Church and the Power of the Throne

Seeing that is so, it is necessary for us always to bear in mind that, while for ourselves, as sinners, God's throne is a throne of grace, it is also a throne of judgment for the enemy. What to us is the throne of grace is the throne of destruction to Satan. We have not only to come in boldness to the throne of grace for ourselves and for the Lord's people needing grace, we have with equal boldness to come to that same throne as the throne which spells the undoing of Satan. Always remember there are two sides to that throne. There is the grace side and the judgment side ; the grace side for us because of the precious blood, and the judgment side for the Adversary.

This latter aspect of the throne is that which comes so prominently into view with Esther. It had to do with the undoing of Haman's devices. We have to recognize that the throne has not only to be in the midst of the Church as the throne of grace, but in all its meaning as the throne of Divine power for undoing the work of Satan. It is a different aspect of prayer, a very important one. You and I should know the touch with the throne against the enemy on behalf of the Lord's people. That throne must be in the Church.

A Final Word on the Trust Committed to the Church

Well now, we must close, and we do so by just gathering it up in this way. This whole trust of the life of the people of God is given to the Church. That is a tremendous thing to say, and an equally tremendous thing to contemplate. I know that, in a very true sense, all is secured in Christ in glory, but it is equally true, according to Divine revelation, that there has to be an outworking, and this latter is committed to the Church. We are workers together with God. We were created in Christ Jesus unto good works which God foreordained that we should walk in them. The Lord has put this tremendous trust upon His people, the working out of His purpose, which is the deliverance and life of His people unto that glorious consummation—the display of the greatness of

Christ in His people, through His people.

You see, when Christ comes, He is not just coming to be seen in glory, to be manifested as the glorified, glorious Christ ; not just that. He is coming to be glorified in His saints and to be marvelled at in all them that believe. Christ's glorification is to be something in the Church at last. Unto that, you and I and all the Lord's people are given the trust of working it out. The Lord gives us light. Then, while He is not out of touch with us, in a sense He stands back and says, Now then, that is your business ; I have given you light, now get on with it! We are all the time appealing back to the Lord to do it. Lord, come in and do this! Lord, come in and do that! The Lord's attitude is, Get on with it! I am here, I give you the supply of the Spirit, but I have made known to you what your business is: do your business! Oh, that the Lord's people would rise up and recognize that He has committed to them this great trust of working out His purpose, of ministering to the life of His people unto that glorious consummation, when the very greatness of Christ shall be displayed in that people. That is our business: and so it is not for us continually to appeal to the Lord for Him to do it as apart from us, but for us to get to the business of prayer and intercession, and in this way minister His life to His people, bring about the deliverance of His people by prayer, standing in touch with His throne for their deliverance from the Evil One and the power of death.

Now, if the very deliverance and life of God's people is at our door by God's appointment, that is no small thing. I believe that the Word clearly reveals that the Church exists for the purpose of taking up this question of the Lord's glory, the Lord's triumph, the Lord's greatness, as that which is to be ultimately displayed in the triumph of His people. It is our responsibility. The Lord give us grace to accept it and to commit ourselves to it, and may we be very much before Him that we shall be found, not as those coerced to pray, but marked by the Spirit of intercession as the very evidence of our life.

CHAPTER 4.

A Representation of Christ in Every Place

"And Simon Peter answered and said, Thou art the Christ, the Son of the living God. And Jesus answered and said unto him, Blessed art thou, Simon Bar-Jonah: for flesh and blood hath not revealed it unto thee, but my Father which is in heaven. And I also say unto thee, that thou art Peter, and upon this rock I will build my church; and the gates of Hades shall not prevail against it" (Matt. xvi. 16-18).

"And if he refuse to hear them, tell it unto the church: and if he refuse to hear the church also, let him be unto thee as the Gentile and the publican" (Matt. xviii. 17). "For where two or three are gathered together in my name, there am I in the midst of them" (Matt. xviii. 20).

"Now ye are the body of Christ, and members each in his part" (I Cor. xii. 27. R.V. MARGIN).

"...being built upon the foundation of the apostles and prophets, Christ Jesus himself being the chief corner stone; in whom each several building, fitly framed together, groweth into a holy temple in the Lord; in whom ye also are builded together for a habitation of God in the Spirit" (Eph. ii. 20-22).

"As he is, even so are we in this world" (I John iv. 17).

In continuing our meditation in connection with the spiritual house, I have an emphasis now in my heart which I feel peculiarly to be of the Lord. For quite a few, it will be no new word or truth, but even for such the fresh emphasis may be of the Lord. In any case, they must seek to co-operate in the word of the Lord for those for whom He may specially mean it. Let us, nevertheless, all seek to enter into the word in a new way.

We are looking at some of the major features and purposes of God's spiritual house to which we belong, and the one which is to occupy us now is this, that this spiritual house is

here as being a representation of Christ in every place. We
have seen that the Church is Christ. He is the Church, He is
God's temple, God's dwelling place. It is in Him that we
find God. He serves the purpose of all that the Church is
intended to mean. The Church is Christ. But now, so far as
this world is concerned, the Church is Christ as distributed,
though not divided ; that is, Christ as in all His members by
His Spirit ; yet not so many Christs, but remaining one Christ.
The Apostle raised the question amongst the Corinthians, as
you know—Is Christ divided?—and there is almost a tone of
scandal at the very idea that Christ should be divided. He
remains one, and He is one, though in so many, and in that
oneness of Christ in all His members we have the Church.
Men will only find the Lord, where we are concerned, so far
as Christ is in us. That is the purpose of the Church.

The Vital Character of the Local Assembly

But now we come to consider the special importance of
local corporate expressions of Christ, Christ as represented
corporately in every place. It is a well-known and understood
thing among us that what the Lord Jesus said as recorded in
the Gospels was but the truth in germ form. Because the
Spirit was not yet given, He could only speak as in an objective
way, putting things in a figurative form or in an undeveloped
way. All that is in the Gospels is like that, awaiting the
day of the Spirit's dwelling within believers so that the much
larger meaning contained in His utterances might be imparted.
And, amongst all the rest, there is this fragment which we have
read in Matt. xviii. 20—"For where two or three are gathered
together in my name, there am I in the midst of them." We
shall lose a very great deal if we take that simply as it stands
in the Gospel. It was never intended to be taken just in that
form. In the later revelation of the Holy Spirit, that passage,
with all others, is taken up and its earlier meaning is made
clear, and what we have as the fuller revelation is this, that
Christ is peculiarly present when two or three are gathered
together, because He has committed Himself to His Body. To
put that round the other way, it is the Body of Christ which is
necessary for the bringing in of the fulness of Christ. "The
body," says the Apostle, "is not one member, but many"
(I Cor. xii. 14). But then the same Apostle says, "Ye are the
body of Christ" (I Cor. xii. 27) ; and he is speaking of a local

company. Christ is peculiarly present when it is a corporate
expression. The Lord has bound Himself up with His Church
for manifestation. It may be true that the Lord is in us
individually: it is true ; and it may equally be true that the
Lord, as in us individually, will express Himself in us and
through us as individuals, but the Lord is limited, and very
severely limited, when it is only an individual matter. His
thought is otherwise, and so He makes this statement. He
might have left a thing like this unsaid. It would seem to have
been quite unnecessary, quite beside the mark. But no, He
said it, and when He has said a thing, it means something.
Indeed, it bears all the significance of such a One as He is
having said it. That means it carries tremendous weight if
He says it ; and He has said this thing in these precise words—
"Where two or three are gathered together in my name, there
am I in the midst of them." He might have said, Wherever
there is one in My Name, there am I! Well, that is true, but
the Lord did not put it in that way: and you notice that He is
dealing with practical matters. He has used the word
"Church." Certain people have to be dealt with by the
Church, and when the Church deals with them, it is the Lord.
That is what He is saying.

You must bring these two things together. Here is someone guilty of remissness in spiritual life. Well, someone go
and tell him, and if he does not hear, take one or two more,
and if he refuse to hear them, tell it to the Church.
"If he refuse to hear the Church also, let him be unto thee
as the Gentile and the publican. Verily I say unto you, What
things soever ye shall bind on earth shall be bound in heaven;
and what things soever ye shall loose on earth shall be loosed
in heaven. Again I say unto you, that if two of you shall
agree on earth as touching anything that they shall ask, it
shall be done for them of my Father who is in heaven. For
where two or three are gathered together in my name, there am
I in the midst of them." The Lord is in the midst in an
executive way in the Church's administration, where two or
three are gathered together. I am not going to deal with
that phase of Church functioning, but I use it to bring out
this principle, that there is a specific value bound up with a
corporate expression of Christ, and a value of very great
importance.

Some Fatal Hindrances to God's Purpose

(a) Individualism

Now, let me stop here for a parenthesis. There are some fatal mistakes into which Christians have fallen, and one of these is the principle of the individual line in the place of the corporate. I say that has been a fatal mistake. It has been fatal to spiritual growth, fatal to spiritual fulness, to spiritual power, to spiritual light and to spiritual life. There are many Christians who are only concerned with individuals. Concern for the individual is of course right, but the Lord only saves the individual with the Church in view, with the corporate Body in mind. We must settle it and be very clear that this dispensation, from the ascension and exaltation of Christ, and the giving of the Holy Spirit, to the taking away of the Church at the end, is marked out by God as the period in all the periods of this world's history for securing, not individuals as so many saved men and women, but a one Body—the Church. Individuals only figure before God in the light of the Church, the one Body, and, if you and I fail to recognize that as the governing law of God's dealings with men in this dispensation, we are going to forfeit a great measure of what the Lord intended for us : limit and straiten our spiritual lives and experiences, and cause weakness in the very work of God itself.

I hope you have understood that. It is of very great importance that we should settle this. You will notice that these two things usually go together. It is the salvation of the individual that engages and occupies so many, and when they have got the individual saved, brought to the Lord, they have no further concern but to go and get more individuals and bring them into salvation. Those two things go together, individualism and salvation in its merely initial sense of souls being brought to the Lord. After that, there is no more. That has proved a fatal thing in the history of God's interests, and to-day we are finding it to be one of the things which is representing the greatest difficulty to Christians themselves and to any fuller work of God. I mean this, that you everywhere meet a large number of people who have just gone that far. All that they have is just their own personal salvation, in the sense of forgiveness of sins, peace with God, those rudiments of the Gospel, and they have been there ten, twenty, thirty, forty, fifty years; and to-day as you meet them and speak with them, you come up against one of two things.

On the one hand, there is an utter inability now to apprehend anything more than the simple elements of salvation; they have not got ability to do it. All those spiritual senses and faculties which ought to have been developed so that they could receive much larger and fuller revelation from God have been stunted, have never been developed by exercise, and in spiritual faculties they remain simply infants after all these years. I am only giving you the Scripture in saying that. You know, Paul had to say that very thing to the Corinthians—"I could not speak unto you as unto spiritual, but as unto carnal, as unto babes in Christ. I fed you with milk, not with meat." To the Hebrews it was the same: "When by reason of the time ye ought to be teachers, ye have need again that some one teach you the rudiments of the first principles of the oracles of God; and are become such as have need of milk...solid food is for fullgrown men, even those who by reason of use have their senses exercised to discern good and evil." Paul had to deplore in his own day that there had been this fatal arrest and he said, in effect, Here I am, just full of Divine light for you, and I have to keep back all this that God has given me for His Church because of that! I say that is fatal for the Church—that the Lord should give abundant revelation for His Church's growth and fulness and functioning, and that there should be, after years and years and years, such a state that people are totally incapable in themselves of receiving it, understanding it. You meet that condition to-day everywhere. They cannot, after so long a time.

On the other hand, of course, you find those who after a lifetime turn to you and say, Oh, that I had known this before! Oh, that I had been told this before! Oh, that I had had this years ago! Why not? It has been here all the time. It is because of this fatal individualistic line. For the greater part, the work of God since the early days of the Church, with the exception of very small things here and there, has been just on this line of getting individuals saved and leaving them there. It is fatal in the long run to all that God intended; and then people come up against the fact that it is so. Oh, that I had known it long ago! Well then, while the individual is very important, and has to be dealt with in the light of the other as an individual, we must note that, if the individual is put in the place of the corporate, nothing but the most sorrowful consequences can follow. That is one fatal mistake.

(b)   The Prevailing " Church System "

Another fatal thing is that which is represented by the present "Church system." The present system which obtains in the largest realm is almost entirely a matter of congregations and preaching places, places where people gather together or congregate in a religious way—yes, maybe an evangelical way, yet but congregations—and they come together to go through a certain rota and, in the main, to hear something preached, and they go away. Now, while there are variations and degrees in that system, that very largely is the position: and that is not a corporate expression of Christ. That is a congregation. That is not a body. That is not the Body locally expressed and functioning. It is something less. What is the result? The same result as in the other case, namely, very little spiritual growth. I am being very frank now. I want to talk out of my heart because I feel the Lord wants to get us somewhere in this hour on this matter, and I must run the risk of treading upon sensibilities in order to get there. The result spiritually in this second instance is very largely the same as in the other case of the merely individualistic, and we are everywhere finding people to-day in that present Church system who have not a glimmer of light on the Lord's fuller purpose and do not know what you are talking about: and multitudes of them have no interest in anything else. This thing, this going to church, this congregation, this going through a rota, this place of the public worship line of things has come into the place of the true local expression of the Body of Christ, and has set that aside. To-day, speaking of the Church in that sense, it is the Church like that which is in a state of terrible spiritual infancy and immaturity and unenlightenment after all these centuries, and people born and brought up in it do not grow spiritually. I know there are some who do grow despite it, but I am speaking of the thing itself. It has become a fatal menace to the real purpose of God.

(c) The Making of " The Gospel Mission " to be Everything

Now, there is a third thing, and that is " The Gospel Mission," which also takes the place of the local church as spiritually formed. Now, this is no denunciation of Gospel Missions, and I am not saying that Gospel Missions ought not to be. I am far, very far from saying that. I am, of course, not speaking now of those evangelistic missions that are held among the churches from time to time, but of that which has assumed the character of a permanent institution in numerous places. If then you take the Gospel Mission and have that as though it were everything that there is, and you remain satisfied just to go to the Gospel Mission where the Gospel is preached to the unsaved, and keep on the Gospel Mission line of things ; well, you are simply dwarfing your own spiritual life. It is a thing which has in multitudes of cases just become a substitute for the spiritually formed local expression of Christ. Christ is much more than that, and you note that the people who live all their lives in the Gospel Mission are the people who are most terribly immature, spiritually ignorant and unenlightened. Oh yes, rejoicing in Christ as their Saviour—I do not question that—glorying in personal salvation ; but oh, where is vocation, where is the fulness of Christ, where is God's eternal purpose being worked out? Not there. That just goes one step, and one step is not the whole road to God's end. Let there be these things, but let them be as auxiliaries to the fuller thought of God, as instrumentalities of the Church, and let them not be the whole thing. If they are, they will fatally affect the life of God's people and spiritual progress.

You see, the difference is this. Take a bunch of flowers, a bunch of roses or any other particular kind of flower. They are of the same species, and they have the same life in them. That is a congregation, not a body! The difference between a bunch of flowers which are all alike, all sharing the same life, and the root and the plant, is a very big one. Give me the rose, root and plant or bush, and what shall I have? Well, I shall have this difference that, whereas the bunch of flowers has the life, it just goes so far. That is all and there it ends. It will never go beyond that. Give me the plant or bush, and it will grow. It may pass through a paroxysm of death for a season, but next year it will come back again and there will be more; and then another experience of dying and resurrection, and again there will be more, all in the same plant. That is a body, that is an organism, not a bunch. And that is the difference between a congregation, so many Christians, units coming together as units, and a spiritual organism, a local expression of the Body of Christ: and it is the Body which is God's thought, not a congregation, not the bunch of flowers. But oh, the Lord's people are so much like the bunch of flowers! It is true they are all of the same species: they are Christians, they are children of God, they are all sharing the same life; but oh, they are not there as one organism in one place growing with the increase of God, passing through corporate convulsions of death and resurrection and making spiritual increase in that way. What I have said about the present system and the missions is just like a bunch of flowers. Yes, they belong to the Lord, and they have the same life, they are all the Lord's children; but they just come to a certain point and they never go beyond that. That is true. I have had enough experience to make me sure it is true. Alas, many of them do not want to go any further, and many of them resent the suggestion that it is necessary to go any further. However, that is not God's thought about it. God's thought is of the root and the plant as a whole, a living organism here and there as representing and expressing Christ Himself. The plant grows and makes increase. The bunch simply goes so far and then it stops.

Now, Satan is not adverse to meetings as such, but Satan is adverse to local families, local expressions of the Body of Christ. Hence you have the great history of Satan's persistent effort to scatter the children of God and break up their corporate life, to bring an end to their practical functioning together.

The Purpose and Function of the Church, as also of its Local Expression

So we have to see exactly what the purpose and the function of a local expression of the Body or the Church or House of God really is, and we can see it if we look at the type that leads to the antitype. What the temple of old was in figure, the Church is in spiritual reality, and what the Church is in spiritual reality as a whole, the local company is to be. It is remarkable that local churches in the New Testament are always viewed in the light of the whole Body. Thus Paul will say to the local church at Corinth, "Ye are the body of Christ." Now, it would not do for Corinth to take hold of that and say, You see, *we* are the Body of Christ! That would be giving a wrong meaning to it. The point in

45

the inspired declaration is this, that every local company is in representation what the whole Body is: what the whole Body is in God's thought is to be seen here and there and there.

(i) The Meeting Place Between God and Man

Now we continue by way of analogy from the temple. What was the temple? In the first place, the temple of old was the meeting place between God and man. That is the first function of the temple, of the House of God. Christ was that in the fullest sense, in a far greater sense than was ever temple of old. Here is Son of Man and Son of God blended in one Person. It is tremendously significant that in Matthew xvi. that very fact comes to light. Christ, interrogating His disciples, uses one term, and, in getting the Divinely-inspired response through Peter, the other term is used. "Who do men say that the Son of man is?" Peter said, "Thou art the Son of the living God." "Son of man," "Son of God": and that is by revelation of God. Here is God and Man met together in one Person, in one place. And of Himself the Lord Jesus later said, Destroy this temple, this sanctuary, and in three days I will raise it up again. Carnally minded Jews thought He was speaking of that material temple, but He was speaking of Himself, His own body. This temple—transition of thought from the temple in Jerusalem to Christ personally, the meeting place of God and man—that is Christ.

Now Christ corporately expressed is the Church according to revelation in the New Testament, and therefore where Christ is corporately found in representation, and livingly functioning, there God should be met with, there God and man should come into a peculiar touch and relationship. The testimony of all who come into such a realm where Christ is really corporately expressed ought to be, I find the Lord there! and that ought to be enough. That is the answer. Do you find the Lord there? Does the Lord meet with you there? Ah, that is the first governing thing, and not other questions associated with gathering together or congregations; no, the Lord Himself, and that not now as a personal thing between myself and the Lord, seeing that I personally can have touch with the Lord anywhere, but now as a matter of the Church. Do I meet the Lord in the midst of that people? If so, I have come into the realm where God's thought is having expression: and that is a realm of tremendous possibilities.

Have you read that little book by A. J. Gordon, "How Christ came to Church"? It might do you good to read it, though rather perhaps from an objective or outside point of view. But let me tell you as quickly as I can the content. Dr. Gordon one Saturday was sitting preparing his sermon for the following day in his study, when he fell asleep: and he dreamt that he was in his own church and in his pulpit on the Lord's day. His was a very fine church with its Gothic pillars and arches. The church was crowded, and he was in the pulpit about to commence the service, when the door opened at the back and a stranger entered and walked down the aisle looking from side to side for a seat. As he got nearer the front, someone stepped out and showed him a vacant seat. Dr. Gordon goes on to describe how he went on with the service, and how his eyes constantly turned to that stranger. If he looked in some other way, he found his eyes coming back to him. Dr. Gordon said, "I registered the resolve that I would go down to speak to the stranger after the service." After it was over, and without showing noticeable hurry, he just as quickly as he could made his way down and tried to intercept the stranger, but before he reached the door, the stranger was gone. With great disappointment, he said to the man at the door, Do you know who that stranger was you let in this morning? The man at the door said, Don't you know who that was? That was Jesus of Nazareth. Oh, said Dr. Gordon, why did you not detain Him? I would love to have spoken to Him. Oh, said the man, do not worry: He was here to-day, He will come again. (Well, as an aside, that double reply bore fruit in two volumes from Dr. Gordon's pen; the one on "The Work of the Holy Spirit," and the other on "The Coming of the Lord.")

Dr. Gordon says he went away with these musings—Jesus of Nazareth has been in my church to-day. What was I saying? I was talking about Him. How did I talk about Him? Did He discern in anything that I was saying the faintest tinge of unreality? Did I speak of Him, not knowing He was present, as I would have if I had known? What did He think of my manner, my matter, my conducting of the service? What did He think about our choir, our singing. It was all about Him, but was it worthy of Him? I wonder what He thought about our Gothic building?

That is the story in brief. But what has come to me is

this: Is that our conception of things? You see, in that the suggestion is that the Church is one thing and Christ another, and that the Church can be in all sorts of respects certain things, and Christ quite another. Oh no, that is not God's Church. God's Church is Christ, and where you find the Church according to God, there you find Christ, and no disparities, no inconsistences, contradictions: it is the Lord. All the other is not Christ at all. The Church is Christ, and if it is Christ who is pre-eminent when the Lord's people come together, God is there Himself. It is on the ground of Christ and Christ's presence that men meet with God. You know as well as I do that men cannot meet with God in us as we are. We cannot of ourselves bring men into touch with God. No priesthood as such can bring men to God. But if the Lord Jesus is in us and we can bring men into touch with the Lord Jesus we have brought them into touch with God. But if He is not there in us either personally or collectively, we may talk about God till Doomsday, but men will not meet Him. That is what the Church is when truly constituted. It is the ground upon which men meet God and God meets men, and that ground is Christ Himself; and there is peculiar and special value and significance bound up with this corporate expression of Christ in the matter of men meeting God. I believe that a far greater impact of the Lord can be registered upon men by a company of Christ-indwelt men and women being together in the power of the Holy Spirit than can be by any number of isolated Christian units. A meeting-place between God and man, the vehicle of Divine life.

You see Ezekiel's temple. The house is now finished according to God's mind, and it is out from the house, down the steps, the river flows, deepening and widening on its way, and wheresoever the river cometh everything lives. Trees are seen on either bank and everything is living, until at length it empties itself into the Dead Sea; and even that death is swallowed up in the life that is out from the sanctuary. It is this corporate expression of Christ, the Church, from which there is the ministration of God's life to men, and that is why the enemy wants to break it up. That was our point in our previous meditation. The scattering or dividing of the Lord's people, the making of the Lord's people into so many individuals and units alone, without a real corporate life, is a

48

strategical move on the part of the enemy against that life. We know in our own experience that, if the enemy can get in between even two of us to set us apart in spirit, our life is under arrest and the river is not released until we mend that bridge, heal that division. That is very significant. The enemy is after that sort of thing. He is against the life, because the Church is the vehicle of God's life.

(ii) The Embodiment and Expression of God's Thoughts

Then again, the temple was the embodiment and expression of God's thoughts. Every stone, everything used, all size, dimensions and measurements, materials, they all represented some thought of God. God's mind was expressed in all. It was a symbol of a spiritual attribute. Peter, following up that word which is before us—"a spiritual house" (I Peter ii. 5) says a little later that the object of the spiritual house is to "show forth the excellencies of him who called you out of darkness into his marvellous light." The temple was to show forth the excellencies of the Lord, the embodiment of Divine thoughts, and the Lord's people in any place should be the embodiment and expression of Divine thoughts. There should be there a disclosing of God's thoughts in a very blessed way, a coming to know the mind of the Lord for His people, a rich unveiling of what is in the heart of God concerning His own. That is how it ought to be ; not just addresses or sermons, but a ministry of revelation under the Holy Spirit through an opened heaven. That is of value to the Lord and to His people. But it wants a living company for that: and oh, how we know it! Sometimes we are not all alive to the Lord for some reason or other when we come together. Perhaps we are tired, or have been bothered, something has come in to cast down, and although the Lord has prepared for us some rich feast, something He wants to make known, He cannot ; He is held back, and there is just a state of lifelessness. But let us come together in the Spirit, alive unto the Lord, and the Lord's thoughts come out and they flow. The condition of the company of the Lord's people very largely determines what kind of time we have. It very largely depends upon us how much the Lord can give us. The company of the Lord's people is to be the expression and embodiment of God's thoughts. That is what it exists for.

(iii) The Sphere of Divine Government and Authority

Then the temple was the place of God's government. Things were brought there to be decided upon, to be judged: and Peter says, "Judgment must begin at the house of God" ; and that is Matt. xviii. again. Tell it to the Church, let the Church decide on this. It is the place of Divine government. I cannot stay with that, but you see that the corporate company, livingly constituted according to Christ, is of very real and practical consequence to God in this world now: and oh, how important it is for life's sake, for light's sake, for power's sake, that we all be consciously and livingly a part of such a local expression of God.

I do want to say this to you from my heart, that it is necessary for you, dear friends, to be a part of, to be in the midst of, to have behind you, a living, functioning company of the Lord's people on this basis. I know the difference, and many of you know the difference, the difference it makes in depth, in strength. For many years, I was a minister, as we say, of different churches, congregations ; but oh, I know the difference between that and what has obtained since. It is not a difference of the natural calibre of the people at all, but a difference in kind. The one was a part of a system largely organized and run by man for religious purposes: the other is something formed of the Spirit ; and that is an immense difference. I know the difference when I meet things. All you can say is that those who have a living local company of the Lord's people of whom they are a part, have something that other people have not. There is measure about them. There is something about them that is more than you will find in the other things of which I have spoken, where it is purely individualistic or formal. It is very important. The Church is intended to be this, and a thing can only know its Divinely appointed resources as it functions according to God's intention. If therefore we are called for this as the Church, then we must be the Church in order to fulfil our great purpose and know our great fulness. I do ask you to think about this very seriously. It is a thing of no little importance, is this matter of the local fellowship of the Lord's people.

I know it may raise problems for some of you. "There is nothing in our neighbourhood and I do not know how it is possible." But there is an answer, and the answer is a simple one, although it may test you. If this is God's mind, you go to the Lord about it. 'Lord, if this is your mind, either bring me into such a thing or bring about such a thing where I am.' Hold on to the Lord for that. Brother Nee, when he was here, speaking about this matter and talking with one and another about it, spoke of how in one place this very thing arose between someone and the Lord, and how that one held on to the Lord for several years over the matter; and then how that, after holding on for so long, gradually the formation commenced, a second being joined to the first, and then a third, and then another. But they were greatly exercised for a long time, standing themselves into the meaning and value of God's thought and holding on to Him for it to find expression and become a reality. You see, that is just it. That is our ministry: through prayer to bring into being what God intends. If we can be put off easily, well then, we have not seen the vision, the thing has not gone very deep. That is only said by way of helping with the problem that arises. Let us be exercised about the Church and let the Church be of greater importance to us than the problem, then I think we shall find a way through.

CHAPTER 5.

The Governing Law of the House of God

READING: Ezek. xlvii. 1-12 ; I Pet. ii. 4-5.

We are not going forward now with a further consideration of the major features of the spiritual house of God, but are leaving that for another time. We are going to bring those features already considered to the measuring line of their own governing law, which is that of life and spirituality. "Living," "spiritual," they are two great words in this passage—"a living stone," "living stones," "a spiritual house," "spiritual sacrifices."

Lest anyone should be in difficulty about that second word, spirituality, let us stay for the briefest moment to say that spirituality just means government by the Holy Spirit ; but a government by the Holy Spirit in such a way as to make us one with the Holy Spirit in all His standards, in all His ways of looking at things, deciding about things, so that, being one with Him, we are not at all influenced or affected by natural judgments, natural standards, natural considerations, but ours are all the Holy Spirit's judgments and values and ways of viewing things. That in brief and comprehensively is what is meant by spirituality, a constituting of us according to the Holy Spirit, which means on the other hand, the ruling out of all that is merely and purely of our own natural life, mind, heart and will.

Well now, let us look at these four features of the spiritual house of God, which house we are if we are the Lord's, and look at them in the light of life and spirituality.

The Exaltation of the Lord Jesus

The first with which we were concerned was that this spiritual house of God exists for the purpose of setting forth, proclaiming, manifesting the exaltation of the Lord Jesus as God's Son, the exaltation of the Lord Jesus to the throne of the Father. It is for that the Church exists, and it is for that we exist if we are of the house of God. But that is not just a truth, a doctrine to be proclaimed. That is not just a part of

51

Being therefore lifted high By & to the right hand of God & having received from the Father the promised blessing which is the Holy Spirit, He has made this outpouring which you yourselves both SEE & HEAR. Rev. 1-3. If we don't have Revelation

the Church's creed—"Jesus Christ has been raised from the
dead and exalted to the right hand of the Majesty on high."
That is not just one of our convictions, as we say. That is
something which has to constitute us spiritually and has to be
expressed by means of life. The exaltation of the Lord Jesus
is, before and above all other things, a matter of life. It was
when He was exalted to the right hand of the Majesty on high,
it was when God made Him both Lord and Christ, it was
when He was actually seated at God's right hand, far above all
rule and authority, principalities and powers, that the Holy
Spirit came out from His presence and made that which was in
heaven, a spiritual reality in the Church ; and that reality was
marked and demonstrated and proved and evidenced by the
mighty power of His ascended life. We have to be spiritually
constituted on the basis of Christ's exaltation. That is to say,
within us something has to be done which brings about in us a
living spiritual oneness with the exaltation, the Lordship, the
supremacy of Jesus Christ. It is not to remain something outside of us, however true it is. We have to be that in fact ; and,
as we have pointed out, the impact of the early believers upon
this world, upon those around them wherever they were, was
the impact of the *fact,* not the doctrine, not the teaching, not
merely the statement, but the *fact* that Jesus Christ was exalted.
That came home upon the situation because that fact has its
supreme significance in the spiritual realm, and we know quite
well that all that is visible, all that is here on this sentient
creation, has behind it a spiritual order.

Never has that been more clearly manifested and demonstrated than in the present world situation. There is a spiritual
order of things which is driving on, mastering, manipulating
everything. It is, as many have been saying for the past
months, Satanic in its background. The exaltation of the Lord
Jesus finds its first registration there, and it is not until the
registration is made there that the foreground is really affected.
To arrest men, to arrest a course of things, to bring the yoke
down upon situations, to harness developments in the seen,
you have to get behind and register some superior reality
against those forces which are creating these things.

Now, that is spirituality. The Apostle Paul said much
about this sort of thing, and we have his language by which he
expressed this reality. For example, "the weapons of our
warfare are not of the flesh, but mighty before God to the

53

casting down of strongholds" (II Cor. x. 4). He did not
actually use the word, but it is quite clear that he meant that
the weapons of our warfare are spiritual, getting behind the
situation: and you know what he was' dealing with at the
moment when he used those words. Here were Corinthians
who were seeking the advantages of natural wisdom, natural
learning, the wisdom and the power of this world, in order to
give them position, influence, standing. They were carnal in
their quest for carnal weapons by which to gain ascendency
in this world. That led the Apostle to that great discourse on
the foolishness and the weakness of this world's wisdom and
this world's strength, and he said that, to overcome this world,
you want something more than this world's weapons, this
world's men. To overcome the carnal, you must have something more than carnal weapons, and the weapons of our warfare are not carnal, but mighty through God. In other words,
they are spiritual. For our wrestling is not against flesh and
blood in the form of wisdom and worldly power, "but against
the principalities, against the powers, against the world-rulers
of this darkness, against the spiritual hosts of wickedness in
the heavenlies." Therefore our weapons must be spiritual,
and spirituality means fundamentally the ability to get behind
the seen, the tangible, to the unseen, the invisible, the intangible powers of evil, and to register your superiority there:
and that superiority is the exaltation of the Lord Jesus far
above all rule and authority and principality and power. That
is a spiritual thing. The house of God is a spiritual house for
that spiritual purpose, namely, to bring home Christ's ascendency in a spiritual way against spiritual forces. Then the
instrumentalities of those evil spiritual forces will in turn come
under arrest. It is no use going directly at things. You must
strike at the cause of things, and then the things themselves
will, according to God's purpose and intention, either be
destroyed, or be brought under arrest or limitation, just as the
Lord intends. It is not the Lord's thought to stop wars
altogether just yet, nor much else that is going on in an evil
way, but there is such a thing as limiting things to the purpose
of God ; and I do feel, and appeal to you as the Lord's
children, that we ought to be engaged in this spiritual registration of the authority and supremacy of the Lord Jesus in
the unseen, in the background of present world situations, with
the object of limiting things to God's purpose. I believe it is
possible for the Lord's people now to take hold of every air

raid on this country and limit it, give it God's limitation, and I believe that that is what is happening. I only use it by way of illustrating my point. It is an amazing thing how things have been limited. We have seen again and again what might have been, and how much the onslaught has been penned in, even where great damage has been done. Oh, how much more might have been, could have been, and the amazement of every day is the limitation that is imposed. Surely that is an encouragement. I believe it is due to something in the unseen which is set in motion through the prayers of the people of God. That is encouraging. Let us be given to our ministry. That is what the Church is for.

Thus the very first thing is that Jesus is exalted above all principality and powers which lie behind this world darkness, and the Church is here, by prayer and testimony and spiritual life, to bring home upon those background forces this superiority of the Lord Jesus. It is a thing, not of words, not of doctrines, not of creeds, but of life, the impact of His ascended life.

Well, we begin there. The principle, you see, the law of the expression of Christ's exaltation, is life and spirituality.

The Ministry of the House to God

The second thing which we were noticing with regard to these features of the spiritual house of God was that it exists to minister to the pleasure and glory of God. It is for God's glory, God's pleasure that the Church has been brought into being, for His satisfaction. And here we bring it right down to this rule: God is glorified and God receives that which is to His pleasure along the line of life and spirituality. You can judge of that by the effect. Wherever you have a real ministration of life, you always have the glory of God, God glorified.

That is, of course, true to the Scriptures. You remember that was the one point which the Lord Jesus made central and supreme in the raising of Lazarus. "This sickness is not unto death, but for the glory of God"; and as He came through all the doubt and unbelief which stood between Him and Lazarus and approached the situation, at least He silently lifted His heart to the Father. "Father, glorify thy name!" Then He cried with a loud voice, "Lazarus, come forth!" The resurrection of Lazarus, the over-powering of death, was for the glory of God, and that was a spiritual thing, that was the triumph of life in Christ. Now, that is the glory of God. It says afterward that many believed on Him. The glory of God is largely seen through the out-working of this principle of life triumphant over death.

Now, that is a big subject. If you go back to the Old Testament, you will see that, in the case of every servant of God, after that servant of God was apprehended by Him, a process of death and resurrection commenced. You can take any one case that you like. Outstandingly, there is Abraham. How significant are the words that mark the apprehending of that servant of God. "The God of glory appeared unto our father Abraham" (Acts vii. 2). That sets the standard of God, and in effect says, Now then, it is according to what I am as the God of glory that I am going to deal with you, and the issue of all My dealings with you will be glory to Me! So, no sooner was Abraham apprehended by the God of glory, than this process of death and resurrection set in. It was a process with constant recurrence. Abraham went into a first stage and phase and measure of death, and then, in resurrection, the glory of God was seen. All the way along, there was this experience of death. I am not speaking now about physical death, but of a working of death in his life in a spiritual way; death to things, death to relationships, death to hopes, death to earthly expectations, death to possessions; and every time death worked, there was a resurrection into something larger of the Lord, the Lord coming and making new covenants, giving him fresh revelations. I am El Shaddai! There were all these positive things when other things were going into death, right up to that last great triumph of resurrection in Isaac. Here is death; yes, death to all the promises, apparently, to all the hopes. If Isaac goes, then God in His faithfulness, God in His Word, God in His covenant, God in His promises, has gone too. It was a mighty death to face, and in spirit it was faced, but it was resurrection finally, full, glorious resurrection: and what glory to God!

Well, you can take many other illustrations of the truth from the Old Testament and then carry them over in a spiritual way to the New Testament, and see that this is exactly what happened with Christ. God received the full quota of glory through the death and the resurrection of His Son, and the exaltation of the Lord Jesus is the testimony to the fact that death has been engulfed and overpowered. Christ being there

56

sets forth that fact in fulness. But then the principle has to be passed on to the Church which is His Body, and the history of the Church since that time has been just a history of successive deaths and resurrections, and every resurrection has meant some fresh contribution to the glory of God, some fresh expression of God's glory ; and what is true of the history of the Church is true in the history of many an individual member of the Church, and probably of some of you. We have known deaths oft, not in the way in which Paul meant, physical and temporal and natural, but in our own life with God we have known what it means to suffer the eclipse of all things, darkness unto death. But that has not been the end. The end has been the God of glory again and again, and it is along this line that God's glory is ministered to, by life, spirituality, and life triumphing over death. We are here for that very purpose. I hope that does not discourage you, but rather that it will help you to recognize that our very being here means that we have to know death again and again to know life. But we do not end with death ; we end with resurrection and glory to God. Let us fasten upon that. Even though the deaths may be many, the end is the glory of God. Eventually, His glory will be displayed in His Son, in His Church, in fulness, when death is finally vanquished, not only in Christ, but in and through the Church.

But this is something for present experience. It is a great truth to contemplate, it is a blessed thing to consider ; but let us bring it right home. What I feel to be the important thing now, the Lord's desire where this hour in concerned, is that we should come very close to these things in reality ; that what we are saying shall not be truth only, but reality in our case. We are the house of God, we are this spiritual house, and we exist for this very purpose, to minister to the pleasure and glory of God, and that is done along the line of life, and that life is the life which overcomes death. So that, with every fresh uprising and experience of spiritual death, we shall write over it, This is not unto death, but for the glory of God ! Oh, may He give us grace to do that. It is easier said than done, I know, but here it is. History sets the seal to this, that this is the way in which the Lord is ministered to in satisfaction and glory, by our being the very vessel in which the power of His resurrection is manifested, and that necessitates experiences of death.

The Ministry of the House to the Elect

Then the third feature of this spiritual house is that it stands for the deliverance and life of others, the others being, of course, God's elect, those who are bound up with God's eternal purpose. We are here to serve the Lord in standing over against the persistent and determined purpose of Satan to bring an end to Christ's life in His Church, and the test of the reality, the spiritual reality, of this spiritual house is just in this direction, How much are we ministering to the life of God's people to deliver them from these recurrent onslaughts of spiritual death? That is the test. We have to get right up close to that. It is all very well to talk about these things, but they have to be true really. It should become impossible to deal with these matters merely as the teaching that goes on in a certain place. The teaching may be all right, quite correct, but what of the practical issue, so far as we are concerned as the Lord's people? The test is not whether we have accepted right doctrine: the test is whether we are functioning according to what we are, whether we are really doing the thing which constitutes our very existence. You see, the Church, the people of God, are not one thing, and the truth another thing, and the Church accepts that truth. It is not that. It is that the Church is that truth or it is nothing at all. I say I am a member of Christ's Body. Well then, I can take the attitude that certain truths are the truths which belong to members of Christ's Body, and therefore I accept those truths: I assent to those truths and henceforth I believe in those truths, and I begin to preach them. That is one thing. Another way is that certain truths are realities concerning the members of Christ's Body, and you cannot divide between the truths and the members, and the very existence of those members means that those truths are operating, and if those truths are not operating, you have serious reason to question the reality of the life of that member of the Body of Christ. Something has gone wrong; it is not normal, it is all wrong. I am not saying that if these truths are not fully manifested in us that has nullified our relationship to Christ as members of His Body, but I am saying that if it is the case that these truths are not being expressed, there is something seriously wrong with us as members of the Body and we are a contradiction to the true meaning of our existence. You and I exist for the life of others and if others are not receiving life through us, then

there is something inconsistent in our very existence. That
sounds very hard, very severe, but that has to come home to
me as much as to you. I never talk to you without having
myself very much in mind, and I have this understanding with
the Lord, that He will make good all truth in my own case
or save me from talking about it.

I challenge you, my dear friends, to face this law of your
existence. Are you ministering to the Lord's people or are

you merely sitting back, or even worse, ministering death?
What does your presence mean to the Lord's people? Does
it mean life? If so, then the house of God is truly represented
by us. If it does not, if it is only neutral or negative or
antagonistic to life, then the house of God has broken down
where such are concerned. All these things are a matter of
life and spirituality, and there is a horrible thing from which
we shall pray earnestly and fervently to be delivered, and that

is, talking truth, holding truths, accepting truths, being associa-
ated with truths as truths, without having the life of those
truths manifested in us. I often fear that is one of the great
and distressing things where such revelation exists, that people
begin to take up the truths, and they stand for the truths that
"Honor Oak" stands for. God deliver us from that way of
speech and that mentality. That is not it. Either we are this
thing, or, however much we may agree with it and talk about
it, we are not it. It is life and spirituality that matters, and we
must be much before God that all shall be real in our case ;
that our presence means that life is ministered, life is passed
on. We are the vehicle of life to the Lord's people for their
deliverance from the onslaught of death. It was for that Paul
besought the believers to pray for him. Oh, this throttling
work of the enemy in the matter of ministering life to the
Lord's people.

An Expression of Christ

Then the fourth thing is that the Church in its corporate
life exists to be a present expression of the Lord Jesus Himself
wherever two or three are gathered together. I wonder if we
have recognized what that word in Matt. xviii. really does
mean? Here is someone who belongs to the Lord, who is
guilty of, or responsible for, something wrong. "If thy brother
sin against thee." The margin says that a good many authorities omit "against thee." Thus it would read, "If thy brother
sin, go, show him his fault . . . if he hear thee, thou hast gained

thy brother. But if he hear thee not, take with thee one or two more, that at the mouth of two witnesses or three every word may be established. And if he refuse to hear them, tell it unto the church: and if he refuse to hear the church also, let him be unto thee as the Gentile and the publican. Verily I say unto you, What things soever ye shall bind on earth shall be bound in heaven: and what things soever ye shall loose on earth shall be loosed in heaven . . . *For* where two or three are gathered together in my name, there am I in the midst of them."

That little word " for " carries with it a tremendous weight of significance. If thy brother sin and after three successive and varied efforts have been made to get him to acknowledge his sin, there is still a withholding, bring it to the Church. Now then, if he refuse to hear the Church, put him out ; let him be as a Gentile and a publican, that is, outside the Church; and in your doing that, it is the Lord doing it. " For where two or three are gathered together in my name, there am I in the midst of them." It is not that the Church has acted as something in itself. The Lord regards that as Himself acting. He is there in the midst, and it is the Lord doing this. The Church's verdict is the Lord's verdict ; the Church's decision is the Lord's decision, when the Church is gathered into His Name.

Now we can leave the specific connection of that and take up the principle. The Church exists to be a corporate expression of Christ wherever He is represented. The Church cannot be represented with less than two, because the Church is a Body, and one brick never made a temple yet. It is a corporate thing, and it is to be an expression of Christ there in its corporate life. That is the purpose of the Church, to be an expression of Christ. That cannot be just official, that cannot be formal. It is not that the Church has a session and in its session has an agenda and discusses certain propositions and comes to certain decisions. No, it is something much deeper than that.

In the first place, the Church is spiritual, that is, the Church has subjected itself to the Holy Spirit and has taken the Holy Spirit for its governance, for its direction. It has put its trust in the Spirit of God to register right courses and right decisions through much prayer. It has altogether submitted itself to the government of the Holy Spirit and in that way become

Prayer

spiritual, so that it livingly functions in a spiritual way; not formally functions, but spiritually and livingly functions, that is, its function is on the witness of the Spirit along the line of life. Issues are raised, difficulties are brought up. How are these going to be met? Well, someone makes a proposition and those who are spiritual feel, Oh, this is death if we take that line! No, we have no liberty to take that line, that would be terrible! It is registered inside. It is not that we have better judgment, but within the Spirit of life says, Do not take that line, that will be disaster! Or someone else may say something and those who are spiritual feel, Yes, that is the Lord's way! It is registered within; the Spirit of life is governing; and that is the basis of the Church's life altogether, and it becomes in that way an expression of Christ, an expression of the mind of the Lord there. The Lord is in evidence along the line, and on the basis, of life and spirituality. But it requires a corporate life for that— "In the mouth of two witnesses or three." That is the corporate principle, you see, at work. I had no intention of going into so much technique about the Church, but it is all to indicate this great truth, that the Church, this spiritual house, exists to be an expression of Christ wherever it is represented by two or three on a corporate basis.

You see, corporate life is spiritual and is life. It is a matter of life. Our union, our relationship with Christ, is on the principle of life. "Unto whom coming, a living stone . . . ye also, as living stones, are built up a spiritual house." Again I say, God is not dealing with us as bricks: God is dealing with us as with living stones. That means that He is treating us as those who have a common life with the Lord Jesus, and our relationship with the living stone is the relationship of one life. It is a spiritual relationship and it is that life which brings about the corporate expression. It is all the difference between this corporate expression on the basis of life, and a society, a club, an institution. You can join a club, you can come into a society, and you may agree on many things with regard to conviction and procedure, and yet not be bound together by a corporate life. But the Church is this latter thing. One life in all the members links all the members with the Head, and thus by that life it expresses Christ wherever it is. It does not just proclaim things about Christ. It brings Christ in and says that here, though it be but in two

It seems good to Holy Spirit & To us.
To Be led of the Spirit we must become obedient to
His Voice. Today if you hear. Do Not Harden
Your heart.

or three or more, here Christ has come in. It is not a claim made. You see, the Roman church will make that claim, that very claim, that where that church is, Christ is. Ah yes, but there is a difference. It is not just a claim, but a fact borne out, that where these spiritual and living stones are, the Lord is there in very truth and people know it, and there comes about that of which the Apostle wrote. When someone comes in from the outside and things are as they should be, when they are after this kind, the outsider comes in and falls down and says, "God is indeed among you." Ah! that is what we want. Whether people begin to fall literally or not, that is not the question. The point is that inwardly they go down : prejudices, suspicions, fears, reservations go down. One thing rises supreme with them and brings down everything. I cannot get away from it, the Lord is there! If only we would surrender to that and all that means it would be very much better for us. But that is the great matter, namely, bringing in the Lord. The Church exists to bring the Lord into every place, even where represented by but two or three. May this all be true in our case. I am sure our hearts respond to that. Well, let us get to the Lord about it, that so far as we individually are concerned as living stones, it may be true in our case ; that we are a ministration of life, a representation of Christ, that we are bringing glory to God, that we are setting forth the exaltation of His Son.

CHAPTER 6.

The School of Sonship unto Adoption

READING: Rom. viii. 14, 17, 19, 21, 23, 29 ; Gal. iv. 5-7 ; Eph. i. 5-6; Heb. i. 1-2; iii. 6-8, 14-15; v. 8-14; xii. 5-7, 9, 11.

Continuing our contemplation of the spiritual house, we are now to consider the matter of the School of sonship unto adoption. I hesitate to go over the ground of technical differences in terms because that has been done so often, but you will suffer just the briefest word in that connection, as it may be necessary for some.

The Divine Conception of "Adoption"

When we come to the things of God, we find that we have to change some of our human ideas, and amongst the many things in which that is so there is this matter of adoption. God's idea about adoption is altogether different from ours. Our idea is that of bringing someone into the family from outside, but that is not God's idea at all about adoption. The word "adoption" literally means "the placing of sons," and you will have recognized, if you were following closely, that adoption comes at the close of things in all those passages of Scripture. It is something which lies ahead. We, who have received the Spirit, wait, groaningly wait, for our adoption. We were foreordained unto adoption as sons. It is something for which we are waiting, according to the Word of God. Thus it is not just the matter of bringing into the family, but it is something which is the result of what has transpired since we came into the family, the result of God's dealings with us as being in His family, and you know quite well that different words are used.

The Revised Version is of peculiar value in this connection. The distinction is made quite clear there that, as children of God, we are such on the ground of birth, whilst we are but sons potentially by that birth. We are actually sons, according to that Divine thought as represented in the word "adoption," after we have been in the family for a time and God has dealt with us. Sonship, in the Divine sense, is something which is being developed in us. To be a child is a question of generation ; " child " is a generic term, but sonship is something received, something given, something imparted. That is something more than being born.

The Scriptural Unfolding of the Subject

This word, as you have recognized, is used in different ways in the Scripture. In Romans and Galatians, for instance, we have some light upon sonship. It is seen to have its genesis in a basic relationship with God through our receiving the Spirit. We have received the Spirit, and are called sons because we have received the Spirit ; but both in the case of Romans and Galatians the object of those letters was to obviate the grave peril which had come amongst believers of stopping short at a certain point in their spiritual life as born-again ones and not going on to perfection. Their peril was that of being turned aside by the work of the Judaisers, who were coming in to try to arrest the spiritual progress of these believers and bringing in the law again and the Jewish system.

We may indicate here at once that the enemy always withstands very fiercely this matter of spiritual progress unto adoption. The most perilous thing to the enemy is " the adoption of sons." That is the end for him and he knows very well the significance for himself of the Lord's people going on with the Lord unto adoption. These Judaisers were the Devil's instruments to prevent the going on of these people to that glorious end.

So the Holy Spirit, through the Apostle, in these two letters, brings in the light of sonship ; that is, he gives the knowledge of sonship in its fuller meaning, and says that basically, by having received the Holy Spirit, we are sons, but that sonship is not realized now in its full meaning and value. That is something unto which we are to go on, in which we are to continue ; for the whole creation is waiting, groaning and waiting, for the literal consummation of that which is potential in our having received the Spirit, namely, "the manifestation of the sons of God." When that day comes, the creation will be delivered from its bondage of corruption. But against that deliverance the powers of evil work, and they worked through Judaisers as well as through many other things and people to prevent that glorious deliverance of the creation in the manifestation of the sons of God. So that what we have in Romans and Galatians is light about sonship, the basis of sonship established, but nothing said which carries with it the definite declaration that we have reached all that sonship means. Even in this word, "As many as are led by the Spirit of God, these are sons of God," there is no saying that every Christian is a son of God ; for is every Christian led by the Spirit of God? It is a spiritual position which is bound up with sonship in God's thought.

Of course, in our birth as children of God, in which sonship is implicit and adoption is prospective, the inheritance is in view, for every one born into this family is a potential heir. If we are children, we are heirs. But it is quite well known that we can be minors while we are heirs, and that is brought out in Galatians. While we may be born heirs, we are still minors, and we cannot have the inheritance until we reach our majority. That is adoption—reaching the majority, coming to full growth, to full manhood.

Full Sonship a Corporate Matter and Greatly Withstood

So that we are brought face to face with this matter of reaching adoption by the development of sonship in us in the School of God. I think I ought to say here that, while this does become an individual and personal matter and must be that in its application, the matter of adoption is one with that of election, and that it is the Church which is in view, not the individual. It is the Church which is the elect body, and it is the Church which is the elect " son," in the sense in which we are speaking of sonship now; and it is the Church which is foreordained unto adoption of sons, not individuals as such, although it has its individual application, and it will be with the manifestation of the sons in the corporate sense, the Church, that God reaches His full end. I say that, because I feel that this matter of sonship involves the truth of the Body of Christ in a very real way. In reality, it depends upon that truth. Now, you may not grasp what I mean. I mean that sonship requires the Body of Christ, is involved in that truth of the Body of Christ, and it is in our relatedness in Christ as fellow-heirs that we shall be developed, that we shall come to fulness, to God's full end. You and I cannot inherit singly, individually: we can only inherit in a related way.

I think that truth goes further than I am now intending to indicate ; but let us recognize that the enemy has something very much in view in keeping the light of the Body of Christ from the Lord's people. The reason for that, you see, is on account of our being foreordained unto adoption as sons by Jesus Christ unto Himself, and all that it means to the enemy ; for to him it means everything. He loses his place, he loses his kingdom, he loses his title, he loses everything, when this "Corporate Son" is manifested in glory, when this work is completed in the Church and it is found in the throne. It is therefore up to him to keep the light of the Body of Christ from believers : and it is for this reason that, when the Apostle has been led to make the declaration of the truth, " foreordained unto adoption as sons," he gets on his knees, so to speak, and prays :

"That the God of our Lord Jesus Christ, the Father of glory, may give unto you a spirit of wisdom and revelation in the knowledge of him ; having the eyes of your heart enlightened, that ye may know what is the hope of his calling, what the riches of the glory of his inheritance in the saints . . ." (Eph. i. 17-18).

It is fervent prayer against this blinding, darkening, withholding work of the adversary as to the light concerning the Church's nature, calling and destiny. You will agree with me that there are comparatively few Christians, when you go over the whole range of Christians to-day in all the world, comparatively few who have light, the revelation of the Body of Christ ; and that represents a most disastrous result of Satanic activity, the blinding of the saints. Oh no, this is not some truth which is an optional thing. This is something which is bound up with the very purpose of God and the undoing of all Satanic work.

Well, Romans viii. is a tremendous chapter along many lines, but that great summing up is immense. The creation, subjected to vanity, is seen groaning and travailing unto the manifestation of the sons of God, when it will be delivered from the bondage of corruption: and then, unto that, the elect instrument is shown—"Whom he foreknew, he also foreordained to be conformed to the image of his Son." It is the Church being brought in and it is a thing of immense importance, and it is necessary to see that, before we can appreciate this training of sons unto adoption.

We are in a school for a tremendous destiny. We are in
the school which has as its end something of such significance
and importance that we can scarce imagine ; and so we have
not to regard lightly the child-training of the Lord. Oh, again
our human ideas must not be brought into the Divine realm
when we use the word "chastening." What a poor translation!
Even the Revisers have not helped us very much. It is simply
"child-training." I think that, as a youngster, that chapter in
Hebrews was my pet aversion in the Bible when I heard it
read! My whole being rose up against that. I suppose that is
quite natural ; but if only we had been given the two words
instead of that deplorable word "chastening." It might at
least have taken the edge off things. "My son, despise not
thou the child-training of the Lord." There is something
better about that. "Whom the Lord loveth, He trains," He
child-trains.

Well, we come to the business of child-training right away.
Here, in this fifth chapter of the Hebrew letter, we have these
school features mentioned in various words, as you notice.

"Though he was a Son, yet learned he obedience by the
things which he suffered."

That is a school verse.

"When by reason of the time ye ought to be teachers. . ."
It is another school verse.

"Every one that partaketh of milk is without experience . . ."

That is a school verse.

". . . by reason of use have their senses exercised . . ."
That is what happens at school. Here we are found right in
the School of sonship.

The Practical Difference Between " Children " and " Sons "

Now, in the practical way, let us note the difference between
infants, spiritually, called children in the New Testament, and
sons. The difference is simply this, that infants or children
have everything done for them and they live in the good of
that for which they themselves have had no exercise. That is
the difference. An infant is one who lives on the good of
other people's exercise and has never had any exercise for

itself. Everything has been done and prepared for it. Everything is coming to it as from the outside, and nothing has been done by the child itself. I think that is the main mark of an infant. But a son, in the spiritual and Scriptural sense, is one who is in the way of having the root of the matter in himself, who is progressively coming out of the realm where everything is done for him and where he has no exercise at all about things, to the place where it is going on in him and he is becoming one who is competent in himself, and no longer dependent upon what others do and say. Everything is not being brought ready made to him. There is a sense in which it is being made in him and he is making it in his own experience by the exercise of his own senses. That is the main difference, spiritually, between an infant or child, and a son.

These two words here are very helpful words—"senses exercised." As children of God, we are regarded as having spiritual senses, and the object of God's dealings with us in His child-training is to bring those senses into exercise, so that by that exercise we may have experience: and what a tremendous thing is experience, and of what value. They are the people who count, these who have experience, and experience comes through the exercise of the senses.

But there are a great many people who never graduate from spiritual childhood and infancy to sonship; and why is it? You see, God does not sovereignly and by determination make sons of us. Oh no, God is not going to make sons of everybody on His own initiative, by His own power. We have a place in this. The responsibility, as you notice, in every one of these Scriptures, is thrown back upon believers themselves, and it is made very clear in very strong words, that the responsibility does rest upon them. The bringing up so frequently of those words relating to Israel's downfall in the wilderness shows what responsibility rests upon the children of God in this matter.

"To-day if ye shall hear his voice, harden not your hearts, as in the provocation" (Heb. iii. 15).

That has usually been used as a text for a Gospel address to unbelievers; but in the New Testament, it was never used in that way. It may be legitimate, but it was never used in that way in the New Testament. It was always used for Christians, for believers, as a warning, and to bring home to believers this matter of responsibility, of something resting with us.

Purposefulness a Requirement in Would-be Sons

Now, that means there is something basic to sonship unto adoption, and that is a purposefulness to go on with God. There must be about us this sense of purpose, this factor and feature of purpose, purposefulness to go on with God, and the Lord calls for that. Oh, the New Testament might be said to be one continuous urge to that, an urge to be characterized by a spiritual purpose, of meaning to go on, and it is upon that the Lord operates. Now I say that to lead to this. It is just that very purposefulness of heart which brings us into all the trouble. Perhaps if we recognized what that means, it would be as helpful a thing as could be said to us. The people who are not characterized by that spirit of purpose and are just content to be little babes all their lives and to have everything done for them and dished up to them and who never have any exercise for themselves, usually have a fairly comfortable time. They are fairly satisfied and pleased with life and they do not want anything else. But let a man become marked by this sense of earnest purpose, and it will not be long before he is in trouble! If you mean to go on, then you have come out of the nursery into the school, and the nature of this school is a very difficult one.

The Discipline that Makes All Inward and Living

It just means this, that God is going to put and precipitate us into the most difficult situations. A situation is only difficult if you cannot cope with it. If you find the thing altogether beyond your measure : your measure of strength, your measure of wisdom, your measure of knowledge, then you are in difficulty: and that is the sort of thing the Lord does with people who mean business with Him. He puts them into difficult situations, and His whole object is to get their spiritual senses exercised, so that they may gain experience, may have the root of the matter in themselves. Thus all our nice, comfortable line of things falls away at once and we find ourselves in a realm with which we cannot cope, for which we are not sufficient. We have been in the habit of asking questions and getting them answered: now, no one can answer our questions, no answer comes from the outside. Of course, people can say things to us and we may get a measure of help from those who have experience ; but God is going to shut us up to the fact that it has to become ours by experience and in truth.

It does not matter what anyone else says, we know quite well that we have to prove that for ourselves: they cannot lift us out of our difficulty. We constantly revert to the old childish way of running around asking somebody to solve our problems, but we have to come out of that. That is not going to work any longer. Really, deep down in us, we know that it does not work. We are not getting what we are after. We know now we have not to have something said to us, but something done in us. We have to be brought ourselves to a position, not to a mental solution; and if you are all the time trying to get intellectual solutions to your spiritual problems, you are still in the nursery. If you are going really to come through to God's full and intended end, you have to know the Lord for yourself in an inward way, and unto that it may be necessary for the Lord to suspend all external helps and render all others incapable of coming to your rescue, flinging you wholly back upon Himself; to prove Him, to know Him, to be deeply, deeply exercised in your own spirit. That exercise enlarges capacity, and enlarged capacity means enlarged impartation from the Lord. That is the School of sonship unto adoption.

You see, spirituality, which is the nature of sonship, is not mental at all. That is to say, it is not a matter of having all our mental problems answered for us by somebody who has an answer to give us. You can never reach spirituality philosophically, logically, academically. You may go all over the world and get many questions answered, but that does not mean that you have come into spiritual enlargement. No, that is a very small realm, after all. Most of us have been there. We know quite well it never got us anywhere at all: and what a time we had and how disappointed we were!

In my own experience in that realm, where it was all a matter of getting answers to spiritual problems, or trying to get them, along intellectual lines, with a very wide search for satisfaction of mind and heart along that line, I reached a point that Robert Browning (a very much bigger man that I am) reached, as the goal of all his enquiry along that line, namely, that it is as difficult not to believe in God as to believe in Him. Well, how far does that get you? But that is the boundary of all inquiry philosophically! You may have decided not to believe anything about God: then there is a sunset and all your decisions are tested at once. You have to

say, Man never made that ; where did it come from? and you
are back to your old questions.

The Lord Jesus Christ says, "If any man willeth to do his
will, he shall know of the teaching" (John vii. 17). That is
only the Gospel way of putting in germ form this great truth of
sonship, namely, that you know by experience and not by
intellectual inquiry and by people telling you from the outside.
You do not come into anything by that way, for what logic
can build up, logic can pull down. No, God dealeth with us
as with—what? Students in the academic sense? No, as
with sons. And where do we locate sonship? God is the
Father of our spirits ; therefore our spirits are the seat of sonship and all His dealings are with our spirits. Thus it is a
matter of spiritual growth, spiritual enlargement: that is
growth in sonship unto adoption. Oh yes, it is experience.

A Final Emphasis and Exhortation

Now, I wonder if you have grasped what I have been
saying and are going to be helped by it ; that, so soon as you
mean business with God, you have put yourself in the way of
numerous difficulties and all that has been so wonderful to
you is going to fall away : all that has been your satisfaction is
probably going for a time to cease to be that, and you are
coming into a realm where you have to find God in a new
way, in a manner in which you have never hitherto
known Him, and where you can no longer really get help
from the outside ; I mean final help. You may just be helped,
but the Lord does not allow those ready-made things to come
and put you into the position to which He is leading you.
You have to get there for yourself. You may be helped as
to how to get there, and as to what is God's goal for you, and
as to how other people came through to that end ; but no one
now from the outside can do it for you and you know that
God has shut you up to have this thing done in you and it is
solely a matter between you and the Lord in your spiritual
history. You may be right in the midst of the most mature
Christians who have gone that way and who know and you
may be as one alone. You know you do not know as they
know ; but do not despair. If you are marked by this spirit
of purposefulness with God, that means He has you in His
school, and it is a good indication when you begin to get real
deep spiritual exercise. We have all met those people who

have lived on the basis of spiritual infancy all their lives, and they can never help us at all in our deepest need. Indeed, everything was so cut and dried with them they would not investigate anything deeper. They regarded anything deeper as quite superfluous and were quite satisfied and had a kind of answer to everything. But in our heart need they could not touch us at all. We have all been that way.

There was an hour in my own experience when I was there, after years of seeking that answer to a deep sense of need ; and, not getting it, I began to go the round to try to see if someone could help me, and I went some hundreds of miles to visit a man who was outstanding as a religious teacher, as a Bible teacher, and as a name in Christianity. I went to see him to get spiritual help: I was in desperate need, and it was a spiritual situation ; and when I put my case before him and told him of my sense of need of a new knowledge of the Lord, he said, "Oh, Sparks, the trouble with you is that you are a bit overtired. You had better go and play golf." He could not understand, could not enter into the situation. I know now why he could not help me and why I got help from no one during that terrible period. I know that God was shutting me up to Himself. I had to come to the place where I could really be a help to others in their hour of need, at least point the way because I had come the way, explaining what God was doing because I had had an experience of His dealings. In order to be of any use at all to those who are going to be sons, to have a ministry for the sons of God, a ministry which, though so imperfectly, so inadequately, touches that great end of adoption ; in order to have the smallest part in such a ministry, God has had to shut us up to Himself so that no one could help us.

Do not take that wrongly. Do not take that to mean that you are to cut yourself off from fellowship and from all help that may be available. That would be a misapprehension of what I am saying and might make things infinitely more difficult and put you in a false position. But I am saying that in your heart of hearts you will find, while there may be help given to you by ministries, fellowship, advice, counsel, by explanation, the real thing has to be born and developed in your own self. You have to have the root of the matter in you and no one can bring that about but the Lord Himself by His own dealings with you. So you will be plunged into darkness. I do not mean the darkness of being out of union with God, the darkness of lost assurance of salvation ; but you will be plunged into darkness in experience in order to make new discoveries, in order that the Lord may give you light through exercise. God dealeth with you as with—not bricks, but living stones, sons. That is an honour, that is a great thing, that ought to inspire us. If we have boys, they always feel tremendously encouraged if we put our hand on their shoulder and say, "Now, old boy . . ." and begin to talk to them as responsible persons, not just dealing with them all the time as babes. My son, I want you to do this for me ; I want you to take this bit of responsibility ; I want you to look after things for me while I am away. Then something rises up and there is a reach out to be what father wants.

Now, in a sense, that is what God is doing. He is saying, I do not want you to be babes always, I want to put responsibility upon you ; I have some big things for you to do. Now, come along! He may put us into some very difficult situation, but the very sense of being called to the responsibility will make us seek to know how to meet this situation. A man flung into the sea to learn to swim learns far better than the man who has the doctrine about swimming. The Lord does that in love : but He does it. Whom the Lord loveth He child-trains.

I wonder how many of us would be very pleased if our parents had always done things for us, always sheltered us from having the trouble, the bother, the worry, the necessity of doing things or finding out how to do them for ourselves. I am quite sure none of us would think that was love in our parents. I think we would come to a time when we would say, I have nothing good to say of my parents ; they have landed me into very very great difficulty by their false idea of love. Here I am: everybody knows I am no good, and I know it myself! But "whom the Lord loveth, he child-trains."

Look ahead to see all that is going to be. You see, there is a throne in view, there is government in view. I do not know how men manage in the governments of this world. It seems to me that they are able to pass from one department to another in the State. I do not know how that is done, but I do not believe that it is because it is in them. So much is a matter of routine, of form. It can be taken up as something already highly organized and arranged.

Of course, I would not say of all statesmen that it was not in them, but I am speaking generally. Now, the Lord is having no official appointments in the great administration of His Kingdom. He is going to have people who have had quality wrought in them. It is unto that the Church, the Body of Christ, is called, and it has to be in us. That is no child's play. That is a thing for full-grown men. If that is not true, then I do not understand the teaching of the New Testament about going on to full growth, nor do I understand the Lord's dealings with His Church. If all that matters is just that we should be born again, have forgiveness of sins, and go to heaven, why all this in the Bible and in our experience? It is certainly not for something here. There may be values here, but they are not commensurate with what we have to go through. It is just at the time when we are beginning to get mature and are a little use to the Lord that He takes us away. We cannot pass it on. There may be some fruit, some value of it here, but not at all commensurate with all this training. No, it is for some other purpose. We say, "Higher Service." Well, yes, that is what it is.

The Lord give us grace then to endure chastening as sons, so that He may have that company upon which He can place the great responsibility which it is His will to give.

CHAPTER 7.

Graduation from the School of Sonship

READING: Rom. viii. 19, 21-23 ; Heb. i. 2 ; ii. 5-8, 9-11 ; iii. 1, 7-8 ; xii. 5-6 ; Rev. xii. 5.

In our previous meditation, we were occupied with the School of sonship unto adoption. We are now going to follow that on to the next stage.

We were seeing a little of the nature, meaning and need for transition from spiritual infancy to the School of sonship. A very real experience is that transition and a very deep one for those who enter into it. A whole new set of conditions perfectly strange to us is connected with that further movement in the life of the child of God which marks the passage from spiritual childhood to spiritual sonship, or the School of sonship. I suppose most of us remember when we went to a new school, or when we went to school for the first time. Everything was strange, everything was new. We had to take up things from the very first point. It was an entirely new world: and so it is in the life of the child of God. It is an entirely new world, a new set of conditions, something with which we are altogether unfamiliar when that point is reached where God takes us in hand to see that we are no longer children, but are brought into the School of sonship with adoption in view ; adoption, of course, according to the Divine meaning of that word, not our natural meaning.

The Purpose of our Graduation as Sons

Now we are going for a little while to consider the graduation from the School of sonship, graduating to that for which school has been going on, all that child-training which, as the Lord Himself knows and let us know that He knows, is for the present not joyous but grievous. But there is the graduation day. The whole creation waits for that graduation day with bated breath and an inward yearning, the day of the manifestation of the sons of God, the *placing* of sons to which we referred in our previous meditation, which is the meaning of the word " adoption " ; not bringing into the family, but the placing of sons who have qualified through the school. And what is the graduation of sonship, unto what is it? It is unto the Throne.

"Not unto angels" (not unto angels of any rank, not even the highest rank of archangels) "did he subject the world to come, whereof we speak. But one hath somewhere testified saying, What is man, that thou art mindful of him? Or the son of man, that thou settest him apart? "

That is the true rendering of the latter sentence ; not "visitest him" as we commonly use the word, but "settest him apart" ; that man, in a word, is in view with God from eternity for this purpose, to have the throne, the government, the dominion over the world to come in union with God's Son, as the sons brought by that Son to glory.

There is the Heir in Hebrews i. 2—

". . . whom he appointed heir of all things . . ."

There are the heirs in chapter ii.—

". . . bringing many sons unto glory . . ."

The throne is that which is in view at the end of school, the graduation, and it is that which is referred to in Rev. xii. The governing principle of Rev. xii. is sonship brought out to completion, a man child.

"She was delivered of a son, a man child, who is to rule all nations with a rod of iron." (This is sonship.) "And her child was caught up unto God, and unto the throne." That is the graduation.

The Man Child of Revelation xii.

Now, I am going to stay for the miserable business of getting rid of a few misconceptions about this chapter. The accepted and firmly held view concerning this chapter is, that this woman is Israel and that this man child is Christ. I will not impute motives and reasons to the holders of that view, but it does seem to me that only a prejudiced mind could hold it, a mind not willing to accept what is, I think, quite patently the truth.

This book of Revelation begins with a pronouncement from heaven that what is going to be shown is "things which must shortly come to pass," and that pronouncement was made years and years after Christ had gone to heaven. It was future. Moreover, when Christ went to heaven, Satan was not cast out of heaven as is the case in Rev. xii. ; for, nearly forty years after Christ went to heaven, Paul wrote his letter to the Ephesians, and in chapter vi. we have this revelation of the nature and sphere of the Church's warfare: "Our wrestling is not against flesh and blood, but against the principalities, against the powers, against the world-rulers of this darkness, against the spiritual hosts of wickedness in the heavenlies." Satan was not deposed when Christ was caught up to the throne. Thirdly, the dragon was not cheated of his prey in the case of the Lord Jesus. The Lord Jesus was slain by the dragon, and it is a part of the great and glorious truth that it was through death that He destroyed him that had the power of death, namely, the Devil. Satan, the dragon, thought he had swallowed up Christ perhaps, but he discovered that he had been swallowed up. But the Lord Jesus did not escape the great red dragon by a rapture: not at all. The dragon got him so far and slew him. But therein is the glorious sovereignty of God, and that is another line of truth altogether: God's sovereignty wrought in the very presence of Satan's triumph. But that is not this.

Then this woman is a paradox, a contradiction. She is at one and the same time in heaven clothed in glory and on the earth clothed with trouble and travail. She is clothed with the sun in heaven, and yet in the next breath she is travailing on the earth. Is not that just exactly what we have in the letter to the Ephesians about the Church? In the heavenlies, in Christ Jesus blessed with every spiritual blessing, and yet at the same time the letter shows us very clearly right at the heart of it that the Church is down here and in conflict. She has an earthly walk and is meeting things down here while at the same time in the heavenlies. A contradiction apparently: at one and the same time in heaven glorious and yet on earth in tribulation. That is the Church. Well, is not that enough, though there is a lot more here?

I know there is another interpretation ; that this was not only Israel but Christ Himself, and that we are the seed of Christ. But that is only just allowed to go so far. It does not carry us through satisfactorily. But this is the main position held about Israel and Christ, and I say I do not see how it can hold water in the light of even the two or three things that we have just noted.

You see, you have a correspondence here. In Rev. ii. you have these very words addressed to the overcomers in the Church at Thyatira—"He that overcometh . . . to him will I give authority over the nations, and he shall rule them with a rod of iron." Then in the letter to the church in Laodicea we have these further words: "He that overcometh, I will give to him to sit down with me in my throne, as I also overcame, and sat down with my Father in his throne." There is the throne for overcomers and the rule of the nations. Then those very words are reiterated in Chapter xii. about the man child caught up to the throne to rule the nation with a rod of iron. And I do not see that we can divorce those words from Hebrews ii.—"Thou madest him (man) in order to have" (that is the sense of the word) "dominion over the works of thy hands." Of course there is the union between Christ and His own: that is what Hebrews is speaking about. "Christ as a son over God's house, whose house are we. . . ."

So then, having said that much—and I think it is enough, I am not dealing with all the data and points in this chapter—having said that much, we want to come right to our point in this meditation.

The graduation from the School of sonship is to the throne, and it is that throne, with what it means with regard to vocation, to service, to purpose in relation to God's eternal intention, that is in view while God is dealing with us, when God takes us out of the comfortable, pleasant time of spiritual infancy and childhood, where everything is done for us, and puts us into that experience where the thing has to be wrought in us and where, through this deep exercise of our spiritual faculties or senses, we become spiritually responsible sons of God. It is with this in view that God deals with us as with sons. Now, do grasp the meaning of that, what it implies. It implies one or two rather important things.

Spiritual Increase Related to the Throne and the Glory of the Lord

Firstly, it does mean that the deepening of spiritual life, as it is called, or any other terms used for the same thing, is not a matter which is just to issue in our fuller blessing. So often people will bring it right down there to that level of fuller blessing, and we are very often tempted even there, in the time of fire and adversity, to react to this whole thing by saying, Well, if I have heaven, why need I trouble about all this, and why should I go through all this? Here are plenty of people just very happy and contented ; they are saved and they know they are saved, and here am I who have sought to go on with God, and I am having the most awful time. It seems to me that I have got the worst of the bargain, by wanting to go right on with God! If we look at it like that, purely from the personal point of view of blessing, we have missed our way, and we shall get into difficulties ; because, as we have always sought to point out, when you come out of this spiritual infancy into the School of sonship, you graduate from what is personal as to your own interest and blessing into what is for the Lord and not for you. From that time forward the whole motive is, not what I am going to get, but what God is going to get. That is Ephesians. "That ye may know what is . . . the riches of the glory of *his* inheritance in the saints." Not what I am going to get now: that will follow, that will be all right, the Lord will be faithful ; but it is something else. We have come into the school on the basis of God's eternal purpose, and God's eternal purpose does not begin and end when He has got us born again. God's eternal purpose is only reached when He has got us in the throne. Thus it is the Lord, for the Lord, and what the Lord is after that is the one consideration. It will be glory for me, but that is not the motive of it now. It is this great purpose with which we are called : that is what is governing everything, and it is in the terms of the throne.

So the transition from infancy to the School of sonship, being a very painful thing, and fraught with all sorts of difficulties, brings us nevertheless into relation with that which has been in God's mind from before the world was where we are concerned. Chosen in Christ Jesus "that we should be to the praise of *his* glory." All the dealings of the Lord with us in this school have that throne in view.

World Dominion the Pressing Issue of the Hour

What I want to say with special emphasis now is that this matter, as I see and feel it—and I leave it to you to judge whether there is any truth in this—is most fitting in relation to what is happening in the world to-day. It does seem to me that this is a time when this issue is put in a way in which it has never been put before ; that is, the issue of the dominion of this world, the issue of Antichrist, is so patent. It is the control and domination of this inhabited earth, and everything connected with this fresh drive to that end is to set aside God and His Christ. It is an evil thing, and it does not need a spiritually minded preacher of the truth to discern that ; for many of our leaders of the State to-day have seen it and are using these words. How far they see, we do not know. But they are seeing that all that Christianity stands for is at stake. They are saying, This is a Satanic thing! and they are using the very phrase—Antichrist. It is discerned by men as to what the nature of things is, and we are able, in a special way as enlightened by the Lord, to see what the end of this is. It is the most far-reaching and terrible bid for the throne of this world that has been known. That is what lies behind it and that is what is in view. Therefore I say that this word is most fit for a time like this, and I am asking myself and I ask you prayerfully to consider whether there must not come something in the nature of a summons to the people of God to recognize this fact, with reference to their calling, namely, that they have to get behind that which is behind the present situation, and that the saints must take the kingdom spiritually now, in a spiritual way, in order that they may come to the place of the throne for the age to come.

We here perhaps—though let us not think too highly of ourselves, more highly than we ought to think—but it may be that our little gathering here with all its earthly insignificance has yet a significance which is very far reaching, seeing that we are here in the audience chamber of God concerning this great matter of the dominion of this world. In a small way, it affects us very seriously. I ask you to pray about this, very earnestly and continually that there might be a movement of God's Spirit within the circle of His own people in a new way, to produce this man child that overcomes and takes the throne. It is quite clear, from Rev. ii. and iii., that all do not come to that position, and equally so from all these exhortations and warnings about Israel missing the goal in the wilderness, falling by the way, as warnings to the Church to beware of the same calamity. "To-day if ye shall hear his voice, harden not your hearts." I wonder if any of us have a hardened heart, not against the Lord in a general way, but against this. You harden by using special terms. Oh, how people have sought to close the door by sticking labels on!

Get rid of terms. Call it Selective Rapture, if you like: I do not call it that. Call it Overcomer Testimony, if you like. It makes little difference, if you mean by that, That is an interpretation, that is a peculiar teaching! Well, that is a hardening of the heart. What if this should happen to be true! We have to look this thing square in the eyes. Is there any possibility that this is true? If there is, it is a tremendous thing; the biggest issue in the history of this world is bound up with it, nothing less than the dominion, the throne. I suggest to you that there is a good deal to-day which would lead us to open the door to possibilities, to suppositions.

An Object Lesson and the Need for Open-hearted Inquiry

You know certain nations at our own door are suffering untold misery, because as long as seven years ago they were told of secret propaganda going on within the borders of their own country, and working its way secretly and subtly into high places, but would not believe it. They were told what that was going to end in, what the object was, what the result would be, and they said, No, impossible! I ask you this: If nine months ago a prophet had stood up in some prominent place in this world and prophesied the history of the following nine months, what would have happened to him? Seven or eight countries overrun and surprised, and this final terrible collapse of France! He would have been put in a lunatic asylum or have been lynched, he would have been shut up for safety. But it has happened: the unbelievable has happened and is happening. No one would believe it or accept it. See how they are suffering for saying, Impossible! Ridiculous!

Ah, I say to you that this should be a lesson to us. That is a trick of Satan. It is a part of his strategy, to work subtly and at the same time to make people believe there is nothing, that all is well; to be working underneath to the internal disintegration and downfall of a people, and yet on the surface to be making nice speeches. This is a Satanic method, and again and again Satan has gained his strategical advantage by that same means. And I say to you that at least we ought to come to a thing like this and say, Well, it is just possible that may be right, and if there is the remotest possibility of its being right, it is such a big thing we had better attend to it! I know many have managed to get past that, but I say again, from the lowest level of making this appeal, that it just may be that the Lord's Word is true after all. It just may be that this is the true revelation of God's thought and intention ; that He chose an elect people, a company which has come to be called the Church, He chose that company, that Body, that corporate entity in Christ before the world was, with a view to it coming through at length to take the throne as His vessel and instrument for governing His universe. I say, that may be true. All I ask you to do is to consider the possibility of its being true, and if only you will allow that, it will give you real pause: and then to see that this is quite true so far as the Scripture and the experience of the Lord's people is concerned in a spiritual way. God is doing a certain thing in His people, in many at least who are pressing on with Him, those of whom we were speaking in our previous meditation who are marked by a purposefulness with God. In these He begins to do something deep and strange and painful, the end of which is never, never reached in this earthly life, the value of which is never entered into by anybody during their time here on earth. It is unto something: it is the preparation of sons unto adoption to take the throne ; and I urge you to pray with regard to your own place in this, and to pray for a movement of God's Spirit within the compass of His people to produce this man child. The Church, as a whole, is moving steadily into this travail.

Then will you not pray that the Lord's people may be enlightened on this matter, enlightened as to what the issue is. It is between Christ and Antichrist, between the Church which is Christ's Body and the whole Antichrist system ; for it is quite clear that Antichrist, though he may be an individual opposed to Christ personally, is also a church, a system, a terrible system. Satan has his Church opposed to Christ's Church. Blessed be God, we have this assurance, "I will build my church, and the gates of hell shall not prevail against it"!

The Explanation of the Mystifying and Painful Preparation

Well then, that is the matter before us in this School of sonship, namely, the throne. My dear friends, I want to get hold of that in my own heart, and I want you to get hold of it. You see, we are so prone to make our sojourn on this earth the big thing ; I mean in the matter of what we are able to do, how much we can do and realize and see in our lifetime, and when we find the Lord shutting us up and limiting us and seeming to put us in prison, ofttimes under the strain and pressure of it, when the iron enters into our soul as with Joseph, we begin to think we have missed the way. Life is going, and it is all unfruitful ; we are not doing anything. It is other people who are doing the thing, we are not. Thus we make so much of this present life in the matter of what we are able to do, as though that were everything, whereas (and this, of course, is no argument why we should be slack about doing) so often the Lord has got His greatest effectiveness in those who have been just shut right up, unable to do anything outside. Is not that the truth about Paul himself? Of yes, it is, and Paul, as we have often pointed out, was the embodiment of the revelation which was given to him of the dispensation of the Church, and when we come to the end of his life, we have Paul, who had had such a wide scope of ministry, who had been able to do so much, we have this man, with all the values that are in him, put into prison. But we get the concentrated essence of value from those prison experiences. We get the letter to the Ephesians, and that was worth Paul's going to prison, and anything like that will be worth all that we undergo in the School of sonship, which sees a very great deal of what is here on the earth closed down, if only the heavenly may become the far more real and valuable as an expression in us and through us.

But I say I want this to get into my heart, into your hearts, that the Lord is not so much concerned—please do not misunderstand me—the Lord is not so much concerned with how much we do now in this life. He is more concerned with the measure of Christ to which He can bring us in this life . . . "till we all attain unto the . . . measure of the stature of the fulness of Christ" (Eph. iv. 13). It will be Christ corporate who will come to take the kingdom of this world in the coming ages, and it is unto that—the fulness of Christ—that God is working pre-eminently in our experience, and that is the thing that matters most. It is the most difficult thing for us to accept ; a supremely difficult thing for any active temperament to accept. To some it is martyrdom not to be doing something. It may be God's way of getting the enlargement of His Son in His members, the patience of Jesus Christ, among other things.

God has this great thing in view. The issue comes up acutely and in an intensified form as we get near to the great end. •In order to answer Satan, to have His answer in a corporate Man, God has to prepare you and me and a company of his people to take the throne, to be caught up unto God and to His throne, to rule the nations with a rod of iron. That, of course, has reference to to-morrow, the to-morrow of the ages I mean, and there is something beyond that, namely, our reigning with Him for ever and ever, another form of reigning. I aspire rather to the day after to-morrow than to to-morrow. Ruling with a rod of iron may appeal to us naturally, but we would sooner have the glorious reign where nothing wants a rod of iron. "Now unto him . . . be the glory in the church and in Christ Jesus unto all the generations of the age of the ages" (Eph. iii. 20-21). It is a big thing for which we go to school for a few years and suffer as we are suffering. It is easy to say that, but it is a painful thing, this school. The Lord knows what He is doing with us. It is the matter of this overcoming, and, in the light of this school or this schooling, we can appreciate the word "overcomer." There is a lot of overcoming to be done. We have to get on top of a very great deal, and the getting on top of many things is leading us to get on top of the Devil and his kingdom. Presently, in the great hour when the sons are manifested, when the man child is caught to the throne, the creation is to be delivered from the bondage of corruption.

See then the meaning of the day in which we live. See the meaning of the suffering into which we may go yet more deeply, and how it is to be God's answer to this working of Satan that has been going on ever since he made a bid for the place of God's Heir, the Heir of all things. Ever since Satan made that bid and was cast down from the higher to the lower heavens it has been going on, and now it is being brought out in a new way. That is what it is, and you and I, as part of Christ's Body, are called to be God's answer to that, and it is to be so now in a spiritual way. Presently it will be in the full way, the literal way, that the saints will take the kingdom, and He shall come whose right it is to reign. The dominion shall be given unto the saints of the Most High.

CHAPTER 8.

"Over All—Faith," and a Final Consideration

READING: Eze. xliii. 1-2, 4-5, 7 ; Eph. i. 12 ; iii. 21 ; v. 25-27 ; Col. i. 27 ; I Pet. iv. 14 ; Heb. x. 37-39 ; xi. 1.

In these meditations, we have been looking at some of the major features of God's spiritual house in which we who are the Lord's are living stones. We have been seeking to see what our being living parts of a spiritual house means, and there are two things which remain for this present time, which we trust the Lord will enable us to say. One is something which governs all these matters, and the other is the final feature of this spiritual house. I put it in that way because I think it will be most helpful to deal with these remaining matters in that order, and the one will lead quite naturally to the other, as you will see.

This thing which governs all the features, the spiritual features, of this spiritual house of God is faith.

Faith in Relation to
(i) The exaltation of the Lord Jesus

The first feature which we considered was that this spiritual house, of which we are a living part if we are in Christ, stands for the setting forth in a living way of the exaltation of the Lord Jesus. We saw how that was the first great note in the Church's history on the day of Pentecost.

"God hath made him both Lord and Christ, this Jesus whom ye crucified" (Acts ii. 36).

"Being at the right hand of God exalted . . . he hath poured forth this, which ye see and hear" (Acts ii. 33).

It was a glorious expression of, and testimony to, the exaltation of the Lord Jesus, and the Church is constituted for that purpose, to maintain that, not firstly as a part of its doctrine, but as being in itself the living exhibit thereof throughout the dispensation and to hold that testimony in a living way right to the end.

But we shall find that, in that matter, as in all the others, it very soon becomes a question of a living faith. It was not

84

that so much on the day of Pentecost. The Spirit came, and filled them that had believed, baptized them within and without, and in that mighty .tidal-wave of the Spirit it was not difficult for them to proclaim and give expression to the exaltation of the Lord Jesus. And that is true in principle, although perhaps not in the same outward way, in the case of every child of God, when they first come into a living union with the Lord Jesus. It is not difficult at that time for us to proclaim, and by our very faces to announce, that Jesus is exalted, Jesus is Lord, Jesus lives. That is our first note of testimony when we receive the Spirit. It is the first thing which expresses itself in a believer. But we all have lived to know that it is not always as easy as that. It does not always come as spontaneously as that. We move into a time when, while the fact remains, we have to hold on to the fact in sheer and grim faith. We have to answer to apparent contradictions to the fact with an attestation of faith ; for things rise up and there is a mighty reaction of the enemy to our testimony and to our position, and we have to hold the position in blind faith ; not in feeling faith, not in seeing faith, but in cold, blind faith we have to maintain our position that Jesus is Lord, Jesus is exalted, Jesus is on the throne ; and it is only by faith being put forth in the fact that we win through, and that testimony becomes a powerful thing in our deliverance, in our very life.

So faith governs this matter, and we shall find that, as we get nearer to the end, the challenge to the Lordship, the exaltation, the Kingship, the enthronement of the Lord Jesus will become intensely severe. It will be a bitter challenge and there will be a situation in which nothing but just faith, naked faith, on the part of God's elect, will keep them standing in the good of that truth, that Jesus Christ, after all, has the reins of government in His hands. If one thing is true about overcomers who do overcome, it is that they overcome by reason of faith ; and faith is faith. So let us not, after all that we have heard and all that in which we have gloried, expect that this is going to be anything other than a testimony in faith. It is not going to be a life of knowing by every evidence, by every proof, by every sign, by every sensation, that Jesus is reigning without any question at all. It is not going to be like that. Do not expect that it is going to be like that. The Word of God makes it very clear that it is not the case. Mark the context, for example, of the verses we read from Hebrews x.

"For yet a very little while,
He that cometh shall come, and shall not tarry.
But my righteous one shall live by *faith.*"

(ii) Ministering Unto the Lord

Then we spoke about another feature of this spiritual house, that it is in existence to minister to God's satisfaction and pleasure. That is a very nice idea! It is a very pleasant thought, a very beautiful thing, to think of being in existence to minister to God's pleasure, to God's satisfaction, to God's glory, and perhaps again at the outset we feel it is not such a big proposition. When we are in those first days of the blossom of spiritual experience, we think that the Lord is very well pleased and happy about us, and we are very happy with the Lord, and it is all right, the Lord is getting something. It is not so difficult to think about this matter of ministering to the Lord's good pleasure. But we discover again that, as the Lord's, we are led out into the wilderness. There is a side of our being which has to be dealt with, that side which has been in the habit of having the upper hand, of having the pre-eminence, of doing all the dictating and the governing, and that has to be put down and another side, namely, that which is of the Lord, has to be brought up, and we come into that realm of which the Apostle speaks—"The flesh lusteth against the Spirit, and the Spirit against the flesh ; for these are contrary the one to the other" (Gal. v. 17). There is something going on in us and when we get out there in that wilderness and are in the deep realities of trial, the demand on faith is no light thing. I am thinking of Israel's forty years in the wilderness while the Lord was dealing with them along the line of discipline, to bring them to that aspect of the Cross as represented by the Jordan, where it is no longer just a matter of their being justified by faith, but of being delivered from themselves by faith: and that required a great exercise of faith when the Jordan overflowed all its banks. But it was in the wilderness, and it is in the wilderness that we, under the hand of the Lord, are brought to understand that no flesh can glory in His presence ; that in us, that is, in our flesh, no good thing dwelleth, and we have to have that brought home to us so that it is not just a theory, but a desperate and awful reality. So we cry, "Oh wretched man that I am!"

At such a time you have great questions as to whether there is any ministry to the glory and pleasure of God. It seems anything but that! And yet, beloved, when we are going through all that under the hand of God, out there in the wilderness, the very fact that we repose faith in the Lord to perfect that which concerneth us, to carry through that which He has commenced unto the day of Jesus Christ, is something which very much ministers to God's pleasure and satisfaction. Just picture it in its figurative setting with Israel in the wilderness. There was the Tabernacle in the midst, and there was God right in that Tabernacle in the Most Holy Place in the Shekinah glory. He was there all the time in the Shekinah glory inside, but on the outside, well, it was a wilderness all right, and there were those horribly ugly covers of the Tabernacle and the glory was hidden. All the beauty was concealed and the outer covers were anything but beautiful and glorious, and the Lord's people were having a very trying time. But at any moment, in the darkest day, the most difficult hour, when things seemed to be most hopeless, at any moment had you looked inside, the glory was to be found there, and it was just a matter of their faith. If they took the appearances as the criterion, they could say, Oh, we cannot see the Lord ; everything looks very uninteresting and anything but glorious, and the situation is a very deplorable one and all this that we are going through and all this lack of sight with regard to the Lord's presence—well, there is nothing in it! We give it up! Again and again in the New Testament, the Lord comes back upon that to warn the Church against such an attitude. "They could not enter in because of unbelief" (Heb. iii. 19). And their unbelief worked in this way, "Is the Lord among us or not?" That was the thing that upset the Lord so much that He refused to allow that generation to go into the land. They asked the ultimate question, Is the Lord among us or not?

Why did they ask that? Because of appearances and difficulties. The glory was veiled, and it was only at rare intervals that the glory was displayed. For the greater part, the glory was not seen. Ah, what then of that word, Christ in you, the hope of glory? Now, that is the word the Apostle by the Spirit addresses to the Church, in the Church's time of difficulty, adversity, discipline, trial, of going through things, and he says, in effect, "Ah, yes, that is how it is on the outside, that is how it is in the matter of circumstances, but Christ in you is the hope of glory": and hope that is seen is not hope. Even this is a matter of faith. We do not always feel Christ in us. We do not live every moment in the consciousness that the Lord is inside: but He is, as truly as the Shekinah glory was there within the Most Holy Place when there was nothing on the outside to evidence it. At any moment you would have been able to prove it could you have looked within. So is it with the Lord's spiritual house, whose house are we. He is there and you have to take an attitude towards this outside situation by which the Lord is bringing us into a new realm, a new position, that, after all, it is not the ultimate thing, the pre-eminent thing: the Lord Himself has said, "I will never leave thee." Faith laying hold of that when it seems there is nothing whatever that contributes to the Lord's glory and satisfaction in us, faith laying hold of the faithfulness of God and trusting Him to carry His work in us through to perfection, is itself a ministration to God's pleasure.

You see that by the contrary. How displeased God was with that generation. Of them He said, They shall not enter into My rest. Why was He displeased? Because they did not trust Him to get them through. They surrendered to the appearances of things in their own lives.

(iii) Ministering to the Life of Others

Then the third thing we spoke about was that the Church is here as a spiritual house for the purpose of ministering to the life of others, of the Lord's people, and here the same principle holds good. It is such a good idea, it is such a fine thought: ministering to the life of others, that is splendid! If only that can be, well, it is a great thing to minister to the life of others, and the very suggestion makes us rise up and feel better. But you remember what the Apostle Paul said: "Death worketh in us, but life in you" (II Cor. iv. 12). You see, it is Gideon's fleece all over again, wrung out, dried, and all around wet, and our ministering to the life of others is like that very often. We are just as dry as dry bones, wrung out. We are not conscious of being full of life and ministering life to others, and yet it is often just then that others do receive something, and that is to the glory of God. Oh, we said, we never thought there could be any blessing in it! Well, the

Lord was not letting our flesh glory in the giving of life to others, but they were getting it.

You see, it is again a matter of faith. Do not think that this ministering to the life of others is always going to be something of which we are conscious, that we are just full and overflowing with life, and people are getting it. I think more often than not it is the other way round. For us it is a grim holding on to God in faith and others are getting the blessing and we are amazed. It can be so. Have faith then: fulfil your ministry in faith.

"He that goeth forth and weepeth, bearing precious seed,
Shall doubtless come again with rejoicing, bringing his
sheaves with him." (Psa. cxxvi. 6.)

Weeping, but in faith. The reward of faith is a great "doubtless."

(iv) A Local Corporate Representation of Christ

Then our fourth feature of the spiritual house was that it is here to be a local corporate representation of the Lord Jesus. We meditated upon that word of His, "Where two or three are gathered together in my name, there am I in the midst of them" (Matt. xviii. 20), and dwelt upon it as a statement pointing on to the great truth of the Body of Christ, that, wherever there are two or three members of His Body, that is a representation and expression of Christ in that place.

But I again see that so often this is only made good by faith. "Where two or three are gathered together in my name, there am I in the midst"—but faith has to rise up very strongly and very deliberately and lay hold of that. You see, you may be two or three gathered somewhere, but there may be nothing whatever of an expression and manifestation of the presence of Christ. You have to come together in faith. You have to stand together in faith. You have to put your feet squarely upon His assurance and declare yourself as resting upon that assurance, and as we take hold of the truth that where the Body is the Lord is, it is then that the thing becomes a reality. We do not make it a reality by faith, but we bring out the reality by faith. The Lord looks for a definite standing upon these things and an assertion of faith. We are here ; yes, but we are not here just as two or three gathered in the name of Jesus in a passive way. There will be no expression of the Lord's presence when things are like that. We come together in faith and we stand in faith that there is going to be an expression of the Lord by our very being here ; and, unless we come together like that, it will be but a congregation, a service, a coming and going. When we come together in a living way with a living faith, it is not an address we have come to listen to, but we have come definitely to meet with the Lord, and the Lord has assured us that, as we are gathered together in His name, we shall meet Him. If that is our spirit, our attitude, there will be something of a living expression of the Lord. Faith is a great factor in the matter of corporate life to make its values real. I cannot go further than that.

(v) Testimony to the Overthrow of Satan

The fifth feature was that this spiritual house is here to testify in a living way to the overthrow of Satan. Well, that is a fact ; Satan has been overthrown by Christ. So far as the Lord Jesus is concerned, the overthrow of Satan has been accomplished and established, and on the day of Pentecost there was no difficulty in their believing it, enjoying it and proclaiming it. But they lived to see other days when it was not just like that. They lived to see days when it seemed that Satan was anything but overthrown, anything but disposed. They saw him apparently doing just as he wanted to do, having it all his own way. They saw him bringing to death their fellow-believers and colleagues in ministry. They saw the ravages of the Devil on the right hand and on the left. Does this mean that the thing they once said so strongly and with such conviction is no longer true and they were mistaken even then? Not at all! This matter has to become a matter of the faith of the Lord's people. The overthrow of Satan, so far as this world is concerned, is a matter of the militant faith of the Church.

I simply draw from Ephesians this. When the Apostle has told us of all the armour that we are to put on in this spiritual warfare against the wiles of the Devil, he says, Now above all take the shield of faith. Our English language is poor in expressing what Paul said. Paul did not say "above all" in the sense in which we should mean it. He said, Now *over* all take the big shield of faith. As you know, the Roman legions had more than one kind of shield. They had the little round shield, which was only for the protection of the face and head against arrows and darts. But then they had the big shield, which could shield them completely, and often an army marched into battle with it over them. As they put the big shields side by side, it was like forming a solid mail roof. They marched under it, the big shield being over every thing, covering everything. All else requires this one thing. All else may yield, prove insufficient. With everything, over and above everything—faith! It requires the militant faith of the Church to bring about here what Christ has brought about in heaven, namely, the overthrow of the Evil One. It is by faith now that Satan is overthrown, so far as the Church is concerned, and so far as things here are concerned. But of course, our faith is not in something which is going to be, it is in something which already is, namely, Christ's victory.

(vi) Present Testimony to the Coming Day of Glory

Now I come to the last thing, which has not been mentioned. The final feature of this spiritual house, which comes up with the passages we have read, is that the spiritual house, the Church, is here in the light of the coming day of the fulness of Glory, to stand in the light of that, to receive upon itself the light of that, and to reflect the light of that day that is coming.

In Ezekiel's Temple, you notice how we read that, after all those goings in and out and round about and through and up and down, at last the man led him by the way of the gate which is toward the east and toward the glory. The east is the sunrise, the new day, and it is by that way that the fulness of the glory comes in. The house, you see, stands right in the way of the coming glory. It is there with its face toward the sunrise, toward the glory. That is the type in Ezekiel, but we have many other passages.

"We should be unto the praise of his glory." That is the Church in Ephesians. But there is this passage in Hebrews.

"For yet a very little while,
He that cometh shall come, and shall not tarry.
But my righteous one shall live by faith . . .
Now faith is assurance of things hoped for, a conviction of things not seen."

Here, you see, is a standing by faith in the light of that glorious hope, that blessed hope, and knowing in the heart the assurance of that unseen glory. We are here as the Lord's house to be a present testimony to the coming day of glory. But that is not testimony in word, in doctrine; it is to be in life, in reality. But that can only be in a spiritual way, and therefore it can only be along the line of faith. We have to apprehend the day of the Lord, the day of glory, the coming of the Lord in glory ; we have to apprehend that in a spiritual way. There are a lot of people who are apprehending it in a prophetical way, but I do not always find that the study of prophecy results in glory. I find very often that it results in a good deal of death and confusion, and it is not all prophetical students who are living in the glory of the coming day. They are living in the belief of it, in the argument about it, but not in the glory of it. It is no mere doctrinal or mental apprehension of that great truth that will bring the glory of it into our lives, but a spiritual apprehension.

I used to study prophecy a good deal, and the book of the Revelation had a very prominent place in it. But the more I studied it, the more confused I got, the more difficulties I found. It did not get me through very far to glory. But then the Lord gave me a clue, and showed me the spiritual principles lying behind the book of the Revelation, and I was able to apprehend that book in a spiritual way. I do not mean that I spiritualized everything, but I was able to apprehend it in a spiritual way. The cloud was lifted and there was life.

Take this matter of the coming of the Lord ; and, of course, that is the coming of the Lord in glory, when He shall come in the clouds of glory, when He shall come to be glorified in His saints—the coming in by the east of the glory of the Lord. Have you noticed that in any time in the dispensation, when spiritual people have been gathered together, and in their gathering together have been speaking or singing of the coming of the Lord, how spontaneously the glory rises and comes in? Have you noticed that? Now, I do not believe that is merely psychological, and I do not believe it is because we are all thinking of ourselves, and of how great a day it will be when we are delivered from all our bonds. I believe rather this rising of glory is in spite of a very great deal. We have lived long enough, most of us, to know many people who believed fervently and said with emphasis that the Lord was coming in their lifetime and they would be raptured, and they have been in their graves for years. That is enough to turn you away from the whole subject and say, We have heard that before! It is enough to put you among those scoffers of whom Peter writes, who say, "Where is the promise of his coming? for, from the day that the fathers fell asleep, all things continue as they were from the beginning of the creation" (II Pet. iii. 4). You may take that attitude, if you like ; but it is in spite of all that that, when you contemplate the coming of the Lord, something gets the better of your mentality, your arguments, and all that bad history, and you find the glory rising. It is so, in spite of it all. Why is it? It was so at the beginning of the Church dispensation, and it has been so in every age : yet the Holy Spirit knew at the beginning that the Lord's coming would not be for a couple of thousand years, at any rate. But nevertheless there has been this spontaneous breaking out of real joy and glory at any moment when spiritual people have been dwelling upon the coming of the Lord. Why is it? Because the Holy Spirit does not live in time at all, He does not belong to time. The Holy Spirit is outside of time and He already has the end with Him and He is the Spirit of the end, and when we really get into the Spirit we are in the Holy Spirit's end. If we dwell in the mind—oh, this reasoning line of things!—out of the Spirit, there is no joy. But when we let go and we are in the Spirit, we find ourselves with the Holy Spirit right at the end. We are outside of time, we are in the glory already in foreshadowing. The Holy Spirit is timeless and you get outside of time and you have everything ; you have your finality, your fulness. Thus, when John was in the Spirit in the isle of Patmos, he got right through to the end of things very quickly, the thing which we in time have not reached yet. That is what I mean by apprehending this matter spiritually. Beware of apprehending prophecy as a mental thing. The Holy Spirit in you in a living way will bring you into the good of things. Thus by the Spirit to-day we should stand with the light of the glorious fulness of the day of the Lord. We should be here as a testimony, not to prophetic things, not to teaching or doctrine about the Second Advent and all the problems connected therewith, but to the spiritual meaning of that. What is it? Why, that is the end to which God has been working right through the centuries, the one thing upon which His heart is set, in which He has His satisfaction, His glory, His praise, His fulness, and the Holy Spirit is always there to make good something of that when we dwell upon it. He is there to be to us "the earnest of our inheritance," and to make us know it is a matter of faith, after all.

We do not always feel the glory of the coming of the Lord, we are not always living in the bright shining of that day, but "faith is the substance of things hoped for, the proving of things not seen," and when we let go our arguments and get into the Spirit, that is, get really into fellowship with the Holy Spirit, the weight of those arguments disappears, all the seeming contradictions in history go out. The glory of the Lord comes in by the gate which is toward the east.

"Yet a very little while,
He that cometh shall come, and shall not tarry.
But my righteous one shall live by faith."

The Lord then strengthen our faith and keep our hearts in faith.

But Ye Are
Come Unto
Mount Zion

CONTENTS

Chapter   Page

Note:
  The Scriptures used in this book are from various translations of the Bible.

Dear brothers and sisters in Christ:

Greetings in the Name of our Lord Jesus! Again we come to you, placing into your hands a series of messages given by T. Austin-Sparks. Again, we are sure that you will reap a great spiritual harvest from these messages shared at a Bible conference not so many years ago. We find them to be still fresh with the dew of the Spirit, and, surely, they are *"seed left over for planting."*

The reader should put himself in the place of one who is attending a Bible conference and read this volume from that vantage point. Also, it will be of great benefit to the reader, before beginning this book, to read Hebrews 1:1-2 and Hebrews 12:18-29.

The punctuation used in preserving these messages from tape was not used to adhere so much to the correctness of English grammar, but was used, we trust, to facilitate the spiritual message given: we were not so much thinking of literary accuracy as we were praying to the Lord to preserve and pass on the spiritual content of these meetings by the anointing of the Holy Spirit.

"Strong meat" was, and is, given in these sessions where *"Zion gathered."* We are sure there was much Holy Spirit conviction upon these words as they were shared amongst the Lord's people, for it is a message of strong words concerning the much-needed spiritual apprehension of Christ. There is much here to encourage, to invigorate, and to strengthen the Body of Christ as it walks in the truth: *"Ye have come to Mount Zion."* But, also, there is much *"shaking"* in these messages: *"the removing of those things . . . as of things that are made"*; and, as our brother said to the brethren at that conference then, so now we say to all who read:

"Be ready for a crisis."

Your brethren in Christ

Chapter One

The Crisis Of Our Times

We remember, O Lord, that it is written: "He spake, and it was done; He commanded, and it stood fast." By the Word of the Lord were the heavens, the earth, created. Our prayer, Lord, is that Thou would speak acts. That Thy Word may be Thine act. Not just words, Lord, but words of power—Divine fiat, by the Word something done. Make it like that, even now. In the Name of the Lord Jesus, Amen.

The matter that the Lord has laid on my heart for these first morning sessions is that of what has come to us, and what we have come to, by the coming of the Lord Jesus. For this present hour, I just want to lay down two fragments of Scripture upon which we shall move at present. The first is found in the Old Testament in the First Book of the Chronicles, chapter twelve at verse 32: *"And of the children of Issachar, which were men that had understanding of the times, to know what Israel ought to do."* The second is in the New Testament in the Letter to the Hebrews, chapter one at verses one and two: *"God, having of old time spoken unto the fathers in the prophets by divers portions and in divers manners, hath at the end of these days spoken unto us in His Son."* Knowledge of the times . . . at the end of these times . . . hath spoken in His Son . . . spoken "in Son":—SONWISE.

You will notice that these scriptures and their context are set in a time of crisis and change, very big crises, very significant change. In the Letter to the Hebrews, the reference to the end of certain times and the introduction of other times represents a tremendous crisis, what Dr. Campbell Morgan called The Crisis of the Christ. That is what is before us now: the crisis of the Christ, which is, the crisis of the dispensations.

Then the Hebrew Letter brings us to the crisis of our own time. It brings us not only to the great general movement from one regime to another, but also to the specific application of that movement to our own time. And as in the setting of the passage in Chronicles, so in this Letter to the Hebrews, the important thing is not just to know of a change of times, of regime, of Divine economy, but it is to have understanding of what the change is. I think we shall see that it is of immense conse-

5

quence not only to know that there are different dispensations, different economies in the Divine sovereignty, but it is vitally important for the Lord's people to know the nature of the times in which they live. I would venture to suggest to you, as far as God is concerned, that perhaps the most important thing, just now, is for the people of God to know the nature of the time in which they live, seeing that there is such a tremendous amount of confusion, and complications are immense and far-reaching just now in Christianity. Many, many people do not know where they are. Many do not know what is right, and what is not right; what is the truth, and what is not the truth, etc. And, I repeat, **the supremely important thing is to have knowledge,**—"*understanding of the times, to know what Israel ought to do*" now—to know what we as Christians ought to do now because of the peculiar and particular nature of what God is doing now. I think you will agree with me that is very vital.

In the Scriptures, throughout the Bible, we do have many crises, many movements through a crisis from one state, position, order, to another. I am not going to mention them, but you know that the Bible is marked throughout by reaching a point from which everything takes a new complexion, a point that represents a new phase of the movement in the going of God. The Bible is full of that sort of thing. God moving, moving by stages, and every stage marked by some crisis. When we use the word *crisis,* we mean we are brought face to face with something of tremendous significance which is going to govern the whole future and make all the difference in the future.

From the Divine side, these crises are onward movements: they are God moving on. From the human side, they are God moving back because things have deviated on the human side. Things have gone off the direct line of God and other things have come in which God never intended in His original pattern; and since there has been deviation, a crisis arises which has this twofold meaning: God is going on, but in order to go on He must bring back. He must take His people back to the point from which they departed. That is exactly where we are. God is going on, He is not giving up, He is not defeated, He is not having to revise His program: He is going on. But from the standpoint or side of His people, He is having to pull them back and say: "Look here, you have gone off the line, you have moved away from My intention, you have deviated, you must come back to the point from which you departed and pick things up again with Me. I am going on; if you want to go on, you must come back and rejoin Me at the point where you deviated."

I think it is perfectly clear that the two aspects of any crisis are always those; and the crisis therefore, very often, is one of leaving an entire regime (what I have called economy, order, development) leaving it in its entirety, leaving it behind and **moving with God in a new entirety, moving with God on new ground to what is wholly and originally, exactly, according to His Mind.** These are things involved in these crises. This is the method of God. I believe that the Lord wants to show us this week something of the present crisis in Christianity, and if that seems too objective, then let us simply say the Lord wants to show us the present crisis in your life and in mine in relation to His original thought and His full thought.

True Spiritual Discernment: A Knowing By Experience

Now we have to insert here that men never really learn anything theoretically. You are not going to learn anything by volumes of words being poured out upon you from this desk this week. Then, you may ask, "Why come here, why do you men talk to us?" No, you are not really going to learn anything by all this: I say, really learn. Man never really learns anything except by experience. Take that in, underscore it. God knows that, and that is why God is so practical. That is why God will take years and years, centuries, three or four thousand years, governed by this thing that men do not learn by what they are told: they only learn by experience. That is, they have got to have a history with God, under the hand of God, before they will learn anything.

Do you think you know something? How do you know it? How have you come to know it? By attending conferences?—No, there can be a terrible tragedy along that line. I know definitely of people who have had the fullest teaching for many years,—20, 30, 40 years—people could hardly have more teaching than they have had, and at the end they have jettisoned the whole thing, washed their hands of it. They knew it all. They said, "We know it all. We know all that. You can not tell us anymore than we know." So you may come here year after year and think you know. Well, how do you know? God knows that we really know nothing only by history, by experience. This sounds very elementary and simple, but we have got to get down to this: we are

7

coming to this point of spiritual understanding of the times, our times, and knowing *"what Israel ought to do."*

Now I ought to put an hour in, just here, on two Greek words in the New Testament. I took the trouble to go through the New Testament with these two Greek words; and I got a surprise, after a good many years of studying the New Testament, to find that I had sheets of paper full of references on these two words, both of which are translated into English as the word *"know."* Yet, these two Greek words are two entirely different words in two entirely different realms. One Greek word means "knowing by information." You know it, because you have been told. You have heard it, you have read it, and so you know that way. The other Greek word for *"know"* is an entirely different word which means, "you have a personal experience of that thing," and you know it because it has done something in you and become a part of you. It is your history, it is your experience. It is your life—it is you.

The New Testament can be divided by those two Greek words. For example, *"Know":—"This is life eternal, that they may know Thee,"* not by information but the word here is *"experience."*—Have an experience of Thee.—This is life, this is something very definite. I must not go on with that but just indicate it and point it out because our New Testament is built around these two words which are two very different kinds of knowledge. And here we are with Issachar who *"had understanding of . . . what Israel ought to do."*

Now we have said that the Bible is marked by time marks and that we are brought with our New Testament to a new time mark or crisis. And everything for you, for me, for all the Lord's people, is really going to depend upon whether we have this spiritual discernment, this understanding, this spiritual knowledge, this kind of knowledge of the second category of which I have referred—of what God is really doing now, what He is working at now; not in general, but in particular.

Oh, if only this week could bring us all to that kind of discernment, then this will be more than a Bible conference of words and teaching. It will have tremendous issues, which make for a crisis. And let me say at once, I hope you are here for a crisis; and I hope that you are prepared to be turned upside down and inside out, prepared to leave a whole regime if God says, "That is finished with," and to really embrace His present economy and commit yourselves to it. I hope that is the position in which you are, because you will be found out on that as we go on with this important matter of recognizing and understanding, especially and inclusively, of what happened, what really happened, **when the Son of God, Jesus Christ, entered history,** when He came into this world. I am convinced, dear friends, that very, very few Christians today understand what really happened when Jesus Christ came into this world, and that is what we are going to spend hours upon, trusting the Lord to give us the opening of our understanding.

Three Cycles (Phases) In Relation To Christ

You see, the coming of Jesus Christ into this world, into history, split history down the middle. The one side said, **"Finished,"** and the other side said, **"Beginning."** Great, immense divide was represented by the entering into history of Jesus Christ, and we have got to understand that divide.

There have been, of course, three cycles in relation to Christ. Firstly, there has been the historical. When I first came to the Lord and became interested in the things of Christ, it was the time when everything was being made of the historical Jesus. The Jesus of Palestine, the Jesus of Bethlehem, of Nazareth, of Capernaum, Jesus of Jerusalem, Jesus of the mount outside Jerusalem called Calvary, Jesus of Gethsemane, the Jesus of the three and a half years, or the thirty years,—the Jesus of history. Everyone was interested in that: that is what engaged us. There is nothing wrong, of course, with that; it is quite good. That was a phase, and it may be a phase still with some, but then there came a change, and we passed into what we might call the theological or doctrinal Christ. Much was learned about the Person of Christ, the virgin birth, the Deity, Godhead, and all of what is called the fundamentals of the faith of Jesus Christ—the theological and doctrinal Christ. And, my word, what a phase it has been. What a tremendous battleground the Person of Jesus Christ has been.

There is nothing wrong with this second phase. There is nothing wrong with being occupied with the Person, the Deity, the Eternal Sonship, that is all right, but you have to go on because this will not get you through. Your theology is not going to get you through when you move into a realm of such terrific spiritual conflict that your very faith will be struck at its roots. You may be shaken of all that you *"know"* in that way. It will not stand. The Lord's people are not going to get through the final crisis on theology, on Christian doctrine, even though it may be fundamental. They cannot get through on that alone.

Now, there are your two phases. They may run concurrently, or they may be more or less defined as periods. However, there is another one, a third one, which is the ultimate, which is the supreme. It is that phase that we are going to be occupied with this week. It is the spiritual phase. So, you can have the historical and you can have the theological without the spiritual; and though you may have all that, and not have the spiritual, you are not going to survive. You have not touched the real heart and core of the great divide, the great change that has taken place with the coming of Jesus Christ. It is the spiritual life of Christ that matters, not the historical. It is the spiritual understanding of Christ and not the theological that matters. But if you do not understand that as yet, stay with me, for we will be getting nearer to that as we go along.

The Spiritual Revelation Of Jesus Christ, Inwardly

Now these three phases are clearly recognized, and we have come to the last, the spiritual revelation of Jesus Christ inwardly by the Holy Spirit—*Supreme, Absolutely Essential, Indispensable*. As I said, God, when He moves (and He is moving now on this line if you can but discern it) is moving onward, but He is moving backward. And if you can get hold of that last thing that I have just said, you will see how true it is that God is moving back in order to move on.

What is the New Testament based upon? The historical life of Jesus? No. The theological life of Jesus? No. That is all there. That is what is foundational; however, the real root of Christianity, this new dispensation, crisis, and movement, the real root of Christianity is gathered into the words of the Apostle Paul, who so very much represents in himself, in his own experience, in his history with God, the nature of this whole dispensation; and in the simple but profound words, it is all gathered up: *"It pleased God,—it pleased God, . . . to reveal His Son in me."* This is something more than the Damascus Road objective experience. That was just the turning point in the great crisis. That was the impact upon him of a meaning which was to begin then and unfold through all the rest of his life. *"It pleased God, . . . to reveal His Son in me."* That is it. Not to me, in me.

What Paul later wrote was quoted here last night: *"That the God of our Lord Jesus Christ, the Father of glory, may give unto you a spirit of wisdom and revelation in the knowledge* (our second category word, but with a prefix: *in the full knowledge) of Him."* A *spirit* of *wisdom* and revelation in the full knowledge of Him, of Christ. **That is inward:** right deep down at the very source and center of our being, God has made us to see, and to see the significance of His Son, Jesus Christ.—Out of that, Christianity comes, true Christianity, and anything less than that is dangerous Christianity. Dangerous for the individual concerned and dangerous for the Church. This is what I mean by the spiritual crisis, the spiritual aspect, above and beyond and more than the historical and the theological or the doctrinal. **The spiritual: the revelation of Jesus Christ within.**

The Lord alone can do that. We all have to pray to the Father of Glory to do it. But it can be done, and it can be done here. It can be done so that we go away from this place saying, "I have seen. I have seen. I can never be the same. A whole regime is left behind, an entirely new order has come in for me. I am out of something, and I am in something else, and I have seen. I have seen Jesus Christ." This is the focal point, dear friends, of the message that I have to bring to you.

The Great Divide: The Cross

Now the Bible is divided into two main divisions, what we call the Old Testament and the New Testament; but, note, it is more than a division of books—Genesis to Malachi comprising so many books, one half of the Bible: then from Matthew to Revelation, so many books, and thus the Bible is divided into two. Oh, but it is much more than a division of books. It is this great divide, this spiritual divide.

The four Gospels,—what do they really mean? When you have stood back and asked yourself that question,—what do they represent? First of all, they introduce the Person Who Himself is the crisis and Who brings in and precipitates the crisis and changes the dispensation in its entirety. The Gospels have introduced the Person Who does that and Who is that: this is the crisis of the Christ.

But you notice, of course, that all the four Gospels, while differing in details of content, all four Gospels head straight, direct, up to the Cross. Every one of them has this characteristic in common, whatever

11

other differences there may be, they all have this in common, that they climax with the Cross. The Person of the crisis is introduced, and the crisis itself is the crisis of the Cross. **The Cross is the crisis of the change that has come in with the Person.** And this is what it amounts to: here is the Person, here is His earthly life and walk, work and teaching, but none of that can become of any value to you until the Cross has been planted over it all. You can have all there is about the historic Jesus and the theological Christ, but nothing will happen until all that is in those Gospels is brought right up to the Cross, and the Cross makes effective the crisis of the Person.

The result and the issue is that between the two divisions of the Bible, between the Old Testament and the New Testament, right there is the Cross. Right there you have got to put the Cross. Between Malachi and Matthew, so far as books are concerned (and I am not speaking of the chronological order of the Bible, but about the spiritual understanding of it), so far as books are concerned, you must put the Cross right there—because on the one side of the Cross, all that goes before and leads up to Malachi, all that has been from Genesis to Malachi, on that side of the Cross, to that side the Cross says: "No more, no more. No, finished! That is done with." And then from that point on, from Matthew to Revelation, to that side the Cross says what? "Yes, all things new!"

If I were to illustrate, I would draw a big cross and I would draw a thick line right down the center from the top of the Cross to the bottom of it, not only would I draw this line on the Cross but I would begin drawing the line above the Cross right down from heaven through the Cross to the devil, a wide line—no man's land—and then on one side of the Cross I would write one word, one big comprehensive word, **"NOT,"** as big as the Cross. Then on the other side of the Cross, the onward side, not the backward side, I would put one other word, **"BUT."**

"Not"—"But"

Now brethren, I have just said something that to experience can take up all your time for the rest of your life. Do you know those two words are two governing words throughout the whole of your New Testament; and if you would care to make a very close, analytical study of your New Testament in the light of this, underlining every occurrence

Not I But Christ.

where these two words are used together, you will have an immense, new comprehension (revelation) of the meaning of Christ and of the difference that He has made, of the great divide, and of what we are in.

The *"not"* and the *"but"* applies to everything. It is made to apply to the very beginning of Christian history in the individual. Open your Gospel by John. Where are you at once? *"Which were born, not of bloods, nor of the will of the flesh, nor of the will of man, but of God."* Here is your big *"Not"—"But"* at the very beginning, and if I went on to show you how this applies to everything in the New Testament [and we are going to come to it later on in some particulars] you would see the Cross, with its great divide and center looking backward over all that has been right up to that closed door, no way through. This is God's great *"NOT"*—ah, but in the resurrection, and remember resurrection is in the positive always, and in the resurrection *"BUT"* is in the positive.

Now *"neither"* is only another word for *"not"*: *"For in Christ Jesus neither circumcision availeth any thing, nor uncircumcision, but a new creature (creation)"*—**"Not-But,"** and so you could go on. It is just wonderful how those two words open up everything and give us an insight into what has come to us and what we have come into with the coming of Jesus Christ. And here is this great division—with the Cross there between the testaments, there at the end of Malachi [which is a tragic, tragic book of the failure of everything in the past] and at the beginning of Matthew [which is a book of hope, light, life, everything fresh, new]. With this division is the great *"BUT"* of a new order of things: it is the end of a system and the beginning of an entirely new one. The Cross of the Lord Jesus has written these two words over the whole history covered by the Bible. The Bible is intended to comprehend human history, and human history is comprehended in these two words: *"Not"—"But."*

Now there is something here that I must say, and I hope that it may be helpful. The Cross is a very practical thing. With God, the Cross is not the doctrine, or just the doctrine, of the way of salvation, the way of redemption. The Cross is not just the theology of the atonement, and all such doctrine, and it is certainly not just the historic thing represented by the crucifix. The Cross is an immensely practical thing with God, intended to make actual this divide; and although you may know all about the message of the Cross (or believe that you do), although you may be full of the teaching of the Cross, the real test of the knowledge that you have about the Cross is where this divide has been made in you, where the Cross has resulted in the leaving behind of one entire regime and system and order.

Oh, I know you say, "The Cross has meant that I have left the world and the things of the world." Oh, that is only nonsense to talk like that. You really do not know what you have got to leave behind. Nevertheless, you will learn under the hand of God what the Cross means about the elimination, the moving away, further and further away, from the old order. We are coming to that in Hebrews. We are going into this Letter to the Hebrews, and you will come to a phrase which you know: *"Let us therefore go forth to Him without the camp, bearing His reproach."* What does that mean to you?—*"without the camp."*

It takes a lot of time to learn what that means, and it means going through some literally terrific, devastating experiences of our soul life. This is the work of the Cross: it is a going out on the one side, a going out of an immensity, of one entire regime, but it is **"to Him."** Oh, it is to Him—that is another immensity, is it not? You see, the Cross is a tremendously practical thing, forcing this gap, this divide, wider and wider as we go on so that the fact is [like it or not like it] the fact is that as we move more and more in spiritual understanding and apprehension of the meaning of Christ, we find ourselves more and more alone, so far as many Christians are concerned, and certainly so far as the traditional system of Christianity is concerned.

Now to bring this preparatory introduction to a close, let me again come back to the starting point and say that progress in the life and purpose of God depends upon spiritual discernment [that with which this Letter to the Hebrews has to do in its entirety, remember what it says? —*"Let us . . ."*—that is one of the key words, key phrases, to the whole letter. *"Let us therefore go forth—let us leave, let us beware, let us go on unto perfection"].* What I am saying is that progress in the life and purpose of God, for the individual and for the Church, depends (and if you forget everything else, write this inside) depends upon spiritual discernment, this kind of spiritual knowledge and understanding as to the nature of this great change that has come in with the Lord Jesus.—DISCERNMENT—!

Knowledge [Spiritual Understanding] Of The Times

Now let us go back for a moment to our Old Testament passage in I Chronicles 12 and scan the chapter. It is a new movement, it is a crisis, a turning point. David is out there, outside the camp. He is in the wilderness, he is in his cave; and now there are coming to him men of many of the tribes, just nuclei, just a few, a kind of remnant of Israel, coming to him outside the camp. There in this chapter are described the various characteristics of these men, men of valour, men of courage, men of strength, great strength, men of ability to make war, men who are committed with all their might, for it says: *"These came with a perfect heart."*

Very good, and so there are all these coming ones, who are falling away to David, characterized by these things; and then right there in the midst of this are the men of Issachar who had knowledge of the times (understanding of the times) and knew what Israel ought to do. Right at the heart of this return movement, this new movement of God which is a recovery movement, right at the heart of it, there is put this contrasting, almost striking thing: *"men that had understanding of the times, to know what Israel ought to do."* And I venture to suggest that with all the driving force of these other men, with all their muscles, all their physical force, and all that side of things, but for these men of Issachar there would have been something lacking which might have spoiled the whole movement. I believe it is put there to show that with all that is being done (with all that is right and well-meaning) the thing that must be here right at the heart of everything is spiritual understanding, spiritual discernment, spiritual knowledge,—men who know what the significance of this time is, men who have knowledge of the times and what this means.

Oh, this is not just something happening that men are doing. No, this has a meaning—a deep, profound, Divine meaning; and these people have seen it. They have understanding as to the meaning of this present time; and because they have understanding, they know what Israel ought to do. Do you not feel that is important, very vital?! Well, what did the men of Issachar really see? What was it that they understood? What was it that they knew Israel ought to do? Pause and think. Look at the context again. Of course, it is historic in illustration <u>but spiritual in principle</u>, and the answer to that in this dispensation is the Letter to the

Hebrews. Where do you read it in your Letter to the Hebrews? *"God, having in time past (old times)* proceeded in this way, adopted this method [He is finished with those times] *hath at the end of such times and methods spoken in His Son, Whom He appointed Heir of all things."*

This brings us back to what Israel ought to do concerning David, and why they ought to do it. We have come to David. God's chosen, sovereignly chosen, God's elect, God's appointed, God's intended ruler, God's principle of heavenly authority amongst the Lord's people—David means all that. They knew that Israel ought to turn back to David and put David in the place for which he had been anointed of God.

Now that is simple, in language, but do not forget it represented something. You still have got Saul alive, you still have got the old regime of Saul. He is not dead yet, he has his forty years run and, my word, what a problem for Israel! God's man, God's anointed man is not in his place fully, he is on the way there; but this is God's way. Turn over to your Letter to the Hebrews and there you are! What is the movement, the final movement, the full movement, which embraces all the parts, the fragments, comprehends all and makes everything final?—**Fulness and finality** are the words to write over the Letter to the Hebrews: it is a Christ movement with spiritual understanding of what He is, Who He Is, what He represents in the universe of God—it is the spiritual apprehension of Christ.

Oh, the words sound so full, do they not? Perhaps familiarity robs them of their strength and point; but, dear friends, everything for Christianity, for destiny, depends now upon an adequate apprehension of the meaning of Jesus Christ in God's order of things. And this is going to be devastating to a whole system, and a Christian system, so called. This is just devastating for you, for me. It will be that for us. The thing is going to disintegrate; our Christianity may disintegrate. Perhaps you do not understand what I mean. Yes, there is going to be a big "No" of God written over a whole Christian system. And men, although they are not intelligent as to this, they do sense, strongly and growingly sense, that they have got to do something to keep Christianity intact. I believe that the whole ecumenical movement is a tremendous effort to save Christianity from collapsing. The whole World Council of Churches is to put Christianity on crutches and save its reputation. Men are doing this, making a tremendous effort, because there are those who are saying Christianity has had its day, it no longer means anything. And you may say that that is infidelity, that is apostasy, but, dear friends, do not make any mistake—if you are going on with God, you are going to come into spiritual experiences in your life with God where you will be tested on every point of your Christian life as to whether this is valid, as to whether this will stand up to the situation, as to whether this is going to get you through. Yes, on the things that you believe most strongly and think you know most fully, you are going to be tested. Do not make any mistake about it—the time may come in your life when you will be tempted to question the very deepest realities of your past conviction.

There are men and women in this world who are going through that now. I think of some of those who have spent long years in prison for the sake of Christ and I read what they wrote before, and I have to say, "I wonder if they believe that now? I wonder if they hold to that now? I wonder if that is getting them through now? That is a tremendous statement that they made about the all-sufficiency of Christ, and so on and so on, but I wonder if it is getting them through?" I believe they will come through because He is Lord, because the heart is right with Him; but, mark you, I am simply saying this—that this great question of the real, spiritual significance of our faith, of our Christianity, is going to be put sorely to the test. It is going to be found out then whether it is Christian tradition, Christian doctrine, Christian theology, the Christian system generally accepted, or **whether it is Christ!!** We are going to be stripped down to Christ, stripped down to the place where we say, "All I have left (after all my learning and teaching and Christian work) all I have left is the Lord Himself." But is that going to be a fatal position?—Not at all! You know about the old woman on the ship, do you not? In a tremendous storm, she looked at the captain and said, "Captain, are we going to be sunk? Is this the end?" The captain said, "You had better pray." And she said, "Oh! Has it come to that?" Yes, we will be wrecked on Christ and then we will be found out whether we are under the "*Not*" or under the "*But.*" Shall we pray . . .

Now, Lord, for Thee it is to interpret, explain and apply and give the understanding. Our reaction to it all is—this flesh cannot, this flesh cannot. We in ourselves cannot. We know it, but Thou art sufficient. Our hearts are open to Thee. Lord, our hearts, we trust, are truly toward Thee. Make use of this feeble ministry to give us interpretation of future experiences in Thy dealings with us, Thy strange ways. O Lord, open our eyes and give us spiritual understanding, we ask in the Name of Thy Son, Amen.

Chapter Two

A New Israel

Lord, not as a part of our program but from our very hearts we say, "Break Thou the bread of life to me." Thou art the Bread of Life. Give us of Thyself this morning. May there be a true ministration of Christ in this hour. Send Thy Spirit, Lord, in a new way to us. Open our eyes that we may see Thee. Lord, answer this prayer for Thine Own Name's Sake, Amen.

In the Letter to the Hebrews, at chapter one, let us again read verses one and part of two: *"God, having of old time spoken unto the fathers in the prophets by divers portions and in divers manners, hath at the end of these days spoken unto us in His Son, Whom He appointed Heir of all things. . . ."* And the peril running immediately alongside of our reading of those words is the peril of familiarity. What I mean is this, that after more than sixty years of being actively in ministry of the Word, therefore closely acquainted with the Scriptures, these words are more alive and more meaningful today than ever. So it ought to be. My trouble is that I have not long enough to live with these words and with this letter.

In a certain sense, you ought not to know your Bible. You ought, and we ought, to be coming to the Bible every time as though we did not know it, and it ought to be to us like that, something which we really, after all, do not know. I cannot convey to you my own sensing of this. I can only make a statement like that, as to how it ought to be. The trouble is, the difficulty is, to convey that sense of immensity, vitality, urgency that is present with me in this Letter to the Hebrews. It must come to you in that way and that is why we pray: *"Oh, send Thy Spirit, Lord, now unto me that He may touch mine eyes and make me see beyond the sacred page." Beyond the sacred page—that is where we have to see. We see the letter, we see the page, we see the words, we know them. They are so familiar, but it is something in the beyond, beyond the actual writing, that we have got to see. The Lord help us this morning.*

Now having repeated those words at the beginning of this letter, I trust that you have already grasped the significance of the introductory

19

words which are really a comprehending of the whole letter or the truth that is in this Letter to the Hebrews. I trust you have seen the two things that comprehend this letter. In times past, there have been fragments, pieces, portions, bits, aspects, but now all that and much more is gathered up together, is comprehended, is brought together in completeness. There are no more different portions, no more different times, no more different ways, but now there is one time, one way, one all "comprehensiveness." It is all here. Fulness is reached, and this is the other time, the subsequent time, the ultimate time of fulness, completeness.

So this Letter to the Hebrews, brings us **the ultimate fulness of all things in the Son**, not only comprehending, not only fulness, but finality. This is the ultimate, the end, there is nothing beyond this. It is the end of all God's speaking. God, Who did speak in those many different ways, forms, methods, has now spoken fully and finally, there is nothing beyond. We ought to be impressed with that.

I do not know what you are looking for, what you are expecting, what you are praying for, but God has given all that you could ever ask or pray for. It is present, it is now. He has no more revelation to give, only of what He has given. Revelation, now and henceforth, is not new truth, it is only light on The Truth.

Now I want you to go over to chapter twelve of this letter, just to pick out again our governing words. Remember what we said yesterday about the two all-inclusive, governing words which are running right through the New Testament? Chapter twelve, verse eighteen: *"For ye are not come. . . ."*—Then what? Verse twenty-two: *"But ye are come. . . ."* Not-But. Here in verses 18 through 21, you have a comprehending of all that has been. It is very comprehensive; and all that is ruled out, finalized, with this word *"not."* Then with verse twenty-two, there is the introduction of another great order of things, wonderful, beyond our fathoming.

I am not exaggerating, dear friends, when I say that we could spend a whole year on verses twenty-two and onward. The fulness and profundity is so great because it comprehends the Bible. It is this great divide between the *"not"* and the *"but"*; and as I said beginning yesterday, we are at this time concerned with what we have come to in the advent of Christ and His Cross. What we have come to, what we are.

Not - But.

I wonder if you will ask this simple question, "What are you?" I wonder what your answer or answers would be. Perhaps you would say, "Well, I am a child of God. Well, I am a Christian." Oh, the answers would be manifold. So now, this morning, as the Lord enables, I want to focus on what we are.

God's Intervention: A Divine Act

Here then in chapter twelve within these verses is the great, great divide between the *"Not"* and the *"But"* as concentrated in this one letter. Other letters are very far reaching, very great and comprehensive; but in this letter, the particular meaning is that all that lies on the two sides of the Cross is concentrated in this letter called the Letter to the Hebrews.

Now you will notice [and I am not dealing with the detail of these verses, only with the general statement], under the *not—"ye are not come to . . ."*—under that *"not,"* you have the constituting of the former Israel. You are taken to Sinai, and at Sinai the former Israel was constituted a nation. They were a people, a rabble, a multitude before, and a mixed multitude at that; but now here at Sinai, they are constituted the ancient Israel, the former Israel. They were Hebrews made into Israel. First Hebrews, Jews, now Israel as a nation. I know the name Israel goes back before that as to the person. It goes back to Jacob's new name and his family, but here they are constituted as a nation out from the nations, separate from the nations, distinct among the nations, a nation called collectively Israel.

This is something new in history, something new among the nations, something new in this world on this earth. It is a new beginning of God,—God's act, God's doing. I need only to take time to quote the Scriptures: *"I have chosen you,"* says the Lord. *"You are My people,"* implying, "You are the result of My action in history."

The first word in this Book of Hebrews is *"GOD,"* and that word always stands right at the head of every new movement of God. What does it say in Genesis? *"In the beginning God . . ."*—God in action at the beginning. It is God taking the initiative; and this people (Israel) is the result of Divine intervention in the history of this world with a Divine action, God's Own prerogative, wholly, completely, uniquely of Himself. God in creation, a new beginning, that is the Old.

Then you come to the New, and the New opens with the Gospel by John: *"In the beginning was the Word, and the Word was with God, and the Word was God."*—*"In the beginning God"*!—But this is another new movement. *"A new creation"* is here indicated, pinpointed, and it is described. *"In the beginning God created . . . man."*[1] But here in John a new humanity, mankind, is brought into view under a *"Not"* and a **"But."** *"Which were born, not of bloods, nor of the will of the flesh, nor of the will of man, but of God."*

"Not of bloods"? In the Greek text, *"bloods"* is in the plural. Why is it in the plural? All right, we will not assay to tackle our liberal theologians, but the Holy Spirit is always very exact and correct, and the Holy Spirit causes it to be put in a way that you almost overlook it, so that you are hardly struck by it, and He puts it this way, *"not of bloods,"* not of Joseph and Mary. That is the mingling of bloods, is it not?! That is the ordinary, natural mankind, the mingling of bloods, two sexes. *"Not of bloods"*—this is a direct application to the virgin birth. Not of all that (two sexes), *"but of God"*!

As the people of God, we are not born that way. You are never born a Christian. You are never born naturally a child of God. You never inherit Divine life by natural birth. Well, that goes without saying, but we are *"born of God."* We are God's act! It is God's act to produce a new mankind, a new and different humanity never produced by the will of man, never produced along natural lines at all, *"but of God"* a new humanity, a spiritual race. Not a natural race at all, but a spiritual race.

So then, what is the implication both of this letter, comprehensively, and of the New Testament, as a whole. What is it?—a new Israel, that is what this letter is saying to Hebrews: not those Hebrews of history, a new Israel has come in.

I think you ought to note, if you have not, it is a very simple thing, of course, everybody should be familiar with it; but I am very glad to notice that in a late translation and interpretation of the Bible called The Amplified, I am very glad and happy to note that wherever the name *"Christ"* is mentioned in the New Testament, this Amplified links the name and word *"Christ"* with *"Messiah."* It puts them together: they are one because, as you know, *"Messiah"* is the Hebrew of which *"Christ"* is

---

[1] Genesis 1:1,26

only the Greek, meaning the same, *"The Lord's Anointed."* Keep that in mind. The Christ is the Messiah. The Messiah in the history of Hebrew mentality, concept and expectation, the Messiah of the old Israel is the Christ of a new Israel. One name, same name, same meaning, but carried over now; and so wherever you read the word *"Christ"* in your New Testament, do not forget the hyphen, say *"Christ-Messiah."*

It is most impressive as you read that version: every time you come on the mention of *"Christ"* and then it says, *"Messiah."* Do you see the meaning? Do you see the significance? Do you see what this is driving at? It is a new Israel because this is, shall we say, a "new" Messiah? Is that quite correct? It is the One Messiah, it is the old Messiah; and here this letter is saying that all of the old Israel's hopes, expectations, conceptions, of their coming Messiah—all they ever had associated with that name of the Coming Messiah, is taken up in Christ, comprehended in Christ. He comprehends and fulfills it and goes beyond their conception; and, as we shall see, beyond their acceptance.

Well, it is a new Israel, not that one of their limited, narrow, exclusive conception, mentality, or even expectations. It is much, much greater and much bigger than all that which the old Israel ever hoped for, looked for, prayed for, expected. It is much bigger indeed, and we will come back to that in a minute. It is a new Israel beginning with the [and I must use the word, though it is not quite right] "new" Messiah, the Christ, the "Christos," the Anointed One.

Now this, as we have said, is a new act of God. A new act of God is *the Messiah, the Christ,* and a new act of God is the new Israel; and there are two governing, dominating features and factors in this new Israel as the act of God. There are two aspects. One is *the Resurrection of Christ,* God's act, God's unique act, for the Resurrection is God's specific, peculiar act in history. It is the act of God. God raised Him! God raised Him! This is not resuscitation: this is resurrection; and, of course, God saw to it that there was no doubt whatsoever that He died, that He was dead. So far as He, as a man, was concerned, He was dead and buried. And if you are in the grave for three days and three nights, you have pretty good ground to conclude that that person is dead. All right! No resuscitation, no breathilizing, no! nothing of that. He is dead. He died, and now only God . . . only God and the intervention of God can make for anything further. **He is God's Act, in His Resurrection.**

But then, the other aspect of this act of God is Pentecost. Pentecost was God's act. God did it! It is the intervention of God by the Third Person of the Trinity, the intervention of God in history to bring as from death this new race. I do wish that all people who are so interested in this word "Pentecost" would recognize really what Pentecost was. They limit it to this and that and something else. The Lord save us from this restricted conception. **Pentecost is the act of God in bringing to birth a new, altogether new, humanity.** It is God producing a new kind of humanity, unique, different. It is God's act! Resurrection and Pentecost are one thing as God's act, firstly in the One Son and then in the sons to be. That is all very simple I know, but I am working on toward my object.

The Growing Light:—
Increasing Understanding Of This New Dispensation

Now then, you come back to your New Testament, and especially to begin with the Book of the Acts; and what have you in the Book of the Acts? The gradual dawning upon the apostles (yes, upon the apostles) and then upon the believers of what has happened, of what the meaning of Christ was. It is dawning, it is the faint rays seemingly of a new day just coming up over the horizon and shooting across the sky, and in their consciousness there is something happening. Notice, in the beginning, they still continue to go up to the temple, in the ordinances of the temple, the ritual of the temple, the time of prayer at the temple. They are still going up, but something is happening, something is spreading over their sky, and that fades out. It fades out. They are losing that attachment. They are losing that mentality. They are meeting in homes, they are meeting wherever they can: they are not meeting in the temple any longer. No, it is not a sudden thing that happened so that they can make a sudden break. I say it is the dawning of the meaning of a new day. It is so real, so clear; they do not put it into any system of teaching and say, "You must come out of that denomination. You must come out of that system. You must leave that order of things." No, it is just happening. Something is happening, and they are finding themselves out. And note this that I am going to say: first of all, it is not a physical separation. No, first of all, it is an inward spiritual separation. I will put it this way, they find themselves out before they are out. They find that they no longer belong. No one has ever told them that they must leave their denomination, their church, their mission, their organization. No, something has happened inside.

You know, in the old creation, God commenced from the outside: in the new, always from the inside, and in this spiritual dispensation it is that you just find yourself somewhere, perhaps where you never intended to be. Peter never intended to be in the house of Cornelius. He quarreled and argued with the Lord about the house of Cornelius, "No, Lord, not so." All right, Peter, what has happened to you? Do you not know what has happened to you? You are going to know, and Peter does come to know. He will write later on about the spiritual house of God. Do you see what I mean? Something has dawned, has broken. It is a new day, and the dawn has come in, and the light is growing, growing. That is the first movement.

Dear friends, do take hold of this. This is an organic thing. It is a movement of life within. It is not legal, "Ye must" or "Ye must not."—"You must leave this and leave that in order to come to God's fulness." It is not that at all. I say, stay there until you cannot for your very life's sake, for your very walk with God, for your very knowledge of the Holy Spirit within. Stay, stay. "Come out-ism" is a dangerous thing. That is not how it was. It was from the inside. It is the way of the Holy Spirit, the initiative of God, the act of God, the dawning of a new awareness that "Something is happening to me because it is happening in me." I know what that means. I have had crises like that. I have had crises like that when I knew that something had happened to create a divide, and "Now, Lord, what am I to do? If I take action, look what will happen." And so I stuck and on a false pretext went on. At the end of some months, I found myself like this—I was not in it. "No, that is not where I am finding the Lord. That is not where life is," and I have gone back to the Lord and I have said, "Lord, what am I to do?" He said, "So many months ago, I took you out in spirit. Now perhaps you will have to follow in body." Oh, do not put a teaching on that. Do not take hold of that and crystallize it into a doctrine. **It is a spiritual movement because this is a spiritual dispensation**.

That commenced, as I have said, at the beginning of the Book of the Acts, and before you are through with that book, what will you find? You will find that the light has been growing and growing; and you will find in the letters that are compassed by that book the growing revelation of what? The growing revelation of what has happened, of what the meaning of the resurrection of Christ and the advent of the Holy Spirit really meant. It is a growing revelation not of some new thing, as a thing, but of what was at the beginning, at the root of things.

So God is moving (so to speak) backward, in order to move onward; and you have this growing revelation under these two words, *"Not-But."* —This is an inward thing: *"Not-But."* The Day is moving on. It will come to its glorious consummation when what happened at the beginning is found in the consummation of the *"New Jerusalem, coming down from above"*—the sum of this new thing that happened with the coming of the Lord Jesus. And we will be coming back to that in Hebrews later on. But you are marking the way, the growing light, transforming the mentality.

Oh, I have the New Testament, all of it, in mind as I am speaking. The growing Light—increasing the understanding of what this new dispensation means: the light within growing. You will have many, many exact statements in the growing light which has grown from the day when Paul first had Christ revealed in him. Paul did not have it all at once. As he says, it was "the growing light." It was growing all the time, and he will say presently: *"The Jerusalem which is beneath is in bondage. Cast out the bondwoman."* Not that Jerusalem, *"but the Jerusalem which is above is our mother."* You see the language and what it means?!

Remember what the Letter to the Galatians is about? Is it not along this line of contrast between the *"not"* and the *"but"*: *"For in Christ Jesus neither circumcision availeth anything, nor uncircumcision, but a new creation."* And is it not impressive that right at the end of that letter, in Galatians 6:16, Paul uses this significant phrase: *"the Israel of God,"* the whole Israel of God, the new Israel? Yes, and that throws light upon the whole letter. You see, one Israel is gone, the old Israel is gone. That is the argument of the letter, and that is why Paul got into such trouble. That is why this letter is such a battleground. That Israel no more, but now another with its Jerusalem headquarters above, its birthplace above, a new Israel entirely. Dear friends, this is a very vital point in our consideration, or in what the Lord is trying to say to us—we must recognize the new dimensions of God in this that has now come in on the *"But"* side.

What was the tragedy of the old Israel? Of course, the tragedy of the old Israel, finally, is their dismissal. Their dismissal: *"The kingdom of God shall be taken away from you, and shall be given to a nation bringing forth the fruits thereof.*" That happened! and it stands today. The kingdom of heaven taken away—not for that Israel, but for another! The tragedy of Israel is that they are dismissed from the dispensation, or the dispensational movement of God. This has lasted for two thousand years. How many more years we do not know, probably, not so long, but you leave that alone.

Here I am going to upset a lot of you: you leave Israel alone for the time being. You will only get into terrible confusion if you get down on this earth with an earth touch in these things. Some of us have lived through things,—we remember the Kaiser (forgive me, that is not an attack upon any nation or people) but we do remember him going to Jerusalem and having a new door broken into the wall of Jerusalem so that he never went in through any of the old gates of that city. No, but because of who he thought he was, a new gate must be broken in the wall for him. And some people fitted that into prophecy and said, "Therefore, the Kaiser is . . . the Messiah!?" All right, was he? And when General Allenby entered Jerusalem and brought the Turkish rule to an end, the prophetic school laid hold of it, brought it down to earth and said, "The end of the time of the Gentiles has come." How long ago was that? Was it the end? And then there was a dear man of God who got caught up in this kind of thing and went from Belgium to Rome to see Mussolini to say to him, "You are the last Cæsar to reconstitute the Roman Empire." Whereupon Mussolini had a great statue made of himself as the last Cæsar and put a great relief map of the revived Roman Empire with ten kingdoms behind his statue. The last Cæsar of the revived Roman Empire? Need we say anymore? You see, you go on like that and it leads to confusion if you come down onto this earth. Leave it alone and see what God is doing, and God is doing a spiritual thing, not a temporal thing.

I could take an hour to enlarge upon that last phrase, "not a temporal thing." Do you see, in the sovereign activities of God, that now He is confounding and confusing and breaking down all temporal representations of His heavenly kingdom?! Men are trying to set up local churches after New Testament order. You have never had more confusion in local churches than you have today. They are trying to set up things, constitute things, Christian movements, Christian institutions, Christian organizations, and they are all in confusion and do not know what to do

No Breath No Life Transform
what is God Breathing on? - Always on humans.
Where is God's Breath Blowing on your heart?
is it just a Location on Earth
What is This Rushing wind
"   "   "   Tongue of fire.

with one another. You may think that is an exaggeration, but you see what I mean?—God is breathing upon every temporal representation in order to have a spiritual expression of Christ!! That is the heart of what we are saying, and that is what is here.

Now I was saying, we must recognize the spiritual dimensions of this that has come in with Christ and this into which we have come. The spiritual dimensions are diverted from Israel's tragedy, because Israel's tragedy is that of being set aside in this dispensation. But why? Have you ever wondered why Israel has been set aside? The answer is in one word—exclusive-ism. "We are the people. Truth begins and ends with us. You will never be able to get anywhere with God if you are not circumcised. Except ye be circumcised, ye cannot be saved. The nations are dogs, are dirt. [Poor Jonah, poor Jonah was caught in this.] We are the people. We are the beginning and the end of all God's Word. You have got to come on to our ground, be on our ground, or you are out." Dear friends, you never will be on God's ground if you do not come up out of that.

Exclusive-ism—God never meant that when He took Israel out of the nations, made them a distinct people, constituted them His Own peculiar people. He never meant that. He only meant to plant them in the nations to show the nations what a God He is, WHAT A GREAT GOD HE IS; and this startled and stunned Jonah that God could ever think in mercy upon anybody outside of Israel, that God could ever think in mercy upon Nineveh.

And so you have this exclusive-ism all the way through, and that is the trouble in the New Testament with the Lord Jesus: it is the exclusive-ism of Judaism, that is the battleground. The battle in the life of the Apostle Paul was that. He was hammering at this brick wall of Jewish exclusive-ism, and all his sufferings are because of that.

This new Israel is so much greater than the old because Christ, this Messiah, is so much greater than their conception of a Messiah. We have got to recognize the immense dimensions of the new Israel and resist exclusive-ism where Christ is concerned, as we would resist a plague. I am not talking about fundamental truths and the personality of Christ; I am talking about the greatness of this One Who is introduced in Hebrews: *"God, . . . hath at the end of these days spoken in His Son, Whom He appointed Heir of . . ."* an exclusive party?—No, *"of all things."* That is Paul's great word all the way through: *"all things, . . . all things,*

. . . *all things,"* and in the end, *"to sum up all things in Christ."* And if I need to safeguard, I am not talking about universalism. I am talking about God's ultimate realm and sphere where it **will be nothing but Christ**. The rest will be outside altogether; wherever that outside is, it will be outside and not inside. *"For without . . ."*—that is the last word of Revelation, *"For without are the dogs,* (and so on), *and everyone loving and making a lie."* That is false, that is out, that is gone.

The Meaning of Sonship: Superior Is Christ

Note

Now, what is the governing concept here in this letter right at the beginning? It is that God hath spoken at the end of these times *"in Son."* There is no article—*"in Son."* What is the meaning of Son or sonship?—**Always fulness. Always fulness**! The fulness of the Father is in the Son, Divinely conceived. The Son is the fulness of the Father: the Firstborn is the fulness and takes up all that is of and in the Father. Fulness! Then, as we have said, **sonship is finality, finality**; and then as to this letter, as to the whole revelation of sonship as here revealed, explained through this letter, and in the first chapters particularly, **superiority**! Using that word in its right sense, superiority. Do you notice the superiority of this Son, *"appointed Heir of all things"?* Do you also notice the catalogue here of things?

SUPERIOR to Moses. Superior to Joshua. If Joshua had brought them into the rest, there would be no more: he did not, therefore, he never reached finality. This One, this Son, superior to Moses, superior to Joshua.

SUPERIOR to angels. To angels? Yes, superior to angels, and think of the angelic ministries right through the Bible, their ministries, visitations, deliverances, activities. One angel in one night by a breath of his nostrils wiping out a whole, mighty army that was besieging Jerusalem, one angel. Think of all that was mediated by angels. This letter is arguing about the angels who ministered the old covenant. Yes, this Son is superior to angels.

SUPERIOR to Aaron and all his system and economy of priesthood. All that system comes under the *"not."* The tabernacle that was. This letter says there was a tabernacle. Past tense. There was a tabernacle and there was a Holy of Holies and there was a Holy Place. Superior is Christ to all that, and what a place it had.

SUPERIOR to the old covenant, and this letter deals with the old covenant and *"the days come,"* quoting Jeremiah 31:31, *". . . the days come, saith the LORD, that I will make a new covenant."* This letter has a lot to say about the new covenant.

SUPERIOR to all the sacrifices, millions upon millions of sacrifices slain through the generations, and the river and ocean of blood of those sacrifices immeasurable, covering centuries. How vast! One Sacrifice only, One Shedding of Blood only, *Superior* to the whole lot, Superior to the hundreds of years of sacrifices and blood shedding, and this One Single Sacrifice, Shedding of Blood, **Superior to the whole lot.**

NOT—BUT. This is what we have come to, and this is the substance of the Letter to the Hebrews. How great then is sonship in Christ! How much vaster than any traditional or historical expression, representation, system, order, economy.—This is what we have come to in Christ!

The Quest of Right Standing With God

Now I must close somewhere, but first let me ask: what is the consummate issue of all this? Can we bring all that we have said, and all that can be said, and could be said down to one, inclusive, comprehensive issue? We can, and although I do not know about you (you may have doubts as I have about some translations, new translations of the New Testament), but I do thank God for this Amplified. I do, because at this very point it has helped.

You see, I have studied theology. I have studied Christian doctrine. I know the doctrines of grace. I know the Letter to the Romans. I think I do: at any rate, I am fairly well-acquainted with what is there and of what the theologians and the doctrinaires have said about it. And when you mention the Letter to the Romans, of course, Luther and all the rest spring into view with their phrase *"justified by faith,"* —*"righteousness . . . by faith."* Oh, I tell you, friends, theology strikes me cold. It may not you. It may mean more to you, but to me as one who has had to deal with all this theology and doctrine and system of Christianity in its doctrines, and so on, it is awfully wearisome. Theology is a very wearisome thing, you know, (deadly thing, I think) but here this Amplified version has come to my rescue.

When I heard and read the word *"righteousness,"* what did it mean? Well, in the Old Testament, the symbol of righteousness is brass. Brass? Oh, how hard is brass, how cold is brass, I am not interested in "brass." Are you following what I mean? And that is what that word came to mean to me, even in the New Testament. Oh, a glorious teaching, but I am not talking about the teaching, I am talking about the phraseology, the terminology. What is it that is represented there? Now here my Amplified version has rescued me. Oh, I am basking in the sunlight of this, every day now rejoicing in this. What does it say? Wherever that word *"righteousness"* or *"justified"* occurs in the Amplified New Testament, you have: *"Right standing with God."—"Right standing with God."* Dismiss your theology. That is it.

Right standing with God has been the quest of humanity from the beginning. It does not matter where you go in the darkest heathenism, amongst the most ignorant, unenlightened realms of humanity, right through all the strata, the one thing, whether man will put it into words or not, whether it is in his phraseology or vocabulary, the one thing deep down in every human creature is to be in right standing with God. All these heathen rites, sacrifices, rituals, after all, they are trying to find a place of right standing with, well, they say "God," even though they have no right conception of Who God is or what God is. *"Whom therefore ye ignorantly worship,"* said Paul, *"Him (THE UNKNOWN GOD), declare I unto you."*

I remember very early in my Christian life I tackled a monumental book, Professor Edward Caird's History of Religion and the Greek Philosophists. [Do not tackle that, I nearly "spun round."] But in this magnum opus, Caird concentrated it all into one statement: "There is not a human being on this earth, of any race whatever, who does not have a consciousness of standing in relation to some supreme object of worship whom he calls god." Is that true? Of course it is. Every person has a consciousness of standing in relation to a supreme object of reverence, and he calls that object "god." He does not know anything about that object, but he just calls it god. Now then, here we are, the quest of humanity all through history, whether or not man has greater or lesser enlightenment and understanding, whether man has little, none, or much enlightenment and understanding, the quest within is to be on good terms with this object called God, to be in right standing with God.

Now we ought to start all over again with the beginning of Hebrews. Here is the One, the Son, and the great thing about this Son, the glorious thing about this Son is that **He is in right standing with God**. All this other in the past was an attempt to get in right standing with God, and it never did, it was a failure. But here is the Son, first of all, inclusively, comprehensively, the Beloved of the Father, the Beloved Son. *"My Beloved Son."* Dear ones, could you have terms that more gloriously express right standing with God?! Think on that. Dwell on that. And then the letter goes on to say, *"bringing many sons to glory"*; and all the rest of the letter, which we leave now, is the way of right standing with God in the Son.

Glorious letter! How great! comprehensive! wonderful! this letter is, and that is only the fringe of it. We will get more into it later if the Lord wills, but I think you have really got enough for the time being. The Lord help us, we pray . . .

Oh, send Thy Spirit, Lord, now unto me, unto each one, that He may touch our eyes, make us see, make us see. Oh Lord, that the result of this hour in Thy Word would be, might be, that this people will really be able to say, not mentally but in the heart, "I have seen the Lord, I have in some new, more wonderful way seen God's Son, seen what God is doing," and that we are able, Lord, to understand now what we are—God's new and final Israel. Teach us more of what that means, but set Thy seal upon this time.

Now, Lord, there is a little interval, and immediately when this is closed now, these people are going to turn and talk about all sorts of things. Save us, Lord: the whole value of this can go in five minutes if we are not very watchful in setting a seal against our lips, having the door of our heart kept. Lord, help us for we are not here just for meetings and messages: we are here for life crises. You precipitate them, Lord, for Thy Name's Sake, Amen.

Chapter Three

" Ye Are Come Unto Mount Zion "

While we wait upon Thee [on Thee, Lord, we wait] and while
we do need Thee to bless us and ask Thee to bless us while we wait
on Thee, we would rise even higher and say, Lord, satisfy Thyself.
Get to Thyself the reward of Thy sufferings, the travail of Thy soul.
Lord, find Thine Own Satisfaction. Ours will, we know, follow. We
shall not lose anything if the Lord gets what He wants. And so,
may we find our blessing in Thy Blessing, for Thy Name's Sake,
Amen.

The Letter to the Hebrews; and we are this morning coming to the
concentration of the whole letter in one section. In chapter twelve, you
will note that this concentration of the whole letter in this section is
governed by the two words, *"NOT—BUT."* Verse eighteen:

For ye are not come unto a mount that might be touched,
and that burned with fire, and unto blackness, and
darkness, and tempest, and the sound of a trumpet, and the
voice of words; which voice they that heard entreated that
no word more should be spoken unto them; for they could
not endure that which was enjoined, if even a beast touch
the mountain, it shall be stoned; and so fearful was the
appearance, that Moses said, I exceedingly fear and quake:

BUT ye are come unto Mount Zion, and unto the city of the
living God, the heavenly Jerusalem, and to innumerable
hosts of angels, to the general assembly and church of the
firstborn who are enrolled in heaven, and to God the Judge
of all, and to the spirits of just men made perfect, and to
Jesus the Mediator of a new covenant, and to the blood of
sprinkling that speaketh better things than that of Abel. See
that ye refuse not Him that speaketh.

Not—But. We shall not dwell upon the various details gathered
under the *"not."* We will simply say that this does represent a

tremendous change over from one whole system of Divine activity and method in the past which is, or was, of the nature of the tangible, the sentient, the palpable—what you could see with your natural eyes and hear with your natural ears and touch with your hands and register by all your natural senses of soul and body. That comprehends the past system, and over it is written "Not"--not any more. That kind of thing is left behind. And, mark you, dear friends, it is because that has been overlooked (or not recognized) that Christianity is in the poor state that it is in today, for Christianity is built very largely upon this "not." You will see that more, perhaps, as we go on the positive side. But register that, register what you are not come to. Take it clause by clause in its significance. Take each clause with its significance and see what we are not come to. We are not come to a system that can be appropriated and known by natural senses. That is very comprehensive, touches a very great deal, that is finished. *The Cross* has cut in between that and this **"but we are come."**

Now I want to be very implicit and careful. Did they really come to Sinai? You see the description? The Holy Spirit through the writer is making it very, very definite and positive and emphatic that this was something very real—so real that even Moses, who had such access to God, such fellowship with God, with whom God did speak Face to face as a man to his friend, this man said: *"I exceedingly fear and quake."* Was that real? Was that imaginary? Was that just abstract? No, this thing was very real. People cried out, "Stop, we cannot bear this. We cannot endure this." Very real! That is what they came to. If you had been there, no doubt, you would have said, "There is no imaginary thing here. This is something terrific." *"But we are come,"* and do you mean to say that the *"but"* is less real than the *"not"*? Do you mean to say that this that we are come to is abstract, while that was concrete? Oh, no, I am sure that this is even more real, after its own kind, in its own realm; and, dear friends, that is the point upon which we must focus everything, **the reality of what we are come to.**

When you go on and break this all up into its details, if you are in your own senses, senses of mind and soul, you are just completely baffled. It seems so idealistic or imaginary, so ethereal, so unreal. See, to the natural, the spiritual is unreal. To the natural man, the man of soul, what is essentially and intrinsically spiritual is unreal. Their reaction is "Oh, let us be practical, let us come down to earth, let us get out of the clouds and get our feet solidly on the terra firma, let us get down to things that are more real." That is the reaction of the natural man to the spiritual. But to the spiritual man, spiritual things are far more real than the tangible. And this that we are come to, to say the very least, is as real as what they came to at Sinai, even though after a different order.

Zion: The Consummation Of Everything

Now I want you to note the tense of the verb, because it is very important to get the tense: *"we are come to Mount Zion."* Not we are coming, not we are going, not we shall then arrive at Zion. No, *"we are, we are come. "* I know you will go on singing, "We Are Marching Upward To Zion. " We know what you mean, but we are not marching upward to Zion. The Word says: *"But ye are come to Zion,"* present tense. **We are supposed to be at Zion now.** Have you got that? There is here, of course, a contrast between Sinai and Zion, but it is not only contrast here, but note, in keeping with what I have just said, it is more than contrast, it is consummation!

This Zion was on the horizon for Israel right at the beginning. I think it is an impressive and amazing thing that you find the people through the Red Sea and on the far side; and then you look at Exodus 15 and find them on the far side and you have this, right there, before ever they had marched into the wilderness and on to the land [or got anywhere other than on the other side of the Red Sea] you have this: *"Thou wilt bring them in, and plant them in the mountain of Thine inheritance, the place, O LORD, which Thou hast made for Thee to dwell in, the Sanctuary, O LORD, which Thy hands have established."* Right at the beginning Zion is in view, as the end, the consummation of their journeyings and their experiences. During the next forty years? Ah, yes, and many more. Zion is on the horizon from the beginning. Zion is not the beginning, Zion is the consummation of everything.

This is the Letter to the Hebrews. In old times, they were on the journey, stage by stage, phase by phase, step by step. You remember that chapter which is just full, smothered, with that word in Numbers, "and they journeyed and they journeyed and they journeyed." I think it is forty times in one chapter, "and they journeyed." This is "the old times." The Letter to the Hebrews says, "We have arrived, we have arrived." How? Because all the bits and pieces, phases and stages, steps and movements, have come to their consummation in Jesus Christ. We have arrived, we are come to the end of all God's movements in His Son. He **is the consummation of all!**

Zion: The Perfected Work Of The Lord Jesus Christ

Now then, still this word *"Zion,"* which it says we are come to, remains a bit abstract so far as our mentality is concerned. We must, therefore, get down to see what this Zion is that we have come to. We have said Zion is consummation, comprehension, or comprehensiveness, but what is it? What makes it up? What is the constitution of Zion as God's end?

[1] ZION: A PEOPLE IN THE GOOD OF THE COMPLETE AND PERFECT WORK OF CHRIST

First of all, we say Zion is an inclusive and comprehensive term; in other words, we are come to the all-inclusive and all-comprehending thought and intention of God when we have come into the Lord Jesus. We may have to grow in our apprehension and understanding of what we have come to, but God has nothing whatever to add to what we have come to. We have got it all! In Christ, we have all! God has reached His end in His Son, finished His New Creation in His Son, and entered into His rest. So the letter here says, *"We who have believed do enter into His rest."* It is a comprehensive term, Zion—it is coming into all that God has placed in His Son for us. Christ is the sum total of all God's work over which is written: *"It is finished."* That does not mean just come to an end, it means **it is all completed,** it is all completed, **it is all perfect!**

You know the formula when the priests brought the sacrifice for the atonement and placed their hands upon the head of the sacrifice, they uttered a formula which in the Greek means, "It is perfect." They had gone with their trained eye over that sacrifice, turning up every hair to see if there was one of another color, any minute point of contradiction and inconsistency, through and through, opening its mouth, examining its teeth, every part gone through the trained eye of the meticulous priest; and when he finished his examination, and when the sacrifice had been put up for ten days under that scrutiny to see if there would be any development whatever of an inconsistent, imperfect element—at the end, he brought it forth and put his hands on it and pronounced: "It is perfect." That is the Letter to the Hebrews. By one offering. forever He has perfected, made complete; and when Jesus cried, *"IT IS FINISHED,"* it was the cry of the verdict of an Offering Perfect, without spot or blemish, to God. *IT IS PERFECT. IT IS COMPLETE.* His work and His Person are in right standing with God.

The sum of all God's work is represented in the symbolic name, *"Zion."* But Zion is seen to be not only Christ Personal, but a corporate thing. It is the people of Zion, as well as Zion—the people of Zion, a corporate thing; and Zion then is a people who are in the good of the complete and perfect work of Christ, a people who are the vessel of that work of the Lord which is complete.

Zion? It is so easy to say things like this, and this is Bible teaching, perhaps, you might say, good Bible teaching; but. oh, my friends, we have got to see before we get through this week that it is not just as simple as that. And you will discover almost every day of your life that this position of standing in and being in the good of the finality of Christ's work is not a simple matter—it is challenged, up hill and down dale, all the way along, that you should be moved, we should be moved, from this position of the perfected work of the Lord Jesus. We are come to something perfect, and we should be the people embodying that perfect work of the Lord Jesus! I do not mean that we are perfect, but His work is perfect; and He Who is perfect is with us and in us. The time will come when that perfection will be manifested. I think that is a very wonderful fragment in Thessalonians: *"When He shall come to be glorified in His saints, and to be marvelled at in all them that believed"* —marvelled at!—And I suppose we shall marvel more than anyone else. Well, that is Zion. It is Christ and Christ collective, Christ corporate, the foundation of everything. His perfect work as His perfect Person—that is Zion!

[2] ZION: THE SUPREME VICTORY OF THE LORD

Number two: Now, of course, I am keeping very close to the background, the symbolic and typical background, of the Old Testament because while the things of the Old Testament have gone, the meaning and the spiritual principles are eternal so that the spiritual meaning and principle of Zion is taken over and applied here. That is why the very name, Zion, is taken out of the Old Testament and brought here into the New: so that the next thing about **Zion is that it is the very symbol of His absolute victory.**

Do you remember the beginning of Zion? After they had brought David back from his exile and made him king, the Jebusites occupied this site and they sneered at David from Zion and said, *"Thou shall not come in hither"*; and they fortified it with the blind and the lame and said, "These are enough to keep you out of here. This is an impregnable stronghold, so much so that the weakest can hold it, save it. If the weakest, the blind, and the lame can do it, well, of course, it goes without saying what the strongest can do." The Jebusites considered this Zion to be absolutely impregnable, the last word in the unassailable and "uncapturable." They said: "You shall not come in here, indeed, it is quite impossible for you to do so."—"All right," says David. [They accept the challenge.] "We take up the gauntlet. You will see." We know what happened. He did break through and break in and take the stronghold and destroy the erstwhile impregnability, and it became the city of David, the City of the Great King. His great victory, his immense victory, is centered in, registered in, established in, Zion; and Zion is the very symbol and synonym of the great prowess of God's King, of God's Anointed.

Now, bring that over: *"Ye are come to Zion,"* the City of the Living God, ye are come to Zion. What have we come to? We have come, we have come, to the Supreme Victory of the Lord Jesus Christ over the formerly impregnable—and what was that? We quote from Matthew : *"I will build My church; and the gates of Hades shall not prevail against it."* And what have you heard as the exposition of *"the gates of Hades?"* I am not sure that in the early days I did not make this mistake. "Gates," in the Bible in the Old Testament cities, were the place of the counsels of the elders, where they came to their decision by discussion and counsel and made their decisions for the city and the land; and so we have said the "gates" are the counsels of Hell. Do not make that mistake. That is right, but that is not what it means. What is the otherwise impregnable stronghold of the prince of this world? It is death. It is death. The spiritual stronghold into which the Lord Jesus broke was that impregnable stronghold of *"him, that is, the devil, that had [the hold] the power of death.*"[1] So the Risen Lord in the presentation of Himself in the Book of the Revelation, right at the beginning, says, "*I am He that liveth, I became dead; and, behold, I am alive unto the ages of the ages; and I have the keys of death and of Hades.*"

Spiritual death is a tremendous thing, a terrific thing, so much so that the Apostle Paul almost exhausts the vocabulary in this connection when he says that we should know "*the exceeding greatness of His power, exceeding greatness of God's power.*" Think of that! The psalmist would say, "*Selah.*"—Think of that!

"*The exceeding greatness of His power (which is) to us-ward who believe, according to the working* [the energy, the Greek word here is energy] *of the strength of His might, which He wrought* [or energized] *in Christ, when He raised Him from the dead.*" What language, what language. It is simply beyond Paul's expressions. He had a very good vocabulary, but he is finding himself hard put to express and explain what it meant to raise Jesus from the dead—to overcome death!

Oh, it is so easy to say, "*God raised Him from the dead,*" but do you see what it meant? The illustration in the Word—and, of course, the illustration always fades in the presence of the reality—but the illustration in the Word is Egypt and Pharaoh and the gods of the Egyptians. See how God is just, shall I say, panning out His power in those ten judgments. The first is a great power, the second is a great power and more, and the third is still more, and on to ten. Increasing power, increasing power, breaking down something, steadily, steadily, breaking down a great force; and when you come to the consummate thing, what is it? It is life and death, the death of all the firstborn in Egypt; and when that is registered, the people are free, out they go, resurrected! It is an illustration. Types are always poor things in the presence of the reality, **the reality is the raising of Jesus Christ from the dead by the glory of the Father, by the exceeding greatness of His power—and that is to us-ward.** Dear friends, I do not think we have begun to understand what it cost, and what power lies behind, our being born again, our being brought from death unto life.

Now we come back to Zion. That is Zion. "*Ye are come to Zion.*" Ye are come to the immense victory of the Lord Jesus in the realm that

---

[1] Hebrews 2:14

supremely challenged God and heaven, the realm of death. Death. And so you have here in this letter, especially in the first chapters of Hebrews, so much about death. *"He tasted death for every man."* He tasted death for every man: "He delivered all them who through fear of death were all their lifetime subject to bondage."[2] Underline death in those early chapters because it is basic to all that follows; and when you come to the end of the letter, you have that great note struck again: *"Now the God of peace, Who brought again from the dead the Great Shepherd of the sheep through the blood of the eternal covenant, make you perfect."* We are brought again from the dead. There is the potential, there is the dynamic, of our being made perfect. That death, which put a period to all spiritual perfection before, has now been broken by the Great Shepherd of the sheep.

Did I say put a period? You remember in Hebrews, remember Aaron and all his sons, the priests? It says they could make nothing perfect because they died. Death put a period to their work, and nothing was perfect. But He has perfected forever. Why? Because He lives forever, *"I am alive unto the ages of the ages,"* therefore, that is the hope and dynamic of your being made perfect.

Oh, thank God, *"the exceeding greatness of His power"* which is going, eventually, *"to present us faultless before the presence of His glory in exceeding joy; a glorious Church, not having spot, or wrinkle, or any such thing,"*—presented faultless. Oh, what a word! What a sweep of the board that is! Faultless! My, we down here are just obsessed with one another's faults and with our own faultiness; and that is one's trouble—looking for the perfect assembly, the perfect church, and the perfect Christian, and we are just all the time occupied with what is not perfect. The fault and faults. To present us faultless—*"He is able to present us faultless before the presence of His glory in exceeding joy."* Why? Because He has conquered death. Death is the stronghold, the stronghold, and He has plundered the stronghold of Satan:

He plunged in His imperial strength to gulfs of darkness down:
He brought His trophy up, at length, the foiled usurper's crown.

---

[2]Hebrews 2:15

The crown of Satan is death. The crown of Christ is Life: *"I will give thee the crown of Life."* Well, are we spending too much time on details about Zion? This is what we have come to, or are supposed to have come to. *May we be given strength and faith to apprehend what is being said. May we enter into the marvelous joy of it.*

[3] ZION: THE PLACE OF HIS DWELLING

Number three: Zion, again, was and is in its spiritual meaning, in its reality, the center of His dwelling. His dwelling. The Lord dwelt in Zion. The Lord was found in Zion. You notice the words from Exodus 15? *"Thou wilt bring them in, and plant them in the mountain of Thine inheritance, the place, O Lord, Which Thy hast made for Thee to dwell in. . . ."* We know historically that it was there that God had His Sanctuary; and I ought to say here that without dealing with details, as in Hebrews 12, verse 18 and onward, Jerusalem and Zion look like synonymous terms. They look as though they are interchangeable. They are not exactly the same thing, but dare I stop to deal with the difference that there is? It may come out without any special consideration, but here is *"the city which Thou, O Lord, hast made—the heavenly Jerusalem."*

And so we come then to this place of His dwelling, the place where the Lord is. If you were asked where you would find the Lord, I wonder what you would answer. You might mention many things, such as, "If you want to find the Lord, you come to our meetings. You come to our company, our place of worship, and you will find the Lord there" ; and so you localize the Lord. I know in the Old Testament they had to go to the places where He caused His Name to be. However, in the geographical and literal sense, that is no longer the case.

To understand this, let us see that here is a great danger into which Christendom has fallen; and we are all in danger of localizing the presence of God. I mean literally saying: "This is where you have to come, or that is where you have to go, if you want to find the Lord." Do not be deceived. That is not true. We have passed from that system. That is under the *"not."* That is under the not. It sweeps all that conception away. There are no sacred "Ephesus" or "Philippi" or "Thessalonica" : if there were, they would be today where they were two thousand years ago. They are not. They have gone. The Lord was met there, but you will not meet Him there any longer, not in that way. No, not even in Jerusalem, and not in Rome. But where is the Lord? The Lord Jesus has given us, is it a formula, a prescription? *"For where two or three are gathered together in My name, there I am."* There I AM, that is the only localization (I hesitate to use the word "locality") that is the only localization of the Lord!

Now, at any place where you may have met the Lord, amongst any company of the Lord's people where people may have met Him, as soon as they cease to be spiritually Zion, to be what Zion really is spiritually, the Lord leaves that just as He left the tabernacle in Shiloh. It is not sacred, the tabernacle is not sacred or it would be preserved until today. No, things on this earth are not sacred to God. The place where the Lord is and is to be found is in Zion; ah, but what Zion means, what Zion is, what we have been saying Zion is—that is what we have come to!

Now you can go and put up a building and get a congregation and put over the door—*"Zion."* No! no! no! this is this mentality, you see this mentality? No, Zion is a spiritual thing, a spiritual people, and the great thing about them is . . . you meet the Lord there when you meet them. With them, you just meet the Lord. You are not meeting a technique, a form, a ritual, a doctrine, a teaching, an interpretation and all that. You are just meeting the Lord. *"Ye are come to Zion."*—Oh, let that be a test as well as a statement. We will give up everything, and rightly so, we could let anything go—buildings, places, and all our constitution—we let it all go if people are not finding the Lord when they come where we are. Paul brings that down to the individual: *"Ye are a sanctuary of the Living God."* That is an individual application, *"the temple of God."* The place of His dwelling is the place where Christ is in the finality of His work, the fullness of what He has done, where things are according to Christ. That is Zion!

[4] ZION: THE SEAT OF DIVINE GOVERNMENT

Number four: Zion is the seat of Divine government, so go back again to *"Zion, the city of the great King."* Out of Zion shall the government go forth. Out of Zion shall He rule the nation. Zion, the seat of His sovereignty and His government, where His throne is. I hinted a few minutes ago at the difference between Jerusalem and Zion. Zion, as I understand, is what Jerusalem ought to be; and Jerusalem is not always Zion, but Zion is what Jerusalem ought to be—the governmental center.

All the people of God are not the seat and center and expression of this government; and in the Book of Revelation, you will have something more than *"the holy city, new Jerusalem."* You will have *"nations walking in the light thereof."* You will have an extra circle. Yes, they are in the Kingdom. No, I am not now discriminating between the Church and the Kingdom. That is not my point, but I am saying that there are overcomers. *"To him that overcometh will I grant to sit with me in My Throne."* That is Zion, but Jerusalem does not always conform to that, so far as the Lord's people are concerned.

I think I had better leave it there, but, you see, this is a great difficulty with many. You present the ultimate, full thought of God for the Church, what God's Mind is about the Church, the Heavenly Jerusalem, yes, you present it; but some say, "Look at all these Christians, one foot in the world and the other foot in Christianity." But remember, there is such a thing as God having a governing people. It is one thing to be the citizen of a country, or even of a city, but it is another thing to be a member of the royal household. Do you see what I mean? Zion is the very epitome, the very essence, of God's thought for His Church, to which the Church (as a whole) does not all approximate, but it, Zion, is this governmental thing.

Now at the beginning it was like that. The literal Jerusalem in Judæa of old was the center of the government of the land. You come into your New Testament, and you find that things move from Jerusalem. They move. You say, "Antioch becomes the new center, takes the place of Jerusalem"? Is that right? That is the way expositors put it, they make a geographical movement of it. Well, all right, you can have it if you like, but it is not true. Let us go to Antioch then and have a look and see what this is.

What are they doing in Antioch? There were certain brethren in Antioch and *"they fasted and prayed, and the Holy Ghost said. . . ."* **They are off the earth, they are out of the world, they have left things here, they are linked with heaven.** And by the Holy Spirit sent down from heaven, the Heavenly Government is in operation. The Heavenly Throne is governing there.

No, it is not a board meeting. I do not know if any of you know the cartoons of E.J. Pace, but years ago in the <u>Sunday School Times</u>, he had a very good one. I think it was a humorous one, but very good. He called it, "The First Board Meeting of the New Testament," and here it is: all the believers are gathered in a congregation in Jerusalem, and there are two big Hands with a big board in them. And this big board, this huge piece of timber, smashed down upon that building and *"they were all scattered,"* *scattered* throughout all Judæa, throughout all Samaria, and to the uttermost parts of the earth; and he calls that "The First Board Meeting."

No, the governmental center is not in Jerusalem literally and, no, not in Antioch literally. Zion is where heaven is governing and not men, where the heavenly councils are operating: *"and the Holy Ghost said."* The Holy Ghost. That is what we have come to, or ought to have come to. I hope I have not offended any of you board members, you committee men, you church directors. No, no, we are coming to reality. Zion is testing, challenging our whole system. And here, at this point, Zion means:—it is that where Heaven rules, the Ascended Christ governs through the Holy Spirit, makes the decisions, gives the decisions, directs the courses. *"Separate Me Barnabas and Saul for the work whereunto . . ."* the board meeting has appointed them?—No, *"I have called them."* This is Heaven acting, and that is fruitful.

[5] ZION: THE PLACE OF SECURED AND ESTABLISHED FELLOWSHIP

Number five: Zion is the place of secured and established fellowship. Now this is rather interesting, instructive. Go back to your Old Testament. When the hearts of the men of Israel turned from Saul to David to bring him back and make him king, what happened? The first movement was to Hebron, and there they stayed for seven years at Hebron. What is Hebron? Do you know the meaning of Hebron? —Fellowship, fellowship, that is Hebron. Now you can put that over a fellowship if you like, and call it Hebron, but let it be true of that fellowship. However, they brought David back and, first of all, made him king in Hebron. It was a partial thing. It was a movement unto fulness, but seven years in Hebron, seven years (spiritually interpreted) of securing fellowship. And after the seven years, up to Jerusalem to Zion; and the values of Hebron are now centered in Zion, i.e., Zion is *that* in which the true fellowship of the Spirit is established!

You have got to read the rest of this section of Hebrews. See the marvelous fellowship that is there. What have we come to? Even *"to the spirits of just men made perfect."* We are come to a marvelous fellowship in heaven. *"To hosts of angels,"* in fellowship with the angels; fellowship with *"the spirits of just men made perfect"* ; in fellowship with *"Jesus the Mediator of the new covenant."* It is fellowship that is in Zion, heavenly fellowship, heavenly fellowship. And you know quite well if you just get a little taste of heavenly fellowship, it is heaven.

Some of you have come from far places where you have little or no real spiritual fellowship; and whatever other values there may be about convocations, I have always found that one of the greatest values, even more than the ministry, has been these lonely pilgrims coming from far and near in the songs of ascents up to Zion, and finding that heart-ravishing fellowship which has sent them back to their lonely places feeling and knowing: "Well, I am not alone after all, I thought I was alone. I was Elijah looking for a juniper tree to say, it is enough. Oh, Lord, take away my life. I am the only one left. But I discovered that there are seven thousand in Israel!" Fellowship is a marvelous thing. That is Zion in truth. *"Ye are come."* **Oh, that we might always live in the good of that, and in our loneliness and isolations and exiles know that our fellowship is in heaven.** It took seven years to get that fellowship, and then established in Zion.

In Zion. Well, what is it again? It is the fellowship of Christ being in His right place and His full place. David is now in his right place, and in his full place, for which God chose and anointed him. He is there: Our **Greater** David in His place, right place and full place—and wherever that is true, that is Zion. And it is not Zion unless it is like that.

[6] ZION: THE GROUND OF OUR SPIRITUAL FESTIVITY

Number six: Zion is the ground of our festivities. I have almost said this in what I have just said. What does it say? *"Zion, the city of our solemnities."* That is the phrase in Scripture, *"the city, the place, of our solemnities."* What did that mean? It was the great feasts and festivals of the people which they had in Zion. God had ordained this people should be a festive people. Now this portion in Hebrews says that is what we have come to. We have come to numerous angels in festal array. The city of our festivities. Need I say anymore? I believe this, I know this, that if you have anything that approximates to Zion spiritually, anything that is really and truly spiritual Zion, however small it may be, you will have a feast of good things. Where these things are true, where these five things that I have mentioned are true:

[1] *A people in the good of the Complete and Perfect Work of Christ*
[2] *The Supreme Victory of the Lord*
[3] *The Place of His Dwelling*
[4] *The Seat of Divine Government*
[5] *The Place of Secured and Established Fellowship*

where these things are true, you will never be hungry, spiritually hungry. The Lord will see to it that there is plenty there. You will not be miserable, but full of joy! We need something more than religious picnics: we need Zion's spiritual festivities.

"*Hosts of angels in festal array.*" I do not know that I understand that altogether, but I think I can glimpse it. My, when the angels see Zion, how happy they are! How glad they are! There is certainly joy amongst the angels when you have things like this. When they look at a spiritual Zion, they put on their festal garments and say, "This is it. This is it." The angels rejoice. Perhaps that is an imperfect interpretation: I do not know, but I am sure it is a part of it because we register this when we have anything that approximates to Zion in this way. Zion's fellowship and the King really in His Place of Governing—we register heaven's feeling about it and say, "My, this is good"; and we no longer condemn poor old Simon Peter. We fall into the same wonderful and glorious trap. We say, "*It is good to be here.*" Let us never go away from this place again. "*Let us make three tabernacles.*" We sang, just before this ministry this morning, about the warring world below. We have got to go back to it, but may we go back with something of the joy of Zion, the city of our solemnities, spiritual festivity. I must leave that then and come to the last thing about Zion for this morning; and this is only the first fragment in the whole section. There is another one which will probably take the whole of our time tomorrow, number eight, but that is not coming now.

[7] ZION: THE PLACE OF OUR SPIRITUAL FRANCHISE— I AM REGISTERED IN HEAVEN, I AM A CITIZEN OF HEAVEN

Number seven: Zion, the place of our spiritual franchise. Is that a difficult word, idea? Now if you do not know what I mean, I remind you of Psalm 87: *"The Lord loveth the gates of Zion more than all the dwellings of Jacob."* Then the psalmist picks out those places in the world that men boast of. *"I was born in Philistia. Think of that."*—*"I was born in Tyre. Think of that! I am a Tyrite. I am a citizen of Tyre."* — *"I was born in Ethiopia. Think of that!"* The psalmist (you can almost hear and see his joy) the psalmist says: *"But this man was born in Zion, it shall be said. Of Zion, it shall be said, this man was born there."* Something absolutely superior. This man is a citizen of Zion, he is born there, his name is registered there, and the psalmist concludes that whole survey, comparison, and contrast with: *"All my springs are in thee"* —All my wellsprings are in thee. The place of my franchise: *"I am registered in heaven, I am a citizen of heaven."*

"Our citizenship, says the apostle, *is in heaven; from whence we look for a Saviour."* *"Our life is hid with Christ in God."* We have been *"born from above"* [always correct the translation]; *"not born again,"* but *"born from above,"* that is something more than born again. Not only have we been *"born from above"* and our names *"written in the Lamb's Book of Life";* not only that, that is glorious, but you have the franchise. Paul boasted of his freemanship: "I am a freeman born," and they all had to yield to that, even the Roman Empire had to bow to that, a freeman born. The poor centurion captain had a bad time when he heard that. My word, his life was at stake for having put chains on a free man. *Our citizenship is in heaven,* our franchise is in heaven, we are *"heirs of God and joint-heirs with Christ."* This one was born there at Zion, in Zion.

I must leave that with you, I do trust it is not just a lot of either interesting or even fascinating Bible teaching, but this is a challenge: *"Ye are come to Zion."*

Lord, help us to see what we have come to, what we really are in the Divine Thought. The Lord make this true of us, wherever we may be, and of the little companies with which we may be related and connected, that it is in this true spiritual sense, Zion indeed!

Lord, make this more than teaching and doctrine and truth and Bible exposition. Do put the challenge into it, into every one of our hearts, is this true of me? Am I a citizen of Zion? Are these things real in my life? Help us to attend to it. Answer our prayer, for the Sake of Thine Own Glory and Satisfaction in Thy Son, Amen.

Chapter Four

"The Controversy Of Zion"

Dear Lord, in no formal way, no mere custom, but in a very deep and strong consciousness of need, we pray. We must pray. We are this morning allowing ourselves to be put under new responsibility. If Thou shouldest Speak, as we have asked Thee to do, then the Words that Thou dost Speak will judge us in that day. We realize that it is no small thing even to allow ourselves to hear the Lord Speak, but, Lord, it is a matter of capacity also. We cannot understand unless the Spirit of wisdom and understanding gives us the ability. Things are going to be said which may be the truth, and we will not understand unless something is done by Thee in us. And we certainly cannot follow through in obedience unless Thou, Lord, dost do this thing. As Thou didst Say to a very beloved disciple, "You cannot follow Me now, whither I go you cannot follow Me now. You shall afterward." That "cannot" is over us and on us. We cannot follow through unless, Lord, there is something done by Thee.

Now all this we bring, and what is true of hearing and obeying is just as much true of speaking. We are not authorities. We are not teachers. We cannot speak unless Thou, Lord, dost the Speaking. The anointing must do it. We submit ourselves that this time shall be an anointed time, a Holy Spirit time, in both ways and all ways. It shall be the Lord this morning. Grant it that the Glory may come to Thee and any fruit may accrue to Thy Glory. In the Name of the Lord Jesus, we ask this, Amen.

We return to continue with that first fragment of Hebrews, chapter twelve, verse twenty-two: *"But ye are come unto Mount Zion, and unto the city of the Living God, the heavenly Jerusalem."*—*"Ye are come to Mount Zion."* Now for this morning, I want to link that fragment with one or two other passages of Scripture. First of all, back in the prophecies of Isaiah, chapter thirty at verse eight: *"Now go, write it before them on a tablet, and inscribe it in a book, that it may be for the time to come for ever and ever."* And then will you turn to the Second Psalm, and I want you to read this psalm, perhaps we will begin at verse six. *"Yet have I set My King upon My holy hill of Zion. I will tell of the decree: the Lord said unto Me, Thou art My Son; this day have I begotten Thee."*

Now you keep that psalm in mind, please, as we go on. All the rest of it, from that verse and before, take a glance; but I want you now to turn to the Letter to the Romans, and to your great favorite, chapter eight, at verse nineteen: *"For the earnest expectation of the creation waiteth for the revealing of the sons of God. For the creation was subjected to vanity, not of its own will, but by reason of Him Who subjected it, in hope that the creation itself also shall be delivered from the bondage of corruption into the liberty of the glory of the children of God."* Now I am leaving that and going on to verse twenty-nine: *"For whom He foreknew, He also foreordained to be conformed to the image of His Son, that He might be the Firstborn among many brethren: and whom He foreordained, them He also called: and whom He called, them He also justified: and whom He justified, them He also glorified."*

Now between those two portions that we have just read, we have this, verse twenty-two and twenty-three: *"For we know that the whole creation groaneth and travaileth in pain together until now. And not only so, but ourselves also, who have the firstfruits of the Spirit, even we ourselves groan within ourselves, waiting for our adoption, the redemption of our body."*

We are occupied with what we have come to, **"Ye are come,"** and we have been thinking about Zion, the Zion to which we are come. We have said seven things about Zion, seven things to which we have come, constituting this position; and I come to the eighth this morning, which is of very serious and solemn moment. I feel that if the Lord gets His Word through this morning, very largely (so far as this ministry is concerned) the conference may hang upon it. It is the most practical issue in this whole consideration, position,—what we have come to in coming to Zion. Here, as you note, in this passage in Hebrews, Zion and Jerusalem look to be synonymous. *"You have come to Zion . . . to the heavenly Jerusalem."* In this whole section, you are not dealing with different things in these various matters of dimension. This is all of one. It is all one thing. Here Zion and Jerusalem come together, are spoken of as being one, and that gives us our starting point for this present consideration.

Zion-Jerusalem: The Storm Center Of The Nations

Zion, as the heart of Jerusalem; as the very essence of all that Jerusalem was intended to be; as the real spiritual meaning of Jerusalem; the concentrated point of all that Jerusalem represented; Zion-Jerusalem, in history and in the nations, has always been the storm center, the storm center of history, the storm center of the nations. Of course, it would take a long time for us to even look generally at the history of Jerusalem. You can do that at any time, but how many sieges, how many investments, how much was Jerusalem the object and center of world attention and concern! Again and again and again, eyes were turned toward Jerusalem, for Jerusalem's destruction, for Jerusalem's wiping out, for Jerusalem's possession. A long, troubled history is the history of Jerusalem, even to our own time. It is a world center of conflict and controversy. That fact everybody recognizes. *Zion*, what the prophet calls, *"the controversy of Zion."*

Zion-Jerusalem has been a controversial object in history and in the nations all the way along. It is extraordinary. You wonder, "Why? It is not such a wonderful city, is it? It is not so great. How long would it take you to walk across it, or even to walk around it? What was it, and what is it? Perhaps it is a better specimen of world cities today, so far as structure is concerned and modernization. But what was it and, even now, what is it?" How can it compare with London, New York, Paris, and any of these others you might mention? They might be centers of attraction, truly. There was a tremendous battle in our own lifetime to get hold of London. Oh, if you had been in the battle of London, you would have known. Fourteen months, day and night, without cessation, a city bombed, fired upon, attacked, assailed. If you had been in that, and seen it happening, great areas going up in dust and smoke, you would have said, "Well, London is an object. It counts for something." Of course, most of you people know nothing about it in that way. I hope you never will.

But Jerusalem,—what is Jerusalem? What is that? Not once or twice in a lifetime, but right through the long history of centuries there has been a controversy over Zion; and if you look closer and look into it more carefully, you will come to see this—that Zion, or Jerusalem, was always a sign. It was a sign. There was a significance attached to it, and the significance was not its temporal aspects of buildings and structures and economies and so on. Why, Babylon could go far beyond all that. But Zion's significance was a spiritual thing, for you notice this: whenever the spiritual life of Jerusalem, as representing the people, the nation, whenever the spiritual life was right; whenever it was a matter of right standing with God; Jerusalem was in the ascendancy. Attack if you like, let the hoards of Babylon, or Assyria, come against Jerusalem and encamp. There is a Hezekiah inside! There is a people inside who are right with the Lord! waiting on the Lord! crying to the Lord! making the Lord their trust! And so much the worse for Assyria, for Babylon. In a night, their hosts are wiped out by the Angel of the Lord. When things are spiritually right, it does not matter how fierce, forceful, and great the assault—the antagonism—they stand, they come through.

But from time to time, it was not like that inside. The spiritual state was low. There was declension. There was wrong. The standing before God was not right, and then Jerusalem was always in weakness, always in fear, always in dread. Weakened from the inside, spiritually it could not stand; and at last, at last, after more than one successful assault, or breaking down; at last, simply because of this poor, low, spiritual condition, Jerusalem is destroyed. Finally destroyed, that is, robbed of its place in the Divine economy and purpose. Zion is a sign of a spiritual condition. It has always been such a sign, a barometer of spiritual life.

It is absolutely useless, dear friends, to refer to tradition and say, "Well, God did this in the beginning, and this is the place where the oracles of God are found and the temple of God is and the great tradition of Israel as the chosen people. It is here, and we rest on that." No, tradition will not support now. History will not support now. Institutions will not support now. It seems as though God has no regard, at length, for temple or ark or altar or priesthood. He cries through the prophets: *"Away, away with you. I want none of your sacrifices."* Isaiah 58. What a chapter! *"Cry aloud, spare not, lift up thy voice."* Then, what follows? *"Yet they seek Me daily, and delight to know My ways."* "I will have none of it, says the Lord. I will have none of it. These are not the sacrifices I want. This ritual is not what I am after. This traditional system is not what I desire. It is a spiritual state." And only on that can the Lord associate Himself, ally Himself, to Zion.

I am saying that Zion has always been a sign of spiritual condition, and that has been made evident by whether there was ascendancy—ascendancy, the support of God—making them superior to **every** adverse force; or whether they were a shame among the nations, a reproach among the nations. With the prophetic element pointing on to something else, as is always so in the prophets, you have Jerusalem crying, crying the great heart cry: "Woe is me. Woe is me. All ye that pass by, all ye that pass by, have pity. Have pity, all ye that pass by." What a tragic situation for Zion. A shame amongst the nations! And these two things, ascendancy or shame, glory or dishonour [right at the center of history and the nations] are bound up with a spiritual condition, are dependent upon a spiritual condition.

You know, there is a lot to be gathered into that statement, dear friends. But if you look again at this Letter to the Hebrews, you will see that we are come to Zion. We <u>are not</u> come <u>to some</u> thing, some religious thing, some tradition, we are not come to historic Christianity (if I may put it that way), <u>we</u> <u>are</u> come <u>to a</u> <u>spiritual</u> situation which is calculated to startle us. Oh, we say, "We are in the day of Grace. This is the dispensation of Grace." True! Is the Letter to the Hebrews on any other ground than the ground of Grace? Surely not, but do you know that in this letter the most awful things in the Bible are written? *"How shall we escape* [we, we escape, we Christians, we believers of this dispensation] *how shall we escape if we neglect so great salvation? . . . our God is a consuming fire . . . it is a fearful thing to fall into the hands of the Living God."* This is said to these people, these Christians; and other things like that are said. But I am pointing this out, that this letter is written in the day of Grace; and it is a day which brings into view not some new Christian system, not the formation of a new Christian tradition, but a spiritual condition, without which everything else is as nothing. You have come to Zion, yes, but you have come to the controversy of Zion. You have come, we have come, to the great battle of Zion; and it is a spiritual battle. There it is then. *WHAT A BATTLE!* That is the background of it all.

Well, now, I do not want to make you glum. I see your faces are getting a bit heavy, your chins are dropping, and you would think I am getting back to Sinai from Zion, but no, no, as I have said, this is a very solemn time. You are going to have a lot of teaching this week. It is not going to avail one little bit if there is not a corresponding spiritual position. So having said that and laid that as the background of all, it is the battle—the controversy—of Zion. And, what is the nature of this controversy? Let us look at one or two things about it, and I am working toward a very, very vital thing, which I trust we shall reach before we are finished.

What Is The Nature Of The Controversy?

The nature of the battle? What was the nature of the battle with Israel, centered and represented by Zion-Jerusalem? It was the battle in relation to a calling and a vocation. They were called by God, they were chosen by God, they were an elect race [you see why we came to Romans eight], an elect race, a chosen people, in history on the earth they were the elect of God. Chosen and called and separated, what for? Just to be saved? Just to be different? Just to be that? No! for a vocation, a calling, a testimony in the world, a testimony among the nations. They were called for a mighty, heavenly vocation on the earth, to reveal God! what God is like! the reality of God! the glory of God! the holiness of God! the power of God! A vessel of testimony among the nations, to the nations—to the world. Zion, as we have been saying, is that which represents God's full thought for mankind. The fulness of God's thought is vested in, centered in, Zion, *"the city of the Living God."* And because of that, the battle starts.

In history, Zion was the city of David, God's anointed king. And do you notice the history of David? Up from birth . . . up? It looks like down and out . . . but, no, steadily, steadily up. Let all the forces of Saul and his malice, his devil-driven soul, be concentrated against this young man,—and what that young man suffered! You know the story. He seems to be a marked man, [as we say, I do not know whether you have the phrase in this country] "a speckled bird." He seems just right from the beginning to be a marked man. The devil had put a mark on that man and was watching him, pursuing him. Poor David cries: *"I am like a pelican of the wilderness . . . a sparrow upon the housetop."* Oh yes, he is the object of a fierce and furious, relentless malice, meant for his undoing. But he holds on his way, steadily; not because he is so strong, for there were times when David broke down: *"I shall now perish,"* I shall now be killed. He resorted to some subterfuges, was a man of like-passions with us, very human; nevertheless, through it all, whether it is in the land of the Philistines by compromise (a mistake from which God sovereignly delivered him) or wherever it is—in the cave of Adullam, in the wilderness driven hither and thither for his very life—wherever it is, his spiritual course is on and up, spiritually. It does not look like it outwardly, but on and up until eventually anointed, David comes to the place of the anointing, the throne; and Zion is the place of the consummation of that history of Divine election, Divine choice, Divine [dare I use the word in these days] foreordination. He is there, on the throne. He is in the place of the full thought of God, and that is centered in him. Zion is the place of the absolute sovereignty and Lordship of God's anointed. That is Zion, and we are come to Zion. We have been saying this: there is Another Greater than David that is here, and there is another Zion greater than that is here. But it is on that point, dear friends, just focused upon that one inclusive and consummate point of the Absolute Sovereign Lordship of Jesus Christ that all the conflict rages and is centered.

THE NATURE OF THE CONTROVERSY: THE ABSOLUTE LORDSHIP OF JESUS CHRIST

You turn to your New Testament, you know their message, as they went out into the world that then was, everywhere their message was, "Jesus Christ is Lord: we preach Jesus Christ as Lord." That brought them up against Cæsar, and all the Cæsars, because Cæsar said: "I am lord." The Roman Empire said: "Cæsar is lord," and they worshipped Cæsar; and the argument, contention, accusation, was—*"These men are preaching another king but Cæsar."* Ah, yes, that is where the controversy was, on this one thing: the Absolute Lordship of Jesus Christ. The controversy of Zion is on that point ultimately: God's Anointed.

Now you see why we read Psalm 2. *"Why do the nations rage?"*—Raging nations, we are coming to that in another connection shortly. The raging nations, the kings of the earth, gathering themselves together against the Lord and against His Anointed. "Let us cast their bonds from us, let us get rid of them. They are a menace, a menace.—*"Yet I have set My King upon My Holy Hill of Zion."* I have set My King! The raging, the storming, the controversy, focused about the Anointed One, in the Anointed One, God's Anointed.

But you notice, it was not very long in the New Testament, you only reach in Acts what is marked off mechanically by chapter 4 (and I have said this often, it is a very good thing to wipe those things out and read straight on, blind to the chapters), and you notice when you read chapter 4, as it is marked, you reach a point in the controversy, the controversy of Zion,—oh, the battle is on! The battle is on, the forces of evil and the forces in this world have set their mark upon this Anointed One and the proclamation of Him; and when they are at work killing James and imprisoning Peter, the Church meets, Zion gathers, Zion gathers.[2] And what do they do? They quote the Second Psalm. They quote the Second Psalm to the Lord. *"Lord, Lord,"* and then they quote, *"Why do the heathen [or the nations] rage,and the people imagine a vain thing . . . against the Lord, and against His Anointed?"* They quote it, and what happens? What happens? *"The King is in His Holy Mount Zion"*: He intervenes, He intervenes. Oh, yes, Herod seems to have scored a great success in killing James; and he is so pleased with himself, and the people are so pleased with him, it seems he is going to do the whole business. He takes Peter and puts him in prison. That is all right. So much the worse for you, Herod. What is the end of that story? He was eaten of worms and died, and the next sentence: *"But the Word of the Lord grew and multiplied."* There is the Holy Hill of Zion and the One Enthroned because there was right standing with God then. So they quoted Psalm 2, meaning that time has no place in this, geography has no place in this; but wheresoever there is a true representation of Zion, there may be assaults, seeming successes of the evil one and his powers, yet, the issue is with Him Who is in Zion. The issue is victory. God has set His Holy One upon His Holy Hill Zion. The Anointed is there.

THE NATURE OF THE CONTROVERSY: THE WORLD SPIRIT AGAINST THE TESTIMONY OF JESUS

Now, dear friends, you are listening to all this as Bible exposition. Perhaps I do not know what you are thinking, what your reactions are; but I know what I am after. I am after something, and I hope you will move with me to the object that we are seeking to reach. If we have come to Zion—and you have, perhaps, been very pleased with the seven things about Zion and have been saying, "Oh beautiful! oh, wonderful! oh,

---

[2]In making his point, "Zion gathers," Brother Sparks interchanges chapter 4 and 12 of the Book of Acts. We left this as it is because we felt the Holy Spirit was using it in this way for strong emphasis; and as our brother says, "time . . . and geography has no place in this."

glorious! yes, Zion. Let's sing more about Zion. Let's have it as the city of our solemnities. Let's have some festivities!"—all right, all true, but you have to meet number eight. If we have come to Zion, we have come to the controversy of a spiritual position on the part of a people, the controversy of history over this people in union with the Ascended Exalted Lord. It is a controversial matter in this universe. Principalities, powers, the world rulers of this darkness, hosts of wicked spirits, all focused upon one thing: the denial of the Absolute Lordship of Jesus Christ; and the Church is the custodian of that testimony. That is our calling. That is the vocation of the people of God, to be that testimony. Against that the battle rages. All that is of the enemy forces is against the testimony of Jesus: a terrific battle is on for *"the testimony of Jesus."*

Well, that is the focal point of it, but then the battle, mark you, not only is in the atmosphere, so to speak (it is there, that is its realm, the heavenly places, the atmosphere, in a sense an abstract thing); but notice again, as in the type in the Old Testament, so in the spiritual reality in the New, this antagonism has its media, its vehicles, its channels, its means. And what is it? It is the world spirit. The world spirit, this evil world in its spirit.

I do not think we have really grasped what the New Testament has to say about this world. This world: it is an enemy of God. It is an enemy of all that is of God. *"Love not the world, neither the things that are in the world."* In a great cry from the heart of the Lord Jesus, the prayer just before the Cross is: *"They are not of the world, even as I am not of the world."* *"I pray not that Thou shouldest take them out of the world,* the geographical sphere that is called the world, *but that Thou shouldest keep them from the evil"* one who rules in it. No, this has not registered yet upon the Church. The world spirit—I think you must know something of what I mean.

You see, in the Old Testament, it was these world interests, world forces, the world, that was all the time against Zion. If you had asked them why, they would have had to sit down and think hard. "Why is it that we do not like that silly little city? Those people—who are they, what are they, why don't we like them?" They would have had difficulty in answering their own question, but there is something sinister behind it all. Those sinister intelligences know something. What do they know? They know what the elect is called for, and in the long run the enemy knows that the elect is going to be his undoing. He is going to lose his world power, his world title as prince of this world. He is going to lose it all at the hands of this One in Zion and through that corporate expression of His Sovereignty, His Lordship.—That Zion we are come to. He knows that, and if you are related to that, I am going to comfort you by telling you, "You are a marked man; you are a marked woman"; and do not succumb to second causes and say, "It is my landlord. It is this and that and something else." Oh, that may be the vehicle and the medium, but there is something much more sinister than that behind it all. Our wrestling is not with flesh and blood, landlords, or anybody else, in the ultimate issue. Committees? Organizations? No, there is something behind all this. The world spirit. The world spirit.

I remember that Dr. Campbell Morgan in his lecture on the Letter to the Corinthians simply said this: "The whole reason for those conditions in Corinth—so shameful, so terrible, from which you turn from some matters in disgust and shame—it is because the world spirit in Corinth had got into the church." Well, there you are. **The battle is with the world spirit. As in the old literally, so now in the new spiritually.** I need not dwell upon I Corinthians, need I? The world spirit? The wisdom of this world: the apostle is up against that. The conception of power in this world: he is up against that. *"The wisdom and the power of God are Jesus Christ,"* he says, *"as Lord."* All right, that is another line. Let us go on, and this is the final phase to which I so definitely want to get to this morning. It is what Romans eight, the parts we have read, brings us to as the very sum of all this that we are saying about the controversy of Zion.

THE NATURE OF THE CONTROVERSY: THE WHOLE CREATION TRAVAILETH, GROANETH?—FOR THE ELECT

The tumult of the nations. Psalm 2, of course, is the nations rage, the kings of the earth gather together: tumult in the nations. And the reason for it? Why the tumult in the nations? Is there anybody here this morning who would not agree with me when I have said the nations are in tumult just now?! Was there ever a time when the world, almost in its entirety, if not in its entirety, was in tumult as it is now? Tumult, not only in the peoples and the nations, but convulsions in nature. We have never had it like this, have we? All these convulsions. I do not know how much you are in touch with it, but somehow or other we know about it. The earthquakes, the famines, a disruption of seasons, and what not. There is, and it is the best word for it: "convulsions in the nations." Romans 8—*"The whole creation gro-o-aneth."*

"The whole creation groaneth and travaileth in pain together." There is an integration in a groan. It is integrated by this travail in the whole creation. *"And not only so, but ourselves also, who have the firstfruits of the Spirit, even we ourselves groan within ourselves, waiting, . . ."* Waiting! The creation is groaning inwardly like this and travailing, if we had a spiritual ear to hear, groaning with us for something. It is subjected to vanity, not of its own will, but by the will of Him Who subjected it. What is it groaning for? What is this travail? To bring forth something, and what is it that is to be brought forth? Note the rest of the passage. The elect!

You come on that section, that great controversial section of Romans about predestination, foreordination, the election. Now do not come to me about that. I am not having anything to do with these systems of predestination or the rest of it. What I am saying is, there is such a thing as God's elect hidden, hidden in the nations. God knows. You do not know. I do not know, and I cannot tell you who is elect and who is not elect. God knows. They are there hidden, and within such there is this spirit of travail, longing, groaning: "Oh, that this vanity, void, not attaining, would be removed; and we should emerge, emerge, come out, be born." The travail should precipitate.

There we touch the heart of things. What are all these convulsions in the nations about, and in nature? As we are moving toward the end of the dispensation, why this tumult, convulsions? Why? Because God has something here that is not wanted here by this world and its prince. It is something like Jonah in the big fish. The moment or the hour came when the big fish said, "Oh, look here, what have I got inside? What is this that I have got?" And the fish got a most awful attack of dyspepsia. "Oh, to get rid of this. I will never be comfortable until I have precipitated this that I have got inside. Let me get rid of this. Let me get this out." Of course, under the Sovereignty of God, he makes for shore *"and vomited out Jonah upon the dry land."* And I can think when that fish turned back into the sea he said, "Oh, there, now I feel all right. He is gone. He is gone."

Now am I exaggerating, imagining, but come back with me, to Israel in Egypt. What is happening? Convulsion after convulsion in

Egypt. Convulsion, under the Sovereignty of God, yes, so that steadily, gradually, persistently, Egypt is coming to the place: "Oh, won't it be a good day and a good thing when we get rid of these people." You notice what happens at the end? *"They were thrust out"!* "They precipitated them, they vomited them out"; and I suppose although Pharaoh's army pursued to bring them back, the many (if not all) in Egypt said, "Thank God, they have not succeeded and brought those people back again. We are rid of them, and it is a very good riddance." Now, that is not interpretation. No, there is a people in there, God's elect, and sooner or later the place where they are will want to get rid of them. "They are a menace, a menace."

But come over to Babylon, they are there. The elect are there. We have not very much to indicate, but we have Daniel and his three friends; and we must conclude that they were not the only true ones in Babylon. There is Ezekiel. There is a remnant in Babylon. God has a people. He is doing something through seventy years, and then the seventy years are completed and what happens? The Prophet Isaiah cries, chapter forty-three: *"For your sake have I sent to Babylon, and have brought down all their nobles."* And how did it happen? Belshazzar has his feast, the hand writes on the wall: *"thy kingdom is divided, and removed."* That night was Belshazzar slain, how? Cyrus and his army went stealthily through the night, moved along the wady, the valley, the dry valley, through, into Jerusalem, underground, and to use the phrases of the prophet: *"had broken in pieces the gates of brass, and cut in sunder the bars of iron"* and come up in the middle of Jerusalem. Slain Belshazzar—*"For your sake, for your sake, because of you, the elect, I have sent to Babylon, and have brought down all their nobles,"* their high ones. The people inside are a menace to the world, but they are the object of all God's activities—world convulsions, if you like.

And I believe, dear friends, as we get nearer to the end when the Church is to be extricated, these convulsions are significant, very significant, that the day of our emergence is near. You remember the phrase in the literal Greek, the words of the Lord, the prophetic words of the Lord, about *"the end."* He says, *"The tumult of nations, men's hearts failing them for fear"* for the terrible things which are coming upon the earth;[3] but the literal there is not *"distress of nations,"* the literal Greek is "no way out for the nations." No way out for the nations. Oh, my word, is that not true today—they are trying to find a way out; and there is no way out for the nations. But then note, when that time comes: "Lift up your eyes, for your Way out draws near." Your way out—there is a way out for the elect when there is this investment.

Involvement In The Controversy Of Zion: Intense Spiritual Pressure

Well, you have got the teaching now. *"You have come to Zion."* I wonder, I do not know, of course in the smaller world of the New Testament, it may have been true under those persecutions and martyrdoms, I think it was; but the world is such a much bigger world now than then, this great world compared with the little world of the Roman Empire then—I wonder if there was ever a time in the history of this world when the saints were going through spiritual pressure more than they are now? Spiritual pressure. I am not talking now only of outward persecutions. Some are in that, but even here, at this time, this week, dear children of God said to me: "I never in my life knew so much spiritual conflict, spiritual pressure. It sometimes gets unbearable, intolerable. I wonder how I am going to get through." Many of you may not know anything about that. If you do not, do not worry at the moment. But if you do know that, dear friends, and some of us do, we have never in our lives (and some of us have a long life with the Lord) known such intense and almost naked spiritual pressure. At times it does seem to get to the point where we will break, where it seems we will break. Many dear children of God all over the world write to me on these terms about this. What does it mean? You have come to Zion—that is what it means. Leave your theology of election and predestination. Leave that—that will not get you anywhere, only into trouble and confusion; but take the fact that God has a people in this world, in the nations, hidden in the nations, whom He knows.

"The Lord knoweth them that are His." He knows them, and they are of the greatest interest to the devil. They are marked, and they are

---

[3]Luke 21:25,26

involved in the controversy of Zion. If you would like to leave the word "Zion," if that creates mental pictures, leave it, forget it, see the meaning—the spiritual meaning—of something that is standing for "*the testimony of Jesus*," that is standing for the Absolute Lordship of Jesus Christ, that is standing for the true vocation of the Church! A people like that are not going to have an easy time. I am sorry to say that to you, but we have been told that this week very, very pointedly.

But here it is, and you will go back and perhaps there will be troubles, difficulties, this kind and that, family, business, what not; and then you will say: "What has happened to me? What has gone wrong?!" On the contrary, it has all gone right. Oh, I wish we could believe that. If what I am saying is true, it is the controversy of Zion, the conflict over something very precious to the Lord, because Zion was very precious to the Lord in history. Read the Psalms. Something very precious to the Lord is being challenged, combated, by all the forces of evil, nakedly and by every kind of means; and this is the explanation of the present convulsions. The prince of this world and this world spirit and system, knowingly or unknowingly, is sick of us. The nations are closing their doors, driving out those who represent the Lord. The world is narrowing down its scope for what is of Jesus Christ. It is pressing in. The explanation?—**It is the time of "The Way out for the Church."**

Of course, it is a false hope on the part of the world. It may have been true that the Egyptians were very glad when those people had gone. They got a rest for a time, but it did not last very long. It was a transient thing; their later history was a bit troublesome. Babylon may have felt a bit more comfortable when that remnant had gone back to Jerusalem, but it did not last very long. "*I have brought down. . . .*" The Lord destroyed Babylon, as He destroyed Egypt. And it may be that when the Church is gone, the prince of this world and his kingdom may say: "There, they have gone. They are out. Now we can have it all to ourselves." But, if you notice, the context of that is they do not have it to themselves very long. Then there comes the judgments. The judgment of this world is just waiting until the Church is out, and that time is drawing near.

I think I have said enough. I could say much more as to the aspects of this conflict, the means used by the enemy to try and undo this testimony, to try and destroy Zion. The means used? Well, one is confusion. These evil powers and spirits are spirits of confusion. They always were. There never was a time, I venture to say, in the history of this world, when there was more confusion, and confusion in Christendom, in Christianity; and it is brought down to the least local expression of Zion. Confusion. Is it true? Is it true you do not know what to do? where you are? how to answer? what it means? Spiritual confusion invading everything that is on this earth—confusion.

There are spirits of corruption to defile, to defile—corruption. There are spirits of deception. Was there ever a time when there was more deception? Everywhere, deception. Oh, I dare not stay with that, dare I? But here it is, the things that are misleading, that are assuming a divine complexion, that are false, that are a lie, they will not last. They will have their day and cease to be. The roots, the seeds of their disintegration, are in them. In the semblance of good and right, there is falsehood—deception.

There are divisions. No end to this, no end. To the last two of the Lord's people there will be this attack to divide, to get us apart somehow. Yes, in the Church universal, an attack to split up; in the local churches, yes, division, and division following division; and in the family, and in the two—husband and wife. We are in a battle! It is a terrible thing to say, but you know however much there may be of love and certainty that the Lord brought you and your wife together, or you and your husband together, very often there is a battle over your fellowship. Is that saying too much? But it is true. A battle, misunderstandings, can come in there and divide and isolate. Anywhere! Anywhere! The spirits of division are at work today, and the slogan of their forces is "divide and conquer." It depends on the ground on which you are standing. If you are standing on natural ground; on doctrinal ground; on theological ground; on interpretation ground; if you are standing on any of those grounds, you will not hold together. You will not hold together. If you are standing on the ground of Christ only, and His Lordship, that is the answer.

Now I close with this: Zion is very precious to God, for the reason that His Son is His Appointed King on His Mount Zion. Ah, there is a great love of this testimony of Zion. It is for His Son's Sake. You and I must have His Son's Sake as the motivating part of all our ways. *Ye are come to Zion,* " but you have come to an involvement in a great conflict! So, help us, God.

We just ask Thee, Lord, that all the authority which has been given to Thee in heaven and on earth may cover, encompass, and embrace what has been said here this morning. Thou knowest it is not easy. It is a battle even to get it out; but, Lord, we need to be protected. The Word needs to be protected. We trust Thee, Lord. We trust Thee and all the Mighty Virtue of Thy Blood to Protect, for the Glory of Thy Name, Amen.

Chapter Five

Zion: The Embodiment Of The Spiritual Values Of Jesus Christ

Lord, we are subjects of Thy pity, of Thy compassion; and this morning we do not even know what to ask of Thee, for we perhaps do not really know our truest need. We think we know sometimes. There are things which are very real to us as needs; but, Lord, it is true Thou knowest all the truest need of our hearts, and only Thou knowest. According to Thy knowledge, speak Lord—make it personal—make it individual—as well as collective, that while Eli did not hear the voice of the Lord, even in the tabernacle, there was one who did. Pick us out for speaking this morning. As Thou didst call, "Samuel, Samuel," may we be called by name. May we know the Lord is speaking to us. Do not allow our minds and thoughts to be diverted onto other people or we shall say that is something for them. But do keep it directly, where afterward, we can truly say, "The Lord has spoken to me." Now for all that is needed, Lord, in us and for us—for this, do that by the wisdom and the power and the grace of Thy Holy Spirit. We ask it, in the Name of the Lord Jesus, Amen.

By now I think you know that there is a book in the New Testament which is called the Letter to the Hebrews, and I am going to read again from this book this morning. We are getting very near to the end of this time of gathering, of ministry, and I feel that it is very necessary for things to become very definite and concrete and that we should at this time expect the Lord to be focusing things on very clearly defined issues.

But once again, let us read at the beginning of this letter, chapter one: *"God, having of old time spoken unto the fathers in the prophets by diverse portions and in diverse manners, hath at the end of these days spoken unto us in His Son, Whom He appointed Heir of all things, through Whom also He made the worlds; Who being the effulgence of His glory, and the very image of His substance, and upholding all things by the Word of His Power, when He had made purification of sins, sat down on the right hand of the Majesty on high."* And again at chapter twelve, verse 18: *"Ye are not come unto a mount that might be touched"* ; verse 22, *"But ye are come unto Mount Zion, and unto the city of the living God, the heavenly Jerusalem."*

I could almost wish that we forget that word Zion, as such, if it represents a subject. We must look through Zion because, you see, what we have in the beginning of this letter is *"God hath spoken."* In Zion? No! God hath spoken through Zion. God hath spoken in His Son. If we have used the Old Testament name (which is always a type and a symbol), we have used it to help us by gathering up all the historic associations of that name in the Old; but let us remember, it still belongs to the *"not."* As to a name and as to a place and as to a thing, a mountain and so forth, it belongs to the *"not."* What belongs to the *"but"* is what lies behind that name Zion, its spiritual value, its spiritual meaning, its spiritual lesson. And if we were asked, "What is that, what is its spiritual value, its spiritual meaning?"—we have got to come back and answer: *"God has spoken in His Son, . . . He has spoken in His Son, Whom He appointed Heir of all things, through Whom He made the worlds."*

God has spoken. Now, how has He at the end of those times spoken? The speaking of God from a certain point in history on to the end is *"in His Son."* Is it necessary to clarify that and say His speaking is not "about" His Son?—not the teaching, the doctrine, of Christ, but the Person—in the Person! He hath spoken in a Person. Do try to get hold of that, dear ones. It is in Him, in Christ, that God speaks! Now let us try to break that up for a few moments.

Zion, if you are going to use the name, is in representation the fulness of Christ. That is what this letter is about, fulness and finality in Christ. And Zion, as a name, represents that. The fulness of God's Son—that is Zion; and that fulness is God's speech for and in this dispensation. God's speech is the fulness that is in His Son.

God's Speech Is The Fulness That Is In His Son

Now you remember when you go back to the beginning of the Old Testament and God has intervened in the history of this earth in what is called "the creation," it all begins with that word *"God"*—*"In the beginning, God."* In the beginning, God. And then what? God spake.

God said, *"Let there be light"* and so on. God spoke and out of His speaking everything came. You come over to your New Testament and although the Gospel of John is not arranged first, that is, chronologically (and for quite a good heavenly reason, the Holy Spirit's wisdom), the Gospel of John really does stand at the beginning because the other three gospels begin on this earth in history, they begin at Bethlehem in Matthew and Luke or, as in the case of Mark, at the beginning of the ministry of Jesus. But John overleaps all time and goes right back to the dateless beginning, and he opens with this: *"In the beginning was the Word, and the Word was with God, and the Word was God . . . and the Word became flesh."* Here in this new beginning of a New Creation, of a new order, the *"but"* era, God speaks the Word.

We have heard something this week about *"the Logos."* I am not trying to add, and certainly not to improve, but I am going to say a little more about that. As you know, *"the Logos"* is *"the Word"* there in John, *"In the beginning was the Logos, the Logos was with God, the Logos was God . . . and the Logos became flesh, tabernacled among us."* In the beginning was the Logos. Of course, John has taken that word from the Greek, which in the Greek world had its own particular meaning.

[1]   THE WORD, THE LOGOS, WAS DIVINE THOUGHT:—
THE MIND AND THOUGHT OF GOD BEHIND EVERYTHING ELSE.

First of all, in the Greek mind, the word *"logos"* meant "a thought, something in the mind": that is where it begins, **"the thought"** or, if you like to make it general, "thoughts." Logos is, first of all, thoughts or a thought. Then, keeping to the Greek, *"logos"* is **"the expression of the thought,"** the thought put into expression. It may be words, but it is what is in the mind expressed, given expression. That is the content of *"logos."* It may or may not go beyond that in the Greek, but in the Bible it certainly does.

It is true that *"Logos, the Word,"* was Divine thought, something in the mind of God first before ever there was expression or utterance. Something that was the mind of God. "In the beginning, in the beginning was the mind, the thought, of God." What a large world that door opens up. You have got the whole of our New Testament there, the mind and thought of God behind everything else. But then, that mind and thought of God was expressed, was given expression. *"God said."* Out of His thought, out of His mind—God said. As Paul puts it in II Corinthians: *"God, Who commanded the light to shine out of darkness, hath shined in our hearts."* God said, by expression. And what happened? Ah, that is the point. That is *"the Word, the Logos."*

[2] THE WORD, THE LOGOS, OF THE LORD IS A DIVINE ACT:—WHEN GOD EXPRESSES HIS MIND SOMETHING HAPPENS, IT IS A FIAT.

You see (and follow me closely now for I am going to perhaps be exacting on you for concentration for a little while), when God expresses His mind, it is not something just in language, in verbiage, in diction, but something happens. Whenever God spoke, and whenever God speaks, something happens. God's speaking according to the Bible is always an act. *"He spake, and it was done; He commanded, and it stood fast."* The Word of the Lord is an act. In Hebrews, you come to chapter four: *"The Word of God is quick, powerful, sharper than any twoedged sword, piercing even to the dividing asunder of soul and spirit, and of the joints and marrow,"* and so on. God's Word is an act. It is a *Fiat,* something happens. God's thought put into expression resolves itself into something that was not before. You can never be the same after God has spoken. Even if you were to refuse it, resist it, that has been a crisis. So Jesus will say, *"The word which I spoke, that will judge him in the last day."* They shall judge you, and me, in the last day. If you do not believe in Me, the words that I speak, you will have to meet those in the last day—because this is something not just said but something put into the universe which is a crisis. The Word of God is a crisis. The Word of God is an act: *"He spake, and it was done; He commanded, and it stood fast."*

[3] THE WORD, THE LOGOS, IS A PERSON:—
THE MIND, THE EXPRESSION, THE ACT OF GOD
BECOMES INCARNATE, IT IS IN A PERSON.

But that does not exhaust the word *"Logos"* as used by John and as *"the Word of God"* in the Bible. There is a third aspect to the Word. True, it is the thought, the mind or the mindedness of God. True, the Logos is the expression of God by which something happens. It is the act of God, but then the third aspect of Logos is **Its Person.** It takes up its residence in a Person, it becomes personal; in other words, it becomes

Incarnate. The mind of God, the expression of God is Incarnate. It is in a Person. Any encounter with Jesus Christ is a crisis. Any encounter with Jesus Christ is meeting God. God was in Christ. It is an encounter with God. It is not just what Jesus says, although that is an expression of the mind of God in words, but, it is a personal encounter that has to be. In the first place, it is not an encounter with what is written, not an encounter with words—it is an encounter with a Person. *"The Word became flesh,"*—Incarnate.

So, let us go over again the third aspect of the Logos: the incarnation of the Divine thought in a practical issue in history, in an act, in a Fiat; it was an act of the Incarnate and Glorified Word of God. Ask Saul of Tarsus whether his encounter with Jesus on the Damascus Road was a Fiat. The whole dispensation answers that very loudly. This is the Logos. *"God hath spoken in His Son"*—Who is the embodiment of His Mind, Who is the expression of That Mind, Who is the incarnation of That Mind. And this whole Letter to the Hebrews is just an analyzing of that or a summing up of that: God speaking, God speaking In His Son! God speaking in His Son; and all which follows that, from chapter one at its beginning right through to the end, is just the exposition of God speaking in His Son. You must read the Hebrew Letter in the light of that. God is speaking.

So when you come to Hebrews in chapter twelve, at this section from verse twenty-two onward, what have you?—You have the gathering up of that speaking of God in His Son and concentrating it. And if you break up the section, you will see it is a concentration of what is true about the Person of the Lord Jesus; and you must look at Zion like that. It begins there. *"Ye are come to . . ."* well, we say *"Zion, the city of the living God,the heavenly Jerusalem, . . ."*?—No! that is symbolic language. We are come to the Son of God in all His meaning. God speaking in His Son: the thought of God expressed, the thought of God Incarnate, Personified, so that *"Zion,"* as a typical word or name, is the embodiment of all that.

God speaks, or in the Old Testament God spoke in Zion. He spoke out of Zion. You go through the Psalms and you go through Isaiah's prophecies, especially the last chapters of those prophecies, and refer to them again. You go through them presently and see how God is speaking out of Zion. It even comes to this: *"The Lord . . . shall roar out of Zion."*[4] God speaks out of Zion; in other words, <u>out</u> <u>of</u> <u>His</u> <u>Son</u>, hath spoken in His Son. Now, having stated that, what is the heart of all this, according to the statement at the beginning? *"God, hath at the end of these days, in these times, in this time, hath spoken in Son."* How? How?— SONWISE—"IN SON." The absence of the definite article *"His"* before the word *"Son,"* the absence of *"His"* in the original text, does not make any difference, because the very next statement is: *"Whom He appointed Heir of all things."* So <u>this</u> <u>Son</u> <u>is</u> <u>His</u> <u>Son</u>. We note that and pass on.

The Governing Law Of God's Speaking Is Sonship

The governing law of God's speaking is sonship,—sonship. That is the thing which governs God in all His speaking. Sonship. And as has already been said, sonship is not a beginning thing. It is a final thing, it is an ultimate thing. Here is Romans eight again: *"waiting for our adoption,"* the manifestation of the sons. The end which governs all God's speaking in Christ is sonship. If you would like to change the word, it is *"adoption."* It is put at the end. Sonship—adoption, is an end, an object, toward which God is moving by the speaking in His Son.

By birth, we are children, by adoption, we are sons. And it is just here that we must remember there is a difference between the spiritual conception of adoption and the secular. Someone holding a little baby yesterday, not of the family or even of the same race, said, "You see, I have adopted her." Oh, no, that will not do here. That is not the scriptural conception of adoption. As you have been told, the scriptural meaning of adoption is someone already in the family by birth who has grown to maturity and then comes the day of maturity, the coming of age, the celebration, the festivity, the coming of age day, when the father takes his own child, **now mature,** puts the toga on him, invests him with the symbols and insignia of authority to be as the father in this world. Everyone meeting that adopted son has to reckon with the father. He is, in effect, the father. He has been adopted or, the word really in Hebrews is, placed. <u>Placed</u> <u>in</u> <u>this</u> <u>position</u> <u>of</u> <u>responsibility</u> <u>because</u> <u>of</u> <u>maturity</u>.

---

[4] Joel 3:16

Now we will have to come back to that from another standpoint as we go on.

What I am saying is that this is the end to which God is working. His beginning is begetting. His beginning is birth from above, bringing in a family. But, mark you, even in the born child there is the spirit of adoption. The adoption has not come yet, but there is the spirit of adoption. That is what Paul says, in essence, in Romans and Galatians: *"because we have the spirit of adoption we cry, Abba, Father."*

I think once when I was here before I told you what that really means. What does *"Abba"* mean? Why put the two things together, is it just two words of different languages?—*"Abba"* in one language, *"Father"* in another. What is it? *"Abba"* is the quality, not the relationship, it is the quality of a child, a little child. And when a little child turns to its Father and says, "dear Father"—you have got *"Abba."* It is a heart relationship. Abba—dear Father. There is something very close, very intimate. It is a mark of spiritual infancy. Of course, that is the first thing we lisp, is it not? When we are really born from above, we do not say when we go to pray: "Almighty Most Terrible and Fearful God. . . ." Our first lisp is, *"Our Father."* That is the beginning of the Christian life. We have the Spirit of adoption, although we have not come to the adoption yet. That is coming if we allow the Spirit of adoption to develop us for adoption. **That is the whole course of the spiritual life.**

ALL THE DISCIPLINE OF THE CHILDREN OF GOD IS GOVERNED BY THIS ONE OBJECT: SONSHIP.

Well, that is all here, and I am saying that the final object toward which God the Holy Spirit is working is what is called adoption, sonship. It is governing everything, it is governing everything. It is the end which is brought to bear upon the whole course. What is God doing? Well, Hebrews will tell you. All the discipline, all the discipline of the child of God, of the children of God, is governed by this one object—sonship. So you have: *"My son, despise not thou the chastening of the Lord, for whom the Lord loveth* (His children) *He chasteneth, He disciplines. He scourges every son to be set by Him, to be placed."* That is the discipline of the Christian life. *"And what child, or what potential son, is he who has no discipline, whom the Father chasteneth not?"* As you know, the writer uses a very strong word about such. They are not true sons, they are illegitimate children who have come into a false position, if they be without discipline.

There is a tremendous revolt against discipline in this world, throwing off of authority and all control, all government, all discipline. There is a revolt against it everywhere, especially in youth. The Word says that is how it is going to be at the end: *"disobedient to parents"* and so on. This does not at all go well for God's final purpose of a family, not of infants but of grown sons, chastened for eternal responsibility. God's final purpose, grown sons chastened for eternal responsibility—governmental position in the Kingdom in the ages to come. There is so much about that in the New Testament. That is Ephesians. Discipline, for that. Dealings of God with us in this way **for that!**

Oh, look again at this illustrated. If you want, look again to the history of Zion. What a disciplined thing Zion was. God was having no nonsense with Zion. God was tolerating nothing less than His full thought in Zion. When Zion deprived Him of what He had brought Zion into being for, He then set Zion aside, showed that He had no longer interest in that as a thing. He disciplined Zion. Read again your Psalms. Read again the prophets. They are all concerned, as we shall show, with Zion. What discipline! What discipline! Through the years, and finally the seventy years of exile while in captivity, what discipline of the people of Zion.

Shall we just look for a moment at Isaiah. I did say a little while ago that as you look at the last chapters of Isaiah, you will find these final chapters are all concerned with Zion. Let us look, shall we, at chapter sixty-one, for we are very near the end of Isaiah when we come to sixty-one. Or you can go to sixty, if you like, where it reads, *"Arise, shine; for thy light is come, and the glory of the Lord is risen upon thee."* But go on to sixty-one: *"The Spirit of the Lord God is upon Me . . . the Lord hath anointed Me. . . ."* And here again it is the twofold interpretation. Zion is here pointing on to the other <u>One</u> Who used these very words and applied them to Himself.

Now to chapter sixty-two. (Cut out the numbers sixty-one and sixty-two, the chapter divisions being artificial.) *"For Zion's sake will I not hold My peace, and for Jerusalem's sake I will not rest, until her righteousness* [yes, remember your Amplified, until her right standing with God, until her right standing with God] *go forth as brightness, and her salvation as a lamp that burneth . . . nations shall see thy righteousness* (thy right standing with God), *and all the kings thy glory."—"I will not hold My peace"* until that happens. This is the cry of the prophet, and you can go on in these last chapters of Isaiah and find it is there; and what I am going to come to in that very connection is this, that Zion was the burden, the concern, the heartbreak, of the prophets.

Prophetic ministry always focuses upon Zion. The work of true prophetic ministry (whether in the Old or New Testament) relates to this Divine thought that is enshrined in this word *"Zion,"* as we have it in the Letter to the Hebrews, to have this amongst the nations, this expression of the fulness of Christ in sonship in a corporate body. That is the end toward which God is working and carrying out all His work of discipline.

I do want to apply this in a practical way. You see, we, rightly so, perhaps, are concerned with the work, what we call the Lord's work, concerned with evangelism, getting souls saved. Nothing wrong with that! That is all right! Do not think I am undervaluing that. The work of preaching and teaching, and having meetings and conferences and all that which we can compass by this word or phrase, "the work of the Lord," we are concerned about that. Very much concerned about it. Perhaps you ministers are very much concerned about your ministry, that is, the next address that you are going to give, and you are filling up your notebooks now. You have got a congregation in view. The work of ministry, of evangelism, or whatever else may come within that term, "the work of the Lord," perhaps you are very much more than anything else concerned with that. Perhaps in your concern you say: "We must be in the work, we must be given to the work."

Here my brother[5] is going to forgive me because as I have said, I am trying to focus this thing right down. We have been having something in the evening meetings that I consider to be the very essence of the Lord's interests. It is the same thing that I am talking about only in other language: *"the overcomer,"* the essence of the Divine thought and intention in Zion. Our brother has been laid on his back for many weeks, and we should not have got that if he had not been; and some of us know that the Lord sometimes sees that it is far more economical to take us out of "the work" than to keep us in it, to lay us aside from all our busyness for Him to get the essence of things. He is after the essential, the

---

[5] One of the speakers at the convocation

intrinsic. Men are after the big. Pragmatism governs so much of Christian work. I venture you do not know what I mean by that word, "pragmatism." It means if a thing is successful, then it is right. That is shallow thinking. The devil has got a lot of success, is he right?! Many things are apparently very successful, growing, increasing, and everybody says, "My, that is the thing." Is it? That is pragmatism. If a thing is successful and popular and everybody is flocking to it, it must be right.

All right, then. What of Jesus of Nazareth? How they flocked, they followed. He told why. Why? He said, "... *because you did eat of the loaves and fishes, because you saw the signs and wonders, and a wicked and adulterous generation seeketh after signs,*" and they flock for that. But, but—this is short-lived. Short-lived. Presently they are all forsaking. They are being sifted out. He is being left alone. All the marks of success are being withdrawn from this world's standpoint, and, at last, is this a successful movement with Him hanging on the Cross? Is that pragmatic? Well, we know today!—No, no, a thing is not necessarily right because people are flocking here or there, crowding, rushing; not because a thing seems to be gaining much ground and becoming big, not necessarily. Wait for that. Wait through the tribulation and then you will get "great multitudes, which no man can number." But that is not pragmatic in this earthly sense.

You see what I mean! There is the discipline, the discipline of being sifted down from the husks to the kernel, from the chaff to the wheat. And *wheat corn is bruised,*" says the Prophet Isaiah. Wheat corn is bruised, it is bruised. He is after the true genuine bread, and the constitution of that is something that has been ground to powder, has been bruised. Does this explain something to you, your own history?—It is very true, it is the Word, you see.

Therefore there is this section in Hebrews about sonship, *"the chastening of the Lord,"* chastening of the Lord, and chastening for every one of us may mean something different. What would be chastening to you would not be to me, but what would be chastening to me would not be to you. You can get away with lots of things, but the Lord knows where to find you out, where you cannot get away. I might be able to force myself through something on sheer natural soul force. I do not know whether that is true now, but it might be. Perhaps in the past it has been true, but the Lord knows just how to chasten me, and He knows the thing that is chastening for me and, perhaps, for no one else. Oh, do not just bring that word *"chastening"* into a narrow definition. It is the thing that "gets" us individually, finds us out. It is the thing, which to me, is real discipline.

There are some nice, very patient, forbearing, longsuffering temperaments, and, you know, they can be spoken to and treated ill and they do not ruffle a bit, they just go on. But with someone else, the Lord brings a rather awkward person into their home and, my word, that person is disciplined. See what I mean? Chastening, discipline, is what it means to us individually. But whatever that is, and you may say, "Well, why does the Lord do this with me? Look, He does not do that with all these other people. They are getting away with it"—*"until I went into the sanctuary of God"* and saw things from His standpoint. "The Lord is dealing with me and letting off all these other people in that way, but He has got me." Do I revolt and say, "It is not fair. The Lord is not fair, He does not do this with other people." Oh, no, this attitude will not do. **He is focusing upon this end, this sonship matter, for adoption for eternal responsibility.** Get hold of that, and we will go on.

TRUE SONSHIP: WITHIN A SENSE OF DESTINY— *"THE CALLED ACCORDING TO HIS PURPOSE."*

With Zion again in the background of our thought, let us pick out one more thing about Zion. I expect you well know that in the blood and constitution of a true Israelite, a true Hebrew, a true Jew, in the very constitution and blood, there is a consciousness or sense of destiny. Their thought is: "We are the chosen people, and we are chosen for God's purpose and intention. It is not something that we have taken on as an ideology, as a philosophy, of our existence, it is in our blood." They cannot get away from it. It is themselves. It is like that. A true Jew, citizen, and child of Zion has this inwrought sense and consciousness of destiny. It is the reason, the ground, of why they have been able to suffer so much, why they could go through their persecutions and survive, why they could endure so much. It is not because they make up their minds, not just the strength of their will, it is something born in them, part of their very being, it is elemental to them that they are a people of destiny. They hold on to it, they cling to it, they are still at the wailing wall. It was born out of this; however, that belongs to the *"not."*

Here we are with the *"but,"*—*"we have come to Zion."* And we have come to Zion in this sense: there is by right, if it is a true citizenship in heaven, *"this one was born there"*; if it is a true child of God, there is something about such a true child of God that although they may not define it, they may not know even the Scriptures about it, within them they have this sense of destiny that there is some purpose governing our salvation, there is some meaning beyond our present comprehension for which we have been called, there is something in us in our very constitution that says, "called according to His purpose." A sense of destiny, this is essential to Zion. This is what the New Testament is all about, and this is what this Letter to the Hebrews is all about. This is true sonship.

Now, we do not like these ideas, we do not like this language, but with the Jews, the true Jews, there was this element in them of "selectiveness." You do not like that language, do you? Selective, something separate, something different, something other, something not general but particular. The inwrought consciousness of being called and chosen for something, which we call destiny. And only that will keep us going through the discipline, only that will keep us going through the suffering, the adversity, the perplexity.

Have you not been as I have, more than once and more than twice, at the point where you would have despaired. Been left to yourself, you would have given up, and gone out, and taken another way, and even washed your hands of Christianity. Have you never been pressed? Well, if you have not, all right, thank the Lord; but there is such pressure. Even Paul, with all his wonderful experience and knowledge of the Lord, came to a point where he said: *"I was pressed out of measure, . . . I despaired of life."* Paul? You despaired?! And you are always telling people not to despair. You were writing about the God of hope, and you tell me you despaired? And you told people to be in the ascendant, on top, and you say: **"I was pressed beyond my measure."** Yes, all right, perhaps you do not know all that, perhaps you know a little of it, but the children of Zion are kept by something. They are held by something. It is this indefinable something which we call "destiny." There is a hold on us that will not let us go. There is a grip upon us that even when we say we are going, we cannot go. Even when we come to the depths of despondency, we do not go out after all. We do not. We decided to, but we do not. No, it is not something to analyze and put into a system of teaching, doctrine, but it is some deep reality that is holding us. We are children of destiny, *"the called according to His Purpose."* Oh, if you want a little Bible study, I would like you to go through and underline that word *"according, according as, according to."* A marvelous word that is with Paul. It is all according to something. Zion was elect, chosen, separated, made distinct, because of destiny—its great purpose: and there was that in its very constitution, in the very blood, in the very blood, a sense that "There is something beyond, unto which we have been called."

Now I am coming back to the prophets. The prophets were supremely concerned with Zion, just because of Zion's destiny. Oh, how burdened they were about Zion, and, of course, in their case, their burden and their concern for Zion was the recovery of Zion. Zion had lost out. Zion had ceased to be what it was called to be, what God intended. It had lost out, and so the prophets are all concerned with the recovery of Zion and Zion's testimony. That is prophetic ministry.

Oh, prophetic ministry. What do you mean?—foretelling? foretelling events? All right, if you like to have that, you can. But the real essence of prophetic ministry is the recovery of the fulness of Jesus Christ which has been lost. It is a recovery and a reinstating of the testimony of Jesus in the Church. That is true prophetic ministry, and do not bring prophetic ministry down to this and that and something else. The gift of prophecy. What is the gift of prophecy? Only foretelling? It may be that, or it may never be that at all and still be the gift of prophecy. The gift, the function, the anointing, of prophecy is the recovery of the full testimony of Jesus, the recovery ministry that does not have that as its objective, clear and strong and definite, is not prophetic ministry. The prophets were thus burdened. Read Isaiah 43 again in the light of that.

Test Everything By Its Eternal, Spiritual Value

Well, now, we come near the end of this morning. Again then, Zion is the embodiment of the spiritual values of Jesus Christ. Underline that word "spiritual values." Test everything, test everything by the spiritual values. Test everything not from the standpoint of pragmatism at all but from the standpoint of its spiritual, which means, its eternal value. The ministry of anyone, my own or anyone else's, is not going to be judged by the number of conventions or meetings at which we speak and the amount of Bible teaching that we give—it is never going to be judged by that. Understand that. You may have your diaries full of engagements, preaching engagements; you may be on the way of a very, very busy Bible teacher; you may be very busy, and you may have no time for anything else; and yet, with all the sum total, it is not going to be judged, dear friends, by how much you have done in that way. It is going to be judged by its eternal, spiritual value; what the essential spiritual value is when this life is gone, when I am gone, when you are gone, when all the teachers are gone, and we arrive in heaven and discover **what was taken up then in our lifetime and is there.** *"The things which are seen are temporal,"* in the preachers and the teachers and the conferences. *"The things which are seen are temporal; but the things which are not seen are eternal."* And that is the standpoint of Zion, the essential spiritual value of everything.

Are you, dear preachers, teachers, really burdened in heart that every bit of your ministry shall have a spiritual, eternal value? Not the address, not the address! No, it is not whether my address is successful, accepted, or not. **It is what is the spiritual, lasting value from eternity's and heaven's standpoint of anything.** Surely our ambition ought to be that when it is all over here, when it is all over, when there are no more conferences down here, no more ministries and addresses down here, and we all gather above, our ambition is to find there people who say: "Look here, I would not be here but for what the Lord did in me through your ministry." That is it, is it not? Oh, focus upon that, for Zion is, let me repeat, the embodiment of spiritual values. Not a place, not a sect, not anything temporal. That is not Zion. Now it is the concentrated and intrinsic values of Jesus Christ. That is Zion.

God's Jealousy For Zion

Upon what note shall I finish this morning? Well, with all that in view, of course, the right note would be God's jealousy for Zion. prophets shared the jealousy of God for Zion. The Lord said: *"I am jealous for Zion, with great jealousy, and I am jealous for her with great wrath. I am returned unto Zion, and will dwell in the midst of Jerusalem."* Where is God's heart set? Not on any temporal expression of the old Zion. That is the *"not."* But God's jealousy, God's concern, God's wrath, relates to the true, intrinsic, spiritual values of His Son Jesus Christ. He is focused upon that. He will look after those spiritual values. **He will look after the spiritual values.** That ought to comfort us in the ministry, especially. See, people may repudiate, may discredit, and may go away and leave us. All right, that discipline is pretty hard. But wait awhile, perhaps in their own lifetime, they will come back or they will confess: "Look here, I got something from you which has been my real salvation. I did not recognize it at the time, but I know now that what you were saying, what you were doing, was the thing which has become my deliverance, my salvation, in the time of trouble."

Well, it is like that. God will look after the spiritual values if you are concerned more with spiritual values than building up something big down here. That is where His jealousy is. Sooner or later His wrath will be shown from Zion. In that sense, the enemies will have to bow, they will have to surrender. As in the eternity, *"every knee shall bow, and tongue confess."* All the enemies of Christ are going to be very much humbled. God is going to roar out of Zion. Well, let us be quite sure that it is Zion in this sense: "Ye are come to that, to Zion." Let us leave it there for now. The Lord interpret. We pray:

We do pray that, Lord, this very hour may be used by Thee to produce those essential eternal values. Not just be an hour with ministry, more or less appreciated, but that there may be something wrought, something planted, something put inside us constitutionally, that shall appear in heaven and in glory as the Divine fiat, the Word, the Word of God, which did something. So help us. Seal this time then, in that way; forgiving all mistakes and errors and faults in the human, and take charge of Thine Own Interests, for Thy Name's Sake, Amen.

79

Chapter Six

A Final Shaking

Lord Jesus Christ, we seek Thy Face. It is written, "The Light of the Glory of God is in the Face of Jesus Christ." Oh, Thou, Who didst forfeit, for that one terrible moment, the Countenance of Thy Father in order that we might never come there, that we might be received and abide in the Light of the Countenance of God, do this morning bring us into that very blessed inheritance through Thy Cross. The Face, the Countenance, the Towardness, the Unforsakingness of God. May this indeed be a time within the Veil when we dwell in the Light of the Countenance, the Face of the Lord. Lord Jesus Christ, in all that great and wonderful meaning, we now seek Thy Face. As we wait on Thee, show us Thy Face, Lord. For Thy Name's Sake, Amen.

In this final hour of this particular ministry, it is necessary to seek special grace to gather up and concentrate all that has been said throughout this week. But I think, perhaps I should say I feel, that the leading of the Lord is to gather up and concentrate all with one part of this Letter to the Hebrews before us. As the letter is drawing to a close, we reach that part of it which is marked as chapter twelve; and it is in verses 25 to 28 that it says: *"See that ye refuse not Him That speaketh."*— Remember, the beginning is: *"God hath spoken in His Son."*

See that ye refuse not Him That speaketh. For if they escaped not when they refused Him That warned them on earth, much more shall not we escape if we turn away from Him That warneth from heaven: Whose Voice then shook the earth: but now He hath promised, saying, "Yet once more will I make to tremble not the earth only, but also the heaven." And this word, "Yet once more," signifieth the removing of those things that are shaken, as of things that have been made, that those things which are not shaken may remain. Wherefore, receiving a kingdom that cannot be shaken, let us have grace, whereby we may offer service well-pleasing to God with reverence and awe.

The significance then is a kingdom which cannot be shaken, as we have been trying to see and show. The significance of this letter for the present time is the *"yet once more"*; that is, in this dispensation which has come in with Christ, the shaking firstly of the earth side of things and then the shaking of the heaven side of things.

The earth side, I think, had a special reference to what was just about to happen in old, traditional, historic Judaism. This letter was probably written in the year 69. I cannot be positive about it because all the expositors and scholars are divided about who wrote it and when it was written. To whom it was written exactly, you need not worry about that; but I am fairly sure that it was related to what the Holy Spirit knew was about to take place in the historic Judaism and earthly Israel. The probability is that this letter was written in the year 69, and you know what happened in the year 70. If that is true, it was a very short distance from the writing of this letter to the destruction of Jerusalem which was so utter, so terrible. Some of you, you pastors especially, will have read Josephus; and if you have, the section on the invasion and destruction of Jerusalem is one of the most terrible things you can read in history. It took place in the year 70, when everything in that Jerusalem was devastated and desolated and the Jews scattered, as Peter says, *"throughout Pontus, Galatia, Cappadocia, Asia, and Bithynia"* and everywhere else. The earth side was certainly shaken, not only shaken but brought down and devastated; and from that, it has not yet recovered. There is no temple. There is no integrated Israel on the earth. That is the earth side, and this is the prophecy, as you know, taken out of the Old Testament that this would happen.

It is interesting, very interesting, significant, and instructive, to go back to the setting of that prophecy (which we are not going to do) to see the setting of it in the history of Israel, to see the conditions that were arising in the time of Haggai. The prophecy is taken up, brought right over here so many, many years later, and applied to the situation which is reached in this Letter to the Hebrews at that crisis time: the shaking of the earth. Of course, it applies particularly to the shaking of the earthly Jerusalem, the earthly Israel. We say that and leave it, but that is only half of the statement: *"Yet once more I will shake not only the earth (and the earth side), but also the heaven."*

So in the light of what the Lord has been saying this week and in the light of this letter in its full content, we are surely right in saying that Christianity, which is the other side; if you like, the heaven side, is going to be subjected also to such a shaking. Maybe we will not be far wrong if we say it has begun. It is on, it is proceeding, it is spreading. However, you may feel it has not reached your country yet. Well, if you are talking of merely material things, of outward economies, there may be few symptoms of it as yet; but spiritually, it is world-wide. It is the shaking of Christianity, the shaking of what we may call the heaven side of things, as different from the historic, earthly Israel.

But the point is that there is a universal shaking to take place in the economy of God; in the sovereign ordering of God, a universal shaking. What for? Here it says in order that there shall be nothing left **but what God Himself has established.** Note the little phrase: *"As of things that have been made."* Who made them? Who made them? Things made. The things that God made, has made and established, are the things and the only things which will ultimately remain, and the shaking is for that.

Now this letter is a comprehensive comparison and contrast (or discrimination) between the passing and the permanent, between the temporal and the spiritual, between the earthly and the heavenly. That is the Letter to the Hebrews. That is what we have been emphasizing all the way through—the *"not"* any longer. A comprehensive *"not"*: *"Ye are not come."* And the *"But"*: *"But ye are come."* Two great comprehensive orders, economies, sovereignties, whatever you may call them, this whole letter has to do on the one side with the things which are transient and not abiding; and on the other side, with the things which are permanent and which remain *"that (in order that) the things which cannot be shaken* . . . [here is your *"that"* again] . . . *in order that the things which cannot be shaken may remain."* This is the comparison and contrast, or discrimination, that is made by this letter as a whole.

Here, as a kind of parenthesis, let me put this. It is important for us to remember that this letter was written to a people who for a long period had held the position of a people whom God had taken out of the world to Himself, showing that it is possible for such a people to miss the way. It is possible for such a people to make their position an earthly one, just an earthly one, or make that position earthbound. And that is the pulse of this letter, not to Israel only but to Christians. This is the **"on-high calling"** letter. This is the heavenly side. This is the New Israel which God has taken out of the world to Himself and for Himself;

but through and through this letter runs this reminder that a people who were like that for so long, taken out for God to God, did in the end miss the object, miss the way, did not arrive. Chapter three is all on that. *"They did not enter in, they perished in the wilderness."*

Oh, dismiss your chapter divisions and see chapter three. There you have the people who failed to enter in, who perished in the wilderness. *"They could not enter in"* is the word, *"because of unbelief."* That is chapter three, but chapter four opens, and you are not far into chapter four before you have this: *"the word of God is quick, and powerful, and sharper than any twoedged sword, piercing even to the dividing asunder of soul and spirit."* I am not going to launch out on that; but the point is, that in the wilderness where they perished, it was because they did not discriminate between soul and spirit. They did not understand the doctrine, of course; and, in effect, they lived in their souls.—That is, they lived in the self-life, the self-direction of everything: how this affects us, what we are going to get out of this, what this means in our interests. The self-life is the soul-life. The spirit is not that. **The spirit is unto God, is the God-life**.

However, this cleavage was not made in the wilderness; and although they had come out by such a mighty work of God, and become God's people, and were separated unto Him, yet because they persisted in what we now call in the New Testament terms "soul-life," because as the people of God there was no discrimination between the soul-life and the spirit, because there was no clear-cut between the two as of a *"two-edged sword,"* cutting both ways, up and down, because there was no clear-cut between the self-life and the life of the spirit, they perished in the wilderness. And do you tell me that that is not a possibility for Christians? That is the point of the letter, you see. Dismiss the division of chapter three and four as simply mechanical divisions, and pass right on and say, "Why did they perish in the wilderness? Why did they not enter in?" Why? Because there was not this clean-cut between self and the Lord, between soul and spirit.

Soul and spirit, this is a large matter about which we have heard too much. I think there is too much talk about that just now. It has become a very fascinating subject. You will never capture people more quickly and mentally than when you begin to talk about soul and spirit. It is a very interesting, mental subject; it is most fascinating. I am coming to the place where I want to talk about the things and not the names, the meaning and not the language or the terminology; however, that is by the way.

Now, you see, what I am saying is this letter was addressed to a people who for a long time had held the position of a people separated unto God, but who eventually missed the way and lost the inheritance, lost the meaning of their separation, because of the earthbound. Judaism—earthbound, and God says, *"I will shake"* that,*" I will shake"* that earthboundness, and *"I will shake"* it so devastatingly that there will be no temple and no Jerusalem and no headquarters for the nation at all, the whole thing will be smashed. *"I will shake"* that earth side, and He did, and has done that, and it has gone on all these centuries.

But He does not stop there. Then He goes over to the other side: *"I am going to shake this other thing, too—this Christianity."* It came in from heaven, the Holy Ghost sent down from heaven, but what have men done with Christianity?—brought it down to earth, made it earthbound, made it something. The Lord, foreseeing that, prophesies: *"I will shake"* that also, *"I will shake"* that also, and Christianity as a merely earthly system, will go into the melting pot, it will go into the fire, **and only that which is really and truly heavenly, of the Spirit of God, will survive and come out.**

You see the force of this letter?! Hence, if you go through this letter, you will find that it is divided along two lines: **the line of precaution, of warning; and the line of resolution.** Now here is a little Bible study for you. You go through and mark the nine times in which the word *"lest"* occurs. *"Lest."* First, *"Let us . . . fear, lest, a promise being left us of entering into His rest, any of you should seem to come short. . . ."* *"Lest."* Nine times that word *"lest"* is used through the letter. Trace it and see its context. "Lest, for this reason . . . ; lest, for that reason. . . ." Nine times *"lest"* gives precaution and warning. And then, ten times you have *"let us";* and connected with that phrase, *"let us"* is an admonition to resolution, to be resolved. No use, you cannot take anything for granted about this. You are not going to get there by drift, and that is the first *"lest."* *"We ought to give the more earnest heed to the things which we have heard, lest at any time we . . . let them slip."*—"Lest by any means you drift away, drift past." That is the real language. You drift, and the picture behind this language is a picture which is a very simple one but very, very clear in its implication.

I used to be a yachtsman in Scotland, and we would go out on our day's sail; but the most anxious moment, the most tense moment, was when we came back to pick up our moorings. If the tide of the current was flowing strongly, and if the wind was high, there would be a chance of missing our moorings. You have got to take off your power, take down your sails, get your head toward the mooring; and then everybody would look toward the one with the boat hook-up in the bow, someone lying down flat on the deck with outstretched hands to take hold of that mooring and to grab it and hold it, because the tide or the current flowing would even pull you into the sea if you did not hold tight. Here was tenseness. The peril was that you would miss it and drift past it; and there were rocks over there. **You could drift past.** You could miss and drift, carried by the tide or the current or the wind. Oh, it was a tense moment. You got it and held on and were able to pull the boat up on the moorings and make fast. Then the tension is gone. "We have reached home. It is all right now. Everything is all right." Now that is the picture here which is actually used. *"Lest we drift past." Drift . . . drift . . . drift. "Lest."* Here is caution, warning!

All this is presented (and, oh, what an all it is!), this fulness and finality in Christ brought in with verses one and two of chapter one. And all that fulness and finality is in this letter, the great inheritance, a tremendous "all"; and the first warning is—"You could drift, you could drift; you could be carried past and carried away by the current, by the present breeze." Now Paul puts it in another way: *"carried about with every wind of doctrine, by the sleight of men, and cunning craftiness, . . ."* That is the same thing. That is an illustration of the *"lests,"* and there are nine of them. *"Lest we drift,"* (etc.), and over and alongside of that is the exhortation *"Let us"—"let us hold fast, let us lay hold, let us go on."* And I am just going to put another fragment in because I think it is illuminating, it may have a point of application, *"lest,"* because of the deceitfulness of sin, we are subverted.

The Deceitfulness Of Sin

The deceitfulness of sin.—Have you ever thought about that? What is the deceitfulness of sin, if the word *"sin"* is a comprehensive word? Now do not narrow it down to one of its meanings. Sin has many aspects. It works in many ways. You can call this sin and that sin and something else and a thousand things sin. Yes, but they are only aspects of the one thing. What is the meaning of the word "sin" in the Bible? **Missing the mark, missing the mark.** You may miss it because of this or that or of many things, but in the end it amounts to this: you have missed the mark. Sin, comprehensively, is "missing the mark." It is the deceitfulness of sin to subvert you from the mark, from what Paul calls *"the mark for the prize of the high calling—on-high calling."*

"Missing the mark," the deceitfulness to subvert. You may ask, "What do you mean by that deceitfulness?" Well, for me, at the moment, for this purpose this morning, it is policy in the place of principle. There is nothing more subverting, more spiritually injurious, than policy—being politic. Oh, how I have seen tragedies in the life of godly men, servants of the Lord, on this thing. I know men brought face to face with God's full purpose, but they had a position in the Christian world; and this full purpose requires a lot of adjustment as to position, adjustment as to relationships. "If I do that, my large door of opportunity for the Lord will be closed; if I do that, I will lose my influence for the Lord; if I take that way, maybe I shall be involved in much that will mean loss for the Lord, I am someone responsible for an organization that somehow or other has got to get support, and now, if I take such and such a line as has been indicated, I will lose my clientele. I will lose my financial support." That is policy, politic, alongside of what God has indicated; and the issue is, "Will I trust the Lord to look after what is of Him. I am no longer interested in anything that is not of the Lord, but if it is, can I trust the Lord to look after that while I obey Him, go His indicated way, or shall I hold on to my place of opportunity, open doors, and influences for the Lord and take this other course?"

Do you see what I mean?—The deceitfulness of missing the mark, and I have seen more than one tragedy, that after years (it is so manifest to everybody) that man has missed the way. That man was meant for something more, something other. The Lord meant something for that man, but policy came in and he argued for his policy that it was in the interests of the Lord. The deceitfulness of sin, and this letter says, "You can be subverted by the deceitfulness of sin: policy instead of principle." Does that fit in anywhere? Yes, it is necessary, you see, to pinpoint all this teaching.

The Shakeable And The Unshakeable—
The Ultimate Thing Is The Measure of Christ

So here we come back. Hebrews, the Letter to the Hebrews, is a statement of what is abiding and permanent as over against what is passing and transient; and does not that matter? Surely it does supremely matter! The shakeable and the unshakeable. The New Testament is comprised of twenty-seven books, and most of them were written to combat some form of a universality of effort to destroy what had come in with Jesus Christ. Would you like me to repeat that? Most of the New Testament was written to combat some form of a universal effort to destroy what had come in with Jesus Christ. That is a statement which is very comprehensive, and you have got to break it up and apply it to each book of the New Testament. "Oh," you say, "what then?" Were Matthew and Mark and Luke and John and Acts and on written to combat something?" Yes, and when you take that as the key, my word, are we not in a combat in Matthew? Is not the Lord Jesus in a combat in Matthew and Mark and Luke and John? It is an atmosphere of combativeness, of conflict, of antagonisms. In Acts, is that true? And so you go on with the letters. Here is some form in each one, some form of this universality of effort, to destroy what had come in with Jesus Christ. The New Testament is a comprehensive countering of a many-sided attempt to subvert the Church and pervert the meaning of God's Son. In that statement, you have got your New Testament in its real meaning; and do try to get hold of it, dear friends, in that way.

Now, the chief point of attack in this comprehensive or universal effort has always been, and still is, the measure of Jesus Christ, **the measure of Christ.** The enemy forces say: "We must, in the first place, keep Him out altogether, give Him no foothold." That is the battle of the ages and of the nations. As soon as you bring Jesus Christ into a vicinity, trouble arises, conflict begins. You must keep Him out. Oh, look how it was with Paul as he went from city to city. He is hardly there, hardly said anything, and look what happens. I do not know how much he had said in Philippi—what he had said he said to just a little handful; we do not know exactly how many were by the riverside, outside the city—and he went into the city, not preaching as far as we know, not raising issues as far as we know, but the devil knew. The devil had possession of that damsel, that priesthood, the priest-woman of the temple; and how subtle are the words spoken: *"These men are the servants of the Most High God, which shew unto us the way of salvation."* Why, the devil is preaching the Gospel; it looks as though the very devil himself is glorifying the Lord Jesus! Ah, there is something very subtle here, as the issue shows. But the point is, from the unseen world where the real intelligence of the significance of Christ is recognized, is possessed, there is this combativeness coming in wherever that which is representative of Christ, or that which is Christ in effect, arrives. There trouble arises at once. The thought is, "Keep Him out, keep Him out; and if He has got in, drive Him out. Do everything to drive out what is of Jesus Christ if He has got anywhere at all."

But then, that is not all. The plan is not only to drive Him out, but to subvert those who are His embodiment there. The plan is to subvert, to deceive, to turn aside, to bring in false teaching, false Christian ideologies, that which is "other" in its essence, that which is not essentially Christ, something put on to Christ, Christ plus, Christ plus, something put on. There are many things which are being imposed upon Christianity with all good meaning, but they are not the essence of Christ. That is the point of attack. The attack is in some way either to prevent, to force out, or to limit the measure of Christ. And do you know, dear friends, that it is the measure of Christ which is the governing thing. Not only that Christ has got in, but the measure of Christ. That is Ephesians. **The ultimate thing is the measure of Christ.**

The measure of Christ, and if you were to use that word *"measure,"* you are always transported to Ezekiel. The end of Ezekiel, what is it? It is the temple. Now I am not putting any interpretation on that, whether that is going to be literal and the Old Testament sacrifices restored. You can have your own interpretation about that, I am not touching that; but what I have there is that when the temple does come into view, it is a Heavenly Temple, and the Heavenly Messenger has His measuring line and taking the prophet round about—*"he took me around, he took me in; round, about, in and up"*—how detailed, how meticulously detailed that is with every point, every fragment, every iota, given a measurement. It is according to this measure, this Heavenly measuring reed or line. It is measured by that. Its place is only by reason of its having that measure; and I believe that stands right at the heart of the Letter to the Ephesians and the New Testament and to this Letter to the Hebrews.

Spiritually, we have come to a New Jerusalem, we have come to the dwelling of the Most High God. We are come to Zion. We are come to that which Ezekiel spiritually saw—a Spiritual Temple. We have come now to that which in every detail is measured *"according to Christ."* Let us ask ourselves: "Is this Christ? How much of Christ is here?" *"According to the measure of the stature of the fulness of Christ"*; that is the beginning of Hebrews, as well as Ephesians. And so, the chief point of the attack is always to take something of Christ away, divert from Christ, put something in the place of the very essence, the very essential, of Christ. Anyhow, anything, so long as the end of it is less of Christ, not so much of Christ, not more of Christ. It has to do then with the Lordship of Christ in everything.

The Lordship of Christ? We used to open our gathering with singing: "Crown Him, crown Him Lord of all." Lovely idea, beautiful thought, wonderful thing! But do you see what it means? Not only the thing as a whole, this wonderful Temple, House, Sanctuary; but to the last detail in the whole heavenly order, to the last detail:—Christ. **Christ in your life, in mine, He is the decision! He is the controlling principle! This is the Kingdom!**

Oh, how Christian phraseology does need redeeming and revising. We talk about the kingdom, the kingdom. "We are out in the work of the kingdom, for the spread of the kingdom." I say these words, "kingdom," "church," and all the others, need redeeming. They need revision. What is the kingdom? Well, in the original language it is quite clear, but we have missed it by some other mentality. The Kingdom of God is the sovereign rule of God. The sovereign rule of God, that is the meaning of it; and that here is brought down to a detail. It is not just some comprehensive conception of a king. No, it is where I go today, what I do today, what the Lord would have about me today. That is the Kingdom of God. A Kingdom which cannot be shaken is of that kind, where it is all Christ; hence, the necessity for making known the ground upon which security rests, the ground which cannot be shaken.

Security is a very debated thing today, a very lively concern in this world. Security, security. In every realm, this word, "security," is governing. There is nothing secure, eternally secure, but what is established by God; and that is concerning His Son, Jesus Christ, our Lord.

That is the positive side to the New Testament always, and so I am going to conclude by reminding you of the nine and the ten. Why nine precautions? Why nine times does it say, beware, *"lest"*; beware, *"lest"*?! How precautionary the Lord is, even with His best servants, His most used servants. If they are really under His Sovereign Government, what precautions He takes. Do you remember the Apostle Paul? Had the Lord ever a greater servant than the Apostle Paul? Was there ever a servant more used of God than he? I venture to say in the annals of eternity that man stands very high in preciousness to the Lord. And what did that servant say? He said, *"Lest, lest by reason of the . . . greatness of the revelations, I should . . . be exalted above measure, . . . there was given to me a thorn in the flesh, a messenger of Satan to buffet me . . . I besought the Lord three times that it might depart. And He said unto me, My grace is sufficient."* The Lord is always positive. He did not say "no"—instead He said, *"My grace is sufficient."* But the precaution of the Lord is to keep a most used and valuable servant from deviating, to keep from the awful snare of pride, even in holy things, the things of God and heaven (for spiritual pride is the worst kind of pride); and so God moves to keep from pride, from the devastation of pride: *"Lest I should be exalted."* God's precaution is *"Lest, lest"*; and here you have these nine *"lests."* Look at them, friends. Go through **them** not just as Bible study which is interesting, but note the peril that is associated with each *"lest."* **Be on your guard. Watch!** Is this that kind that abides forever, indestructible and unshakeable? **Is this Christ?**

Be Utterly Committed To The Increase Of Christ

Then you have: "Be utterly committed." And that is where the other side comes in: the *"let us, let us, let us"* is ten times, and if you sum it all up, it amounts to this: **"Be unreservedly and utterly committed."** "Committed": I think that means something more than becoming a Christian, for many, many who are children of God, yes, genuinely born-again, are not utterly committed. Not utterly committed?—No, there are some other interests. They have got one foot, or even a toe, in the world—still something where there are alternatives to utterness. But the exhortation, *"let us,"* is mentioned ten times. *"Let us, let us, etc."* Why? Because of this peril. Let us go on, do not drift, do not leave yourself to the mercy of the present current, the tide, the wind. There is nothing that will keep us safer than being positive.

I like that Moffatt translation of the phrase, *"fervent in spirit, serving the Lord."* I think it is Moffatt who has translated it: *"maintain the spiritual glow!"* Oh, it is a safeguard. There is nothing more safeguarding than being positive. Remember David on the housetop?! The tragedy, catastrophe, calamity of David's life, which left its scar on him, was being on the housetop when he ought to have been in the battle, reclining when he ought to have been <u>going</u>. Israel dilly-dallied in the wilderness for forty years instead of getting on with it, instead of going. *"Let us go on to full growth; not laying again the foundations ... but, let us go on, **go on**."* This is the great *"let us"* of chapter 6:1.

So often we are in weariness, tiredness, discouragement, despondency, perplexity, disappointment. The enemy's plan is to make us sad, make us sad, take the initiative out of us, and we are inclined to sink down; and then again and again in our spiritual history, we have to gird up the loins of our mind and say: "No, this will not do! This will not do. This is a cul-de-sac. If I get down here, there is no way through, and the only way is to come out of it and go on." Beware of your cul-de-sacs, your backwaters, your no thoroughfares. Keep on the high road, the main thoroughfare. In this sense, if you like, in this sense you can be marching to Zion; whether the doctrine is right or not, have the spirit of it. And you will sing again in that hymn, "I'll walk the golden streets." How often we carried on with that tune, and the Bible says there are no streets in the New Jerusalem, there is only one—a street of gold—all of God is in the New Jerusalem, the heavenly Jerusalem, only one, only one thing, a golden street. You are not going to choose your locality there. You are going to be put on to the Lord's highway. You see figurativeness? It is just that—all of God as represented by a golden street, and only one. We will have to learn how to live together someday.

Do you see the point? The integrating, uniting thing is: *"Let us go on to full growth."* If we are all of that mind, we will not be caught by these subverting things, these alternatives, these impositions. We will not be caught. No! The question for us is: "<u>Is this going to mean, really and truly mean, an increase of Christ, a greater fulness of Christ</u>; or is it some interesting thing, some fascinating thing, something that is going to be for the moment, for the time being, and then presently it is going to fade out, and I am going to be left high and dry." That is what happens with so many of these things. They are just for a time. You can see history strewn with the wreck of things which at one time seemed to be the thing, the ultimate thing. Well, the only thing that is the thing is the increase of Jesus Christ. That is the test of everything: the increase of Jesus Christ. And the universal challenge, contest, is on that.

I have said enough. I close there praying, as I trust you will do, that this will not be a subject of a conference, just a man's theme morning by morning. The Lord will make the challenge of it, *"For yet, yet again, I will shake not the earth only, but the heavens"*; and the shaking has begun. It has begun. Christianity has entered the great shaking. **What is going to remain?** Not the things that are made, not the earthbound things of Christianity; but that Kingdom, that Sovereign Rule, which cannot be shaken. It is Zion's citizens, *"as the mountains are round about Jerusalem,"* it cannot be shaken. That is the Old Testament idea, but here it is. It is what is really and truly Spiritual and Heavenly that is in us and that we are in. It is that, to use our first word these mornings, to which we *"are come."* The Lord help us.

Lord, with the indelible pen of the Spirit of the Living God, write the terms of the New Covenant on our hearts, on the fleshy tablets of our hearts. Write indelibly, so that it may not pass with the week, with the ministry, with the gathering of the people—however all this may be blessed and joyous—but that the Lord's Own intention, revealed to us, may abide in our hearts. Continually check us up; arbitrate between the two courses; keep us from the options, the alternatives; and may we always come back to this: "Does this mean more of Christ?" Lord, so help us. We ask with thanksgiving, in the Name of the Lord Jesus, Amen.

The Gold
of the
Sanctuary

CONTENTS

Chapter One

THE SUPREME IMPORTANCE
OF THE INCORRUPTIBLE

I WOULD LIKE AT THE VERY OUTSET to seek to put into two or three concise statements what I believe to be the Lord's object for this time.

In the first place, God is supremely concerned with ultimate and time-outlasting values. Then, He would have those values secured as directly and immediately as possible. Further, the effectiveness of a believer's life, and of the life of God's people together, is all a matter of the measure of intrinsic value ; not of comparative or superficial, but of intrinsic value. And therefore, finally, it is a matter of primary importance that the Lord's people should recognise this and be committed to it. Now, probably these statements will take on significance as we move from chapter to chapter, and so it will be profitable if they are repeated from time to time ; but I hope that the outstanding word in it has struck you— that you recognise that really what the Lord is after is intrinsic value, not comparative value, and that therefore He works with that object in view. Surely, if time is shortening, He will press that issue more and more closely.

Now will you turn with me to a passage of Scripture—II Timothy i. 8 – 10. We read this whole section because what we are after is included in it and is a part of it.

" *Be not ashamed therefore of the testimony of our Lord, nor of me his prisoner : but suffer hardship with the gospel according to the power of God ; who saved us, and called us with a holy calling, not according to our works, but ac-*

7

cording to his own purpose and grace, which was given us in Christ Jesus before times eternal, but hath now been manifested by the appearing of our Saviour Jesus Christ, who abolished death, and brought life and immortality (incorruption, A.R.V. margin) to light through the gospel ".

The clause which we take out as the key to our present consideration is this—" who abolished death, and brought life and incorruption to light ", or, to cut that down still further —" life and incorruption ".

THE GREAT ISSUE OF CHRIST'S COMING

This is a statement as to the grand issue of the coming into this world of the Lord Jesus ; as to His life, His death, His resurrection. The one great issue here is stated to be the bringing to light of life and incorruption. That coming, that living, that dying, that being raised, had secured the substance of the Gospel, so the Apostle says here, and that Gospel brought to light that great issue. This whole great matter was brought to light by the Gospel. The issue of the preaching, of the proclaiming of the good news, was life and incorruption.

Logically, therefore, the conclusion is that, apart from that coming, that living, that dying, that rising, neither life nor incorruption would be known, nor would it be available. Some translations of the passage have the word " immortality " in place of " incorruption "—" life and immortality ": an unfortunate translation for us, because " immortality " has taken on a much more general meaning in the minds of people than the word here allows. It is thought to mean continuance after physical death, survival after the life here ; but, although the Bible teaches the survival of all after physical death, that all have to stand before the judgment seat after death, that is not what is meant by the word as it is used here and in several other places in the New Testament. The word here used is connected with several different things (if I may use that word ' things ' for the moment).

In the first place it is used in connection with God. He is spoken of as "*the incorruptible God*" *(Romans i. 23)*. You would not put the word ' immortal ' there in the place of " incorruptible ", because you at once recognise that there is some element about incorruptibility that is more, and much more, than just eternal existence. He is the incorruptible God.

The word is used in connection with the Lord Jesus—" *Neither wilt thou give thy Holy One to see corruption* " *(Acts ii. 27)*. It was not possible that He should see corruption. The Lord Jesus had an incorruptible nature and life, and that meant that there was something there which conquered death. It was not just death suspended or put aside ; there was some clement that destroyed death. It was that incorruptible element.

The word is also used of the Blood of Christ. " *Ye were redeemed, not with corruptible things, with silver or gold . . . but with precious blood, as of a lamb without blemish* " *(I Peter i. 18 – 19)*. You see, there is an element in incorruption that is extra.

It is also used of the glorified bodies of believers—" *this corruptible must put on incorruption* " *(I Cor. xv. 53)*. That is related to glorification.

And once more it is used by the Apostle in relation to an incorruptible crown. " *Now they do it to receive a corruptible crown* " *(I Cor. ix. 25)*. We know what that means—something that not merely fades and dies, but completely disintegrates, and becomes something very other than glorious. But the incorruptible crown means more than just survival, as of a flower that does not die, an everlasting flower. It is something with an extra element in it.

And that is the word that is used here: " Jesus Christ . . . abolished death, and brought life and incorruption to light through the gospel ". It is the quality of the life, the inherent and intrinsic nature of the life that He has brought to light, that is the incorruptible thing. He *annulled* death, not just only non-existence, but destroying the essential nature of death which is corruption. Life and incorruption, in the way in which the Apostle links them here, are one thing. Incorruption is the nature of the life.

EFFECTIVENESS DEPENDENT UPON INCORRUPTION

What we are concerned with, then, at this time—and you will suffer this preliminary laying down of foundations, because it is a very important thing to do—what we are really concerned with now is the one supremely important thing of being incorruptible. The thing of supreme importance is incorruption. As Christ's concentrated effectiveness depended upon certain spiritual factors, so it will be with us, and the factors upon which that concentrated effectiveness depended were the factors or features of incorruption—those things in the background or constitution of His life which were incorruptible things. It was those that gave to His life its tremendous, its immense, meaning.

What a great amount of intrinsic value was found in three and a half years. That is not much in a lifetime, especially when you are looking back on life. But just consider again all that those three and a half years contained. It has not only taken two thousand years to touch the very fringe of it: it will take all the ages of the ages to exhaust the content of those three and a half years. It is an inexhaustible fulness. From the baptism to the glorification there was a concentrated fulness of value capable of filling eternity. Men through all the cen-

turies have been drinking at the fountain of those three and
a half years, and they are still drinking—all nations, all classes,
all languages—and it is as full as ever. It is still more full than
all that has been taken out of it. How pregnant were the values
of that brief spell of life here! What a seed plot for the whole
universe! How could it be that so much should come out of
so little? How could it be that for ever and ever afterward
there should be this flowing of the mighty river of inexhaustible Divine values ?

That is the question, and that is the question to which, I
believe, at least to some extent, the Lord would give us an
answer here ; and I say again, it was because during those
three and a half years that life was constituted upon incorruptible principles, incorruptible elements. *While Jesus was the
Son of God, and thus fundamentally, infinitely, different from
us as regards Godhead and Deity,* the New Testament makes
it unmistakably clear that the features of an incorruptible
life are to be reproduced and to reappear in His people; not
the features of Deity or Godhead, but these features of His
life. Otherwise what is the meaning of this—that they are
' brought to light by the Gospel '? What is brought to light?
Just certain facts? No. Certain values for us, which are to
become ours and are to be true of us as of Him, the incorruptible values and features and characteristics of Jesus
Christ as the Son of Man. And so we say again that concentration of effectiveness, of values, depended upon these incorruptible elements ; and our effectiveness, our value, will
correspond to the measure in which there are incorruptible
values in our life. Therefore certain things follow.

INCORRUPTION THE STANDARD MEASURE OF HEAVEN

Firstly, the standard weights and measures of God, of
Christ, of the Holy Spirit, of heaven, of eternity, are the one

standard of incorruption ; that is, everything is weighed and measured, from the Divine standpoint, from Heaven's standpoint, from Eternity's standpoint, according to its incorruptible characteristics. Have you grasped that? It is a tremendous statement, but it is a very true statement. Heaven has no other standard of values, God has no other standard of values, the Holy Spirit has no other standard of values, Eternity has no other standard of values. Everything is weighed and measured by its incorruptibility. Heaven takes this attitude—How much will reappear and abide throughout eternity? How much will come through when all else has gone? What will be found ultimately as glorified? That is heaven's standard ; that is the law of the incorruptible.

THE STANDARD OF INCORRUPTION APPLIED TO OUR LIVES

Therefore again we should judge everything of our lives and in our lives by its incorruptible nature and value. You have to sit down with that and think. Everything that makes up my life, everything in my life, brought to the bar of the incorruptible, *i.e.* that which can take on glory. How much will stand the test, how much will pass, how much of all that makes up my life will go when time goes, when I leave this world, when all that is here ceases where I am concerned? How much will go on and appear again with eternal glory? It is a very serious challenge ; but that is how heaven is viewing things all the time, and that is what heaven is at work upon. All the dealings of the Lord with us are according to that law, that standard—to make very, very little of the corruptible, the passing, the transient, whatever it is, and to make everything of the incorruptible. What will be the proportion of the incorruptible to the corruptible resultant from our time here? I suggest that very few more solemn and serious ques-

The real value is Eternity — Can we cause
eternity to be different? Would our time spent
here make a difference in all Eternity — yes

OR, THE FINAL CRITERION   13

tions could be asked or faced than that. Oh, how much there
is that makes up life, that we are interested in, that we are
dealing with, that we are accumulating, how much time, how
much expenditure, how much worry, how much there is that
is going and will show nothing afterward, will not stand, will
not reappear! How much in all this and through all this is
incorruptible? How much of it is being turned really to account for the incorruptible, or is just being spent on our
corruptible?

I said that our first statement would take on significance
when we began to look into this matter. God is primarily concerned with intrinsic value, and that is not with Him a comparative matter—it is an absolute matter. " The fire . . . shall
prove each man's work of what sort it is " (I Cor. iii. 13), the
Word says. That is a universal and an imperative dictum.
" The fire shall . . ."—that is imperative—" prove each man's
work "—that is universal ; and I think, in the light of the New
Testament, we would be right in adding ' the fire shall try
every man ', and not only his work. The fire shall try every
man. Fire may mean many things. It may mean the personal
fiery trials of which Peter speaks, the fiery trial trying faith,
proving the gold. It may be the ordeal of the Church in persecution and suffering—and God knows how much more that
may be, in the near future, than it has been in many parts of
this world—the fiery ordeal for the Church. But whatever the
fire may mean in its manifold application, it is that which
puts things into the categories to which they belong. The fire
puts the corruptible into the category of the corruptible, and
makes it know that it is corruptible, that it belongs there : the
fire declares it. The fire, on the other hand, puts the incorruptible into its category, and shows it has no power over that :
that belongs to the incorruptible, and the fire has no power
over it. It has defined its nature : either that it is of the perish-

Burn in me Holy Spirit.

able and the passing, or that it is of the imperishable and the
permanent. The fire does that.

And do not let us think merely objectively. Are you in the
fire now? Is the fire not at work in your life now—the fiery
trial of testing, of adversity? How many words could define
the work of the fire in us! Yes, it is a *burning* in our experience. We know already the individual ordeal of fire. What is
the fire doing? Why the fire? For one thing only, under the
hand and in the intent of God—to put things in their place,
to make us think ever more lightly of the corruptible and to
lay store by the incorruptible, to make the incorruptible the
transcendent in our standard of values. The fire shall try every
man and every man's work.

Therefore, again, this law of the incorruptible must be applied to everything. It must be applied firstly to ourselves.
When we have lived our lives and have gone hence, what will
go on as the substance of the incorruptible resultant from our
having been here at all?—a universal question, though a difficult one. What will there be that defeats time, defeats decay,
defeats death, defeats the whole realm of corruption, and appears again in glory for ever, as the outcome of our having
been on this brief journey on the earth? We have to apply this
question of the incorruptible to ourselves.

APPLIED TO OUR KNOWLEDGE

What about all our Christian knowledge—all the teaching
we have had, all the truth we possess? We have to apply the
question here. How much of that great store of teaching and
truth, doctrine and knowledge, is producing the incorruptible
in us, is going to appear again in eternity? We must test our
conferences by this. We have been, perhaps, to many conferences, we have had a great deal of teaching by one means and
another. Well what is the upshot of it all for eternity, when the

fire tests our teaching, when the fire tests all our knowledge, perhaps in this life? That is what is going on in the East. A great deal of teaching has been given and now the fire is testing the incorruptible value of that teaching. What can survive and triumph over the fire? In all that we know, in our Christian profession, as we bear the name of Christ embodied in the title 'Christian', Christ's one, how much of that very profession is more than a profession? Is it a possession, an intrinsic value, incorruptible reality? All our Christian tradition handed down from our fathers, all that we inherit through the centuries of Christianity: how much of it now is of this particular quality, this essential value, this essence of Christ, and how much is just form, habit, an established and recognised and accepted thing? How much of it in our case is incorruptible? All our emotion, our excitability, our noisiness—is there behind it all that substantial element that will stand up against the fury of Satan, the hatred of hell?

As to ourselves, this matter of the incorruptible is a very pertinent thing, and, if I mistake not, this is going to be the kind of thing that will be pressed home by God to the nth degree at the end-time. If, therefore, we are in the end-time, and it is not easy to doubt that, such a word is of importance. If we were to turn aside to consider that matter, we should find that never before was there so much in the Scriptures that was never understood, even by its writers, which to-day is intelligible with a mere modicum of intelligence. The very language of Scripture which could not possibly have been understood at the time when it was written is as patent as anything can be patent to-day. —But that is an aside. We are unmistakably and undoubtedly at an end-time. Therefore God would gather His people, those who really mean business with Him, and He would begin to say, ' That is good, but there is something very much more than that: this is the thing that

16   THE GOLD OF THE SANCTUARY,

matters—the intrinsic value, the essential value '. He would put His finger upon the absolute essentials. How much of the very essence of Christ is wrought into us? That is the point.

APPLIED TO CHRISTIAN WORK

This question of the incorruptible has to be applied, of course, to Christian work and works, and everything must be tested by it. It is all very well—size, appearance, seeming, immediate effects, the trappings and the means—but what about the essential, intrinsic value? God does not judge by the size of a thing as it appears, by the seeming of things, nor by the immediate effects produced by man's means and methods. God is looking through, His eyes are the eyes as of flame, and He looks right in to find the measure of the incorruptible that will not be gone in a week, a month, a year or a few years, but will go right on and appear again. He is looking for that.

There are two kinds of starting-point you know—man's and God's. Man usually starts with big frameworks, with a big plant, machinery, publicity, structures and so on. That is how man usually starts when he is going to do something for God. It is a propensity ; it is our way. We may argue that God is worthy of something big. That is man's way. God's way is never like that—it never was. You search in vain to find any instance of God beginning like that. Pentecost came out of very deep and drastic dealings with twelve men. God's starting-point is always the intrinsic. God has always begun with life, with the inherent, with the potential. Man's beginnings usually end in only a small percentage of lasting value. God's beginnings always end in a very great percentage of lasting value. But God's beginnings seem so small, they appear so little. But so does a seed: it is a small thing, a little thing ; yet look at the potentialities in one seed, one grain of wheat.

One seed

It is the intrinsic with God. That is where God begins. That is why anything really of God has a long and hidden history of deep dealings on His part.

GOD'S SECRET WORK

The thirty years of our Lord's hidden life had a great bearing on the three and a half. The forty years of Moses away back there in the desert, looking after those sheep of his father-in-law, had a great bearing upon the rest of his life. They were not lost, wasted, futile years. And so we could take up one after another—Abraham, David, and others, who had a long, deep, secret hidden history: it was out of that that the effectiveness came. Very often more is done, when God has been at work, in the last few years of a life than in all the years previously. That does not mean that all the previous years have been of no account, having no place. It means that God has been working to get intrinsic values, and now at last these values are coming out. Be careful, young people, that you do not write off older saints as back numbers. You may be violating the very principle of your own life —that of intrinsic value. But God have mercy upon an old man or an old woman who has no intrinsic values. As we get older, we ought to be the substance for the generation to follow. And God help the generation that follows that has not an inheritance of intrinsic value. No, let us be careful how we judge things. It must not be by time, but by the incorruptible.

Let me repeat that God begins with the intrinsic. His greatest things are the coming out of intrinsic values to make themselves known. Therefore He takes a lot of time and a lot of pains in secret history with that one object, and it may be that, though you may be thinking the years are going, and what does it all amount to? —soon life will be past, all over, and

B

you have missed the way, and it has all been a problem, an enigma—it may be that in a few years an infinitude of spiritual value will come out of the time through which you are going, out of this which you think is lost time. Only adjust yourself to this, that God is not careful at all about our standards of values, either in time or in method or in any other way. What God is careful about is to have the inherent, the potential, the essential, the intrinsic. Lay that up in your hearts and cherish it and let it be a real governing factor with you. God works for depths, God works for solidity, God works for intensity: therefore He works through testing, through hiddenness, and with very, very little appeal to our natural pleasure. Incorruption is therefore a very testing thing, and may demand a complete adjustment of our whole mentality.

Having reached this point, we are committed to an enquiry into the nature of the incorruptible. If all the foregoing was true of the Lord Jesus, and if it is true that the Word of God teaches that, Deity and Godhead apart, what was true of Him in this way is to be reproduced in His own, then we want to know what were the incorruptible things that constituted such a life, and we shall go on to look at these, for it is in this way that we shall have the best explanation of what we have already been considering.

Yes Lord—To your dealings with me
Yes Lord—To your timing
Yes Lord to your training
Yes Lord to your teaching
Yes Lord to your discipline
Yes Lord to your Voice
Yes Lord to your spirit
Yes Lord to your revelation.
Yes Lord only to you & to your all
the time yes Lord.

Chapter Two

THE INCORRUPTIBLE CHARACTERISTIC OF
UNION WITH GOD AS FATHER

Reading : II Timothy i. 8 – 10

WE CAME IN OUR LAST CHAPTER to the point where we were found committed to investigate, to enquire, and seek to know, what were and what are the incorruptible characteristics of the life of the Lord Jesus, because the real value of life, the real value of work, of service, in the sight of God and heaven, will be on the same basis as was His.

Sometimes, in connection with our printing work, we have samples sent to us from different firms, and recently I had some samples of stocktaking sheets, which could be supplied with narrow or wide margins. While these were lying on my desk, they said something. Stocktaking with narrow or wide margins. What is in the margin? A wide margin of surplus, in the stocktaking, that does not stand for any value, and a small area of intrinsic worth, or a large area of the intrinsic and a very narrow margin of the worthless? For there is going to be a great stocktaking. Yes, we all have to go the way of the stocktaking of life and of work, and then there will arise the question of the width of the margin and what is in it. Of all that life has contained, of all that we have done and have had and have used, have expended or drawn in, how wide will be the margin of that which just did not matter or count in the light of heaven and eternity? That is a very serious matter, and it surely is a way of bringing us back very forcibly to this important consideration. God is after no margin at all, but the whole page filled with that which is of intrinsic value. God does not want to have to draw lines and say, 'On the one side of that line there is so much that is more or less good ; on the other side no good at all'. He wants no lines, and if the Lord has His way—and, mark you, He does seek by every means to have His way in this connection—He will get as full a measure as we will let Him of real intrinsic value.

With this preliminary word, let us go on. We have said that the Lord Jesus is the great example of a life without any margin, a life reaching wholly to the edge, on every side, full of intrinsic value, and that such a life has an explanation. He, then, was the embodiment of the incorruptible. Life and incorruption were embodied in Jesus Christ in terms of Manhood, as Man. We are now leaving out of our consideration His Deity, His Godhead. It would not need to be discussed at all in this connection. Very God of very God leaves no room for discussion or argument concerning incorruption. But when it comes to man, it is another matter. And so we are concerned with Him on that side of His person and personality in which He is called the Son of Man. This whole question and issue of the incorruptible is therefore a human question. It is a matter which relates to and concerns man.

Man, or Man-hood, is a big and specific thought of God. The idea of Man, of Humanity, was born in the mind of God. He is a peculiar creation in the mind of God for a special purpose. The writer of the letter to the Hebrews says—" Not unto angels . . . But . . . What is man? " (Heb. ii. 5 – 6). ' Not unto angels . . . but man '. This is not a matter, then, which concerns angels and it is certainly not a matter of abstract and unrelated ideas. There is a testimony which has to be found in the concrete expression of man and manhood. The Bible makes it perfectly clear from beginning to end that the idea connected with man or manhood is that of representation, re-presentation of Divine thoughts. "In the image of God", in the likeness of God—that is representation, and that idea in relation to man runs right through the Bible. The question all the way through is—Does man, or does man not, fulfil the purpose of his being, which is to represent God, to express God?

Now, man was made for incorruption, for incorruptible life issuing eventually in his glorification. If that is not understood at once, just hold it for the present as a statement. Man was made for incorruptible life, so that at length he might be glorified, might be endowed with Divine glory. I am not going to argue that from Scripture : those of you who know your Bibles will at once be able to support the statement—Those of you who do not, go and read your Bible! But man missed the purpose of his creation, he missed the incorruptible life by his disobedience and unbelief, by his rebellion against God, his self-will, his pride. He missed his incorruptible inheritance or heritage. He is no longer a candidate for glory in his na-tural condition. Glory is not possible for man as man is found outside of Christ. But Christ came, and in His coming fulfil-led a work by which the destiny and purpose of man was re-covered and secured. That is, in Christ incorruptible life is recovered and secured for man. Christ was a man *who could not be corrupted*, and, therefore, because He could not be corrupted, corruption was kept out of the very stream of His life. It was not possible that He should see corruption even in the grave. "He whom God raised up saw no corruption" (Acts xiii. 37): that is the statement of Scripture. He was in-corruptible in His life and therefore triumphant over corruption in His death. So Christ was constituted on incorruptible characteristics, and we are now going to ask what they were. In the ensuing pages we shall say something about the first of these incorruptible characteristics of Christ, which are to be reproduced in those who are in Christ by faith.

A RELATIONSHIP ESTABLISHED BY THE HOLY SPIRIT

The first, then, of these characteristics was His union with God as His Father—a simple statement, but oh, how much was in that union with God as His Father! We are aware how often He used that word ' Father, and how often He said ' My Father ' and then ' the Father and I '. His enemies saw the point ; they were not slow to pick on what they thought was heresy and blasphemy. ' He makes Himself equal with God ' (John v. 18). That union between Him and the Father was of such a kind that their relationship was absolute and final. That relationship was established by the Holy Spirit. I am speaking now of Christ as Son of Man. The relationship between Him as Son of Man and God as His Father was established by the Holy Spirit. In His birth He was begotten of the Holy Ghost. In His work He received through anointing the Holy Spirit. In His walk, it was ever in and by the Spirit. In His Cross, He offered Himself up by the eternal Spirit (Hebrews ix. 14) ; and we can complete the circle by saying that it was through that eternal Spirit that He was raised. The Holy Spirit initiated, maintained, and consummated that relationship with the Father. That union with the Father was the governing thing of His whole life. At every point, at all times, He referred and deferred to God as His Father. All His works were out from the Father. " *The Father abiding in me doeth his works*" *(John xiv. 10).* His words were out from the Father. " *The word which ye hear is not mine, but the Father's who sent me" (John xiv. 24).* You are well aware of that. Everything for Him was out from the Father, by way of this union, this oneness, and this was the very occasion of all the conflict in His life. It was the very point of all the attack and assault of the enemy. The one thing that the Evil One and all the evil powers were ever focusing upon was this oneness and fellowship with the Father, in order to try somehow to drive in a wedge, to get that relationship ruptured. That was the point of the attack all the time, and that is very significant. If an enemy concentrates all his attention and all his resources upon any one point, it is clear that he regards that as the point upon which the whole thing will collapse, everything is gathered up in that one point of concentrated attention ; and it did not matter which method the enemy used of the many ways which he did use—whether open antagonism or friendly suggestion or subtle subterfuge or bribery or any other means —that is the point. ' If only I can get between these two somehow, the Father and the Son ! ' I say again, that was tremendously significant.

THE RELATIONSHIP THE EXPLANATION OF SUFFERING

That union, then, that relationship, was the explanation of all His sufferings and His testings—indeed, of the whole ordeal of His life. Would He, on any consideration, with wonderful offers, bribes or threats, or the presentation of a dark shadow of suffering, the awful anguish of the Cross ; would He, on any consideration, let go, violate, the principles of that union?—and to maintain it, to preserve it, to adhere to it, was no small, light thing for Him. For that one thing, the most terrible cost that ever a man has paid in the history of this universe was paid: the cost of that dark moment of the Cross when everything seemed to have gone out of His universe. There was not one glimmer of light even from the Father's face while He was under that test. Yes, this was a costly thing, because there was something involved in it. There must have been some very great issue involved in this union. There was nothing superficial about this. It must have been something unspeakably great that was bound up with it. What was it?

PROVIDING GOD WITH A PLACE

It can be answered in one brief sentence. Primarily, it was the issue of providing God with a place. Go back to the first man. God created that man in order that He might have a place in that man and in all his seed ; and not just *a* place, but *the* place. In a sense God's place had been taken from Him. God had been rejected and put out of His place with man. He still remained sovereign Creator, of course. He still remained Ruler and Lord, the original Owner, but there was a difference. Let us look at it like this. Pardon the descent to such a low level to try to illustrate such infinite and holy things.

Here is a landlord. He builds a house and he is the owner of that house. In kindness and friendliness he lets that house to some people, and to begin with the relationship is quite a happy one, so happy that he is able to visit that house and is welcomed and has a place in the family ; they are always glad to see him. But someone comes along while he is not there and begins to say things about him that are unworthy and that are scandalous, begins to defame him, to insinuate motives, make suggestions, with a view to getting him out of his place in that home and that family, and this evil one succeeds so well that no longer has he a place in the heart of that family. He is still the landlord, the rightful owner, and all the law is on his side, but there is a difference between being a land-lord and having the law on your side, and the thing being yours and having a place in the heart of the family. That is what I mean. God lost His place. He is still sovereign Owner of this universe, He is still Lord, and one day He will assert His legal rights over His creation. But do you think that is good enough? Within His creation He wants to have a place.

There is all the difference between sovereignty and fellowship. The union between Christ and His Father was not the relationship of a sovereign and a subject. He did not live that life and do that work under the sovereign government of God. God was not just acting sovereignly in the case of this Man —doing His own will, asserting His own rights, claiming His own place, demanding His own recognition and carrying through His own programme in a sovereign way. No, it was all on a very different footing from that. It was fellowship. God can do a lot of things with us and through us and by means of us in a sovereign way, but that is never, never good enough for God. He wants us in fellowship. He wants a place, not as sovereign and as despot, but as Father—*Father*. That is the significance of the word on the lips of the Lord Jesus. He taught them to pray, " Father ". The significance, then, of the relationship between Christ and God as His Father was that God had a place, a place in the heart of a Man.

Now the whole Bible is occupied with that one concern ; that is the issue arising all the way through. God is seeking to have a place in the heart of man—somewhere where He has a place, not just as sovereign Creator, but in terms of fellowship, in terms of love, in terms of delight to have Him. The Old Testament is full of that in type and illustration. He seeks some place for His Name, where His Name is loved, some place where He can meet men on the ground of fellowship and love. The New Testament brings that out into bold relief. Its beginnings contain links between the Old and the New. Christ, as Son of Man, is the inclusive Link. Here again is the law of incorruptibility. There is that which will go through to eternity, there is something there that Satan cannot destroy, there is something there that death cannot annul, there is something there that is so precious to God that it will appear again for ever. When all that is capable of corruption has gone, the love relationship as between Christ and His Father will abide. Oh, what a difference between this and much of the relationship with God that exists in general.

This, of course, is clearly seen to be the idea of the New Testament as to the *individual*. What is God after with us? It is just that—to have a place in our hearts, on the basis of love and of fellowship. " My Father will love him, and we will come unto him, and make our abode with him " (John xiv. 23). " I and the Father are one " (John x. 30). That, too, is the idea concerning the *nucleus*—that they, little companies of two or three, should give Him a place. " Where two or three are gathered together in my name, there am I " (Matt. xviii. 20), and " I come unto you " (John xiv. 18). And it is the New Testament idea of the whole *Church*. What does the Church mean in the Divine thought? Just a place for God in love relationship, in joyous relationship, in perfect fellowship. That is the idea of the Church.

So then, if Christ meant anything, He signified the coming of God into this world in terms of fellowship. And this is an eternal issue. If we could project ourselves into the ages of ages, the eternal hereafter, and see the nature of things, the very nature of things, as it will be then, we should find it was just this: a perfect harmony between God and man, so harmonious that it is all music, there is no discord, there is no strain, there is no shadow, there is no suspicion, there is no prejudice, there is no fear. All those things have gone, with the corruptible : the incorruptible remains ; and in this first instance the incorruptible is this—fellowship with God. It is this *kind* of relationship. It is an *eternal* issue. I underline ' eternal '

because that is only another word for the incorruptible.

THE TEST OF EVERYTHING

Therefore, the test of everything with us will be: How much of God really came in by our having been here? That is a fairly thorough-going test. It may sound very exacting, but it is just this—how much of God came in by your and my having been here? How much, afterward, will it be possible for others to say, ' Well, through that life I came to know God, I came to fellowship with God, to enjoy more of Him '?

Yes, that is testing and that is discriminating. The test of everything, of all our teaching, is, how much of it results in more of God—not more of knowledge, not more of mental apprehension, but how much more of God. Two of us were talking one day. We were talking about certain men of God of the past, and their life-work and teaching, and at the end this is what we agreed—that, although there were those things in their teaching which we did not feel able to accept, they themselves have left us a heritage, they have given us a deposit of God, there is something of the Lord that has come through them to us ; and *that* is the thing which marks their life for us. It is not that they were great teachers, not that they were great organisers of Christian work, not that they were great missionary statesmen, but that somehow they have passed to us a deposit of God ; God has come through them to the enrichment and enlargement of our lives.

That is the test of everything. For me, at least, it is a terrible test—one that I wonder whether I can face. Is it going to be like that—that after all the speaking, after all the teaching, there is a heritage of the Lord Himself left behind? Teaching, truth ; the truth of the Church, the teaching of the House of God—all very well in themselves ; but oh, let us be careful of any of these things *as such*, of putting the emphasis upon the *truth* of the thing, the *truth* of the House of God, the *truth* of this, that and the other! Beware of your emphasis. The emphasis is—what is the House of God for, how does it work out, what is the issue of all the teaching about it? The issue is this— that God comes in. His place is provided, He is there. We may have meetings, and all the rest of the paraphernalia of Christianity, but if it does not issue in this, that the people concerned have more of the Lord Himself, then the whole thing is futile. Yes, with all our exact technique, and the rest—if the Lord is not found there, it is meaningless, it is valueless. All must be related to this one issue—God having a place, and God being there, and God being there without a margin, right to the edge. That is the incorruptible element.

That is what the Apostle says in the passage that we read. *" Be not ashamed . . . of the testimony of our Lord."* The testimony of our Lord—what is it? *"Who annulled death, and brought life and incorruption to light through the gospel."* The testimony of our Lord is His incorruptible life. The testimony of His life, the testimony in His death, of His resurrection—the " testimony of our Lord " is found in that word ' incorruption'.

We have been considering the first of the incorruptible characteristics of the life of the Lord Jesus, which must be reproduced in us. Our conferences will go, our meetings will go, the whole set-up will go, and what will remain will be the measure in which the Lord has come in, the Lord has found an abiding place, the Lord is there intrinsically. That will be the issue. One thing about heaven and about eternity will be that the Lord is there and the Lord fills everything : there is no room for anything else. That was the life of Jesus. He provided a place for God, and there was no other place in His life for anything else at all. Oh, that we might come to that! It will be that, may I say again, which will determine the measure of the permanent, the eternal, the intrinsic value of our lives and of everything—how much there is of the Lord.

Chapter Three

THE 'PLUS' AND 'OTHER' OF HEAVEN

Reading : II Timothy i. 8 – 10

THE INCORRUPTIBLE CHARACTERISTIC of the life of the Lord Jesus upon which we shall dwell just now—all too insufficiently, I am afraid—is what I will call the ' plus ' and ' other ' of heaven. That is rather an awkward phrase, I know, but you will understand it better as I go on: the ' plus ', or extra, and ' other ', of heaven.

You have no doubt been impressed, as you have read the Gospels, with the frequency with which the word ' heaven ' was on the lips of the Lord Jesus. It occurred, so far as I can see, nearly one hundred times, and when one word is so frequently on anyone's lips you are not left in very much doubt as to their main preoccupation. When we go abroad, and meet people there who are from our own land, we find that they are always eager and anxious to talk about ' the Old Country ', and either that phrase, or else the name of the country, is continually on their lips as they meet us and we are in conversation. So it was with the Lord Jesus here. He was always talking about what to Him was the ' Old Country ': He was always referring to heaven. You look it up again, and get a fresh impression, from His constant reference to heaven and His relationship thereto.

This, in Christ's case, indicated three things, or three aspects of one thing.

THE BACKGROUND

Firstly, there was His own personal background. The background against which He lived and moved was heaven. That was always in His consciousness. Secondly, there was His 'extra' to this life and this world. It was something which to Him was a great 'plus' to life, a great extra to everything here. Thirdly, to Him it was a great and wonderful difference. There were these things, then, about Jesus as Son of Man, so that when you met Him, met Him, so to speak, on the surface, face to face, as a man, it was just impossible to feel that you had met everything, that that was all. There are some people whom you meet—and that is all. You meet them, you perhaps have an interchange with them, pass the time of day or have a few words with them, and then you part, and that is all. They came and they went, and there was no more to it than that. It was never so with the Lord Jesus. If you had met Him, you would have immediately met something more than the ordinary, but you would also be left with the consciousness— 'That is not all; there is something very much more there than I have touched or seen. He implies a vast amount more than I have been able to recognise or grasp. The impression that is left with me is that that is not all, there is something more than that. That man has a lot more behind Him than is on the face of things.'

That is very simple, but that helps us toward this whole matter of the incorruptible. Suppose, instead of waiting till later on, we begin to make our application at once—because that was the thing, that was the incorruptible thing about Him, the undying thing, the thing that would abide—the fact that He did not put all His goods in the shop window, so to speak :

it was not all there so that you could comprehend it all at once, and that was all there was to it. You were conscious of something there of a vast and profound fulness and depth, and that left a mighty impress. And let me say at once—If that is not true of you and me and of the Church of God, then we are sadly lacking in the material of the incorruptible.

Let me apply that here. Suppose we are a company of Christians and we are moving about the same world as the Lord Jesus—with, of course, many changes ; but it is the same world, and people are more or less the same in all generations. When people meet you and meet me, when people come into the midst of us as companies of the Lord's people, what is left afterward? Can we move amongst them, can they come into touch with us, can we touch them in this world, and then part, and that is all there is to it—that is the beginning, and that is the end? ' He has gone—well, a nice fellow, a nice woman, a nice girl '—superficial impressions, judgments formed, and then fading and passing away—nothing more than that? Oh, no ; that is not the incorruptible, the eternal, the abiding, the thing that will appear again in glory for ever. Not at all. That was not so with the Lord Jesus, and it must not be so with us. It must really be that when we have gone this way and touched lives, moved through this earth and gone our way, there is something left which is the plus of our lives which will abide for ever. People have to say, ' There is something more in them than was just on the face of them '.

Do you feel that is too simple? But oh, how it applies to everything! How concerned about this matter we must be, as to what we leave when we have made a contact, what the impression is. It may not be that they can define it, it may not be that they even sit down to think about it, but somehow or other they are aware, whether they take thoughtful account of it or not, that 'having met him and having met her, I have not met everything, there is something more there'. And it is just that something more that is the ground of the Lord's activity in lives. He knows where there are people who are looking for something more than this world can give, something more than they have. They are disappointed, they are hungry; or they may have been peculiarly in the Lord's thought to be brought into something more for a specific purpose, a chosen vessel unto Him to bear His Name. The Lord knows where that Saul of Tarsus is, where that Ethiopian eunuch is, where that Cornelius is, marked out and recognised, and hungry deep down for something more. And where is something more to be found? The Lord must have it available—He must have it in a Philip. He must have it in a Peter, in an Ananias; He must have it in you and in me: that is, the incorruptible, the immortal, the eternal factor: so that there is a point of contact made between heaven and lives by means of this heavenly background and heavenly place in you and in me.

That is the principle of service. You think of the work of the Lord, the service of the Lord, as giving up business and coming out and taking a course of Bible study and then going out preaching. That is not what the Lord thinks about it at all. What He thinks about is—Where can I find something which is an extra, a real extra, a mighty extra, that I can use as the ground of bringing about contacts, touching lives? That is ' evangelization ', that is ' the extension of the Kingdom ', if you like to use those phrases. It is that something is there to which the Lord can bring as the point of His contact.

You can test that. So often it is not what we *say* at all. We try to persuade, we try to argue, we try to urge, we try to bring about issues in other lives—and we are missing the way all the time. The real upshot rests upon this—Was there some-

C

thing more than our argument, something more than our effort, something more than our persuasiveness?—so that if
something happens, those in whom it happens will afterwards
say, ' It was not your argument, it was not the way you put
things, and it was not even your earnestness. There was something about you ; you have got something, and that found me
out.' Unless that is there, we seek to persuade and argue in
vain. That is the incorruptible thing. The Lord Jesus had a
background, something behind Him, and men knew when they
met Him that that was not all. Now you and I are moving
about and we are contacting people all the time ; and what is
the impression? You see how important it is for us to have
this plus of heaven.

THE EXTRA

Then not only was there something more behind Christ, but
it was to Him an extra world—an extra world of resources
that He could draw upon, an extra world of knowledge that
was available to Him, an extra world of relationships, heavenly relationships: with the Father, with the Spirit—yes, and
with other intelligences, celestial intelligences ; an extra world,
another world of relationships. What a big world He had
behind Him to draw upon in this life down here, in its
vicissitudes, its difficulties, its trials, its adversities, when He
was alone and no one could help Him. Even those who would
want to seek to help Him could not. He was alone here. Without the resources of this world, He had another world to draw
upon, a wonderful other world of resource.

And what is the incorruptible world? It is that which gives
the real value to our life here, which says that this is not all.
The knowledge that we possess and the knowledge that this
world possesses which is available to us comes to a point
where it can no longer help us. Have we something beyond
that? Is there a realm of knowledge which is altogether be-

yond and above this world's knowledge at its greatest and our knowledge at its fullest? When we have exhausted things here, we are only beginning with the resources of heaven. That is no exaggeration ; for, after all, most of us, as the Lord's people, know in experience something about this, if it has not been put that way in our minds: we are after all living out from and drawing upon another extra, plus world. When we pray, we do that ; whenever we go to the Lord, we are doing that, we are drawing out from a realm which is more than this one.

Oh, how much more real that must be to us and in our consciousness! ' Here I have come to an end of my resources, here I am right up in a corner, here I am, not knowing, so far as this world is concerned, which way to turn: I am at a standstill, a deadlock, an *impasse ;* but I have another world to draw upon, a very real world, and that other world can come right into my situation.' And it is just as we are living out from heaven, out from our extra, our plus, world, that things will partake of the character of the eternal, and that into this life will come the imperishable: so that there is something in that solved problem, that overcome difficulty, which is not just the result of human ingenuity, but of Divine intervention and undertaking. That is the incorruptible, and God is always seeking to have it like that. Perhaps that is why He allows the problems and the *impasses,* to make us know that this is not all. There is another world of resource, all so infinitely in advance of what is here.

THE DIFFERENCE

Once more, not only a background, and an extra, but a difference. Looking at the Lord Jesus, speaking as men speak, we could say that that Man was governed by different standards, by different conceptions, by different ideas, from anything

here. He did not act just as people usually act here. His conduct was different from the usual conduct of people, from the
established and accepted order of things, of how it is done,
and how people think it ought to be done and all that kind
of thing. No ; He did not belong to that realm at all, He
seemed to have entirely different standards and different ideas
and different conceptions. He could not be involved in our
system of ideas and procedure and conduct at all. He just
would not allow Himself to be roped into our order. He had
another world with an altogether different set of conceptions,
and He acted according to them and was governed by them,
and that made Him so strange amongst us. We thought the
way was *this*—this is the ordinary way, the usual way, the
accepted way ; but He did not do it our way at all. He had a
strange way of doing things.

Now that word ' strange ' means ' not just as we do things '.
You can of course use it in another sense. We sometimes talk
about people and say, ' A strange person ', meaning that they
are a little mentally out of order. But the Lord Jesus was
strange in the sense that He was a foreigner to this set-up, to
this whole order of things. He belonged to another world, and
He had that other world's conceptions. There was a great difference about Him. They just could not keep Him in, they just
could not make Him conform, they just could not understand
Him at all.

Well, it was those very heavenly standards and conceptions and ideas which were the incorruptible things. This
world's ways of going on—what do they lead to? They lead
to corruption. At their fullest, highest, greatest, they lead to
corruption. Never, never was that more apparent than in our
own day. The greatest development of human ideas and ingenuity is leading to the greatest development of corruption.
In every realm, corruption. Men are talking very freely now,

men who know best—talking almost with bated breath, yet talking quite a lot, of the end of the human race now within sight. Well, that is the end of human ingenuity, of this world's wisdom—corruption.

His ideas did not work out that way. You and I—we have come to know something of the Lord, something of the Lord's standards, the Lord's conception of heavenly things, and we know quite well that this is not corruption, this is life and incorruption. We know it, do we not? We are rejoicing in something because we have come to know the Lord ; but what have we come to know? Something from outside of this world altogether, something different.

Now let us apply this. Let us be very careful that we do not just seek to be all of a piece with men here, all in tune with them, all in step with this world, just falling into line and being one. If we do, we forfeit the very essential of our heavenly birth and our heavenly relationship, which is this something so other and so different. Paul is saying here to Timothy, " Be not ashamed therefore of the testimony of our Lord, nor of me his prisoner: but suffer hardship with the gospel according to the power of God ". Why this " be not ashamed "? Oh, for shame, we try to be on good terms with the world, we are ashamed to be otherwise, we think we will lose prestige, we think we will lose influence if we do not just come into line and be hail-fellow-well-met with everybody. What a deception! We simply throw overboard the very values of our Christian life when we do anything like that. See how it worked out in the case of the Lord Jesus. This other—well, it worked out and resulted in contacts, yes, but without connections. Can you make that discrimination—contacts without connections? Oh, He was in contact with people, He was in contact with things, He was moving amongst them, meeting them, yes very definitely in contact, but there was no connection. He was not all of a piece. Associations—yes, He associated Himself—a marriage, a funeral, a feast, and the rest, but no compromise or acquiescence. A gap was always kept between association and compromise or acquiescence. It was not kept formally, it was not kept in a kind of strain or pretension—You belong there and I belong here, you keep on your ground and I am keeping on mine. That may not be said in word, but so many people, I am afraid, give the impression. It was something spiritual. He associated, it was a charge laid against Him, that He was a friend of publicans and sinners (Matt. xi. 19), but He was not a publican nor a sinner. Association, but no compromise, no letting down, no letting go, no acquiescence, no acceptance of what was there. It was that relationship with heaven, that extra, and that other which kept Him incorruptible. He was the incorruptible One in it all. It was all summed up in one precise phrase of His—" I am not of this world " (John viii. 23).

There never was another who so filled his time seeing to things, carrying the burden of other people's lives, no, never anyone else whose life was so full of things in relation to other people's interests, but at the same time so marked by a detachment. There was something there that made Him different, that still made Him a kind of outsider, and everybody knew it. That is a very important thing. The Christian life in the New Testament is clearly shown to be heavenly in every respect, heavenly in birth, born from above, heavenly in sustenance, sustenance from above, heavenly in consummation, in translation or rapture, yes heavenly in vocation, a heavenly calling, everything heavenly makes up the Christian life according to the Word of God. The Holy Spirit coming down from heaven has not come just to make us successful in this world, not just to prosper

our ventures here, nor to be used by us to realise the thing
in which we are interested and to further those plans of ours.
He has not come down from heaven for anything like that.
He has come down to reconstitute us as heavenly people, and
then translate us to heaven. That is His whole work, the re-
constituting of our whole being according to heaven's ideas.
That is what He is getting at if we understood the work of the
Holy Spirit in our lives, which is only the work of God in our
lives, His dealings with us, His ways with us, if we understood
the ways and the workings of the Spirit we should see that
what He is after is not to make us something here at all, not
to make a lot of this life, but to get us to turn everything to
heavenly account, to make us according to heaven's pattern.
He is after the incorruptible. All this other will go.

That is a very simple word, but let us follow it through
again. We must ask ourselves this question continually—When
I have been met or when I have met others, when I have gone
through this world, in my business, my social, my domestic
contacts, in my religious activities, I have come and I have
gone, is that all, is that all there is to it? That is that! Is it?
In the deepest consciousness of others, whether they will admit it or not, whether they try to explain it or not, whether
they can define it or not, deep in their consciousness they know
somewhere remotely at the back of their mind—' I did not
meet everything when I met them, there is something more
there than I am wholly aware of, there is something more,
and it is that something more that is the thing in their life,
that accounts for them, and that something more is something
not of this world. You do not get that sort of thing here, you
do not get that sort of thing in the ordinary run of men and
women and there is something different about them '. That is
the testimony of the incorruptible. That is the first challenge
to us. Let us ask the Lord very much about that and about

everything. It must be like that. In our teaching, in our meetings, our whole Christian procedure, there is something extra
and something different, the incorruptible, that has been
brought to light through the Gospel of our Lord Jesus who
annulled death and brought life and incorruption to light.

Chapter Four

THE NATURE AND REALITY
OF SPIRITUAL ENERGY

IN OUR PREVIOUS MEDITATION, we were speaking about
the extra world of resource which the Lord had at His
service, at His command, with which He was in communi-
cation and from which He was drawing. Everything for Him
was from above—that is, out from heaven. We are now going
to consider a further element in His unseen reserve and resource, namely, the nature and reality of the spiritual energy
that resulted in His activity and movement. That is something
about which you and I will have to learn a great deal, if there
is going to be anything commensurate with His life as the result of our own activities here on this earth.

THE PURPOSEFULNESS OF CHRIST

No one can read the Gospels without being greatly impressed with the purposefulness of Christ. It characterized
Him from His youth, or even childhood. At the age of twelve,
it was one thing which came out pre-eminently in the, shall
we call it, altercation that took place between Him and His
parents, when they had been to Jerusalem and had returned,
not found Him amongst them, and gone back seeking Him
for three days. In all their anxiety and concern He just quietly
explained it all. *" Knew ye not that I must be in my Father's
house ? " (Luke ii. 49)*—with the emphasis upon the ' must '.
' I just must, I am governed, I am controlled, I am under the
mighty persuasion and girding of a heavenly thing, a heavenly

41

relationship.' And how often afterwards, when He had taken up His life-work from the Jordan days, that word came from His lips. " *We must work the works of him that sent me, while it is day : the night cometh, when no man can work* " *(John ix. 4).* " *Other sheep I have, which are not of this fold : them also I must bring* " *(John x. 16).* You see this tremendous imperative in His life of purposefulness, leading to so much of vital activity and involving or expressing such a tremendous energy

Whilst I was reading in this connection, I naturally turned to the Gospel by Mark, and I thought that I might perhaps be able to put down on paper His movements in the first few chapters of that Gospel. But I found that by the time I reached the end of the fourth chapter, it was necessary to give it up. You just look at the movement—quick, rapid, incisive movement. ' Straightway He . . .', ' straightway He was . . .', and on from place to place. It is a picture of continuous activity and constant movement, from place to place, here and there, this and that ; a life just crowded and crammed, the working out of some tremendous energy that was in Him. That was His life.

And when you move to the book of the Acts, it is impossible not to recognise that same energy in the apostles and in the Church. It is a book of continual goings, of tremendous energies, of vital activities. It is the Spirit of God in action. And when you move still further, into the letters of the New Testament, you find this same thing ; but now it is carried into the spiritual life of the Church, the spiritual life of believers, and the constant urge is to go on, go on—" let us go on ". It is the spirit of movement, of progress, of advance. It is the expression of the mighty energies of the Spirit, the goings of the Spirit of God in the Church and in believers.

Surely this is a true fulfilment of Ezekiel's vision of the

cherubim, and the wheels, and the Spirit in the wheels, going straight forward, turning neither to the right nor to the left, but going. " The Spirit . . . was in the wheels ", and they were going straight forward. And again, it seems to be so much the counterpart of what we have in the book of Numbers. There, as you know, the Spirit is in charge, in the symbol of the cloud. When the cloud rises and moves, the tabernacle has to be taken down and moved, because the Spirit is on the move. The Spirit stops, and the tabernacle is set up—but only for a time ; presently the Spirit rises and goes on, and the same thing is repeated—all under this forward movement of the Spirit, this going. The tabernacle, as you know, is that which sets forth the whole heavenly Person of Christ, Christ from every standpoint, and here it is the matter of all things con- cerning Christ being in the hands of the Holy Spirit, and con- stantly projected forward. It is the fulfilment of His own words in John xvi. 13, that " the Spirit . . . shall guide you into all the truth ". All the truth ; ever on. Christ is the fulness, the whole heavenly revelation, and the Spirit is here to bring the Church ever on. There may be a pause, for a purpose ; but the pause, when the purpose is accomplished, is termina- ted, and on we go again.

My point is to indicate the tremendous energy that there is related to God's purpose as embodied in the Lord Jesus. Per- haps we have in the past put too much emphasis upon the negative side of this. So often we have quoted the words of the Lord, " I can of myself do nothing " (John v. 30), " The Son can do nothing of himself " (John v. 19), and similar passages of Scripture which indicate the negative side, the impossible side, the side of limitation. I say, perhaps we have put too much emphasis on that. It is a most impressive thing that the Lord who said that—" I can of myself do nothing ", " The Son can do nothing of himself ", " The words that I speak unto you, I speak not from myself: the Father abiding in me doeth his works " (John xiv. 10)—the Lord who said all that was the most active and energetic person that has ever been on this earth: His was a life more crowded with move- ment—I mean movement to effect, movement with an issue, movement with values of eternal character—a life more crowded with that kind of thing than any other life has ever been.

Perhaps therefore we should pass over to the positive side ; but, as we do so, we must understand that this is not just bare activity, this is not merely energy, this is not a restless, fever- ish drive. There is a *nature* here, and it is that nature of things, of the energy and of the movements, which contains the quality of the result. There have been, and there are, many full lives, tremendously active lives, but again we come back to our great test of everything—how much is of the incorrupt- ible character which will appear again, and what proportion of it all will be there in glory for ever? That is the test ; that is the question. My point is not just to say that the Lord Jesus had a very busy life, that He was always on the move. My point is to say that there was something in it which was not just the movement of a very energetic person ; there was some- thing very much more about it than that.

THE GOINGS OF GOD

In the first place, these goings were the goings of God. They were not goings initiated by man. These goings were not of the planning of man ; these movements were not promoted by man. They were the goings of God, and the Lord made it perfectly clear that, with all that He was doing, He was get- ting it from above, it was what the Father was doing that He did, and He did nothing other than that. It came from above.

All the plan, all the purpose, all the activity, every work, and the time of every work, was given Him through the eternal Spirit from above: that is why it is all eternal, that is why it was so full of potentiality, and all so tremendous in its effectiveness.

We can, of course, easily test that. We know quite well that that is not true of a great mass of energetic activity, even in Christianity. The percentage of the really eternal, incorruptible value is very small in all our work for the Lord. What the Lord is wanting to say to us at this time is this: that He wants the maximum of the intrinsic, the maximum of the eternal, the maximum of that which will not pass when its vessels pass, when those used have left the scene ; that which will be established for all time, appearing again and again in the spiritual life of His people, and appearing in glory as the substance of that whole Kingdom which is to be. The maximum of the intrinsic value—if it is to be like that, as it was with our Lord, it must be on this wise, that the goings are the goings of God.

But let me say again that the goings of God are really very, very much in action. I think some people imagine that a life in the Spirit is a life which is very passive, with much waiting and doing nothing. Perhaps we have to adjust ourselves about this. There are times when the Lord keeps us out of action —as we call actions—but there are another lot of actions going on in us. There are times when it seems, outwardly, that we are not being allowed to fulfil any great purpose, but the Lord is doing something which is very vital to His purpose. His goings are in operation all the same. A life in the Spirit is never a passive life, never a quiescent life, never a life without movement. If ever, inwardly or outwardly, you come to the place where there really *is* nothing doing, you may take it that you have got out of the way of the Lord. There is always something doing provided the Holy Spirit is in charge.

You must not put your judgment upon it and say that there is nothing doing. God is at work *if* we are under the government of the Holy Spirit ; there is no doubt about it. We must always keep on the positive side of this, and not think that a spiritual life is a life without purpose or action. It is nothing of the kind. We will come back to that again presently. The goings are the goings of God ; they must be so if the values are to be eternal values ; and the value, the eternal value, will be in proportion to our oneness with God in His goings, not our own.

THE DIRECTION OF GOD

Then the directions are the directions of God. God has never yet asked any man to make a plan for Him—never! You will never find anywhere that God says, ' Please plan My work for Me, please arrange things for Me, please provide Me with a schedule '. God has never done that. God keeps the plan in His own hands. God designs everything ; and mark you, again, the measure of real value from heaven's standpoint will be the measure in which we are moving in God's plan, not in our own, in the way in which God has predetermined He should fulfil His purposes.

THE ENERGY OF GOD

Not only the goings, and not only the directions, must be of God, but the energy must be the energy of God. That is the pivot of our present consideration. It is the energy of God, and this also makes a big and very deep discrimination. Our energies, as such, will never accomplish anything eternal. Let us settle that. We start on that side, and come to the other side in a moment. Our driving force, our strength of will, our strong-mindedness, our determination, our forcefulness, in itself, will get nowhere in eternal things. We admire people who overcome many difficulties, who accomplish great things, and especially who overcome the handicaps of human life, by sheer force of will. Yes, that is heroism, in its own realm to be admired, but never let us think that we are going to accomplish anything of eternal, heavenly value by force of will, by our own energy of mind, soul or body. Not at all! The Lord Jesus had tremendous energy, but He drew it all from above. It was all the energy of the Holy Spirit by whom He was anointed, and that is borne out overwhelmingly by the whole teaching of the New Testament.

Saul, the persecutor, was a man of tremendous will. The driving force of that man was terrific. He was a dynamic force amongst men, and what Saul of Tarsus determined no one would withstand but God. He was a man like that. But what does Paul say about himself, and what did Paul have to learn all through his life? This very thing—" I can do nothing of myself ". He came to the point, to the wonderful height of spiritual attainment, where he said, " *I will not glory, save in my weaknesses* " *(II Cor. xii. 5). " Most gladly . . . will I . . . glory in my weaknesses, that the power of Christ may tabernacle upon me " (II Cor. xii. 9).* That is rising very high. It was one of his life lessons, that, with all his natural drive and force, power of will, of mind, nothing was accomplished in that way, by that means. It had to be something coming down like a tent and then enfolding, enwrapping him, so that he was moving within the sphere of another mighty energy that he called " the power of Christ ". He spoke of himself as being insufficient, wholly insufficient, for these things ; he cried, " Who is sufficient . . . ? " And he answered, " *Our sufficiency is from God ; who also made us sufficient as ministers of a new covenant " (II Cor. iii. 5, 6).*

The real effectiveness of that man's life, which was by no means a passive or negative life, came from heaven. It was not because Paul was such a forceful man, with such a tremendous will—so energetic that he could never stop going. No. He put it all down to one thing, when he summed it up like this : *" according to the power that worketh in us " (Eph. iii. 20).* Here is another energy which is responsible for all things. There were certainly many times in the life of Paul, as no doubt also in the life of the Lord Jesus, when he could not have gone on, when he would have just had to give up in sheer exhaustion, under a " sentence of death ". But how many times did this servant of God rise and go on when it was humanly impossible! The energy is the energy of God, not the driving force of man.

THE IMPACT OF GOD

And yet once more—the impact of these lives and of all this activity was the impact of heaven, the registration of heaven. We make a mistake when we attribute things to the natural side of servants of God. When we attribute anything to what Paul was himself, we make a big mistake. Men have got into the habit of talking about Paul's wonderful powers of intellect, of Paul's wonderful powers of recuperation, of Paul's wonderful powers of survival and continuance. Paul may have had a wonderful brain, but that wonderful brain did not produce the revelation that we have got through him. The Lord may have had a very useful channel and vessel, but the knowledge, the revelation, was not there until the Lord put it there—that is, it was all from heaven. All this purpose, execution, realisation, impact, effectiveness, is because of some incorruptible resource, because there is that ' plus ' of energy to draw upon. Thank God for that inexhaustible fountain of spiritual energy! It is a very great reality. You and I

need to learn what we have, in the way of resources in Christ,
for *doing*, for accomplishing and for finishing.

A PRACTICAL LIFE

Now we must come to this very important point. While this
is all from God—and it *is* all from God, the work and the
works, the plan and the procedure, the energy and the accomplishment, and everything in Christ, and for us according to
His will; it is all of the *Lord*—do not let us make this fatal
mistake, that we are to wait until the Lord moves us, that we
are just to sit down in our armchairs, if you like—literally
or metaphorically—and wait until the Spirit stirs us up. What
I see about the Lord Jesus is this, that the Holy Spirit moved
Him to a great many practical things here on this earth in
relation to the needs of others. His was an immensely practical life. He was alive to need, and He was alive to need by
the Holy Spirit actuating Him. He was *alive* to it.

Oh, how much we wait to be told what needs to be done,
to have it pointed out to us. And how selective we are. ' Well,
that is not spiritual, that is merely temporal, that is secular.'
We begin to put things into categories like that, and become
—may I use the phrase?—far *too* ' spiritual'! We are up in
the clouds somewhere, and men or women governed by the
Holy Spirit will never have their feet off this earth. You
understand what I mean. We may expand that in the next
chapter. But there are Christians who are all the time thinking that a really spiritual life is a life intensely occupied with
studying the Scriptures, and with prayer, and with all kinds
of spiritual exercises, and any *spiritual* work, well, that is all
right; but this and that, the menial, the ordinary, the everyday, the things of this life and this earth, no, they belong to
another realm.

They do not! The Holy Spirit is going to manifest energy

D

for the simplest and for the most difficult tasks down here.
The thing does not appeal to our natures at all, that He is for
that, and in *that*. In these things it can be proved—and He
would have it proved—that there is a heavenly resource. Oh,
be careful of your selectiveness! Be careful of the dividing
between what is called 'spiritual' and something else. I see
the Lord Jesus alive to need, and alive by the Holy Spirit to
need, not having to be coerced, to be persuaded; 'on the
spot', as we would put it; and that is where the testimony
is. It is a very practical thing, this testimony of the heavenly
life. I am always afraid of using that very phrase 'heavenly',
in case people get the idea that somewhere or other we are
going to float about on clouds and be out of everything. Not
a bit of it! We shall find the Holy Ghost drives us into a
wilderness, the Holy Ghost brings us into very practical situations and says, 'Now then, test your resources, test your
heavenly resources, in that situation, and in that!' We are
all the time wanting to come out of business and get into
'spiritual' work, but that is not the way of the Spirit. I
believe that really spiritual people are alive to situations and
are very practical and active in all manner of things. Much
more could be said about that, but no more for the present.

The point is this, when all is said: that in everything, in
all sorts of ways, by very many different practical, everyday
courses, heaven would insinuate itself, heaven would come
in and say, 'Yes, in *this* there is to be the testimony of the
Lord Jesus, which is that He has brought life and incorruption to light. In *this* there is something extra to what it is
in itself. In *this* there can be a testimony to that other resource
that is yours.'

When the Lord Jesus was here, and touching so many of
the ordinary things of this life, as we said in our last chapter
—a wedding, a funeral, a market-place, a feast that they made

for Him—when He came in, something extra always came in with Him. That extra at the marriage of Cana of Galilee ; that was no ordinary earthly affair. " This beginning of his signs did Jesus in Cana of Galilee, and manifested his glory " (John ii. 11). Something of heaven came in to what otherwise would have been an ordinary affair—that is, viewed from the outside. Perhaps marriages are never ordinary affairs in the case of the people who are concerned! But here was one of a million marriages—yet it was not just ' lost in the crowd '. It was something distinguished : He brought into it His ' plus '.

There is a funeral. Oh, there are many funerals, a daily occurrence, but this was an exceptional funeral. There probably never was a funeral like that one. Jesus came into it, and He brought in something that made all the difference. Then there was that feast that they made for Him. Wherever He was, He touched the situation with something that lived and has gone on and will show its value throughout eternity. This is what the Lord needs, this is the Lord's testimony : that we should be here on this earth, not apart from the everyday things of life, in what we call the ' spiritual '—which really means the ' abstract '—but that here, in this world, heaven should be coming through, something more should be registering ; there should be an energy, a vitality, which is more than human, more than natural, which will not just pass when that thing is done, but which will appear again. So it was with Him, so it was with the Apostles, so it was with New Testament Christians. So it is shown to be the mind of God for the Church, and so it should be with you and with me—that we should be here as living embodiments of the fact that there is something all the time coming through which is not of this world, something of heaven that is our resource.

Chapter Five

THE CROWN OF THE INCORRUPTIBLE

" *Our Saviour Christ Jesus . . . abolished death, and brought life and incorruption to light* " *(II Timothy i. 10).*

" *Now unto the King of the ages, incorruptible, invisible, the only God, be honour and glory unto the ages of the ages* " *(I Timothy i. 17,* R.V. margin*).*

" *But one hath somewhere testified, saying, What is man, that thou art mindful of him ? or the son of man, that thou visitest him? Thou madest him a little lower than the angels ; thou crownedst him with glory and honour* " *(Hebrews ii. 6, 7).*

" *Blessed be the God and Father of our Lord Jesus Christ, who according to his great mercy begat us again unto a living hope by the resurrection of Jesus Christ from the dead, unto an inheritance incorruptible, and undefiled, and that fadeth not away* " *(I Peter i. 3, 4).*

" *Who annulled death and brought life and incorruption to light* ".

> ' O loving wisdom of our God!
>   When all was sin and shame,
> A final Adam to the fight
>   And to the rescue came.

52

'O wisest love! that flesh and blood,
Which did in Adam fail,
Should strive afresh against the foe,
Should strive and should prevail'.

THE VERDICT OF THE 'LONG RUN'—I think we could gather all that has been said so far into that—the verdict of the long run, that is, what abides as incorruptible when all else has passed, is the verdict upon life and work: How much will be found afterward to the praise and glory of God? That word 'incorruptible', then, is the word which governs all, tests all, is the standard of all.

GLORY THE CROWN OF THE INCORRUPTIBLE

We are going to think for a little while about the crown of the incorruptible. The crown of the incorruptible is glory. That is implicit and explicit in the passages which we have just read. The verdict upon the life of the Lord Jesus is just that verdict. John says, many years afterwards, "*we beheld his glory*" *(John i. 14)*. That was the issue. Neither John nor any of his fellow-apostles was alive to it, or very much alive to it, while the Lord was with them; nevertheless He was gaining on them all the time, He was overtaking them, He was registering. Eventually they were left with one deep and indelible impression, which stood the test of many years, many experiences, many trials, much suffering; and at last, at the end of that particular phase, the apostolic age, John, the one lonely remaining apostle of the whole group, wrote the verdict: " We beheld his glory "—the glory of the incorruptible.

Peter also, at the end of his life, when he was saying that he was about to be offered up, recorded the same verdict. Referring to that wonderful experience on the Mount of Transfiguration, he wrote, " *we were eye-witnesses of his majesty. For he received from God the Father honour and glory*" *(II Peter i. 16, 17)*—the verdict of the incorruptible.

The writer of the letter to the Hebrews, whom I always suspect as being Paul, said what we have just read: "*We behold him who hath been made a little lower than the angels, even Jesus, because of the suffering of death crowned with glory and honour*" *(Hebrews ii. 9).* Whether that was Paul or not, it was someone who passed the same verdict ; but Paul did join in as in the words we read from his first letter to Timothy : "*Now unto the King eternal, incorruptible . . . be honour and glory*". The verdict of the incorruptible is glory.

We have been seeing that the glory of Christ was due to certain incorruptible characteristics. First, His union with His Father, something so deep, so real, so unshakeable, as to abide all tests and go right through, in spite of all the efforts of man and demons and the very devil himself to part the Two, to come between. That union with the Father was uninterrupted ; it went through. And we said that the Lord Jesus made it perfectly clear that such a union as existed between Him and His Father could exist between us and Himself, and with the Father ; not in Deity, Godhead, but in real, living organic oneness and fellowship ; by being born of God ; and that union is the basis of glory. It is something incorruptible.

MAN MADE FOR GLORY

Let us come to this matter of the crown of the incorruptible—glory. I have prefixed two hymn-verses to this chapter. Paul it is who calls Jesus " the second man ", " the last Adam ". Our hymn-writer made a little slip, and so we correct: not a second Adam, but a *last* Adam ; a second *man*, a last Adam. Paul indicates that God takes another step in a second man, and a final and inclusive step in a last Adam. Christ is God's next move, and Christ is God's final move, but Christ comes into the place which the first Adam held as representing the intention of God concerning man. As we are thrown back, by this way in which Paul speaks of Him, to the first man Adam, we are shown by the Scriptures, in particular that passage read from the letter to the Hebrews, that God's intention for man was that he was to be glorified, to be "crowned with glory". He was made for glory. That is the definite statement of Scripture.

GLORY CONDITIONED UPON LIFE

But that glory was conditioned upon life, a peculiar life, the particular life of God, Divine life. The glory was contingent upon man having that life, because the glory was the very essence of that life ; that particular Divine life held all the nature and potentiality of glory. So the glory depended upon his having that life, and that life was dependent upon faith and obedience—upon whether man would believe God to be true, to be honest, to be faithful, that God meant what He said, that He was to be trusted ; and, so believing, would act accordingly, that is, be obedient to God. The life was contingent or dependent upon that.

MAN'S FALLING SHORT OF GOD'S GLORY

But we know that man did not believe God, did not trust God, did not take the attitude that God was to be trusted, believed. He disbelieved, and acted accordingly: he disobeyed. The result was that he brought into his own being, and into all his seed, first corruption and then death. A state of corruption entered into his moral being, and that corruption led to death. Thus, for that man, the prospect of glory ended, the intention of his being came to a full-stop. No glory for that man. Heaven is closed, the glory departs ; man is excluded, shut out, with no prospect.

But man strangely did not accept that Divine verdict, so rebellious had he become. This thing had become such a positive factor in his being, this corruption was so active, that he refused to accept the verdict, and set out upon a course of making his own glory, getting glory for himself. The history of man is the history of an effort to get glory without getting it from God. That covers a very great deal. It started very early in the Bible story, and we see it going all the way through ; but the glory of man, as we have said earlier, always ends in corruption. However much glory he draws to himself, however much he achieves of that which is called the 'glory of man', it ends in corruption. We who are at the end of the history of this world—and that is no exaggeration, that is no false statement ; it is the end of the history of this present world, as it now is—are seeing how the glory of man is bringing his own undoing: the most universal corruption, the threat, as we have put it, of the blotting out of the human race. That is the glory of man. Is that glory? He cannot help himself, he is energized by another power, he is not his own master. He calls it glory, and the thing which is so strange is the blindness of man all the time. He wages a war and calls it a 'war to end war', and he wages a worse war and thinks and believes that this surely is the end of war, and on he goes and still it gets worse and worse ; and now it is true that we are in sight of the disintegration of humanity, and the possibility of the wiping out of the human race. We understand to-day, more than ever it could possibly have been understood in this world's history, the meaning of our Lord's words : " except those days had been shortened, no flesh would have been saved" (Matthew xxiv. 22). Is that not true? There has already been a foretaste, in certain parts of the world, of how easy that would be, were it to spread.

Well, that is our present condition—corruption with false glory.

A FINAL ADAM

But another Adam came.

> ' A final Adam to the fight
> And to the rescue came.'

There are three statements made regarding Him. " The Word was made flesh." That is the incarnation. " In him was life." That is the incorruption. " We beheld his glory." That is the effect of the life. Glory works out from the life, and this final Adam, this last Adam, retrieves the loss of the first: He secures a life that was missed, secures the incorruptibility that was never known, and secures the glory. That is the story of Christ in three words—life, incorruptibility, glory. In those three words He comes to us and says: ' Have faith in Me, believe in Me, and life, that life, is for you '—hence also that incorruptibility, and further, that glory. The crown of incorruptibility is glory.

CHRISTIANITY A SYSTEM OF GLORY

Christianity may be described, from one point of view, as a system of glory. God is called " the God of glory " (Acts vii. 2). Christianity is a family; its Father is called " the Father of glory ". Paul spoke of " the God of our Lord Jesus Christ, the Father of glory " (Eph. i. 17). Christ, who brought this ' Christianity ' into being, is called " the Lord of glory " (I Cor. ii. 8). The Holy Spirit, the energy of this whole heavenly system, is called " the Spirit of glory " (I Peter iv. 14). So the three Persons of the Divine Trinity are all related to glory, all interested in glory.

The Father produces the whole system of glory: it emanates from Him as Father.

The Son, as the Lord of glory, is governing everything in relation to glory. What a glorious statement that is ; how much there is gathered into that—' governing everything in relation to glory ' ; " the Lord of glory ". So we have in our Bible a whole book containing the record of the activities of the Lord of glory. Situations and positions seem at first sight all the work of the devil, all the work of devil-inspired and -energized people—situations so difficult that they look hopeless. And that book contains the verdict of the long run, that every one of those situations was turned to glory, something glorious came out of every hopeless and impossible position. The Lord of glory was seeing to that. Yes, there is much comfort in that title " the Lord of glory ".

The Spirit of glory, so called by Peter, if you will look to see the context, is this. Here are believers passing through fiery trial ; they are persecuted, they are misunderstood, they are slandered, they are misrepresented. And Peter says, ' It is all right, if you take this humbly, if you take this without bitterness ; the Spirit of glory will rest upon you ': that is, believers in adversity find that, right in the midst of persecution and opposition, something of inexplicable joy rises up, a deep and wonderful peace. The persecutors hurl their stones, or whatever else they may do, and somehow there is glory in the heart. That is the story of many a martyr, of many a murdered servant and child of God—" the Spirit of glory ". Glory is not some place to which we are going presently, although glory may be a sphere in which everything is glorious. Glory is for now. It is a part of the very life that we have now received. It is the essence of Christ as ' in us, the hope of glory '.

It is the very nature of what we have received through faith in Jesus Christ. I say again, Christianity is a system of glory, and the Lord wants us to have a life, and to live according to that life, which will produce more and more glory in us. It will again be only as we live according to that incorruptible life that the glory will be manifested.

So we have to look again at the One who has set for us the pattern, shown the way, indicated the principles of the incorruptible which result in glory ; to look at what was true of Him, as this incorruptible One, that resulted in God giving Him glory. One or two things I will indicate because they are very important.

INWARD SEPARATION FROM SIN

Firstly, it was His inward separation from sin. There was a great gap between Him and sin. It is said of Him that He " knew no sin " (II Cor. v. 21), that He was " separated from sinners " (Heb. vii. 26). That is, in His nature He was separate from the rest of men ; there was an inward separation. Now, we are not constituted as He was, as sinless, but we are told and made to understand, in the New Testament, that that inward separation which was so true of Him, which was so real in His case, can be made true in us. Paul has a way of putting it. He calls it the " circumcision of Christ " (Col. ii. 11), and he says that it is a thing of the heart, an inward separating between what we are in ourselves and what we are in Christ, the putting of a gap between the two. And then the New Testament says that by the Holy Spirit's enablement, by the Holy Spirit's power, you need not live on the ground of what you are in yourself, you can live on the ground of Christ, and living on the ground of Christ you need not be the slave of yourself and your sinfulness, you are delivered. There is something that has separated inside, and if you live on the ground of

what Christ is and not on the ground of what you are in yourself, you are on the ground of the incorruptible and you are on
the ground of the glory.

That sounds very technical, I know, doctrinal or theological, whatever you may call it, but it is very practical. We know
it very well. You and I who are Christians, who are the Lord's
born-again children, know that a cleavage has been made in
us, and that we are now two people. There is that side which
is our new life, our new relationship, which is our Christ-con-
nection. There is that other side which is still our old relationship with the old Adam. It is there ; it is not cauterised,
it is not annihilated. It is there ; and we know now that it is
for us to take continually the power of the Holy Spirit, in
virtue of that separating Cross, to keep on the Christ side, on
the new side ; and, if we do, *we know it is glory*. Very often
we know more of the meaning of the glory by a touch of the
other. Step over on to the other side and give way to the old
Adam, and you know quite well there is no glory there.

Now that very thing existed perfectly, fully and finally, in
the case of the Lord Jesus ; but the Holy Spirit as the Spirit
of that glory has come into us to make the divide, and the
Christian who has the most glory is the Christian who is walking most on the Christ side of the line. There was the Divine
in Him, of course ; there were no two natures, there was no
need for dividing between a sinful nature and a Divine nature
in Him ; but there was a constant gap between Him and sinful man. The enemy, the great enemy of the glory, was ever
seeking to contaminate Him, involve Him, pollute Him, corrupt Him. Do not let us think that He never had to resist anything, that He never had to say No to another. That matter of
how a sinless one could be tempted is of course an old theological problem, but there is no doubt about it that He fought
our battle, in all reality.

So that is the first thing—an inward separation, a divide, and on the one side the new life, the ground of the incorruptible, which is the ground of glory. " This mystery ", says Paul, " which is Christ in you, the hope of glory " (Col. i. 27).

OUTWARD SEPARATION FROM THE WORLD

Then next, an outward separation from the world. The inward separation had its outward effect or outworking in separation from the world, and no one will think for a moment that I am speaking about physical separation from the world. No, He was here right in it, in its throng and press, in its affairs, with everything pressing upon Him ; never seeking to live the life of a hermit, a monk, detached from the world, but right in it—and yet, while in it, rubbing shoulder to shoulder with the world, having all the contacts of this world in every form, there was that distinctiveness about Him that He was not a part of it, but apart from it, a wonderful outward separation. While being able to talk with the grossest and the most defiled and the most involved people in this world, He was yet by no means a part of them, their system, their order, their life, their nature, but outwardly separate from the world. I think you will agree with me when I say the most unhappy people in this world are Christians who try to have both worlds. It is my experience that if you want to find a miserable Christian, find what is called a ' worldly Christian ', in whom a constant civil war goes on between two worlds, two kingdoms. Yes, a *Christian* involved in this world, a *Christian* trying to get something out of this world —of course a contradiction in name—is a miserable creature. I used to illustrate it by the old Border battles between Scotland and England, the Picts and the Scots. The people who lived in the Border country never had a day's rest all their lives. One day it would be the overrunning from one side, the next day from the other side, and these poor people on the Border line had the most miserable existence possible, and it is like that. You try to live a border-line or border-land Christian life, and you will be a miserable person, without rest or peace or joy or anything else. You will never know exactly where you are, who is your master, which way you are going, to whom you belong. It is a miserable existence.

The Lord Jesus was not like that. He was on one side, and absolutely on one side. The border line was a very wide one for Him. Indeed, there was no border line. He was attached to heaven, and He maintained that attachment. You and I, if we are going to know glory now and glory afterward, will have to be on the same ground as He was in this matter—no compromise or trucking with this world ; in it, having to do our work here, having to meet people, having to be friendly in a way, yet not one with their nature, their realm, their way. It is a difficult thing—it is not as easy to do as it is to say—it is truly a difficult thing to be in it and not to be of it, and you know quite well what I mean. You know that in practical ways it works out like that, that you must not allow yourself to be involved or you involve the glory of your Christian life. Christ was wholly for God, that is the point ; and because He was wholly for God, His Father was the Father of glory, and the Spirit of glory rested upon Him, and the Father could give Him glory.

CHRIST'S HUMANITY WAS GLORIFIABLE

Now one brief word on a matter that needs very much more time, and is perhaps the most difficult matter in all the realm of Christian things to make clear—this whole matter of Christ's humanity as becoming glorified. *His humanity was a glorifiable humanity.* Of course, that is a statement that requires explanation ; but it is a statement worth making because not all humanity, indeed no other humanity, is glorifiable, as we have seen. His was a unique humanity, capable of being glorified, and it was glorified. Paul speaks of His body as a glorified body. He said that we are to be "conformed to the body of his glory " or " his glorious " or " glorified body " (Phil. iii. 21). He was capable of being glorified, and that actually took place on the Mount of Transfiguration. He had fought through all those tests and trials, all those efforts to compromise Him, to make Him let go and become involved. He had fought them right through to the pinnacle of that mount. There was nothing more for Him to do, so far as He Himself was concerned ; anything more was for us. At that point He had proved Himself worthy of being glorified, and, as Peter says, on that mount God gave Him glory. In the transfiguration of the Lord Jesus, God is showing in a representative Man what He intends for you and for me and for all—that we shall be transfigured, glorified, " made like unto his glorious body ". His was a glorifiable humanity. His humanity as glorified is the standard in heaven to which God is working for every believer in Jesus Christ. It is a Man in glory glorified, and He is there as the last Adam, the second Man. Those very titles have no significance apart from other men of the same kind. What does ' Adam ' mean? What does ' man ' mean, if it is not an inclusive and comprehensive and representative designation? The Scripture states that quite clearly. " The firstborn among many brethren " (Rom. viii. 29) He was to be. Many Scriptures could be quoted to prove that.

I believe that was the secret of the Apostle Paul's life, from the very day of his conversion, right up to the end, when, after so many years, and after seeing and knowing so much, he was still found aspiring, still stretched out. He had seen Jesus of Nazareth glorified, and he said, ' That is the on-high calling! ' And that is so much in keeping with what we have read in the letter to the Hebrews: " We behold . . . Jesus . . . crowned with glory and honour ". And then the writer goes on: " Wherefore, holy brethren, partakers of a heavenly calling . . ." (Heb. iii. 1). What is it? It is Jesus crowned with glory, as the Man according to God's eternal intention for man. God is calling " unto his eternal glory in Christ " Jesus (1 Peter v. 10). Christ in a glorified humanity is the model, the pattern, the stature, the representation of God's intention for all who believe in the Lord Jesus.

So then, if we have received that eternal life, if Christ is in us, ' dwelling in our hearts ', as the Apostle puts it, ' through faith ', our destiny is that. We have the basis of an incorruptible life, which will eventually emerge in the fullness of that glory which He as our representative now knows. Faith not only believes for the forgiveness of sins, not only for pardon, not only for remission, not only for atonement, not only for justification and redemption. Faith in Jesus Christ apprehends Him as the very humanity to which we are to be conformed. Faith takes hold of Him as He is now, and says, ' He is as He is because God wants me like that ' ; and, if we did but know, the Spirit of glory is operating for us on that basis every day, to make us like Him, to transform us that we may be transfigured, to conform us to His image. All the meaning of the activities and methods of the Spirit of God in our lives is to lay a foundation for glory.

And it is on these principles of the incorruptible. May the Lord teach us how to keep clear of this corrupted world, how to keep clear of that wretched, corrupt old man. You remember that magnificent, though so very simple, picture that Bunyan has given us—the man with the muck rake, with the crown of glory over his head, but so occupied with his rake and obsessed with what is down there in the mud, that he sees not the glory, he misses it all. That muck is our old man, and we are always turning him over to see if we can find something good in him, some glory. We are seemingly incapable of learning this one lesson, that there is no glory there and we had better finish all the investigations in that realm. Do write that old man off altogether, and do not get turning him over again, looking into him, or having anything to do with him. Lift up your eyes from him to the Lord of glory—and you will find the way of glory.

We are " called . . . unto his eternal glory " (I Peter v. 10), we are begotten again " by the resurrection of Jesus Christ . . . to an inheritance incorruptible . . . that fadeth not away, reserved in heaven " (I Peter i. 3, 4). How great is the wonder of this calling, of this life, of what we have through faith in Jesus Christ, and of how it is all going to work out! But be sure, as a dear old servant of God now gone to be with Him always used to say, to ' keep on the glory line ' ; do not touch that other. Get in the way of the glory, and keep in the way of the glory, for you are called unto glory.

E

Chapter Six

MANHOOD IN RELATION TO
THE LORD'S TESTIMONY

Reading : II Corinthians xii

IN PURSUING THIS MATTER of life and incorruption, we shall now consider particularly a little phrase used by the Apostle Paul about himself, occurring in II Corinthians xii. 2 : " I know a man in Christ ". *"A man in Christ."* I want to link with that one very small and simple clause, which occurs in different connections at different places. We begin right at the end of the book of the Revelation.

" I JESUS *have sent mine angel to testify unto you these things for the churches " (Rev. xxii. 16).*

It is just that single clause at the beginning—" *I Jesus* ". Then, working backwards, we have—

" I JOHN, *your brother and partaker with you in the tribulation and kingdom and patience which are in Jesus" (Rev. i. 9).*

" Now I PAUL *myself entreat you " (II Cor. x. 1).*

" Behold, I PAUL *say unto you" (Gal. v. 2).*

" I DANIEL *understood by the books . . ." (Dan. ix. 2).*

" I Jesus ", " I John ", " I Paul ", " I Daniel " ; and that is not only permitted but evidently inspired by the Holy Spirit, a fact which carries its own significance.

The object of our consideration, then, is " a man in Christ ", or manhood in relation to the Lord's testimony.

66

We have already said that man-hood, or humanity, is a Divine conception, something taking its origin in the mind of God. Being, then, in the eternal thought of God, it has come to stay. There is nothing in all the Scriptures to indicate that God at some time, at some point, is going to finish that order of things and replace it with another order—an angelic order or some other conception of His mind as to the inhabitant or occupant of His creation. No, manhood has come to stay. It is of the substance of incorruption, the undying, the permanent, and in God's thought therefore manhood or humanity must take a very high place—higher than the angelic order, so the Scripture makes clear. In the Divine thought, manhood is a very noble thing with a very great and high destiny. Hence God is greatly concerned with our humanity.

THE DIGNITY OF MAN IN GOD'S THOUGHT

Now in this chapter we shall be largely occupied with the correcting of faulty ideas in order to get at the true. Our ideas about man have become a little confused ; there are many defects in our conception of man. Evangelical Christianity has placed a very great deal of emphasis upon the total depravity of man. It is a fundamental doctrine of the Evangelical position. I have nothing to take from that : we can support that quite strongly ; but we need to remember that every truth runs so very close to a peril and an error. It is just as true on the other side, that man is a very wonderful creation. " fearfully and wonderfully made " (Ps. cxxxix. 14). Humanity is something very, very complex and very wonderful. We are constantly discovering new factors and realms within the human soul, and it is the soul of man which is the very core of humanity. I am not going to embark upon an analysis of the human soul : but are we not sometimes ourselves surprised at what there is in us, all unsuspected, of capability and capacity, of unsuspected forces at work? There are two sides to this matter of humanity, the one, which is perfectly true, man's total depravity ; the other, the wonderful dignity of man, the dignity of the human idea in the mind of God ; and these two things have somehow got to be balanced, or many other evils will result.

So there is a faulty idea which must be corrected before we can get to the real thought of God about man. Let us be careful.

OUR INDIVIDUALITY NOT ANNIHILATED BY THE CROSS

Now running closely alongside of what is so often our unbalanced and one-sided conception of man, there is our conception of the meaning of the Cross as to man. We place a great deal of emphasis upon that side of the Cross which relates to our identification with Christ in His death : not only the removal in that death, by that Cross, of our sins, but of ourselves, the putting away of one kind of man wholly and utterly ; and there is nothing to take from that. That stands, and we can add nothing to it ; it is true. But again, there is a very great peril running immediately alongside of that fact. *Our individuality is not annihilated by the Cross.* We as human beings do not go out in the Cross. The Cross does not destroy our entity. It deals with the basis of our humanity upon which we are living now in relation to Adam, but it does not destroy *us,* and we have to be very careful how we carry the Cross into realms where it is never supposed to be carried. Some people seem to think that the apprehension of the meaning of the Cross, as our identification with Christ in death and burial, means that somehow or other we have to disappear from the universe and never in any way be seen or known or recognised or felt. There is to be a kind of vacuum between our very existence and this world. We have to walk as—well, not existing at all! The Cross is not meant to create or minister to asceticism. You can carry this matter into a realm which is wrong. Let me repeat, our personality and our individuality is not touched by the Cross in the way of destroying it. Now you will have to sit down and think about how these things are to be balanced. I am making these statements because we are getting at a very important matter.

OUR INDIVIDUALITY NOT LOST IN THE BODY OF CHRIST

Then we must correct another faulty conception. I have referred to the Cross. Now I refer to the Body of Christ. Well, a great truth, a great reality, a wonderful thing, is the Body of Christ. There is nothing that we need to take away from all the revelation and truth and doctrine of the Body of Christ. But we must be very careful how that affects our thoughts, because a false conception of the Body, " the church, which is his body ", may result in our having the idea that individual distinctiveness is destroyed and that we all merge as it were into a general lump ; that all the identification of us passes out, and we lose any personal form, in some thing called the Body. Now Paul himself was very careful to point out the fault in any such idea. " If the whole body were an eye . . . If the whole were hearing . . ." (I Cor. xii. 17). That was his way of approaching this peril—the peril of supposing that the Body involves generalisation, leading to the loss of individual distinctiveness.

And again we have only to consider our bodies, both inside and out, and we will find that down to the smallest part, the smallest organ, there is something absolutely distinctive. Each has a distinct form and a distinct function, something that belongs to it and is quite distinctive. One of the effects of disease is to destroy the distinctiveness of an organ, so that it loses its own particular and peculiar function and character-istics. That is disease in the human body. We must therefore adjust our minds about this matter of the Body. We confuse _individuality_ with _individualism,_ and that is just where we go wrong. Yes, individual_ism_ has got to go out ; but individual-ity—never!

Need we pursue that to the creation? Why this vast and inexhaustible variety in God's creation? It is one of the won-ders of creation, its endless variety. And yet the whole of crea-tion is interdependent: every branch depends on another branch—the flower on the bee, and the bee on the flower, and so on. This principle is shot through the creation, one form, one department, one organism, being absolutely dependent up-on another for the justification of its existence and the reali-sation of its destiny.

And what is true in the whole creation is peculiarly true in our bodies. When the body is taken as a figure of the Church, it is like that, a vast variety. There is at the same time a won-derful unity, but each part has its distinctiveness of contribu-tion and function, as something which belongs to it, which is indispensable, and this is the argument of Paul to the Cor-inthians. 'We cannot say that we have no need of this, we cannot dispense with that.' The whole depends upon and de-mands that, because it is something in itself of value to the Lord.

GOD'S IDEA IS A MAN

Then there is a further matter that needs to be corrected— a faulty idea that has to do with being a thing rather than a person—and when I say a ' thing ', people who bear the de-signations that I am going to mention will need, of course, to

be very forbearing. It is possible for some people to be
'teachers' and 'missionaries' and 'ministers' and 'Christian workers' and 'helpers'—designations, titles—and they
become just that: a preacher, a Christian worker, or what
not, falling under one or another of the many possible titles
or designations. They cease to be persons, and become things,
and when you meet them you meet the teacher, you meet the
preacher, you meet the minister, you meet the Christian
worker. That has in many cases resulted in wearing special
kinds of clothes, both men and women. You meet the minister,
the clergyman, the deaconess. You are meeting some *thing*;
it is so easy for us to become a thing, something that belongs
to a platform or a class, and that thing wipes out our personality. That is to say, we are not met as persons, and
we do not meet people as persons, as men: we meet them
as that or that or that—some *thing*—and this is a faulty conception that needs to be adjusted and corrected, because God's
idea is a man. God's idea is not a preacher, not a teacher,
a Christian worker, a missionary. God has never yet sent out
a *missionary*. God has sent out a man and He always sends out
a man. If God has His way, He will see to it that it is a man
He sends, not a missionary. You understand what I mean.
Men with their organizations send out missionaries, send out
preachers, send out workers. God always sends out people,
and He is very particular that it is people, not things. Occupa-
tions can become more than persons, and that is always a
danger. The thing with which we are most occupied becomes
the thing which veils the person, stands in front of the
person.

GOD WANTS ORIGINALITY

Then again as to the matter of originality. Here is a very
important point—and you will recognise that here we are get-

ting more closely to business. This matter of originality—of course it is quite true that there is nothing in itself original. But while that is true—as Solomon said, " There is nothing new under the sun "—yet God can do that *in us* which makes " all things new ". Things may have existed for long, many others may have known and wondered at them, but not until there is a touch of the Divine hand upon our eyes or hearts do they spring into real being for us, and are as though they had never been. We exclaim—" I never saw *that* before! " So it may be with the Word of God which was written centuries ago. It might only have been written to-day when that touch of God's hand rests upon our eyes. That is what I mean by originality. For all its value it might not have existed at all. But now, from mere existence, things become experience.

How is that? It is not because someone has thrown some new light upon it, but because the Lord has done something. The Lord has done something in us, so that out from the realm of the long-existent there has come something that might never have existed before. There must be something in us which makes everything original. We cannot take these things at their face value, merely as things. We are not supposed to be like tape-recorders. When I speak into the microphone, it all goes on to the tape. Presently, if occasion requires, I can just turn it back and it will all come through again. You would hear my voice and every word that is said, but that is not a personality. It has got it all, all the message, all the truth ; in a sense it knows it all, it contains it all ; but there is no personality there, and there is no originality there—it is mechanical.

The Lord does not want us to be machines ; He wants nothing mechanical, no kind of tape-recording of truth. He wants originality, and originality relates to ourselves and not to our matter. You may have all the information in your notebooks, just as the tape has it ; but until it gets somewhere else it is of no use to you—there is no real value about it. It has to get into you, to become you. Something has to happen, so that you are able to say, ' Well, I have all that ; I know the words, the phrases, the sentences, the ideas ; but I have something much more—that has become a part of my being, something on which I live.'

THE PRINCIPLE OF SPIRITUAL AUTHORITY

This is the very principle of spiritual authority. When it was said of the Lord that He spoke with authority and not as the scribes (Matt. vii. 29), that did not mean that He had more ordinary knowledge than the scribes. Probably they had a great deal more knowledge—school knowledge—than He had. He did not have the knowledge of the schools. They had all that. Their authority was academic or technical authority. When they made His authority superior to that of the scribes, what they meant was: ' This man is talking out of his experience, he is talking out of what he knows in himself ; this is coming from him, not from books ; this is not the latest address he has heard, the latest book he has read, not something that has caught on with him, that he has got from someone else, that he thought was a bright idea and developed. No, this is the result of something God has done in him, and it comes from Him.'

This is all getting down to this whole matter of manhood in relation to the testimony of the Lord, a man in Christ.

GOD DEMANDS HISTORY BEHIND EVERYTHING

Now because the Lord is so concerned about this, that we will call the *human* factor in His testimony ; because this is

His own Divine idea, and therefore has in it the element of the incorruptible, that is, that which is to be eternal, because God made man for incorruption and for glory, and that eternal thought is bound up with man: because it is so, *He demands history* behind everything else. That is, He demands history behind all that we say. If we are giving out truth, if we are teaching or preaching or working or in any way seeking to influence other lives, if we are here in relation to the whole purpose of God in relation to other lives, our part, our place, our influence must have a history behind it. We are not here just to stand as a kind of middle man and to take from a store and pass on to others in that mechanical way, to study up subjects from the Bible and pass them on, retailing Divine products. God demands history behind everything, and only as there is a history will there be a real value. The testimony is constituted not by words, ideas, truths, but by history in relation to them. God is very careful about this and very intent upon it, that you and I shall never go beyond ourselves in truth, that we are never found talking beyond ourselves, because, if only we knew it, we ourselves are the measure of the truth that we are uttering. There is something there behind the truth which gives to that truth its incorruptible nature, that makes that truth living and permanent and effective. It is not the truth itself—it is knowing the truth ; the knowing is the knowledge of experience. The real value in all our teaching and speaking and trying, as we say, to further the testimony, to stand for the testimony—I do not know that I like the phraseology, but that is how we talk or what we mean —is that everything has to have spiritual history behind it.

 It is, as I have said before, spiritual history which makes authority, and nothing else can make authority. And it is spiritual history which creates originality. Do not forget that originality is essential. Everything has got to begin with us before we can give it to others with any effect or value. The words of the Lord to Pilate might very often be addressed to us: " Sayest thou this of thyself, or did others tell it thee concerning me? " (John xviii. 34). " Sayest thou this of thyself? " It has to begin there, it has to come up out of our own history. The fact is that thousands and thousands may have gone the same way as we are going under the hand of God, but for all practical purposes no one might ever have gone this way before. We just cannot live on the experience of others, though there be thousands of them. When God gets us into His hands it is as though no one had ever gone this way before. We are alone in this, this is something original. For us the sense is that no one *has* ever experienced this before, they cannot have done—' I am the only one who has ever had anything like this! '—and yet thousands have gone this way. You see the point of originality. The Lord makes spiritual experience to be to us as though no one had ever had it before.

" I Jesus." Does it not impress you, that right at the end of the Bible the last utterance of the Lord Jesus, speaking to the churches, should be couched in that Name? Not ' I the Lord ', but " I Jesus ". You Bible students know quite well that the Name ' Jesus ' invariably belongs in the New Testament to Him in the days of His humiliation. After His exaltation they called Him ' Lord ', ' the Lord Jesus ', ' the Lord Jesus Christ ', ' Jesus Christ our Lord ', but when ' Jesus ' is used by itself it always in some way relates to, refers back to, His life of humiliation when He took the form of a man. He was " found in fashion as a man " (Phil. ii. 7). The word ' fashion ' is an interesting word there. It means that in all outward appearance, according to all outward judgments, He was like other men. There is another word used of what He was inside ; that was something other. But here He is having taken outwardly the form of a man, and in so doing He took the Name Jesus, the name which was the most common name in Palestine, Jesus, Jeshua ; and so that Name carries back to the day when He was going through all that which made spiritual history in Himself—tried, tested, tempted in all points like as we (Heb. iv. 15) ; so that, strangely enough, it could be said of Him that He was made " perfect through sufferings " (Heb. ii. 10). " Though he was a Son, yet learned [he] obedience by the things which he suffered " (Heb. v. 8). History was being made in His humanity. It was a man learning. No one will think that I set aside His Deity ; yet here is a man, a human being—God incarnate, true, but here in the form of a human being—knowing all about human life, having spiritual history made, out of which, as we have sought to point out so much in these pages, should come those intrinsic values that should be for all the ages of the ages. That was all being done in manhood, and now at last He presents Himself to the churches—" I Jesus "—the sum of spiritual history in a man's life, something completed in humanity.

" I John ". Yes, John is permitted to say—on a much smaller scale, it is true—' What I am writing, what I am going to write, is not just something that has mechanically come to me, but things which our eyes saw, our hands handled, something that has come into vital relationship with ourselves, become a part of us, so that we are now in a position where we are allowed to mention ourselves in relation to the testimony of Jesus.' " I John . . . for the testimony of Jesus."

And Paul—" I Paul ": he is allowed to bring himself into view with the authority of a man who has history behind him. " I know a man . . . caught up even to the third heaven. And . . . he . . . heard unspeakable words " (II Cor. xii. 2 – 4). ' This has become the substance of my very being. I am not talking to you about abstract truths : I am talking to you about something that has happened to me. I have been taken into it and it has been taken into me. In effect that has become me and I have become it: therefore I am allowed to say " I Paul say unto you ".'

Was that not true of Daniel? " O *man* greatly beloved " (Dan. x. 19). Not ' O prophet greatly beloved ', ' O servant of the Lord greatly beloved ', ' O exponent of Divine truth greatly beloved ', but " O *man* greatly beloved ". " I Daniel " : you see the *man*—it is the man of God, the man in the Lord, the man in Christ.

When I use the word ' man ', I am of course speaking of humanity—that includes the woman. It is what God was after. These were all human beings. John was a human being. Paul was a human being. Daniel was a human being. Christ had been a human being ; He was a human being *plus*—the mighty plus of Deity. It is where God makes something of Himself a part of a human life, and in so doing constitutes the testimony of Jesus.

Well, you see what God is after. God is not after making you a Bible teacher, a preacher, a missionary, a Christian worker. Those things may emerge, that may be just a form which the other will take, but before, over and through and after all, it is us, ourselves, that the Lord is after, and therefore He takes infinite pains with us. Do understand that, because you will misunderstand the Lord unless you recognise that. You are after your work all the time, you are after your job, you are after your function ; you are troubled about things. The Lord is troubled about *you*, and if the Lord is suspending the things, do not just get worked up into a terrible state about it and get upset with the Lord. He is after you. He is more concerned with your humanity than with anything else. If He has that in Christ, according to Christ, the other will spontaneously flow. You will not have to don any uniform, take any title or name ; you will not have to be called by any particular designation. You will be that, and what does the other matter? It does not matter at all. Oh, let us see the emptiness of names—minister, pastor, teacher and all that—if there is not there the thing that it means. But if that is there then the other is unnecessary.

" I Jesus ", and then standing alongside Him as the great Head, " I John ", " I Paul ", " I Daniel ", and ' I ——' —you may put your name there if this is true.

Chapter Seven

THE FULL STATURE OF MANHOOD

" I know a man in Christ " (II Corinthians xii. 2)
". . . till we all attain unto . . . a full-grown man . . . the stature
of . . . Christ " (Ephesians iv. 13)
" Not unto angels did he subject the world to come, whereof
we speak. But one hath somewhere testified, saying, What is
man, that thou art mindful of him ? or the son of man, that
thou visitest him ? " (Hebrews ii. 5)

WE ARE NOW GOING TO CONSIDER one particular aspect of this matter of manhood, namely, the full stature of manhood and how it is reached.

THE GREAT UNIVERSE OF MAN

We begin by a word about the creation of man, in which, through the incarnation of Christ, all the wonderful thoughts and realities of God, Deity apart, are intended to be expressed in mankind. The creation of man, and the subsequent incarnation of Christ, represented the carrying into effect of that great mind of God to express Himself ' manwise '. It is a wonderful thing to think that God chose to make a peculiar kind of creature called ' man ', bring into being something that is called ' humanity ', in order that by that means He might write for the revelation to the universe, the education of the universe, His own thoughts, His own mind. The knowledge of man is still in a very imperfect stage, after all the time that man has been on the earth. On the side of potential evil it

79

is sometimes beyond human comprehension what man is capable of. Under grace and in union with God through Jesus Christ the potentialities of redeemed humanity are correspondingly high and beyond comprehension. It was this incomprehensible destiny of man in Christ that exhausted all the superlatives of language of which the Apostle Paul was capable.

Take some of the departments of the science of man. I am not going to give them their scientific names ; you can quote the names to yourself, if you wish, but here are five distinct sciences of man. There is, firstly, that which has to do with the functions and phenomena of his physical being, the thing with which physicians and surgeons and all in that realm are trying to cope. After all the centuries of man's existence on the earth, they are still finding that there are new complexes and complications and depths and difficulties which are beyond them, just beyond them ; always new situations arising in the physical bodies of people, causing considerable concern and perplexity, even to those who know most about it and, as we say, know all that there is to know about it ; and so it goes on. The additional names that are accumulating to the maladies and the disorders of the human frame are very significant. In the realm of man's human body there is still, after all this time, with all this study, research and knowledge, a depth unfathomed, that is beyond the experts. They are so often at a standstill, at a loss what to do about it, and the whole question of reconstructing this human body, this physical life, and making it perfect, is as far from its realisation as ever it was. It breaks down just when it is thought that we are getting on.

Then there is that science of the human mind, so very largely developed in recent years, in our own lifetime. A new name has sprung up in this connection, and it is a world which is finding many giving themselves wholly to its study, to its exploration; a wonderful world and kingdom—the human mind being probed, analysed, investigated—you know that whole realm of things; and still the human mind is beyond the grasp of the experts. It still defeats and defies the best efforts to solve its problems, to put it right.

Further, there is the third realm of humanity, the realm of human relationships: human beings living together, whether it be two or whether it be communities or nations. It is what is called 'society', or human relationships. That again is a department of study and investigation, and much hard work, which is the whole-time, and whole lifetime, occupation, of a vast number of people—and what a complex world it is! You know it if it is only two people, and when you have to deal with a larger number, you understand what a burden it was that rested upon Paul when it made him refer, almost with a groan, to " that which presseth upon me daily, anxiety for all the churches " (II Cor. xi. 28). It is the problem of people living together, getting on together, and, as I have said, when you expand that to nations the problem of human relationships is a tremendous thing. It has killed many of our greatest statesmen, trying to solve this problem of getting people and nations to go on together in amity, in good relationship.

Again expanding, there is that great science which has to do with human races, the races of people; not only the nations, but the races. We cannot go into that now, but you know how much time and money has been expended in the attempt to get down to the peculiar constitution of different races, with a view to solving human problems. This race is characterized by certain things and that race by another set of things, and this creates a great world problem of racial life and relationships, and demands constantly an immense amount of work

F

and anxious thought ; yet the racial problem to-day is as great as ever it was. Look at South Africa! The racial problem is completely beyond man.

And finally, there is that whole realm, which again is a complete science in itself, which has to do with human nature, and particularly with sin or evil in human nature. That goes by a name of its own. Well, that has occupied man from the beginning: this sin in human nature—this evil, this wicked, human nature. What a world it is—what an ocean, what a depth!

There you have five great worlds, a constellation of worlds, forming a very universe, all related to man himself, to mankind. All this came in when man came in ; all this is bound up with humanity, with this being called man. How vast and far from fully explored is this whole question of man!

CHRIST THE EMBODIMENT OF GOD-INTENDED HUMANITY

Now, why all this? It is not just a point of interest, some matter to throw in. This leads to something.

Christ is the comprehensive embodiment of all this in a new kind of humanity, in the God-intended kind of humanity. He affects the whole of those five realms pertaining to mankind.

He relates to the whole problem of this physical life of man, and the whole problem of the physical life of man is going to be solved in the humanity of Jesus Christ, " when this corruptible shall . . . put on incorruption, and this mortal . . . put on immortality " (I Cor. xv. 54). When this body of our corruption is made like unto His body of glory (Phil. iii. 21), the whole problem of man's physical world will be finally solved. And that is not just a statement of fact concerning some future time. He has given us that life to indwell us *now*, so that even now, in a body of corruption, we may know the power of His resurrection, we may know a life which triumphs over that corruption until God has finished with us here. We have that very life given to us *now*, so that our mortal, our dying, bodies can be quickened by the Divine Spirit to fulfil a work of God here on this earth contrary to all human possibilities. When we ought to be dead—ought, indeed, to have died a good many times!—it is not so because there is a life in us which is triumphing until our work is done. He has solved the whole problem of that world of the physical, and in giving us eternal life has already given us the earnest of that solution, and on the basis of that this body will be conformed to the body of His glory. " Then shall come to pass the saying that is written, Death is swallowed up in victory " (I Cor. xv. 54).

And what is true in that whole realm of the physical man, the human physical side, is true of all the others. Take this matter of the mind of man which is such a problem. The New Testament teaches us that there is another mind, the mind of Christ, and " God gave us not a spirit of fearfulness ; but of power and love and discipline " (" a sound mind ", A.V.) (II Tim. i. 7). It is another mind, a heavenly mind, the mind of Christ ; a ' new-mindedness '. You have no need that I gather up the Scriptures on that. The problem of psychology (now I have given it its name!) is solved by the Holy Spirit in the believer. It is part of our inheritance in Christ to have a sound mind, not to be unbalanced. We will go no further with that, because we have so much ground to cover.

Again, in this whole matter of human relationships—what we call society, the relationships of people on this earth—has not Christ solved that? There is a testimony whenever the Lord's children from many lands come together. He has not changed our temperaments, He has not changed our basic individuality. He has not annihilated our varied personalities. He has not put out of existence our different nationalities, but He has made us one. We have one life, we have one language. All those things which separate us humanly, that is, in the old humanity, are touched in Christ. Oh, that we recognised this more! When divisions come, when there is strife and schism and the like, we are in the realm of the old creation, we are not in the realm of Christ. He, in His own humanity, makes a different kind of corporate entity. It is a wonderful thing, this corporate entity, the " one new man " (Eph. ii. 15), " where there cannot be Greek and Jew, circumcision and uncircumcision, barbarian, Scythian, bondman, freeman " (Col. iii. 11) ; all are one, there is one new man. The problem of society is solved in Christ.

But then there is this question of race, the races on the earth with all the problems of racial differences and conflicts. Oh, I do not understand people who call themselves Christians, with their New Testament in their hands, putting up colour bars! I understand the problems, but I believe there is another way through the problem than the colour bar. I think that is a perfect contradiction of the New Testament ; it seems to me to clearly say: ' This New Testament teaching about the oneness of the Body of Christ, where there is neither Greek nor Jew, neither coloured nor white, is an impossible thing. It cannot be ; it will not work.' Very well, then ; scrap the New Testament and cease calling yourselves Christians. This thing is solved in Christ. It has been proved possible, and it has been and is being proved workable. It only wants the grace of God to get into both sides, the government of the Holy Spirit on both sides—not on one side only, but on both sides—and the problem is solved. It may require patience, instruction, building up, but the basis is there when we are all baptized in one Spirit into one Body, whether bond or free, whether this or that. Christ touches this thing.

Finally, this whole matter of human sin. Well, I need not stop to say much about that—the great problem of sin in human nature, of evil in mankind himself. We need not look beyond ourselves ; we know in ourselves that Christ has solved that problem, which is still such an awful problem for the people who are interested in ethics, the problem which is defeating the moral philosophers all the time. That is settled in Christ.

THE GREATNESS OF CHRIST

Christ affects this whole universe of man on all his sides and aspects. Is not Christ great? He is the comprehensive embodiment of a new type of humanity in which these other things are solved and settled and put away. How great Christ is! And therefore how great the new man is, the man in Christ! Christ is so great that He can give character altogether different from, and altogether higher than, that which we know belonging to humanity. He can give character to a vast multitude, for the Church ultimately is no little thing. We are, I am afraid, inclined, as we look out on the world and take note of how ' few there are that be saved ', of the small percentage of real believers in the multitudes, the millions, on this earth, we are inclined to think that the Church must be a very little thing. But when we come to the sum at the end we shall find that the Church is no little thing, but a great multitude, a vast concourse, and that vast concourse, that immense thing, is taking its whole character from one Man. How great Christ is!

SPIRITUAL FULL STATURE

Having said that—and that is only my introduction—I want to come to this matter of spiritual full stature. The first thing, of course, standing over it all is seeing how great Christ is.

How great is this humanity of Christ! And then how wonderful must be the purpose of our being in Christ! To Paul it was an unceasing wonder to be able to say of himself: " I know a man in Christ ". It is no little thing to be " a man in Christ " And then of course the meaning of God's work in us comes in here: for it is in the light of this that God is pursuing all His work in us and all His dealings with us. If He is breaking down one humanity in us, it is only to build up another. If He is putting us through fiery testings and trials, and experiences that constitute great difficulties to our own natural humanity, it is only to produce this other humanity. God's dealings with us. His ways with us. are all explained by the great purpose, the great destiny unto which we are called—conformity to the image of His Son.

Now, taking a little phrase which occurs in the Bible in a number of connections, I want to say something about this matter of full stature and how it is reached, and I am going to take some Old Testament illustrations of this.

THE POWER OF RESURRECTION

"And Isaac sowed in that land, and found in the same year a hundredfold : and the Lord blessed him. And the man waxed great, and grew more and more until he became very great " (Genesis xxvi. 12 – 13).

The man did. Here is a type of manhood come to full stature —Isaac. Now we who are familiar with the typology of the Old Testament know that Isaac is the embodiment of the power of resurrection. I need not go over the ground to prove that. Abraham through faith received him back from the dead. and so Isaac stands out as the great example or type of resurrection power. And then, on resurrection ground. Isaac engages in agriculture, the realm in which, more than in any other realm, resurrection is known. In that realm, where the predominant law is the law of resurrection, he becomes very great. The law of resurrection operates so that he increases more and more and becomes very great.

We lay stress on this. The increase, this greatness of Isaac, is through resurrection—that is the point. He knows in his own person, his own history, his own experience, in his very being, he knows the power of resurrection, and by reason of that very experience, that experimental knowledge, he becomes very great. Through all the demands and processes of agriculture he came to know this: for, although it says only that he sowed and in the same year reaped a hundredfold, there is no sowing without a good deal of ploughing ; he had to do the ploughing, and then the sowing and all the other labour, with all the endurance, all the patience, all the courage, all the persistence, all the faith, all the hope. All these things are drawn into the work of agriculture. I think it is a realm in which perhaps heroism lies more deeply than in any other realm. To see all the hard work of ploughing and harrowing and sowing blotted out in a night's storm and then go and start again— that calls for something ; it calls for there being something in *you* before there is something in the soil ; you are not going to have that from the soil unless that is in yourself ; what comes from the soil will be because of what is in you—the power of resurrection. You have to believe in the power of resurrection to be a good farmer, especially in the days of the blight and the adversity and the ruin of everything. The power of resurrection—Isaac knew that.

CONCERN FOR REPRODUCTION AND INCREASE

Now what did it amount to in his case? What does it amount to in any man in that particular realm and sphere of life? It amounts to this—a tremendous concern for reproduction and increase. That is the secret of spiritual full-growth—a real and mighty and triumphant concern for increase and reproduction. Whether it be the Church as a whole or a local company or an individual believer, spiritual growth, enlargement, ' greatness ', will depend upon a deep concern for reproduction. It used to be said, and it is still said in some circles, that a non-missionary church is a dead church—it never grows ; and there is much truth in that. Where there is no concern for reproduction, for the salvation of souls, for the expansion of the church, there is no growth. The kind of spirit that does the ploughing, the sowing, the hard work, the grind ; that endures, that exercises patience and courage against adversity and disappointment, and persists because it believes that this thing can be and should be, because the Lord of resurrection dictates it: that kind of spirit is going to lead to much enlargement, spiritually, of the individual, the local church, and the whole Church. So Isaac is not only the embodiment, but the expression, of the power of resurrection, and that is shown by this great concern for increase.

Are you concerned for spiritual increase, or are you just sitting passively, indifferently, a passenger, a parasite, drawing everything to yourself and giving nothing? Are you one being carried all through the years, or are you one who is a true farmer in this spiritual sense, really concerned about increase? This thing must be a hundredfold ; nothing less than that can really mark the full blessing of God—a hundredfold in me and in others. Oh, how that would correct a great deal of our attitude toward others. Our attitude is far too often one that would limit other people's spiritual life. We criticize, we talk about them, we point out their faults, what is going on. How do we use our tongues about the Lord's people and His servants? What is going on in our homes in that matter? If it really did touch those people of God directly, would it be to their enlargement or be to their undoing or their limitation? What is our attitude? Are we true Isaacs in this, that we are concerned for their growth, for their increase, and are not going to do anything, by lip or hand or any other way, that would hinder the spiritual growth of other people, whether individuals or the Church? It is a very pertinent thing, this. You may take it as a settled thing that if you are using your tongue detrimentally to the people of God, you are cutting across your own spiritual growth, you are dwarfing your own spiritual stature. These people are little people, contemptible people ; they are of small spiritual stature. Oh, may we grow up!—and we shall grow up as we have a heart enlarged for spiritual increase.

DIGNITY, DISCERNMENT, AUTHORITY

" *The man, the lord of the land, spake roughly with us, and took us for spies of the country . . . And the man, the lord of the land, said unto us . . ." (Genesis xlii. 30. 33).*

" *And Judah spake unto him, saying, The man did solemnly protest unto us . . . but if thou wilt not send him, we will not go down ; for the man said unto us, Ye shall not see my face, except your brother be with you . . . And they said, The man asked straitly concerning ourselves . . . take also your brother, and arise, go again unto the man : and God Almighty give you mercy before the man . . . And Joseph said unto them, What deed is this that ye have done ? know ye not that such a man as I can indeed divine ? " (Gen. xliii. verses 3, 5, 7, 13, 14 ; xliv. 15).*

Here is " the man ". What are the features of this man? This is a man of stature. He is a big man, he is a great man. This man is marked by great dignity. That is patent ; it lies on the surface of the story. These brothers of his are all aware

of the dignity of this man. This man is marked by discernment
—" Know ye not that such a man as I can indeed divine?".
You remember that that was how he got to his position—Pharaoh had his dream, and Joseph was the only one who could
interpret, and the verdict was that the Spirit of God was in
him. He could discern, he had power of discernment and interpretation. And he had authority. Everything is in this man's
hands. He has them completely in his hands. Those three
things are the characteristics of Joseph—dignity, discernment,
authority.

That is stature. Those are the things that mark spiritual
full-growth. We could spend a lot of time on that. In one who
has spiritual dignity there is nothing mean, nothing contemptible, nothing small, nothing petty ; he is one who has to be
recognised as a man of stature, as one who counts for something. The man who has discernment is one who can see
through beyond his own nose, who is far-seeing, ' in-seeing ',
who has what we call vision ; he is a man who has a secret
knowledge of the meaning of things. And the possession of
spiritual authority means that there is something about that
man or woman which is more than themselves. They themselves, perhaps, would not command much respect and certainly not command obedience, but there is something about
them that you have to take account of. They have got what
we were speaking about in the last chapter—history with God.
That gives them something that makes itself known and felt
in the presence of other people. They have to say, ' They know
what they are talking about, you cannot just twist them round
your finger ; they know where they stand ; there is something
about them that you are compelled to recognise, acknowledge
and bow to '. That is spiritual authority. Let us not interpret
these things physically—I was going to say literally. These
are spiritual factors, spiritual features, these are the marks

of spiritual growth ; and here is a big man, a great man, who has reached full stature.

Are not these the features of Christ? Look at Him again. Is there not dignity about Him? There is nothing small, nothing petty, nothing mean or contemptible about Christ. There is dignity right the way through. There is insight, discernment, perception, vision, knowledge beyond the ordinary. As for authority, He was someone to be reckoned with, even in the day of His humiliation. Sometimes when we are in a bad way physically and having a bad time, we lose out. But there He is, in the deepest humiliation, mocked, spat upon, crowned with thorns, suffering—and the great Roman representative is in His hands. It is Pilate in the hands and before the bar of Jesus, not the other way round. He is there in His dignity and His authority, which is a spiritual thing from heaven. These are the features of Christ. Now, those are to be reproduced in us, and these are the things which will appear as we grow. They will be marks of growth.

But how did Joseph come to it? By emptying and suffering, in exactly the same way as Christ. That is how he came to growth ; out of this deep and dire distress, out of this anguish, out of all this suffering through which he went, came these very virtues, these very features. You can see Joseph being developed in the fire. In Potiphar's house, in the fiery trial, the dignity develops: ' Should such a one as I do this thing?'. It was in the fire, in the dungeon, that these features were developed. It was through suffering. It will be the same with us : but that is what God is after, to develop these things. It is a wonderful thing that the grace of God just reverses the order of things. Ordinarily in suffering the unregenerate man loses calibre and often loses character ; but in the case of the believer, with the grace of God suffering only adds to character and calibre. Something comes up and grows which is fine, which is grand. That is the story of so many a suffering child of God. It is grand to see them, to be with them. Oh, that is not natural, that is not something that they inherit. That is something that has come by the grace of God, something that has come out of the fires.

MEEKNESS

" Now the man Moses was very meek, above all the men that were upon the face of the earth " (Numbers xii. 3).

What a verdict! *" above* all men " : head and shoulders above all other men! And how was he head and shoulders above all other men? It says it was in meekness, a tremendous summing up of a man's life! You could say about Moses that he was great in many respects. very great, but the Bible does not make a lot of his greatness in other respects. The Bible passes its verdict upon him that he was the meekest man upon the earth. See God's estimate of greatness, what God calls greatness—meekness. We need not stay with it. What is it? Well, meekness is what he thought of himself : it is what a man is in himself and toward himself. When Moses was alone and when Moses had any thought about himself at all, those thoughts about himself were very poor. He never, when thinking about himself, recognised that there was any reason why he should assert himself, that there was any ground on which he could stand up for his rights or could be something, any reason why they ought to take account of what he was in his own inner life. There was none of that—it was the other way. His thoughts about himself were very small thoughts, and he was only in his position because he had great thoughts of of God and little thoughts about himself. That is all we need say. That is meekness. It works, of course, in many ways, it comes out in many ways ; but that is the heart of the matter

—what we are in our own eyes about ourselves, and therefore how we behave.

Moses was not always meek, as we know from his early life in Egypt ; but, under the hand of God, his weakest point became his strongest.

Now look at the Lord Jesus. There did come a Man on the earth greater than Moses, and His greatness was superior greatness even to that of Moses. He was on the same ground. " I am meek and lowly in heart ", He said ; " learn of me " (Matt. xi. 29). That is the way to grow. Pride is one of the most ruinous things in the realm of spiritual growth.

DEVOTION TO THE LORD'S TESTIMONY IN HIS PEOPLE

" Mordecai was great in the king's house, and his fame went forth throughout all the provinces ; for the man Mordecai waxed greater and greater " (Esther ix. 4).
" The man . . . waxed greater and greater." You see how this little phrase " the man " in every connection is related to stature, to growth, to greatness. " The man Mordecai waxed greater and greater." Why? What was the secret of his greatness? Why did God sovereignly act to bring that man right up, in that startling way, from sitting at the door as a kind of eavesdropper and beggar—bring him up and up and up, until at last this could be said of him: " the man Mordecai waxed greater and greater "? Why? There is only one reason. Here was a man who at any cost was devoted to the interests of the Lord's people and to the Lord's testimony as vested in the Lord's people. That is the answer. You know the story of Mordecai and of Esther. Here is a man whose whole story is summed up in this deep, overwhelming concern for the Lord's people, because they embodied the Lord's testimony. We need, of course, to go over that whole ground of how Israel,

chosen of God, was chosen as a people in the earth to be the vessel of His testimony, and here these people are at the point of being wiped out to the last child by this cunning, evil work, the devil-inspired device of Haman, " this wicked Haman ", the Agagite. This man Mordecai set himself right in the full tide and flood of that iniquity, which was nothing less than the destruction of the life of the people of God in order to carry away the Lord's testimony from the earth. He set himself, and the tide broke on him, and God honoured him and raised him up and saw to it that he became great. His greatness was not the mere turn of fortune in his favour. It was because of what God was in him ; and it is ever like that. Whatever other people try to do, however much they try to keep us down and under and out, spiritual greatness will be brought about by the Lord in us, if only we have this over-whelming concern for His interests in His people.

These are the features of greatness, because they are the features of Christ, and it is by these things that we come to the full stature of " a man in Christ ". How important it is for us to recognise that all this is to be true in us as men and women —not as glorified saints hereafter, and certainly not as angels, but as men and women on this earth now, as human beings down here. How wonderful to know that it can commence and develop right away, even here and now, through the grace of God.

Thus, I trust we have been helped to see what God is really after ; what intrinsic value is ; and what will be the nature of incorruption. Man thinks much of Christian *work*. God thinks most of Christian *men* ! There is no grander title than " O, man of God " (or woman). This is the Gold of the Sanctuary, and The Final Criterion.

Spiritual Sight

CHAPTER ONE

THE MAN WHOSE EYE IS OPENED

"Then Jehovah opened the eyes of Balaam, and he saw the angel of Jehovah standing in the way" (Num. 22:31).
"Balaam the son of Beor saith, and the man whose eye is opened saith ... falling down, and having his eyes open" (Num. 24:3,4, A.R.V. Margin).
"And they come to Jericho: and as he went out from Jericho, with his disciples and a great multitude, the son of Timaeus, Bartimaeus, a blind beggar, was sitting by the way side ... And Jesus answered him, and said, What wilt thou that I should do unto thee? And the blind man said unto him, Rabboni, that I may receive my sight. And Jesus said unto him, Go thy way; thy faith hath made thee whole. And straightway he received his sight, and followed him in the way" (Mark 10:46,51,52).
"And he took hold of the blind man by the hand, and brought him out of the village; and when he had spit on his eyes, and laid his hands upon him, he asked him, Seest thou aught? And he looked up, and said, I see men; for I behold them as trees, walking. Then again he laid his hands upon his eyes; and he looked steadfastly, and was restored, and saw all things clearly" (Mark 8:23-25).
"And as he passed by, he saw a man blind from his birth ... and said unto him, Go, wash in the pool of Siloam ... He went away therefore, and washed, and came seeing ... He therefore answered, Whether he is a sinner, I know not: one thing I know, that, whereas I was blind, now I see" (John 9:1,7,25).
"... that the God of our Lord Jesus Christ, the Father of glory, may give unto you a spirit of wisdom and revelation in the knowledge of him; having the eyes of your heart enlightened, that ye may know what is the hope of his calling, what the riches of the glory of his inheritance in the saints" (Eph. 1:17,18).
"I counsel thee to buy of me gold refined by fire, that thou mayest become rich; and white garments, that thou mayest clothe thyself, and

3

*that the shame of thy nakedness be not made manifest; and eye-salve to
anoint thine eyes, that thou mayest see" (Rev. 3:18).*

*"... to open their eyes, that they may turn from darkness to light and from
the power of Satan unto God, that they may receive remission of sins and
an inheritance among them that are sanctified by faith in me"
(Acts 26:18).*

I think the phrase used by Balaam might very well stand at the head
of our present meditation — "the man whose eye is opened."

The root malady of our time

As we contemplate the state of things in the world today, we are
very deeply impressed and oppressed with the prevailing malady of
spiritual blindness. It is the root malady of the time. We should not be far
wrong if we said that most, if not all, of the troubles from which the
world is suffering, are traceable to that root namely, blindness*. The
masses are blind; there is no doubt about that. In a day which is supposed
to be a day of unequalled enlightenment, the masses are blind. The
leaders are blind, blind leaders of the blind. But in a very large measure,
the same is true of the Lord's people. Speaking quite generally, Christians are today very blind.

A general survey of the ground of spiritual blindness

The passages which we have just read cover in a general way a great
deal, if not all, of the ground of spiritual blindness. They begin with those
who never have seen, those born blind.

Then there are those who have been given vision, but are not seeing
very much, nor very clearly — "men as trees walking" — but who come
to see yet more perfectly under a further work of grace.

Then there are those who have true and clear sight as far as it goes,
but for whom a vast realm of divine thought and purpose still waits upon
a fuller work of the Holy Spirit. "That He would grant unto you a spirit of
wisdom and revelation in the knowledge of him; having the eyes of your
heart enlightened, that ye may know what is the hope of his calling, what
the riches of the glory of his inheritance in the saints, and what the

---

*Written in 1992, Second World War

exceeding greatness of his power to usward who believe." Those words are addressed to people who have sight, but for whom this great realm of divine meaning still waits upon their knowing a fuller work of the Holy Spirit in the matter of spiritual sight.

Then, again, there are those who have seen and have followed, but who have lost spiritual sight, of which they were once possessed, and are now blind, but with the most fatal additional factor: they think they see and they are blind to their own blindness. That was the tragedy of Laodicea.

Further, there are those two classes represented by Balaam and Saul of Tarsus, from whom we have quoted. Balaam, blinded by gain, or the prospect of gain. That is, I think, what is meant in the New Testament by following in the way of Balaam; being taken up so much with the question of gain and loss as to be blind to the great thoughts of God and purpose of God, not seeing the Lord Himself in the way, and by this blindness coming very near to being smitten down on the road. The statement is quite definite there. Balaam did not see the Lord until the Lord opened his eyes, and then he saw the Lord. "The angel of the Lord"; that is the way in which it is put. I have not much doubt but that it is the Lord Himself. Then he saw. Later he made that double statement about the matter — "the man whose eye is opened", "falling down, and having his eyes open". Such is Balaam, a man blinded by considerations of a personal character, of a personal nature, how things would affect him. That is what it amounts to. And what a blinding thing that is where spiritual matters are concerned. If ever you or I pause on that question, we are in very grave peril. If ever for a moment we allow ourselves to be influenced by such questions as: How will this affect me? What will this cost me? What do I stand to get out of this or to lose by this? That is a moment when darkness may very well take possession of our hearts and we go in the way of Balaam.

Then, on the other hand we have Saul of Tarsus. There is no doubt about his blindness. His was the blindness of his very religious zeal, his zeal for God, his zeal for tradition, his zeal for historic religion, his zeal for the established and accepted thing in the religious world. It was a blind zeal about which afterward he had to say: "I verily thought that I ought to do many things contrary to the name of Jesus of Nazareth" (Acts 26:9). "I thought I ought." What a tremendous turn round it was when he discovered that the things which he thought, and passionately thought he ought to do, in order to please God and to satisfy his own conscience,

5

were utterly and diametrically opposed to God and the way of right and truth. What blindness! Surely he stands as an abiding warning to us all that zeal for anything is not necessarily a proof that the thing is right, and that we are on the right road. Our very zeal as a thing in itself may be a blinding thing, our devotion to tradition may be our blindness.

I think eyes have a very large place in Paul's life. When his eyes spiritually were opened, his eyes naturally were blinded, and you can use that as a metaphor. The using of natural eyes religiously too strongly may be just the indication of how blind we are, and it may be that, when those natural eyes religiously are blinded, we will see something, and not until they are do we see something. For a lot of people, the thing that is in the way of their real seeing is that they see too much and see in the wrong way. They are seeing with natural senses, natural faculties of reason and intellect and learning, and all that is in the way. Paul stands to tell us that sometimes, in order really to see, it is necessary to be blinded. Evidently that left its mark upon him, just as the finger of the Lord left its mark upon Jacob, for the rest of his days. He went into Galatia and later wrote the letter to the Galatians; and you remember he said: "I bear you witness, that, if possible, ye would have plucked out your eyes and given them to me" (4:15). He meant that they noted his affliction, were aware of that mark which had lasted from the Damascus road, and so felt for him, that, if they could have done so, they would have plucked out their very eyes for him. But it is wonderful that the commission which came when he was naturally blinded on the Damascus road was all about eyes. He was blind, and they led him by the hand into Damascus. But the Lord had said in that hour: "to whom I send thee to open their eyes, that they may turn from darkness to light and from the power of Satan unto God."

These passages have their own message for us, but they cover the ground fairly generally in relation to spiritual sight. There are, of course, many details, but we will not seek to search those out at the moment. We will get on with this general consideration.

Spiritual sight always a miracle

When we have covered the whole ground in a general way, we come back to notice one particular and peculiar feature in every case, and that is, that spiritual sight is always a miracle. That fact carries with it the whole significance of the coming into this world of God's Son. The very justification of the coming into this world of the Lord Jesus

Christ is found in the thing which is assumed in the Word of God;
because it is a settled matter with God Himself that man now is born
blind. "I am come a light into the world" (John 12:46); "I am the light of
the world" (John 9:5). That statement, as you know was made right there
in that section of John's Gospel where the Lord Jesus is dealing with
blindness. "When I am in the world, I am the light of the world," and He
illustrates that by dealing with the man born blind.

So spiritual sight is a miracle from heaven every time. That means
that the one who really sees spiritually has a miracle right at the foundation of his life. His whole spiritual life springs out of a miracle, and it is
the miracle of having sight given to eyes which never have seen. That is
just where the spiritual life begins, just where the Christian life has its
commencement: it is in seeing.

And whoever preaches must have that miracle in his history. He
himself is dependent entirely upon that miracle being repeated in the case
of every one who listens to him. That is where he is so helpless and so
foolish. Perhaps it is here that, in one sense, we find "the foolishness of
preaching". A man may have seen, and may be preaching what he has
seen, but no one listening to him has seen or does see. So he is saying to
the blind: "See!" and they see not. He is dependent entirely upon the
Spirit of God coming and, there and then, working a miracle. Unless that
miracle is wrought, his preaching is vain, so far as the desired effect is
concerned. I do not know what you say when you come into a gathering
and bow your head in prayer, but there is a suggestion for you. There may
be present that which has come out of a miracle in the one who is giving
it forth in preaching or teaching, and you may miss it all. The suggestion
is that you ever and always ask the Holy Spirit to work that miracle in
you afresh in this hour, that you may see.

But we go further. Every bit of new seeing is a work from heaven. It
is not something done fully once for all. It is possible for us to go on
seeing and seeing, and yet more fully seeing, but with every fresh
fragment of truth, this work, which is not in our power to do, has to be
done. Spiritual life is not only a miracle in its inception; it is a continuous
miracle in this matter right on to the last. That is what arises from the
passages we have read. A man may have had a touch, and, whereas
before he was blind and saw nothing, now he sees. However, he sees only
a little, both in its measure and in its range, and he sees imperfectly.
There is a certain amount of distortion about his vision yet. Another
touch is required from heaven in order that he may see all things cor-

7

rectly, perfectly. But even then it is not the end, for those who are seeing things correctly, perfectly, within that measure, have yet possibilities from God of seeing such vast ranges. But it is still a spirit of wisdom and revelation which is required to effect it. All the way along it is from heaven. And who would have it otherwise, for is not this the thing which gives to a true spiritual life its real value, that there should forever remain in it the miraculous element?

The effect of the loss of spiritual sight

Then we come to that final word. To lose spiritual vision is to lose the supernatural feature of the spiritual life, and that produces the Laodicean state. If you seek to get to the heart of this thing, this state of things represented by Laodicea, neither hot nor cold, the state which provokes the Lord to say: "I will spew thee out of my mouth;" if you seek to get to the heart of it and say: Why is this, what is the thing lying behind this? There is one thing that explains it: it is simply this, that it has lost its supernatural feature, it has come down to earth; it is religious, but it has come out if its heavenly place. And then, you see, you get the corresponding rebound to overcomers in Laodicea. "He that overcometh, I will give to him to sit down with me in my throne." You have gone down a long way to earth, you have lost your heavenly feature. However for overcomers in the midst of such conditions there is still a place above, showing the Lord's thought as over against this condition. To lose spiritual vision is to lose the supernatural feature of the spiritual life. When that has gone out, be as religious as you like, the Lord only has one word to say: Buy eye-salve; that is your need.

The need of the hour

That brings us, then, to the need of the hour, the need which, of course, is the need of every hour, of every day, of every age. But we are made more and more aware in our time of this need. In a sense, we can say there never was a time when there was a greater need for people who could say and can say: "I see!" That is the need just now. Great and terrible is that need, and not until that need is met will there be any hope. Hope hangs upon this, that there should arise people in this world, this dark world of confusion and chaos and tragedy and contradiction, people who are able to say: "I see!" If there should arise a man today who had

To See makes all the difference.

position, to exercise influence and be taken account of, and such a man who saw, what new hope would arise with him, what a new prospect! That is the need, whether that need will be met in a public, national, international way or not, I do not know, but that need must be met in a spiritual way by people on this earth who are in that position, who really can say: "I see!"

You see, Christianity has so largely become a tradition. The truth has been resolved into truths and put into a Blue Book, the Blue Book of Evangelical Doctrine, a set and fenced up thing. These are the evangelical doctrines. They set the bounds of evangelical Christianity in preaching and in teaching. Yes, they are presented in many and various forms. They are served up with interesting and attractive anecdotes and illustrations, and with studied originality and uniqueness, so that the old truths will not be too obvious. They will stand some chance of getting over because of the clothes in which they are dressed up. A very great deal also depends upon the ability and the personality of the preacher or the teacher. People say: "I like his style, I like his manner, I like his way of saying things!" — and much depends upon that. However, when all those trappings have been stripped off, the stories, the anecdotes, the illustrations, and the personality and the ability of the preacher or teacher, when that has all gone you have simply got again the same old things. Some of us also come along and outdo the last man in the way of presenting them in order to gain for them some acceptance, some impression. I do not think that is unkind criticism, for that is what it amounts to. No one will think that I am asking for a change or dismissal of the old truths.

But what I am trying to get at is this: it is not new truths, it is not the changing of the truth, but it is that there shall be those who, in presenting the truth, can be recognised by those who listen as men who have seen. That makes all the difference. They are not men who have read and studied and prepared; but men who have seen, about whom there is that which we find in this man in John 9, the element of wonder. "Whether he is a sinner, I know not: one thing I know, that, whereas I was blind, now I see." And you know whether a person has seen or not, you know where it has come from and how it has come. That is the need: that something, that indefinable something, which works out in wonder, and you have to say: "That man has seen something, that woman has seen something!" It is that seeing factor which makes all the difference.

Oh yes, it is a far bigger thing than you and I have yet appreciated.

Let me tell you forthwith that all hell is banded together against that, and the man who has had his eyes opened is going to meet hell. This man in John 9 was up against it at once. They cast him out, and even his own parents were afraid to take sides with him because of the cost. "He is of age; ask him." "Yes, this is our son, but do not press us too much, do not involve us in this thing; go to him, get it cleared up with him, leave us alone!" They saw a red light, and so they were seeking to bypass this issue. It costs to see, and it may cost everything, because of the immense value of seeing to the Lord, and as it is against Satan, the god of this age, who hath blinded the minds of the unbelieving. It is the undoing of his work. "I send thee to open their eyes, that they may turn from darkness to light and from the power of Satan unto God." Satan is not going to take that, neither at the beginning nor in any measure. It is a tremendous thing, to see.

But oh, what a need today for men and women who can stand spiritually in the position in which this man stood and say: "I was blind, but now I see, and this one thing I know!" It is a great thing to be there. How much I do not know, one thing I do know, I see! That was not the case before. There is an impact, a registration, with that. Life and light always go together in the Word of God. If a man sees really, there is life, and there is uplift. If he is giving you something secondhand, studied, read, worked up, there is no lift in it, other than, perhaps, that temporary and false lift of interest, passing fascination. But there is no real life which makes people live.

So one does not plead for changing the truth or having new truths, but for spiritual sight into the truth. "The Lord hath yet more light and truth to break forth from His Word," which is true. Let me get rid of that thing which has been fastened upon us here if I can. We do not seek for new revelation, and we do not say or suggest or hint that you may have anything extra to the Word of God. However we do claim that there is a vast amount in the Word of God that we have never seen, which we may see. Surely everybody agrees with that, and it is just that: to see, and the more you see, really see, the more overwhelmed you feel about the whole thing, because you know that you have come to the borders of the land of far distances, lying far beyond a short lifetime's power of experience.

Now just to close, let me repeat, that, at every stage from initiation to consummation, spiritual life must have this secret in it: I see! Right at the commencement when we are born again, that should be the spontaneous expression or ejaculation in the life. Our Christian life ought to begin

10

there. But all the way along to the final consummation it must be that, the working-out of this miracle, so that you and I are maintained in this atmosphere of wonder, the wonder-factor repeated again and again, so that every fresh occasion is as though we had never yet seen anything at all. We have heard it put this way, that "what has now come by the Lord's grace has eclipsed all that ever went before and is greater even than my conversion." We have heard it said like that, and not by ordinary folk at that. We have heard that said by leaders. We have come to see in a new way! It has to be like that.

But I may as well say at once that usually a new breaking-in of the Spirit in that way follows the eclipse of all that has gone before. It seems that the Lord has to make it necessary, so that we come to the place where we cry out: "Unless the Lord shows, unless the Lord reveals, unless the Lord does a new thing, all that ever has been is as nothing, it will not save me now!" Thus He leads us into a dark place, a dark time. We feel that what has been has lost the power which it once had to make us buoyant, triumphant. That is the Lord's way of keeping us moving on. If you and I were allowed to be perfectly satisfied with what we have got at any stage, and not to feel the absolute necessity for something we never have had, should we go on? Of course not! To keep us going on, the Lord has to bring about those experiences where it is absolutely necessary for us to see the Lord, and know the Lord in a new way, and it must just be so all the way along to the end. It may be a series of crises of seeing and seeing again, and yet again, as the Lord opens our eyes, and we are able to say, as never before: "I see!" So it is not our study, our learning, our book knowledge, but it is a spirit of wisdom and revelation in the knowledge of Him, the eyes of our hearts being enlightened, and it is that seeing which brings the note of authority that is so much needed. That is the element, the feature, that is required today. It is not just seeing for seeing's sake, but it is to bring in a new note of authority.

Where is the voice of authority today? Where are those who are really speaking with authority? We are languishing terribly in every department of life for the voice of authority. The church is languishing for want of a voice of spiritual authority, want of that prophetic note: Thus saith the Lord! The world is languishing for want of authority, and that authority is with those who have seen. There is far more authority in the man born blind seeing, in his testimony — One thing I know that, whereas I was blind, now I see — than there is in all Israel, with all Israel's tradition and learning. And may it not be that that was the thing

11

about the Lord Jesus that carried such weight for "He spoke as one having authority, and not as the scribes" (Matt. 7:29). That is rather invidious. The scribes were the authorities. If anybody wanted an interpretation of the law, they went to the scribes. If they wanted to know what the authoritative position was, they went to the scribes. But He spoke as one having authority, and not as the scribes. Wherein lay that authority? Just that in all things He could say: "I know!" It is not what I have read, what I have been told, what I have studied, that is with power, but this: "I know! I have seen!"

The Lord make us all to be of those who have eyes opened.

CHAPTER TWO

THE ISSUE OF SPIRITUAL SIGHT

Reading: Num. 24:3,4; Mark 10:46,51,52; 8:23-25; John 9:1,7,25; Eph. 1:17-19; Rev. 3:17; Acts 26:17,18.

At the outset of our previous meditation we were speaking of the root-malady of our time, which is spiritual blindness. We took those passages which we have read and noted how they, in a very general way, cover the full ground of spiritual blindness and spiritual sight. Then we went on to speak about the common factor in all these cases, which is that spiritual sight is always a miracle. No one has real spiritual sight by nature. It is something which comes out of heaven as a direct act of God, a faculty which is not here naturally, but has to be created. So that the very justification for Christ's coming from heaven into this world is found in this fact, that man is born blind and needed a visitant from heaven to give him sight. Then, finally, to lose spiritual sight is to lose the supernatural element in the Christian life, which was the trouble with Laodicea. We went on to see that the great need of the hour is for those who really can say, I see! Imagine yourself being born blind and living perhaps to maturity without having seen anything or anyone, and suddenly having your eyes opened to see everything and everyone. The sense of wonder would be there. The world would be a wonderful world. I suppose when that man in John 9 went home, he would be constantly saying: "It is wonderful to see people, wonderful to see all these things!" Wonderful! That would be the word most on his lips. Yes, but there is a spiritual counterpart, and the great need is of people who have that spiritual wonder in their hearts all the time, that which has broken upon them by revelation of the Holy Spirit and is a constant and ever-growing wonder. It is a new world, a new universe. That is the need of the time: I see!

In this meditation we are going to follow up a little now the point that at every stage of the Christian life from initiation to consummation,

13

the secret must just be that: I see. I never saw as I see now! I never saw it like that. I never saw it on this wise, but now I see! It must be like that all the way through, from start to finish, if the life is a true life in the Spirit. So for a little while let us think on one or two phases of the Christian life which must be governed by this great reality of seeing by divine operation. You will be recalling a great deal of the Word as I speak, seeing how much there is in the Scriptures about this matter.

Seeing governs the beginning of the Christian life

What is the beginning of the Christian life? It is a seeing. It must be a seeing. The very logic of things demands that it shall be a seeing, for this reason, that the whole of the Christian life is to be a progressive movement along one line, to one end. That line and that end is Christ. That was the issue with the man born blind in John 9. You will remember how, after they cast him out, Jesus found him, and said to him: "Dost thou believe on the Son of God?" And the man "answered and said, And who is he, Lord, that I may believe on him? Jesus said unto him, Thou hast both seen him, and he it is that speaketh with thee. And he said, Lord, I believe. And he worshipped him." The issue of spiritual sight is the recognition of the Lord Jesus, and it is going to be that all the way through from start to finish.

We may say that our salvation was a matter of seeing ourselves as sinners. But had it been left there, it would have been a poor lookout for us. Or we may say that it is seeing that Christ died for sinners. That is very good, but not good enough. Unless we see Who Christ is, that subtle and fatal thing may find a lodgement in our hearts that asserts that many a British soldier has died just as heroic a death for his fellows as Jesus died, not discerning or discriminating between the one and the other. No, the whole matter is summed up into seeing Jesus. When you really see Jesus, what happens? What happened to Saul of Tarsus? Well, a whole lot of things happened, and mighty things which nothing else would have accomplished. You would never have argued Saul of Tarsus into Christianity. You would never have frightened him into Christianity. You would never have either reasoned or emotionalized him into being a Christian. To get that man out of Judaism needed something more than could have been found on earth. But he saw Jesus of Nazareth, and that did it. He is out, he is an emancipated man, he has seen. Later he is right up against the great difficulty of the Judaisers, tracking and following

14

him everywhere to disturb the faith of his converts, to wreck their position in Christ, and they are inclined to fall away, if they have not already done so (I speak of those converts and churches in Galatia). Then he once again raises the whole question as to what a Christian is, and focuses it upon this very point of what happened on the Damascus road. The letter to the Galatians really can be summed up in this way: a Christian is not one who does this and that and another thing which is prescribed to be done. A Christian is not one who refrains from doing this and that and another thing because they are forbidden. A Christian is not one at all who is governed by the externalities of a way of life, an order, a legalistic system which says: "You must, and You must not." A Christian is comprehended in this saying: "It pleased God to reveal his Son in me" (Gal. 1:15-16). That is only another way of saying: He opened my eyes to see Jesus, for the two things are the same. The Damascus road is the place. "Who art thou, Lord? I am Jesus of Nazareth." "It pleased God to reveal his Son in me." That is one and the same thing. Seeing in an inward way: that makes a Christian. "God ... hath shined in our hearts, to give the light of the knowledge of the glory of God in the face of Jesus Christ" (2 Cor. 4:6). "In our hearts". Christ, so imparted and revealed within, is what makes a Christian. A Christian will do or not do certain things, not at the dictates of any Christian law, any more than Jewish, but as led by the Spirit inwardly, by Christ in the heart. It is that that makes a Christian, and in that the foundation is laid for all the rest, right on to the consummation, because it is just going to be that growingly. So the foundation must be according to the superstructure. They are all of a piece. It is seeing, and it is seeing Christ.

That is a bold statement upon which a very great deal more might be said. But it is a challenge. We have to ask ourselves now: On what foundation does our Christian life rest? Is it upon something outward; something we have read, something we have been told, something we have been commanded, something we have been frightened into, or emotionalized into, or is it based upon this foundation: "it pleased God to reveal his Son in me?" When I saw Him, I saw what a sinner I am, and I saw too what a Saviour He is. It was seeing Him that did it! I know how elementary that is for a conference of Christians, but it is good sometimes to examine our foundations. We never get away from those foundations. We are not going to grow up and be wonderful folk who have left all that behind. It is all of a piece. I do not mean that we stay at the elementary things all our lives, but we take the character of our founda-

15

tions through to the end. The grace which laid the foundation will bring forth the topstone with shoutings of "Grace, grace!" It will all be that, the grace of God in opening our eyes. I will not stay longer with that.

Seeing governs spiritual growth

Let us pass on to growth. Just as the beginning is by seeing, so is growth. Spiritual growth is all a matter of seeing. I want you to think about that. We have to see if we would grow. What is spiritual growth? Answer that carefully in your heart. I think some people imagine that spiritual growth is getting to know a great deal more truth. No, not necessarily. You may increase in such knowledge as you grow, but it is not just that. What is growth? It is conformity to the image of God's Son. That is the end, and it is toward that that we are progressively and steadily and consistently to move. Full growth, spiritual maturity, will be our having been conformed to the image of God's Son. That is growth. Then if that be so, Paul will say to us: "We all, with unveiled face beholding as in a mirror the glory of the Lord, are transformed into the same image from glory to glory, even as from the Lord the Spirit" (2 Cor. 3:18). Conformity by seeing, growth by seeing.

The ministry of the Holy Spirit

Now that contains a very precious and deep principle. How can we illustrate? That very passage which we have just cited helps us, I think. The last clause will give us our clue: "as from the Lord the Spirit". I trust I do not use too hackneyed an illustration in trying to help this out when I go back to Eliezer, Abraham's servant, and Isaac and Rebekah, that classic romance of the Old Testament. You remember the day came when Abraham, getting old, called his faithful household steward, Eliezer, and said: "Put now your hand under my thigh, and swear that you will not take of the women of this country for a bride for my son, but that you will go to my own kith and kin." And he swore. And then Eliezer set out, as you know, with the camels for the distant country across the desert, praying as he went that the Lord would prosper him and give him a sign. The sign was given at the well. Rebekah responded to the man, and, after tarrying a bit and being confronted with the challenge quite definitely, she decided to go with the man. On the way he brought out from his treasures things of his master's house, things of his master's

16

son, and showed them to her. So he occupied her all the time with his master's son and the things which indicated what a son he was, and what possessions he had and what she was coming into. This went on right across the desert until they reached the other side and came into the district of the father's home. Isaac was out in the field meditating, and they lifted up their eyes and saw, and the servant said: "There he is! The one of whom I have been speaking to you all the time, the one whose things I have been showing you. There he is!" And she lighted down from the camel. Do you think she felt strange, as though she had come from a far country? I think the effect of Eliezer's ministry was to make her feel quite at home, to make her feel that she knew the man she was going to marry. She felt no strangeness or distress or foreign element about this thing. They just merged, shall we say? It was the consummation of a process.

"As from the Lord the Spirit". The Lord Jesus said: "When he is come ... he shall take of mine, and show it unto you." "He shall not speak of himself; but what things soever he shall hear, these shall he speak ... he shall take of mine, and shall show it unto you" (John 16:13-14). The Spirit, the faithful servant of the Father's house, has come right across the wilderness to find the bride for the Son, of His own kith and kin. Yes, there is room for wonder here. "Since the children are sharers in flesh and blood, he also himself in like manner partook of the same" (Heb. 2:14). "Both he that sanctifieth and they that are sanctified are all of one" (Heb. 2:11). The Spirit has come to secure that bride now, one with Him, His flesh and His bone. But the Spirit desires to be occupying us with the Lord Jesus all the time, showing us His things. To what effect? That we shall not be strangers when we see Him, that we shall not feel that we are of one kind and He another, but that it may just be: "This is the last step of many which have been leading to this, and every step has been making this oneness more perfect, this harmony more complete." At the end, without any very great crisis, we just go in. We have been going in all the time, and this is the last step. That is conformity to His image, that is spiritual growth: getting to know the Lord, and to become like Him, getting to be perfectly at home with Him, so that there is no clash, no strangeness, no discord, no distance. Oneness with our Lord Jesus deepening all the time unto the consummation, that is spiritual growth. You see, it is something inward again, and it is but the development of that initiation, that beginning. We have seen and are seeing, and seeing and seeing, and as we see we are changed.

17

Is that true of everything you think you see? We have to test everything we think we see and know by its effect in our lives. You and I may have an enormous amount of what we think to be spiritual knowledge. We have all the doctrines, all the truths, we can box the compass of evangelical doctrine, but what is the effect? It is not seeing, beloved, in a true spiritual sense, if we are not changed. Oh, that is the tragedy of so many who have got it all, but who are so small, so puny, so unkind, so cruel, so legalistic. Yes, seeing is to be changed, and it is not seeing if it does not bring that about. It would be far better for us to be stripped of all that and to be brought right down to the point where we really do see just a little that makes a difference. We must be very honest with God about this. Oh, would we not sooner have just a very little indeed that was a hundred per cent effective, than a whole mountain of knowledge, ninety per cent of which counted for nothing? We must ask the Lord to save us from advancing beyond spiritual life, advancing, I mean, with knowledge, a kind of knowledge, presuming to know. You know what I mean. Real seeing, Paul says, is being changed, and being changed is a matter of seeing as by the Lord the Spirit. So we will pray to see.

Some of us knew our Bible, knew our New Testament, knew Romans, knew Ephesians, thought we saw. We could even lecture on the Bible and these books, and on the truths in them, and did so for years. Then one day we saw, and people saw that we saw, and said, What has happened to the minister? He is not saying anything different from what he has always said, but there is a difference; he has seen something! That is it.

Seeing governs ministry

And of course that must lead us to the next thing, though in a very brief word. What is true of the beginning of the Christian life and what is true of growth, is true in the matter of ministry. Now, do not think I am speaking to any particular class of people called "ministers". Ministry, as we have said here before, is a matter of spiritual helpfulness. Any ministry which is not a matter of spiritual helpfulness is not true ministry, and anybody who is spiritually helpful is a minister of Christ. So we are all in the ministry, in God's plan. Now, since that is so, we are all affected, we are all governed by this same law. To be spiritually helpful is a matter of seeing. You know that 2 Corinthians is the letter in the New Testament which has most to do with ministry. "Seeing we have this ministry" (4:1) — and what is this ministry? Well, "God hath shined into our hearts" (4:6). It is very familiar to us that Paul has at the back of his mind as he writes this part of the letter, Moses, the minister of God. That is the designation by which we know Moses, as the servant of God, and Paul is referring to Moses fulfilling his ministry, his service, reading the law and having to put a veil upon his face because of the glory, the people being unable to look upon him. And that was a glory that was passing. Now, says Paul, in the ministry committed to us God hath shined inside and we have no need of a veil. In Christ the veil is taken away; and what you are to see is Christ in us, and Christ is to be ministered through us as He is seen, as we are the vehicles of bringing Christ into view. That is spiritual helpfulness, that is ministry; namely, bringing Christ into view, and "we have this treasure in vessels of fragile clay, that the exceeding greatness of the power may be of God, and not from ourselves" (4:7). "We are ...": and then follows a whole list of things which put us at a discount. But he is saying, in effect: It is Christ! If we are put at a discount, if we are persecuted, pursued, cast down, always bearing about in the body the dying of the Lord Jesus, that is only God's way of bringing Christ into view. If we are pursued and persecuted and cast down and the grace of the Lord Jesus is sufficient, and you see the grace of the Lord Jesus being exhibited in that suffering and trial, then you say, that is a wonderful Christ! You see Christ, and by our sufferings Christ is ministered. That is spiritual helpfulness.

Who has helped you most? I know who has helped me most. It has not been anyone in the pulpit. It was one who passed through intense and terrible suffering for many years, and in whom the grace of God was sufficient. I was able to say: "If I go through suffering like that, then mine will be a Christianity worth having, mine will be a Christ worth having." That helped me most, that is what I want to see. Do not preach to me; live, and you help me most. It is an inspiration, surely, or should be to us, to see that it is in our trial and adversity that others may see the Lord and be most helped. How we go through trial is the thing that is going to help someone else better than all that we can say to them. Oh, the Lord cover us as we say a thing like that, for we know our frailty, how we fail Him under trial. But that is what Paul is saying here about ministry. "We have this treasure in vessels of fragile clay ... we are persecuted, pursued, cast down, always bearing about in the body the dying of the Lord Jesus." But, with Paul, the end of all such things was: "They glorified God in me" (Gal. 1:24). What do you want more than

19

that? That is ministry. If you and I could say that at any time we should not have lived in vain. We should have been of some help if it could be said: "They glorified God in me."

But it is seeing. We, to be spiritually helpful, have to see, that others may have the ground provided for seeing. I put it that way, because we may see, and we may give out what we see, we may be living epistles, but others may not be seeing. But there is the ground for their seeing, and if they are honest in heart and unprejudiced, really open to the Lord, He will give them to see what it is the Lord has revealed to us and in us, and is seeking to reveal of Himself through us. He must have living epistles, men and women in whom He can be read. That is ministry.

Therefore ministry to be given and to be received, is all a matter of this divine work of grace of opening eyes. It all constitutes one great appeal to our hearts to seek the Lord to have our eyes opened. It is never too late to get spiritual sight, however blind we may have been, and for however long, if we really mean business with the Lord. But do not forget that this is a matter of being honest with God. The Lord Jesus said a wonderful thing to Nathanael. Nathanael was perilously near that double blindness. At the moment when he allowed himself to give expression to a popular prejudice, he was very near the danger zone. He said: "Can any good thing come out of Nazareth?" That is a popular prejudice. A popular prejudice has robbed many a man and woman of knowing God's fuller thoughts. Prejudices may take many forms. Let us be careful. But Nathanael was saved. The Lord Jesus said: "Hereafter ye shall see the heaven opened, and the angels of God ascending and descending upon the Son of man" (John 1:51). "Hereafter ..." — He meant, of course, in the day of the Spirit. "As by the Lord the Spirit", Nathanael would see. He was in danger, but he escaped. If you are in danger through your prejudice, beware. Forsake your prejudice, be open-hearted. Be an Israelite in whom there is no Jacob, no guile, open-hearted to the Lord, and you will see.

According to
to
Christ

CHAPTER 1

NOTE. During the many years of this spoken and printed min-istry, very much has been said regarding the Church. This has led to not a few enquiries for advice from many who are in difficulty over this matter. Many of the enquirers are in responsible positions in the Lord's work. It is a sign of the times that there is such a very consid-erable revival of concern in relation to the Church. Many conferences on the subject are being held, many 'church' movements are afoot, and a very considerable literature is being published.

It is not our intention to enter the field of discussion and contro-versy in relation to this matter in general. The questions which reach us are almost entirely to do with the essential nature of a 'New Tes-tament church': how such a church is formed, what are the principles which govern it, and similar questions.

There is a good deal of dissatisfaction and unrest among many sincere believers and servants of God, due largely to the poor or even bad state existing in so many churches. In not a few cases it is due to error in teaching, or disorder and sin. Many complain of spiritual starvation, and still many more are tired of mere formalism and spir-itual death. While the perfect church has never yet existed on this earth, and while there always have been, and always will be, faults and weaknesses, or worse, there really is a need for a reconsideration, and a recovery, of the essential nature and function of the Church; and therefore, while making no claim to be expert in this matter, we feel constrained to offer what we feel we may have of light in this direction.

What is the Church, and what are the churches?

Have we in the New Testament a clearly defined and completely set-out plan of the Church, its order, constitution, methods and work? Is there a concise and worked-out system in the nature of a 'blue-print', which is ready for copying and reproducing everywhere, and can be recognized as true to type in every place? The answer is decidedly No! But if we mean: Is there in the New Testament a revelation of God's mind as to the Church, in its nature, constitution, and vocation?

1

It is no contradiction of the above when we say: Yes, decidedly Yes!

It is possible to take parts of the New Testament, as to doctrines, practices, work, methods, and order, to piece them together, and to frame them into a system to be adopted and applied. This is the mechanical or 'ecclesiastical' method, and it is capable of an almost endless variety of presentations, resulting in a very large variety of organized bodies, every one of which claims the New Testament for its authority. This in turn issues in rivalries, competitiveness, controversy, and, eventually, in the presenting to the world of a Christianity divided into a vast number of independent and unrelated parts, far removed from 'all speaking the same thing'. The external and objective approach to the New Testament, with a view to studying it as a manual or text-book of Christian life, teaching and work, is a false one, a dangerous one, and — so far as any real spiritual outcome is concerned — a dead one. If God had meant successive generations of Christians to *imitate* the first and proceed on the mass-production principle, surely He would have seen to it that in some way a precise and unmistakable prototype existed, with adequate safeguards against all the confusion and misapprehension which has actually eventuated.

When men, Christian men, contemplate a project which is intended to the last for a considerable tenure, they set down precisely their 'Principles and Practice', consisting of their doctrines, their purpose, their practices, their methods, and so on. God did not commission or allow His first Apostles to act in this way, so that we might have a Jerusalem or Antioch Blue Book or Manual for Christian churches. In the divine mind it is all definite, fixed, precise, and permanent, but when we come to the New Testament, and especially the formative period as covered by the Book of the Acts, everything seems so fluid, so open, and so subject to proving. There is the most wonderful and sublime reason for this; but, before we come to that, let us point out that the approach to which we have referred above is the cause of more limitation, stagnation, deadly legality, than can be measured. In doctrine, it means that the doctrinal compass is boxed and no new light is allowed as to God's Word. Of course, this is the peril of orthodoxy. The intense desire to safeguard the Scriptures can lead to a sealing off against any new light from them as to meaning and interpretation, and this makes for a static spiritual position. Spiritual pride, bigotry, exclusiveness, suspicion, are some of the unholy brood of this legalism. If Satan cannot force to the one extreme of superiority to the written

Word, he will try the opposite of bondage to the letter without the spirit.

The merely objective approach of which we have written may or may not be characterized by all of the above-mentioned features, but it will most certainly be limited in its spiritual power and results. It may very well result in the responsibility being made to rest upon men, so that all kinds of devices and expedients have to be resorted to in order that the work and institution can be maintained and furthered. Christianity has almost entirely come to be such a thing now, and it is practically impossible for the vast majority of Christians — their leaders especially — to understand or even believe that God can do His work without committees, boards, machinery, advertisement, organizations, appeals, reports, names, deputations, patronage, propaganda, publicity, the press, etc. Unless these things are present with a 'recognised' backing, the thing is not trusted, even if it is believed to exist.

We are aware that the foregoing is mainly negative, but it is necessary in order to lead to the positive, to which we now proceed.

We have said that the New Testament has within it a revelation, precise, definite, and full, as to God's mind for this dispensation, and that in that revelation there is an answer to all the questions of What? Who? and How? in all matters of the Church's constitution and vocation. What is that revelation? The answer is that it is not a system, as such, but a Person. That which in the New Testament is secondary, and a consequence, has now been made primary. That is, the results have been made the first and governing things, whilst that which comes before them as the cause is overlooked. If we will look again, we shall see that anything that came into being under the Holy Spirit's first activity was the result of a seeing of Christ. By that we mean what the Apostle meant, when he recorded the substance of his prayer for believers: "that the God of our Lord Jesus Christ ... may give unto you a spirit of wisdom and revelation in the knowledge of him: the eyes of your heart being enlightened, that ye may know ...", etc. It is a seeing of the immense significance of Jesus in the eternal and universal order.

With the Apostles that seeing was subsequent to the days of physical association. During the forty days after His resurrection it was like the dawning of a new day. First, those intimations, as when the uncertain light just passes over the heavens. Then more steady and certain rays, leading to the Day of Pentecost, when the sun appeared in full glory over the horizon, dispelling the last shadow of uncertainty. On that day they saw Him as by an opened heaven. The mystery of the

3

past was dispelled. The Bible lay open like a new book. They saw Him in the light of eternity. They began to see that, while He was the glorified, personal, Son of God, He was Himself the embodiment of a great, a vast heavenly and spiritual order and system. This *seeing* was absolutely revolutionary. It was a crisis out of which a new world and a new creation was born. True to this fundamental principle, all that vast revelation, which has come down the centuries from and through the Apostle Paul, took its rise from that crisis described by him as: "It pleased God ... to reveal his Son in me" (Gal. 1:16). "I received it ... by revelation of Jesus Christ" (vs. 12). All the implicates were in the crisis; the full content was a progressive and ever-growing revelation.

While there was some initial testimony, the Apostles did not formulate in conference an enterprise, a mission, with all the related arrangements and organization. The new life forced off the old leaves and dressed the new organism with a new vesture *from within.* The might, energy and urge of the Holy Spirit within produced a *Way* and an order, un-thought-of, unintended by them, and always to their own surprise. What was happening was really that Christ was taking form within them, individually and corporately, by new birth and growth. The believers and the companies were becoming an expression of Christ. Here we come upon the essential nature of the Christian life and the Church.

What, in the thought of God, do Christians exist for? What does the Church exist for? What do local churches exist for? There is only one answer. The existence and the function is to be an expression of Christ. There is nothing less and nothing more than that. Christ is the Alpha and the Omega, the beginning and the end, and all between! Let that be the starting-point; let that be the governing rule and reality in *all matters* of life and work, and see at once the nature and vocation of the Church. This vast, incomprehensible heavenly system, of which Christ is the personal embodiment, touches every detail of life, personally and collectively. But remember, only the Holy Spirit sees and knows how it is so; hence, as at the beginning, there has to be an utter submission to and direction by the Lordship of the Holy Spirit. What the blood-stream is to the human body, the divine life is to and in 'the Church which is His body'. What the nerve system is in the physical realm, the Holy Spirit is in the spiritual. Understand all the workings of those two systems in the natural, and you begin to see how God has written His great heavenly principles, first in the person of His Son,

4

and then in His corporate Body. As an individual believer is the result of a begetting, a conception, a formation, a birth and a likeness, so, in the New Testament, is a true local church. It is a reproduction of Christ by the Holy Spirit. Man cannot make, form, produce or 'establish' this. Neither can anyone 'join' or 'enrol', or make himself or herself a member of this organism. First it is an embryo, and then a 'formation' after Christ.

So, all talk about 'forming New Testament churches' is nonsense. The beginning is in a seeing of Christ, and when two or three in one place have seen Him by the Holy Spirit, and have been "begotten again by the word of God", there is the germ of a church.

That, then, is the starting-point. But, how drastic that is, in the matter of reconsideration and recovery [1]. If we did not know that, both in New Testament times and in the world *to-day*, such churches existed, we should be right in viewing all this as either mysticism or idealism; as unreal and impossible; but it is only when there has not been that vision of Christ, and when there is a weddedness to a merely traditional system, that it can be so regarded.

We shall have to stop looking at the Church and churches, and look again, long and earnestly, at Christ; for to see Him by the Spirit is to see the Church.

Let us summarise what we have said.

1. This consideration is in answer to requests for advice as to the true nature of the Church, and especially of local churches.

2. The objective approach to the New Testament, with a view to formulating therefrom a pattern to be imitated, copied, and reproduced as 'New Testament churches', is wrong. It only either leads to a variety of conclusions, and therefore 'denominations', or results in something fixed, static and legalistic. This in turn leads to rivalries, suspicions, fears of 'sheep-stealing' and loss of 'members', etc.

3. The origin of the Church, and of churches, was a Holy Spirit revelation of Christ. As truly as Jesus said: "He that hath seen me hath seen the Father", so truly, although it does not put it into a similar precise sentence, the New Testament teaches that he that has seen Christ has seen the Church: for, although Christ retains His personality, individuality and distinctive identity, the Church is the corporate expression of Him.

---

[1] See introductory note

5

So truly as there was a "mystery" as to Christ, in the days of His flesh, which could not be truly seen and recognised apart from an intervention of God, as giving sight to the blind, the Church as the Body of Christ demands a similar eye-opening work of the Holy Spirit for a potent and dynamic knowledge of its true nature and vocation. (Eph. 1:17, etc.).

The recognition of the Church is an event which is of such a revolutionary character as to emancipate from all merely traditional, historical and earthly systems: as see the Apostles and especially Paul.

4. The Church was not formed by any conference, convocation, organization, council or plan.

The Church, and likewise the churches, were *born.* A living seed — the truth concerning Jesus, in the power of the Holy Spirit — was deposited. The Word and the Spirit, united with the quickened spirit of believers, formed an embryo, and this produced an organism. The whole process was biological as opposed to mechanical. "Not of blood (bloods), nor of the will of the flesh, nor of the will of man, but of God" (John 1:13). The Church, and any true church, is as much a birth by the action of the Holy Spirit as is any true child of God. "Two or three" in Christ is a local-church nucleus.

5. The function and vocation of the Church, and of the churches, is to bring Christ into any location on this earth. The test is ever and only that of whether, and how much, Christ is found, met with, and ministered *there.* Anything and everything that does not truly bring Christ in, or minister to His increase, has no place in a true church.

In purpose and nature the Church *is* Christ, and so are the churches locally — no more, no less.

Having said that, before we go on to the constructive aspect of this matter, there are two important discriminations and distinctions to be made.

1. The Church is not co-extensive with 'Christianity'.

What is called 'Christianity' is an enormous conglomeration and mass of contradictions. The Church is no contradiction within itself, and it will not allow its name to cover any contradictions. Christ is neither divided nor contradictory. The thing that now goes by the name of 'Christianity' embraces between its two poles almost every conceivable complexion and inconsistency. At one pole it has the complexion of a liberalism which denies every fundamental truth — as to the person of Christ, the authority and trustworthiness of the Scriptures, the atoning work of the Cross, the bodily resurrection of Christ, and so on. But all this is included in the title 'Christianity'. At the other pole we have hard, cruel, bigoted legalism, which can resort to physical force and the use of lethal weapons for its defence or propagation. We know of instances of actual physical fights between leaders of what would be called 'evangelical' (or 'Fundamentalist') bodies. This also is included within the term 'Christianity'. Between the two extremes there are many things which bear a character that is the most violent contradiction of Christ.

No, the Church is not co-extensive with that confusion and Babel of tongues. Anything that refers to the Church in the New Testament shows it to be quite different from what — *in general* — is called Christianity. "Christian", originally, just meant 'Christ one'. It is a master stroke of the great maligner and discreditor of Christ, on the one hand to have put that title upon so much that really will not bear it, and on the other hand to have confused the Church with it, so that the word "Church" can apply to almost anything; a building, an institution, a denomination, etc. The Church is holy, sacred, undivided, heavenly, and all of God. Not merely ceremonially sacred, but intrinsically so.

2. Difference between being in the Church and understanding what that means.

It is not an essential difference, but one that can result either from an imperfect apprehension of Christ or from an inadequate instruction. The bulk of the New Testament is concerned with bridging this gap. That is, it is occupied with making believers understand what they have come into through faith in Jesus Christ. This knowledge is shown to be of *very great* and vital importance. Whatever may be the cheap and frivolous teaching of many, that the only necessity is to be 'saved', and everything is all right — a teaching which accounts for no small measure of the present deplorable condition in Christianity — the Apostles most positively did *not* take that view. They 'laboured

7

night and day' that believers should know what they had come into. All the eternal counsels concerning Christ and God's eternal purpose as to Him are bound up with the Church. There are very many and very great values in a true Church life, that is, a true Body relatedness, and there can only be very great loss in not knowing or apprehending this.

That which is called 'Christianity' is not impregnable; the Church is! 'Christianity', so called, is not eternal; the Church is! 'Christianity', is going to be shaken to its collapse. The Church will not be prevailed against by the very gates of Hades. Someone who speaks with knowledge and authority has recently written: 'It takes no particular prophetic gift with a fair degree of accuracy to see what the outcome will be. From some direction harsh reality will strike swift and hard and the millions who have taken refuge under the glass roof of popular Christianity will find themselves without a cover: then, bitter and disillusioned, they will turn in fury against the gospel, the Church and every form of religion. Cynicism, materialism and unbelief will blanket the world again as it did after World War I.' Those are hard words, but they are only another way of saying what is prophesied in Hebrews 12:26, 27.

The Apostle Paul had given much time to Asia, and had 'not shrunk from declaring the whole counsel of God' there (Acts 20:27). Nevertheless afterward he placed on record the substance of his fervent prayer for those saints; and that prayer concerned that into which they were called in Christ, the context showing that the Church is the very complement — "fulness" — of Christ, without which He is by no means fulfilled. Although there have been, and are, distinguished Bible teachers who hold that not all born again believers are in the Body of Christ, it is not necessary to hold that view to see that the New Testament not only teaches, but thunders, that it is imperative that all born again believers should come to "full knowledge", *and that relates to Christ and His Church.* There is nothing in all the realm of divine revelation that has suffered such furious and many-sided antagonism from the forces of evil as the knowledge of the true nature of the Church. This Paul has clearly indicated at the end of that immense document on this subject — the letter to the Ephesians. Nothing has suffered so much confusion and misapprehension. This is itself significant, and indicates how important it is, and how necessary it is, to have a right and true understanding. It would be well-nigh impossible to describe what a tremendous impact would be made upon this world and the kingdom of darkness by a true realisation and expression of the

8

Church. It would be no less an impact than that of the very throne of Christ, as exalted "far above all". There is also made clear that to believers who have their life on a corporate basis there are many and real values, as contrasted with the weakness, poverty, and perils of mere individualism.

In New Testament times all hell rose up to prevent the local churches from coming into being. The significance of the presence of the Apostles in any city was fully recognised by the evil forces, and they — the Apostles — had either to be driven out or killed. The very existence of a local church was a testimony to, and an embodiment of, Christ's victory and authority over the evil powers. When the Church was born out of such travail, its spiritual life must by any means be shortened. Like Moses at the hands of Pharaoh, and Jesus at the hands of Herod, the babe must be slain. Someone or some few will have to travail initially (and maybe, as with Paul, "again") for churches which are a true representation or embodiment of Christ. The significance of Christ in any place is too great to go unchallenged, and no form of opposition will be left unused in order to prevent or to discredit.

To be able to go on 'happily' and tranquilly in worldly favour is no testimony to spiritual significance. The contemplation of 'New Testament churches' must take these facts into account.

9

CHAPTER 2

The first part of this consideration has been a general survey and statement as to the nature and purpose of the Church (universal) and the churches (local). We proceed now to look at foundations, but some things already said need elucidating and enlarging, and the matter now to be considered will serve this purpose, and touch vitally the beginnings of the Church in both its aspects, the universal and the local. At a point we made a statement which, if not rightly understood, could lead to a false position and to unfortunate results. It was this: 'The recognition of the Church is an event which is of such a revolutionary character as to emancipate from all merely traditional, historical, and earthly systems: as see the Apostles, and especially Paul.'

How important it is that that should be kept in the context. In other words, how necessary it is that the 'recognition' should really be an *event*. There are many who 'break away', and become 'free-lance' people or movements, on any other ground or occasion than a spiritual crisis of seeing the *positive* way of the Lord. This often leads to more limitation and negation than was found in the position which they have left. It is true that Paul, at one point, came to a definite crisis over Judaism, and as from that day said: "Lo, we turn to the Gentiles" (Acts 13:46b). But that is not how he, or the other Apostles, came into the Church. Something happened inside before it happened outside. Their spirits went ahead of their bodies or reason. They inwardly migrated; the Holy Spirit took them even where they had not contemplated — or perhaps intended — going. It was all a spiritual movement, not something of men. It was the Holy Spirit inculcating the significance of Christ.

We are now brought to those more positive features and principles of a divine movement. The first of these is far from easy to state without the risk of misapprehension. Even the very words used are open to a false interpretation. This is because we are in the presence of one of the many paradoxes with which the Bible abounds. The paradox here is that of Christ satisfying the heart, and yet the Spirit reaching on and ever on. Nevertheless, when rightly understood, this first feature is perfectly clear throughout the Bible, and clearly

10

seen in all God's movements. Since the very constitution of man, from his first digression, is always to digress — and history is one long story of human digression from God's way — all God's return movements have been the result of another element powerfully at work. This element is what we may call —

The Divine Discontent

We must very heavily underscore the word *divine*! While 'The word of the Lord' may have come to patriarchs, prophets, judges, apostles, resulting in a commission and a mandate, it is very easy to discern that, either before or by that word, there was found in them an unrest, a dissatisfaction, a sense that there was something more in the intention of God. Inwardly they were not settled and satisfied. Maybe they could not define or explain it. They did not know what they wanted. It was not just a discontented disposition or nature. It was not just criticism, or querulousness, or 'disgruntledness', a spirit of being 'against the government', as of a malcontent. *God* was not satisfied, and He was on the move. These sensitive spirits, like Abraham, and Moses, and Samuel, and Daniel, and Nehemiah, and a host of others in every age — Old Testament, New Testament, and since — have been God's pioneers, because of an inward link with His divine discontent.

Of course, this is one aspect of all spiritual progress, but it is very true of every new thing of God. We shall yet lay down the basis of the difference between natural and spiritual, human and divine, discontent, but for the moment we are concerned with the fact and the principle. If this discontent is a truly divine activity, it will not be a matter of mere human frustration. It will have nothing to do with natural ambition or aggressiveness. It will resolve into a sheer issue of spiritual life or death. It will become a soul-travail.

Personal and worldly interests will fail to govern. What is politic from the standpoint of advantages in this life will fail to dictate the course. There may be a divine restraint as to time, but the inevitable ultimate issue is known deep down. A crisis is known to be imminent, and the issue is one of obedience to the way of the Spirit, or surrender to policy. If the spirit is pure, and the life in God selfless, there will be a growing sense of 'not belonging', of having already

11

moved on, or being out with the Lord, and it is only a matter of being 'obedient to the heavenly vision'.

How often, when we have come into something new of the Lord, we have been able to say: 'This is what I have been looking for and longing for. I did not know what it was, but this answers to a deep call in my heart which has kept me dissatisfied for years'. So, just as the confession or salvation of an individual is always with the sense of having come home, a local church should be to the company a coming home, the supply of a deep need, the answer to a deep longing; just 'my spiritual home'. The spirit has been on a spiritual journey and quest, and now it has found — or is beginning to find — the answer. This quest will never reach its end until we are all at Home at last; but *something* directly in line with the end, and of the very essence of the full, should be found in the local 'family' representation.

Have we made it clear? Do you see that 'churches' should not be just congregations, preaching places, or places for religious observances? They should be, in their inception, constitution, and continuation, the answer to God's dissatisfaction; that which provides Him with the answer to His age-long quest in the hearts of all concerned. If there is one thing that God has made abundantly clear, it is that He is committed to the fulness of His Son, Jesus Christ. That fulness is to find its first realisation in the Church, "which is the fulness of him". Therefore God will only commit Himself to that which is in line with that purpose. As we have said elsewhere, it can be taken as an axiom that, if we are to find God committing Himself, it is essential to be wholly in line with His object at any given time.

But God *must* have a clear and free way. The Church and the churches are not now the starting-point of God, although they should stand very near to it. Some serious work has to be done before there can be a true expression of the Church in any locality. So, a cursory glance through the Bible will make it clear that the very door to the House of God was the altar. It barred the way, and at the same time led the way, to the Sanctuary. In the New Testament, of course, it is Christ crucified in direct line with Pentecost, the Church, and the churches. The Cross bars the way and points the way.

But when the Church is reached (so to speak), that is not the end of the work of the Cross. When we have come in, the Cross still governs. Thus it comes about that, in the New Testament, we have a very great deal about the Cross *in* the Church and the churches. It is quite clear that, when spiritual progress toward the ultimate fulness of Christ was arrested or impeded, or when things became defiled or disordered, the Holy Spirit, through the Apostles' letters, or by a visit, brought in the Cross with fuller meaning or stronger emphasis. This can be seen immediately, when we read such letters as those to the Romans, Corinthians, Galatians, Ephesians, Philippians, Colossians, and Hebrews, with the Cross as the key. It is back to Christ crucified that the Spirit invariably leads or calls, when purity, truth, life, power, and liberty are in question.

What, then, is the particular relationship of the Cross to the Church, and to the churches themselves?

Undoubtedly, the Cross says that in any true expression of Christ, individually and collectively (which is the sole object of their existence), there is no place for man by nature! Christ crucified goes beyond the door, which is atonement, justification, righteousness as acceptance through faith. Christ crucified is, in representation, the devastation of the whole race of the old creation, with its nature. The agonized cry of God-forsakenness, the accompanying signs in a darkened sun, earthquake and rending rocks, all comprised the mighty '*no*' of God and of Heaven to that creation. That was the all-inclusive climax of every pointer by death through the past ages.

The death of Christ was infinitely more than the martyrdom of Jesus. It was universal and eternal. In that all-comprehending veto was involved every realm affected and infected by Satan's corrupting influence and touch. To bring back into any sphere of God anything that lies under that ban is, on the one side, to deny and contradict the Cross; and, on the other hand, sooner or later to meet certain devastation. This was very early demonstrated, as a sign-instance, in the case of Ananias and Sapphira (Acts 5), as well as by others in Acts and at Corinth who intruded natural reasoning, passions, and behaviour into the realm of the Holy Spirit's jurisdiction. It is as though the Holy Spirit took hold of the Cross and smote them to death, or, in some cases, very near it.

There is very much tragic history contained in what we have here said; no least the weakness, reproach, confusion and ineffectiveness of the Church and the churches. The natural man serves himself of the Church. In it he displays his importance, his lust for power, his craving for self-expression (very often in ministry itself), and many

13

other aspects of his selfhood — that satanic thing which was begotten in the race when the supreme 'I' gained man's will for an act of spiritual fornication; for that is what it proved to be.

In the churches, it is all too often — and too much — that we meet people themselves, and not supremely Christ. At the beginning, the essential thing, as we shall see more fully presently, was *spiritual* men, as standing over against the 'natural man'. As the Church universal rests solely upon the foundation of Christ crucified, buried, and raised, so the churches must take their character from the foundation. Every member must be a crucified man or woman. Every minister must be a crucified man, and *evidently* so. No man should preach on any other ground than that he is compelled by the Holy Spirit. He should have no *natural* liking for preaching. Preaching ambition should be crucified! We verily believe that before a true church-expression can emerge, the foundation of the Cross must be deeply and truly laid with devastating effect upon all 'flesh'.

But, if the Lord means to have such an expression, the applying of the Cross will explain the meaning. This will not, and, in the nature of things, cannot, be all done at once. The movement toward fulness is progressive. So, again and again, that movement is marked by the fuller adjustments, releases, cleansings, of new and deeper works of the Cross. For greater fulnesses of Christ, there must be deep despair of any virtue, ability, resource, other than Christ risen and present in the Holy Spirit. We cannot 'form' or 'found' churches like this, but the Lord can bring into being a nucleus of well-crucified leaders, building therewith and thereon. If we put together Matthew 16:18 and John 12:24, we shall see that the first is a declaration of purpose and intention; the second is the way in which it would come about. That way is the organic way, i.e. through death and resurrection, in which every grain shares, and to which all the grains, severally and corporately, are a testimony.

Matt. 16:18 And I say unto Thee That Thou art Peter, and upon This Rock I will Build my Church, and The gates of hell shall not prevail against it.

Jn 12:24 Verily, verily, I say unto you, Except a corn of wheat fall into the ground + die, it abideth alone: but if it die, it bringeth forth much fruit.

14

CHAPTER 3

The occasion of these articles is a widespread and serious exercise concerning the nature of the local expression of the Church. As we pursue this enquiry we are getting ever nearer to the heart of the matter. The fragment at the head is, we trust, becoming clearer as to its real significance for every local representation, from the "two or three" gathered into the Name, to whatever greater number there may be. Let us, then, bring it right back to this: it is not an expression or representation of some *thing*, even be it called 'The Church', as extra to or apart from Christ, but the presence and expression of Christ Himself. To this essential reality we now apply ourselves along one more of the lines which meet in Him.

Peter as Representative

We shall all agree that, while the full revelation of the Church has come through Paul, Peter was the point at which both the intimation was given (Matt. 16:18) and the actuality broke in (Acts 2). While much — too much — has been made of this by historic ecclesiasticism, we do agree that Peter was in an outstandingly significant place in the beginning of the Church in this world. So we are going to look at Peter with a view to getting to the most fundamental factor of all in the Church and the churches.

When Peter sat down to write his circular letter to "the elect, scattered throughout Pontus, Galatia, Cappadocia, Asia, and Bithynia", he began with a doxology. That doxology hinged upon the living hope springing up with the resurrection of Jesus Christ from the dead. Peter, perhaps more than all men, had cause for a doxology over the resurrection of Jesus!

But we take Peter as representative of all those who had become followers of the Lord Jesus in the days of His flesh; not only of the twelve, but evidently quite a large number beyond the twelve. There were the seventy; and, beyond the seventy, many more who followed Jesus, and had some attachment to Him. Peter can be taken as, in a very real sense, representative of them all.

The Devastation of the Cross

We are thinking at this moment particularly of the *effect* of the Cross upon him, and upon them all. The utter devastation, and then the despair, that the Cross of the Lord Jesus brought upon them. For we are told they were 'all scattered abroad'; and we know how, even before the Cross became an actuality, any reference to it brought a terrible reaction. From time to time the Lord did just make some mention of His coming death, and, as He did so, many went away, followed no more with Him (John 6:66). Then again, others said, "This is a hard saying; who can hear it?" (5:60). Apparently off they went as well. The very thought and prospect of the Cross was impossible of acceptance. When it came, Peter, as the very centre of that whole company, is found most vehemently denying, with a terrible denial, any association with Christ — just because of the Cross; and they all shared that, even if not in word and in the same form of expression, for we are told that 'they *all* forsook him and fled' (Matt. 26:56). And He had said to them: 'You will *all* leave Me' (John 16:32) — and it became true.

Then we meet them after His crucifixion. We meet those two on the Emmaus road, the very embodiment of despair. For them, everything had gone, was shattered. All their hopes, and their hope, were eclipsed — 'We had trusted ...', or 'We hoped that it had been He that should redeem Israel' (Luke 24:21). Now, everything was gone, and the hope laid in His grave.

From time to time we meet Thomas, and we know what Thomas thought about the Cross. He again was in the grip of an awful despair and hopelessness — loss of faith, loss of assurance. As we move through those forty days after the resurrection, we find the Lord repeatedly having to upbraid them, rebuke them, because of their unbelief. 'They believed not', it says (Mark 16:11, 13, 14). 'Some doubted' (Matt. 28:17). We can see what a shock the Cross had been. I have not used too strong a word when I have said that the Cross was nothing less than a devastation for every follower of the Lord Jesus. And right at the heart of them all was Peter; we could say that it was all concentrated in him. It must have been, in view of what he had done. Put yourself in his place, if you can, and see if you would have any more hope for anything, or for yourself. No!

The One Supreme Essential

Now, there were forty days of this: forty days of appearances, disappearances, of coming and going; a build-up, steadily, of the fact that He was risen; overcoming day by day that despair and that unbelief; building up a new hope. But even after forty days of all that, the most vital thing is still lacking. You might think, 'Well, given all that, they have enough to go on.' But no: the most vital thing, even at that point, is still lacking. What is it? It is *Christ within!* All that — yes! but not *Christ within* — yet. Hence the restraint: 'Tarry ye in Jerusalem, until ye be endued with power from on high' (Luke 24:49). 'Don't move yet. With all that you have, you really have not yet got the vital thing, the essential thing.' And that thing is *Christ in you, the hope of glory.* Christ *in* you!

That is why the apostles were so particular as to converts receiving the Holy Spirit before ever they felt assurance about their conversion. Thus, there were all the reports — there was no reason to believe they were false reports, mere rumours — about things happening in Samaria. Had not the Lord said that they would be witnesses unto Him in Samaria (Acts 1:8)? The report comes back of things happening, of people turning to the Lord, real conversions taking place in large numbers. Why not be satisfied with the report? It is a good report, and there is surely no reason to doubt it. But no; the apostles are not just satisfied with that. They sent down from Jerusalem, and when they were come down, they laid their hands upon them, that they might receive the Holy Spirit (Acts 8:14-17). We see, again and again, how that happens. For them, things were not really settled until they were sure that Christ was on the *inside* — that Christ was *in* them; which is saying the same thing as 'receiving the Holy Spirit', the Spirit of Jesus. That, I say, is why the Lord said, 'Tarry; don't move yet!' And that is why the apostles were so meticulous on this matter of 'receiving the Holy Spirit'.

That, too, is why the Holy Spirit gave evidences, in those times, that He had come within. We believe that this book, the Book of the Acts, is a book of fundamental principles for the dispensation. When principles are being laid down in the first instance, God always bears them out with mighty evidences that they are true principles — that these are governing things for all time. God puts His seal upon them. So, when they received the Spirit, there were the evidences of the

Spirit. They spoke with tongues; mighty things happened. It was clear to all, without any doubt whatever, that the Spirit was on the inside; Christ had entered in. That universal Christ, transcending all human language; that Christ of Heaven, transcending all earthly things — He had come in, and the evidences were given.

There is no mistaking this, that the matter of *Christ within* is the fundamental essential of Christianity. You may have the mightiest facts — the mightiest facts of His birth, of His marvellous life, His death, His resurrection — and they are the mightiest of facts — you may have them all, and they may all be impotent, non-potent, until He is inside! That is a tremendous statement, but it is borne out by at least this threefold truth: Tarry — don't move yet; the essential has not taken place after all! Make sure; leave nothing to chance; let it not be just an emotional revival in Samaria! Whatever there may seem to be on the outside, to prove that something has happened, make sure that it has got inside! Make sure that Christ is *in* — the Holy Spirit is *in*! Make sure! For, as we shall see as we go on, you may have so much — and then, that vital thing being lacking, there may be calamity, as with them.

This mighty hope does not rest merely upon historic grounds — that is, upon the ground of the historic Jesus. This mighty hope rests upon inward reality — Christ in you! That is super-historic! And for the full, full meaning — the 'mystery which hath been hid from all generations' — it has been there through *all* generations — 'but is now made known, which is Christ in you, the hope of glory' — we have to go to Paul.

The Insufficient Foundation

So much for a general approach to the matter. Let us now in greater detail consider Peter, and the others whom he undoubtedly represents.

Firstly, then as to *the hopelessness*, ultimately, *of a merely outward association with Christ*, however sincere. There is no question about the sincerity of Peter or of any of those followers. They were sincere; there was a devotion to Jesus; their motives could not be called into question; it was well meant — there is no doubt about it. They had left all and followed Him; and to follow Jesus of Nazareth in those days

18

involved them in a considerable amount of trouble, at least with the high-up people, and the prevailing system. Their association with Him undoubtedly meant something.

Moreover, while perhaps they were not able fully to see and understand; while they were not in the full light of who He was — the *fact* of who He was was present with them.

For instance, there is the fact of the *incarnation* — the *fact* of it: that this One amongst them was God incarnate, was the very Son of God, was God come down from Heaven to dwell in human form. There is the fact. They were in closest touch with that fact every day of their lives.

Then, there was the fact of His *personality*: and there is no avoiding this, that that was a personality! I mean, there was a Presence where He was, that was different; that made itself felt, that registered. His was a very, very impressive Presence, beyond that of anyone else with whom they had any association, or of whom they had any other knowledge. There is a mystery about this Man: you cannot fathom Him; you cannot explain Him; you cannot comprehend Him: He is more; He is different. And wherever He comes, His Presence has an effect, and a tremendous effect. The *fact* of His personality!

And then, although we do not know how far it went, there was the fact of *Mary* and her secret. We do not know to how many she spoke of her secret; we are told that she 'hid all these things in her heart' (Luke 2:19, 51). But we do know that some knew about it; and Zachariah knew it; and John the Baptist knew Mary's secret. She was there with them all. There is the *fact* of Mary and her secret — without pressing that too much; but it is there.

Then there is the fact of the *miracles* — we cannot very well get away from them. Miracles in the realm of the elements — the sea and the wind; miracles in the realm of nature — as our hymn says: 'It was spring-time when He took the loaves, and harvest when He brake'. Miracles in the realm of sickness and disease, and even death: His healing, and His raising from the dead, such as the son of the widow of Nain. These were *facts*. And then, in the realm of the powers of evil — muzzling demons and casting them out, and delivering the demon-possessed. These were all *facts* present with them. It is a tremendous accumulation of evidence.

Further, the fact of the *teaching*: that without special education, He bewildered, confounded and defeated the authorities of His time —

all the men of information and knowledge, the scribes, the lawyers, the best representatives of the intellect of Jewry. They picked out on occasions their best intellects, to go and try and catch Him in His words; and these very men had to ask the question: 'Whence hath this Man this, having never learned?' (John 7:15). There was the *fact* of His teaching.

There is a tremendous build-up. What a situation! They had all that (and how much more that embraces!) — and yet, whilst being in possession of that whole mass of mighty facts and realities about Him, and whilst living in the closest association with Him, it was possible for them to know all the havoc and the despair of the Cross. I venture to say that you and I would probably think that, if we had only a bit of that, we should be safe for ever; never have any reason whatever to doubt our salvation. And they had it all, and yet here we have them after the Cross in the abject despair. I have not exaggerated; I do not think one could exaggerate in this matter. When it came to the supreme test, all that did not save them; there was lacking the one essential to make it all vital, to make it the very triumph in the trying hour. That one essential is Christ — *that* Christ — in you. So long as all that is still objective, on the outside, though you may be in the closest association with it all, there is yet something lacking. And that lack may spell disaster, for it did with them.

By the resurrection a new hope was born; by the resurrection a new power came into the world and human life; by the resurrection the way was opened for that Christ to change His position from Heaven — from outside — into the inner life of the believer. It has all got to be 'Christ *in* you, the hope of glory'. This is just the essential nature of this dispensation in which we live. In the former dispensation, the Spirit moved from the outside *upon*. Jesus said: 'When He is come, He shall be *in* you.' That is the change of dispensations; that is the character of this present dispensation — the Spirit within. What is the secret of the Church's power? What is the secret of the believer's life, strength, persistence, endurance, triumph against all hell and the world? What is the secret of ultimate glory? It is Christ *in* you; in other words, that you have really and definitely *received* the Holy Spirit.

How important this is! — that you and I shall *know* that our Christianity, our faith, does not rest upon even the greatest historic facts, but that we *know* that Christ is inside; we *know* that we have received the Holy Spirit. That is the secret of everything.

20

Let us carry this a little further, and consider the next thing: *the hopelessness of work for Christ without Christ within.*

'He called unto Him whom He Himself would; and He appointed twelve, that they might be with Him' (Mark 3:13, 14); and He chose seventy, and sent them forth, and gave them power over unclean spirits, over all manner of diseases; and they went forth, and they returned with great joy saying, 'Even the demons are subject unto us in Thy Name' (Luke 10:1, 17). Tremendous! 'Heal the sick' — yes; 'raise the dead; cast out demons; freely ye have received, freely give' (Matt. 10:8). And they returned with great joy: it was done; they had seen it! And you have this picture after the Cross of these same people — the *same people* — devastated! You say: Is that possible? Is that real? If you know your own heart, you will know it is possible. But what is the meaning of this?

In the case of the 'twelve' and the 'seventy', we have set forth a strange, wonderful, and almost frightening fact. It is that, within the vast scope of the sovereign rule of God — which is only another definition of the 'Kingdom of God' — within the sovereign rule of God, many things obtain which only *express* that sovereignty. They are not of the essential and permanent essence of God Himself, as in the nature of things; they are the *works* of God. I say, within that vast scope of His rule and His reign, God has countless instruments of His sovereignty — be it official, be it providential — which He just uses in His sovereignty in relation to His end. There is a purpose to be served, and end to be reached, concerning His Son, Jesus Christ: it has got to be made known in this world that the Kingdom of God has drawn near, and that Jesus Christ is the centre of that Kingdom. And, in order to make that known, God will employ sovereignly even the devil himself! His sovereignty gathers into it many, many things which are not essentially of the nature of God.

Perhaps you have been amazed sometimes, and perplexed and bewildered, why God should use that, and that and that; and such and such persons. You have been inclined to say: 'It is all contrary to what I believe to be necessary to God for His work. I see that the Bible says that instruments have got to be according to God's mind in order to be used.' But history does not bear that out. As I say, He has used the devil, and the devil is not according to God's mind. There is a sovereignty of God spread over in relation to His end.

But when you have said that, it is a frightening fact when you

21

christ in you
" me.

come to the work of God. I mean this — that we may be working for God, and doing many mighty things as employees of the Kingdom of God, the rule of God, and then, in the end, be cast away! In the end, we ourselves might just go to pieces. Here it is — this strange thing, that these men went out, twelve and seventy, with this 'delegated authority' — this *delegated* authority — and exercised it, and mighty things resulted; and then these same people are found, after the Cross, with their faith shattered; nothing to rest upon. What does it say?

The Deficiency Made Good

Thank God, the book of the Acts transforms the whole situation! Because the book of the Acts brings in this mighty new factor: that Christ, who had delegated the authority, is now indwelling as the authority Himself. And the works now are mighty works, but they are not just works *for* the Lord — they are the works *of* the Lord. It all goes to prove this tremendous fact: that it is "Christ *in* you" that is the indispensable necessity for life and for work. All that they had in their association with Him, and then all that they were allowed to do by His delegated authority — all fell short of being something that could make them triumphant in the hour of the deepest testing. And that is something!

Paul put his finger on it at Ephesus, if you remember, when he said: 'Did you receive the Holy Spirit when you believed?' (Acts 19:2). It was ever the apostles's question, and ever their quest. They knew afterward, if they knew anything at all, that nothing, *nothing*, will stand up to anything, save Christ Himself indwelling.

Now, we can, of course, take that both ways. There is the negative side — the almost frightening possibility that there should be all that, and then disaster at the end. But let us take it positively. What a marvellous thing it is that we are in the dispensation when the one thing, above all others, that God will make true, is "Christ in you" — Christ *in* you! No wonder Peter burst forth with his doxology: "Blessed be the God and Father of our Lord Jesus Christ, who ... hath begotten us again unto a living hope by the resurrection of Jesus Christ from the dead"! You need to be Peter to be able to speak as he spoke; to have gone through the awful shattering, into that unspeakable depth of despair, loss of hope, to be able to say "a living hope" — a *living* hope!

22

And what is it? "Christ *in* you, the hope of glory."

No; there is no hope for us individually; there is no hope for our companies, our churches, our assemblies; there is no hope for Christianity — unless and until the living Christ, with all the tremendous significance of His coming into this world, of His life here, of His Cross, of His resurrection, has come, by the Holy Spirit, on to the inside of things, of people, and churches; until it is "Christ *in* you". All the other may be there — the creed, the teaching; you may, with all sincerity and honesty, say: 'I believe in God the Father...' and so on — it may all be there, and yet there may be disaster where that thing is the most frequently declared.

It is the impact of Christ that matters. In those early days He could not be present without it being known; and that is the thing that you and I need; that is the secret of the Church's power. It is the presence of Christ on the 'inside' of you and of me, and of all of us as people together; "this mystery *among the nations,* which is Christ in you". You are among the nations; and the deepest, the profoundest, the most inexplicable thing is "Christ in you", as you are amongst the nations, "the hope of glory."

It is a question of *hope.* It can be touched by a deep and terrible despair; it can see disintegration and disruption. What we need is a mighty, mighty hope, a living hope — that is, Christ, Christ risen, Christ Himself! We need to get beyond even the resurrection, to where we are able to say: It is Christ present; to what Christ means, as *within* us.

The living hope is Christ in
X on the hope of glory

23

CHAPTER 4

In concluding this brief series of editorials, for the time being, we are going to sum up this matter of the Church and the churches by looking more seriously at the great crisis or turning point which we have in the New Testament.

From what we can discern in the relevant literature, it would seem that very few indeed — and some of these only indistinctly — have recognised the tremendous nature of the events centering around Stephen (Acts 6, 7). A more careful consideration of Acts 7 in the light of the whole context of the New Testament will lead to some very deep and far-reaching conclusions.

In the first place, through Stephen there is given a retrospective confirmation and explanation of some of the most momentous and critical things said by the Lord Himself in the days of His flesh. Too little account has been taken of those intimations or declarations of His that with Him and resultant from Him an entirely new economy and different order was imminent.

In the second place, with Stephen there was the forcefulness of Heaven breaking in with two mighty meanings. One, shock-treatment to the Church, which, with its first leaders, was settling down to a semi-Judaistic Christianity, with the temple, synagogues, and Jerusalem as an accepted system. The other, the divine foreknowledge and prediction that in the approximate period of forty years (a significant period) the whole of that centralized and crystallized order would be shattered, and scattered like the fragments of a smashed vessel over the earth, never again to be reconstituted in the dispensation.

Stephen, in his inspired pronouncement, did some devastating things. He first traced the divine movement from Abraham, along a *spiritual* line (back of all temporal and material instrumentalities), to Christ, showing that what was in the divine mind throughout was a spiritual and heavenly system and order, culminating in Jesus, the Christ. He next showed that historically the people concerned had failed to recognise that spiritual meaning, that heavenly concept, and had done two things. They had made the earthly and temporal an end in itself, and given fulness and finality to *it*. Then they had persecuted, cast out, or killed those who, seeking to make the spiritual and heavenly

24

paramount, had rebuked their shortsightedness and condemned their unspirituality. According to Stephen this was a vicious and evil force that was at work even when the symbols and types of the heavenly were being *formally* and ritualistically practised.

The effect of Stephen's pronouncement, and the significance of his anointing with the Holy Spirit — as will be seen from some of his clauses — was to wipe out and set aside the entire Old Testament order, as represented by and centred in the temple at Jerusalem. The significance of the advent of Christ was the displacing of what was — and is — of time, by that which is eternal; the displacing of that which is of earth by that which is of Heaven; the displacing of the temporal by the spiritual; and the displacing of the *merely* local by the universal. The cult of Israel was finished for the age.

One, perhaps supreme, factor in the significance of Stephen was what he saw at the end and said with almost his last breath: "Behold, I see the heavens opened, and the Son of man standing on the right hand of God" (7:56). Here we have the central and basic reality of true New Testament Christianity, of the Church and the churches — Jesus on the right hand of God. The government, the authority, the headquarters, vested in the ascended Lord, and centred in *Heaven;* not in Jerusalem, nor anywhere else on earth. Then, this is the only occasion on which, after Jesus Himself had used the title, He is spoken of as Son of Man. This is *not* the Jewish title, it is the universal designation. In Daniel we have the Son of Man as receiving from God "dominion, and glory, and a kingdom, that *all the peoples, nations, and languages should serve him*" (Dan. 7:14). That is the meaning of Stephen's vision and utterance.

The Jewish rulers and Stephen's accusers were quick and shrewd enough to recognise the implications, for they had no less and no other import than that the 'temple made with hands' was finished; the dispensation of the Law was ended. There was an implicit call to the Church of Jesus to leave the temple and all that went with it and to move into the greater, the fuller, and the abiding reality. What startling and impressive significance this gives to two other things immediately related. As we see these, we are forced to exclaim: 'Oh, wonderful!'

The first is that Paul comes right into the picture at this very point. Was Stephen God's vessel for this great heavenly revelation? Was he the spearhead of the heavenly movement? Was he the voice of Heaven, proclaiming, in a crucial and dangerous hour in the Church's history, the true and eternal nature of its constitution and vocation? Did they do him to death, driven by the sinister intelligence of the evil powers who know the incalculable importance of a Church on *heavenly ground*? Very well then, heaven answers, and, in the hour of hell's vicious and destructive onrush, brings into immediate view the man who will impart for all time the revelation in fulness of those realities inherent in Stephen's brief ministry. What an answer! What an example of the Son of Man being at the Throne! The same forces of destruction will pursue Paul for his life, but that Throne will see the revelation given in fulness, and destruction suspended until the work is done.

The second impressive thing is that the very work of evil, intended to curtail and end this essential development, was made the very means of effecting it. The Church universal, and its representation worldwide, took its rise from that very hour and event. Peter and James may remain in Jerusalem, and some die-hard legalists may circle around the latter at least; but God is moving on, and they will have either to fall in or be left in limitation.

Now all this, with its tremendously searching implications, has much to say to Christianity to-day.

Because of the close likeness, both of Stephen's position and of his interpretation of the times, to the Letter to the Hebrews, some have attributed that letter to him. There is no value here in pursuing the matter into the realm of authorship or textual criticism, but the identity of position in both is impossible to mistake. Indeed, 'Hebrews' could very rightly be regarded as Stephen's (or, for that matter, Paul's) full presentation of the crisis and change of dispensations.

The tragedy is that, with 'Hebrews' in their hands, responsible leaders of the Church can still adhere to a system and form which is but the extension or carry-over of the Old Testament, with certain changes of phraseology. The *immensity* of the change and gap has certainly not been apprehended. Some of the most terrible things in the whole Bible are contained in that letter in relation to the crisis and the two ways and realms. The issue is no less than that of life and death.

All this has much to say regarding the true nature of the Church and the churches. He that hath eyes to see, let him see!

26

God's End
and
God's Way

God's End and God's Way

"Having made known unto us the mystery of His will . . . To sum up all things in Christ . . . according to the purpose of him who worketh all things after the counsel of his own will: . . . he put all things in subjection under his (Christ's) feet, and gave him to be the head over all things to the church, Which is his body, the fulness of him that filleth all in all." (Eph. i. 9-11, 22).

There are three main parts to that statement.

1. The eternal will and purpose of God.

2. Christ as the center of that purpose.

3. The Church, which is His Body, the vessel of the full expression of the purpose —that is, of Christ.

We are shown God in eternal counsels purposing. In outlining and devising His intentions to create and constitute *"all things,"* "in the heavens and upon the earth" (Eph. 1. 10), He was moved and governed by a specific and definite purpose. This *"Purpose"* is mentioned a number of times in the New Testament, and various things are shown to be related to it. It is most important that we recognize that, however many phases there may be in Divine activity, the purpose of God is one. Nothing is an end in itself. The first law of spiritual *fulness* (and be it observed that fulness is what is in view) is to apprehend the fact and nature of God's all-governing purpose. It is an impressive and painful fact that there is very, very little of what is associated here with the Lord that is really marked by spiritual fulness. Smallness, weakness, limitation, poverty, defeat, ignorance, immaturity, and disappointment characterize so many of the Lord's people, and so much of the Lord's work. This is one of the things that is causing so much distress, inquiry, and effort in some quarters.

May not the explanation be that *nothing that is only a part of a whole can reach and realize the whole purpose?* To be in the way of fulness it is essential that, in the first place, we recognize and realize that God is not just a Busybody in a large number of good and merciful activities; but that He is wholly occupied with one all-inclusive, and all-related purpose! "Who worketh ALL THINGS after the counsel of his own will." The measure of ultimate attainment and accomplishment will be according to our initial apprehension of a single purpose. When that is established, we shall soon move on to see what the purpose is, and how—and by what means—it will be realized. If a masterman has a single purpose to which he has abandoned himself, he will require that all who work *for* him are not just doing various things, however good they may be, even as parts of his whole work, but that they are seeing beyond their own job and part to the whole end and object, and are working positively to that. He will be favourable to any who come to work for him and to any means employed, only in so far as the full purpose is in their heart. The measure of his resource and fulness will be given on this basis alone.

So it is with God. But let it be understood that it is *spiritual* fulness that is in view, not personal gratification.

Then the purpose is to sum up all things in Christ. It is a Person filled full, enlarged, and all-comprehending. The greatness, the magnificence, the universal fulness of Christ is God's goal. Again, it is not sufficient that we see the purpose basic as that is, but that we see—in an ever-growing way—the fulness of Christ. There must be an initial seeing of this greatness, this majesty, this glory, this universality. It was such a seeing that accounted for the power, effectiveness, and glory of the Church's first days. That was the meaning of "Pentecost." It was such a seeing that made the Apostles the men that they were. Paul owed everything to God's revealing of His Son in him. But that seeing must go on. It must become ever fuller. We must not just date our seeing of Christ to some past experience. It is the Lord's will that we shall so live in and walk by the Spirit that we are able to say that what we see of Christ to-day is infinitely greater and more wonderful than ever it has been. That is only in line with God's *purpose*, and it is so for all who have truly come into a spiritual apprehension thereof.

Then in the third place we move to see God's method and means of fulfilling His eternal purpose. This is by the way of "the church, which is His (Christ's) body." The Church is definitely stated to be "the fulness of Him that filleth all in all." That universal fulness of Christ is determined to be revealed and expressed in and through a vessel called the Church. What is this Church?

Firstly, it is said to be an elect company of people. Leaving all theories of election, let us be content, for the moment, to see that God has eternally determined to have such a company, and that election is related to purpose, not primarily—if at all—to salvation. God knows, He cannot help knowing, the ultimate reactions of people to His presentations, and *according to His foreknowledge* He has foreordained to His purpose. But God has never said to any *unsaved* person that he or she is so foreordained. He only calls. The Church is the company of the called who obeyed.

Secondly, the Church is something greater than the churches. Whatever we may mean by the latter, the Church may be in them all, or it may not be in many of them at all. The Church is essentially a spiritual thing; not sectarian, denominational, "ecclesiastical," traditional, etc. It is the spiritual relatedness as of a living organism; a body possessing *one life*; it is a single entity, an "all one in Christ." The measure of light does not make for a more or less membership of that Body, although that may affect functioning. The apprehension of "Church Truth" does not constitute Church membership, although it will greatly affect the matter of fulness. Vital relatedness to Christ is the basis of Body actuality.

But when we have said that, we *must* point out *how* important the recognition of the Church is. Next to the revelation of Christ personally in His greatness, the revelation of the Church is bound up with our practical progress toward fulness. Paul has a far greater fulness in his writings than any other Apostle, and this is mainly due to the specific revelation of the Church which was given to him. What arises from this revelation is that Christ and the Church are one, as Head and members of one Body.

There are one or two things which arise for our apprehension in this matter. Firstly, there is the fact—so clearly and fully given in the Scriptures—that God has just as definitely chosen and appointed the Church for the realization of His eternal purpose as He has chosen and appointed His Son. He has just as positively bound Himself and His fulness to the one as to the other. While one is subject to the other, and the medium and vessel of the other—as the wife to the husband (Eph. v. 22-24), they are one in the matter of purpose. This carries with it the jealousy of God for His Church, and means that for fulness there can be no allowing of an ignoring, belittling, or injuring.

Further; God will keep strictly—in the matter of spiritual fulness—to working

Bodywise. That is, it is *not possible* for any units as such to know fulness. Fulness is a related matter. "The Church is the fulness of him." No individual can be that. Therefore spiritual oneness, inter-relatedness, fellowship, mutuality, and interdependence are basic and indispensable to spiritual attainment of full-growth. "Till *we all* attain unto . . . a full grown man, unto . . . the fulness of Christ" (Eph. iv. 13).

In the Old Testament, when things were constituted according to the heavenly pattern, God spoke out of the Tent of Meeting. So it is in the New Testament. For the answer to his inquiry on the Damascus Road, Paul had to go into the city and get it as out from the Church. For the entering upon his great life-work he had to abide in the Church at Antioch and get his commission confirmed there (Acts xiii). All this does not mean that God has never sovereignly and in grace moved without the recognition of this law by those concerned for His interests, but we are speaking of spiritual fulness, and our ministry is concerned with *that*. It is not a committee, "General," "Executive," or "Advisory," but the "Body" in representation and spiritual functioning that is God's ordained way.

It would take much more space than we have at our disposal to set forth all the values and implications of an apprehension of God's place and purpose for His Church in all things. This is one of the matters which has had a considerable place in our spoken and written ministry through these past years.

This leads on to the churches; that is, the local companies of God's people. Times and conditions have changed greatly since New Testament days; that is, so far as the Western world is concerned. It was simply and straightforward to gather together believers in Christ in those times; there were only believers and non-believers. Today numerous other questions arise; such as "Connection," "Order," "Practice," "Belief," etc. But there are one or two things which must still govern this matter. They are:

1. The local church or assembly is intended to be locally all that the Church as a whole is universally. It must not be smaller in its vision, its vocation, its relatedness. Though locally placed, it is universal in nature, outreach, concern, and function. If it lives unto itself it will die. Fulness is dependent upon its *spiritual* length and breadth, and height and depth.

2. The local church is the spiritual training-ground for all usefulness to the Lord. There all the essential lessons are learned, not by teaching alone, but by spiritual discipline. The very vital lesson of subjection to the Lord—which means so much in the matter of spiritual growth—is learned in a very practical way in a true assembly and fellowship life. All independent, unrelated, and merely personal life is impossible when the "Body" is truly recognized.

The spiritual support, upholding, encompassing, and covering of the Lord's people in something more than a general way is of tremendous value and consequence. Far from

—12—

local expression of the family of God, and to fulfil all the functions and provide all the values of a true family life and relationship. the local church being but a "congregation" or a preaching place, it is intended to be a local expression of the family of God, and to fulfil all the functions and provide all the values of a true family life and relationship.

3. The matter of pre-eminent importance in the local church, as in the universal, is the absolute sovereign headship of Christ. Anything which usurps this, or in any way conflicts with it, will most certainly result in spiritual limitation and proportionate retarding of growth. Is this not why, in the New Testament churches, no one man exercised headship, but elders—not an elder— were appointed. The "Body" principle is upheld in the corporate, and individual sovereignty is prevented. At Antioch the "Holy Ghost said" *to a company of representative men,* who were together in spiritual responsibility. Eldership is representation—spiritual measure, not ecclesiastical. The New Testament plurality of eldership means that the church is brought—as in and

by its representatives—under the complete sovereignty of Christ through the Holy Ghost.

4. We must then see that the Apostles never set out with the plan to form churches. That was the spontaneous and necessitated result of the Holy Spirit's work in every place Christ was preached and accepted, and relatedness spontaneously followed (see Acts ii. 42). That which decides churches is Christ. This is the solution of and the answer to many of the problems and questions which arise, especially in this Western world in these peculiarly complicated times. What is to be our guiding and deciding principle in gathering together? It is to be Christ! We meet on that ground alone. Where God's end is most fully in view, and what provides most fully for its attainment —the fulness of Christ—decides where we ought to be, and no one ought to quarrel with that. It is because of a devotion to and jealousy for some "thing"; a "Mission," "Denomination," "Tradition," "Fellowship," "Movement," etc., that rivalries, and

bad feelings spring up. All the talk about "sheep stealing" and "dividing the Lord's people," or a great deal of it, arises out of a concern for—not spiritual growth—but something here on the earth. How very much of this talk would be impossible if everyone concerned took the attitude that it does not matter what survives or ceases to exist so long as Christ is being increased in a spiritual way. This involves the necessity that all the Lord's people, and particularly those in "official" positions, and positions of influence, should be utterly and only devoted to the increase of Christ. Christ is not divided, therefore Christ is the ground of unity, not the things as mentioned above.

Whose sheep are they? Are they ours? Can Christ's sheep be stolen by those who are devoted to Him? If they are sheep of this or that, then things are in another realm. No, all this sort of thing is the cause of spiritual weakness and smallness, and a new mind as to Christ Himself is needed for fulness.

Finally, in this connection, and for the moment; everything appointed by the Lord is intended to be for the direct and positive "building up of the body." That marks its object and direction, and its unifying law. Evangelism, Teaching, Gifts, personal and spiritual, etc., are all said definitely to be to this one end. The evangelist and evangelism are not an end in themselves, nor something apart. The New Testament overwhelms such an idea or procedure most completely. All these functions are "Body" functions, and for a well-balanced Body they must be kept together; neither emphasized to the detriment of the other; neither left out. A teaching ministry must go hand-in-hand with an evangelistic ministry; and the other way round. Everyone who functions as a member of Christ's Body—and all members *should* function—should have in view—not souls being saved, not saints being instructed, but—through these, and all other means, the increase of Christ. Let us remember that the Church is not large or small; our work is not more or less successful according to the *number* of people represented, but according to the positive measure of Christ.

Increase of Christ this is all that matters. 'Tis Christ & His fulness Here!

I cannot close this review without a brief reference to one or two other matters which are vital to this ministry.

There is the matter of the Cross. It will not be saying anything fresh or unusual when we say that the Cross of Christ is deeply bound up with the question of Divine fulness. But how this is so demands a continuous re-emphasis and growing unfolding. The Scriptures make it quite clear that right to the very end the Adversary will seek with all his might and by every means to revive the question of acceptance and standing with God. He is seen very late in the day (Rev. xii) as the "accuser of the brethren," and the destruction of assurance is one of his most determined endeavours. Everything that carries with it the idea of our doing anything and making ourselves anything to obtain the mercy of God and attain unto acceptance with Him, bears the hall-mark of the Devil himself. Christ's death for us and our death with Him is the only, but the sure ground of full acceptance! Luther said it very utterly when he put it thus—

"O Christ, I am Thy sin, Thy
curse, Thy wrath of God, Thy
hell; and contrariwise, Thou art
my righteousness, my blessing,
my life, my grace of God, my
heaven."

No wonder the Devil hated Martin Luther
and assailed him so bitterly.

But there is not only the basic, initial, perfect value of the Cross for our full and
unquestioned acceptance; there is a meaning
of the Cross in relation to spiritual fulness
and fruitfulness. It is what Paul calls

"Being made conformable to his
death" (Phil. iii. 10).

This let us emphasize, must be kept apart
from our justification and access to God.
How very much of the tragedy, scandal,
defeat, weakness, deadness, limitation and
loveliness of many Christian people and
Christian institutions, communities and
churches is due to uncrucified "flesh" or
natural life! How greatly Christ is hidden
from view by men and things and methods
which bring themselves into prominence!

The need, if He is to come to the place of the Divine intention, and we with Him, is for a continuous and ever-deepening working of the Cross in us. We really must be in a position to say, "I have been crucified with Christ." Yes, but also to complete the statement "It is no longer I, but Christ." Is it true—"No longer I?" "No . . . I"? That is what Paul meant, but who can know the depth of that "I." Only Christ knows how deep and thorough His Cross is, and we must hand ourselves over to Him for the Holy Spirit to work all *His* meaning of the Cross in us, if the way is to be clear for His fulness.

So the twofold meaning and message of the Cross is a very strong part of this ministry. There are many who do not like the latter and will not have it. We can only say that if they represent something far more than the average in spiritual wealth and their apprehension of Christ, and if that with which they are connected is free from the common results of the strength of the natural life; then there is something in their antagonism to the subjective meaning of the Cross to which we must give heed. But we have been there ourselves, and know the difference.

We must close, and we do so with a reference to one other matter. Many may agree with much that we have written, but they will react to it by saying that it is "idealistic"; it is too high; as things are now it is not possible; we cannot hope for such a recovery. Well, there is one answer to that attitude. The Bible has always recognized and provided for a position like that. It was but a small number of the captive nation of Israel who returned voluntarily to rebuild the city, the wall, the house at Jerusalem, and the word which governed and characterized them was, "Whoso is of a willing heart, his God be with him."

In the book of the Revelation it is clear that the majority had left the full thought of the Lord. The appeal there is to those within who have "an ear to hear." We find them called "Overcomers," and this clearly relates to the decadent conditions; a reaction to the Lord's full and original thought. It is hardly to be expected that all Christians will respond to the appeal and standard, but it is clear that they *can*, the Lord wills it, and what He wills is not out of the question. It may be a costly way; and the cost will be mainly acute because of the attitude of other Christians.

Hence, we realize that this ministry will sift the Lord's people, and only those who really mean business with God and to "go on to full-growth" will have a place for it. Our message is therefore one which will affect the "Overcomers," although we do not regard them as an elect of the elect, a select spiritual aristocracy. They will have a place of special honour because in them the Lord will have that upon which His heart has been set from the beginning. The difference will be that which is seen ultimately between Joseph and his brethren.

Such ministry as that of which we have spoken will be the outcome of His very deep and drastic dealings with us. It is not something studied and worked out mentally. We shall never be off the wheel as a vessel finished, but somehow the Lord will combine the moulding and the using. Surely this is as it should be. "The Lord's messenger *in* the Lord's message" contains the vital principle that the instrument should never be in advance of its spiritual history. Even prophets who spoke of things to come, and of many things the meaning of which was not *fully* clear to them, were made to have their ministry inwrought by practical experience. But the drastic handling is ever unto increase and progress. Such a ministry cannot be "taken up," or adopted. We cannot go into it as we go into any other kind of work, by technical or intellectual training or instruction. Indeed, it is something from which to shrink *naturally*, as did Moses, Jeremiah, and others. It is helpful and interesting or enlightening to see that, when the Lord spoke through Jeremiah to Israel about the potter's house, and the potter, and then Himself took the place of the potter, the moulding, shaping, correcting, adjusting, purging, unto usefulness was by means of the assaults and inflictings of enemy activity. There was a connection between the Potter's hands and a foreign ruler's opposition and besieging. So for fuller usefulness the Lord uses the enemy and his work, and we are not for long free from this pressure.

These, then, are the main things to which we are called and committed. "Here we stand, we can do no other, God help us."

The Lord give you all a heart to "follow the Lamb whithersoever he goeth," and to reach unto His fulness.

The Holy Spirit and the Cross, the Church and the Coming Again of the Lord Jesus

The Holy Spirit
and
The Cross,
The Church,
and the
Coming Again of
the Lord Jesus

A spoken message

As to the first part of our theme, the Holy Spirit and the Cross, we can see that the one great and inclusive question in view was, and is, the securing of God's rights in the universe for Himself; the setting forth of God, as the supreme and sole object of all worship, or Worthship.

This was necessitated by the breaking in, before this world was created, of another will and thought on the part of one, Lucifer, to divide that worship, to rob God of it, to dispute His sole right in the universe, and by an uprising to ascend into the heavens above the clouds to be equal with the Most High.

By this his downfall was brought about and, with it, the casting out of heaven of a company of "angels which kept not their first estate", who, we are told, are now "reserved in everlasting chains"—in chains unto everlasting perdition and darkness. Then follows the reappearing of that one upon this earth, assailing the citadel of God in the heart of man and succeeding in dividing the rights of God, the worship of Himself; securing recognition, acknowledgment, obedience, and thus worship. Then right down through the ages we have the two Gods, the true God and the god of this world, who is the false god; the two worships, the worship of God and the worship of this other, which is in many forms, by many systems and in divers manners, but there is always the one object behind everything, and that is to take away

3

from God, and to divide the rights with God. It does not matter how it is done, but it will be done always in the way which is most calculated to succeed.

At one time, it will be to appeal to the dominant faculties of that time, which may be psychical—along the line of superstition, fear, or dread, especially in the realms of little enlightenment or great darkness. Another time it will be in another realm, perhaps along the line of intellect and reason and considerable enlightenment. It does not matter how it is done as long as the end is attained that God has not His place and is not allowed to be supreme in His universe, having undivided and unrivalled sway.

The persistence of this other thing is at times manifested in—one was going to say—an impertinence, for it will even assail the Son of God and say : "If only THOU wilt worship me"—Thou wilt worship me! It stands at nothing and will pay a great price for that recognition.

All this, we have been brought to see, is gathered up in the Cross of the Lord Jesus, and we no longer look upon Calvary as merely the crucifixion of the Jewish Messiah, nor do we talk about the Calvary scene as an historic human tragedy. We look back on it and see that this whole realm and range of contrary worship, the thing which had its own strategy against the Throne of God, was involved there. It was there that Calvary's meaning had its full significance. In that Cross the Lord Jesus met the whole of that thing and gathered it up in His own Person by one all-inclusive sacrifice, whole burnt offering, because He, and He alone, could do it. God and man were united in sinlessness. Such a One was required, for such a One alone could do it, and He did it in this whole burnt offering.

4

He Secured in His Person the Entire
Universal Rights of God

for God, and in thus offering Himself to God, it was as representing many sons whom He would bring to glory, a new creation which He would bring into being. In that Person there is provided a sacrifice by means of which the last remnant of that false thing shall be ultimately plucked, to the end that "God may be all and in all", and worshipped without a rival. The Lord Jesus secured that in the Cross.

The Cross, therefore, represents God's rights secured in Christ, and when we speak about the Cross, let us always have a vision and background large enough to see why the Lord calls us into fellowship with Himself in death, burial and resurrection.

It is of such a range that Satan should never again, so far as we are concerned, have a vestige of ground upon which to work against God. That is the meaning of it, and when we are called into the fellowship of His Cross, it is to wipe out the ground of Satan's rights, claims and activities, and counter his hand against the Throne of God. Oh, that men could see that every bit of un-crucified flesh is the hand of the devil against the Throne of God! It is the hand against the Throne whenever we choose our will against the will of God. It is an expression of the attitude of the enemy who said: "I will be like the Most High."

When the Lord calls us into fellowship with Himself in the Cross, it is not only to remove the ground of the enemy's operation and activity, but it is a declaration that in our risen union with the Lord Jesus we are wholly unto the Lord. No one who will not go the whole way will dare to talk or sing about the Cross, nor has he a right to speak of the Cross

5

of the Lord Jesus as being anything to him.

That Cross is the brazen altar upon which we are utterly consumed unto God, without a vestige left, so that, *in the intention of God*, there should not be one fragment or atom upon which the enemy should have a claim. That is the Cross, that is what it meant in the Person of Christ representatively, and that is what it meant for us as included therein, so that in that Person, that risen, ascended, exalted, glorified Person of the Lord Jesus, everything is secured unto God. Oh, do get the sufficient emphasis upon that! Everything is secured unto God! Take the little phrase: "Unto God", or "Unto the Lord", and trace it through the Word and see its significance!

All that which is redeemed by His precious Blood is redeemed unto God. It is for the Lord. Do we hold everything unto the Lord? Do we hold our business, our home, all our money, our children and our friendships unto the Lord? Do we hold our bodies unto the Lord? Do we hold all our opportunities unto the Lord?

Is everything "unto the Lord", and do we let go of everything that we cannot hold unto the Lord? Is it true with us that there is no longer a question: "Is there any harm in it?" That is negative. There is nothing negative in this life! The question is: Is it positively *unto the Lord?*

That is the meaning of Calvary: "unto the Lord", the whole burnt offering unto the Lord. That is what it means to be in Christ. He is the whole burnt offering, and to be in Him is to be offered wholly unto God. "He died," says the Word of the Spirit, "that they which live should no longer live unto themselves, but unto him. . ." He secured it all. He secured the earth for the Lord in His own Person. He settled the dispute as to who should be the Prince of this world, who should be the God of this world, who should hold the sway of this world, and who should sit upon the throne of this world. That is the dispute of the ages, but He secured the world unto God in His own Person. Therefore, this world, by right of Christ's victory, belongs to God, and therein is our vocation found: to take the world for God, to stand on it, to put our feet down and say: "We stand here for God."

Christ secured the world— "All authority hath been given unto me in heaven and on earth." He secured man, that disputed thing made for the glory of God, but meddled with by Satan, so that even man gave his consent to Satan's will, authority and right, but in His Own Divine Person as *Man*, (oh! the wonder of the incarnation!) He secured man representatively for God, for "since by man came death, by man came also the resurrection of the dead"—the God-Man. He secured man in that Cross as utterly free from the power of Satan. It is in that sense that God has secured man in Christ. He has secured the world, He has secured man, He has dealt with Satan and He has dealt with death, and all in this Cross of Christ.

The issue for the world now is to recognize the rights of God as secured in Christ, to take sides and acknowledge them. That sets up a testimony, the testimony of God in Christ, which becomes the testimony of Jesus, and the testimony is all this as secured in the glorified Person of the Lord Jesus by means of the precious Blood. That testimony has been taken and settled in the heavens. Thereupon the Holy Spirit is sent forth to find some place on this earth in which to establish that testimony, and thus you come to:

7

The Holy Spirit and the Church

The Spirit constitutes that which is the true Church according to the mind of God. It is not what we call the Church, but what God calls the Church, and the Spirit constitutes it—as we have seen—a thing in which that testimony is placed in trust. The Church is left here on the earth, but it has a heavenly life in order that that testimony may be borne and upheld here on the earth; that God has His universal rights, which are secured in the Person of Jesus Christ; and the Cross of Calvary was the scene and is the power of the establishment of that testimony, the message of the Cross being Christ crucified, the power and the wisdom of God.

The Church is here in trust for that purpose. The testimony of all that is secured in Christ to God at Calvary is deposited in the Church, and the fact that God has not wiped the adversary out of the universe but has let him remain and gives him so much liberty is explained along this line—that God is going to work out all the content of that testimony in, and through, the Church.

That explains why, immediately there is an entering into the testimony of Jesus in the power of the Holy Ghost—not in mind, thought, doctrine, teaching, or human association, but in the power of the Holy Ghost—the enemy at once begins his terrific onslaughts and goes over the ground again in order to wipe that testimony out of the earth, wiping the Church out by any means, device or scheme-if he can.

Immediately God brings the Church to light, other things are brought to light. The dark things, the enemy and the devices of the enemy are brought to light; and it is in the face of that that the Church stands. If we are really members of Christ's Body we are here, not merely to present the Gospel to men—though that is a great and vital part of the whole—but that "now unto principalities and the powers in the heavenlies might be made known through the Church the manifold wisdom of God." "Now!" We have heard many times that the vocation of the Church is not limited to flesh and blood, but reaches far beyond to other spheres.

The testimony is universal, not local, even as to the earth, but it is beyond the earth. How, otherwise, are we to explain things? I think I can safely say that nine-tenths of the terrific spiritual conflicts through which we pass have no direct effect upon men and women. They seem to be without any virtue so far as people are concerned.

It seems that men and women are only touched in a manner which is far short of what is commensurate with the terrific conflicts that go on. There is something more involved for, surely, the nine-tenths are counting somewhere! Yes,

God is doing a Thing out of the Sight of Men

in this matter and is displaying His manifold wisdom.

One has to conclude that upon the mere ground of logic or righteousness, but one comes to see that it is definitely stated to be so in the Word of God. We might refer to the Book of Job.

Where is the drama of that book set? In the realm where Satan appears before God and challenges Him concerning the faith and the faithfulness of one of His servants, and God says: "I will prove to you by that very man that he does not serve Me for what he can get out of Me. I will prove to you that there is such a thing as a faith in the

9

universe which believes in Me for what I am." And Job is a type of the Church, stripped and led into affliction and adversity, with the hand of the devil allowed to be against him, as it is against the Church. It might seem that Job's faith is shaken, but the strength of God comes in at a critical moment and triumphs, and the ultimate issue is that God has exhibited to principalities and powers His grace, His glory, and the thing which speaks of Himself—His testimony.

That is the story of the Church, but God is not only doing that on the dark side. He is also doing it on the light side, and angels desire to look into these things. Angels and archangels are being instructed by the Church, so the testimony is a very wide testimony.

The explanation of our spiritual conflicts is far-reaching and goes a long way. You will see it "in that day"!

The Holy Spirit constituted the Church for that, and that is the Church. Is that the Church we know? Is that the Church to which we belong? Is that the nature of the vocation which we are fulfilling? Are we in that, or are we engaged in trying to hold people together into some human association, some organized thing on this earth that we call the Church? Are we trying to get them to live more decent lives, to give some recognition to God once a week, and get them how we will—with an entertainment, a bridge party, or a dance? NO! But that, of course, is a long way off from this about which I am speaking. There are many grades, but God wants the true Church, where Calvary means for every member of Christ's Body that there is only one thing to live for, and that is the glory of God.

So the Church is set up as an earthen vessel to enshrine

10

the heavenly treasure, the testimony, and to minister to the glory of God, to His pleasure. There are the riches of His grace, the manifold wisdom to be displayed.

But there are the six months of myrrh with which Esther was prepared for the intercessory work before the throne—but it is there that the beauty of the Lord comes in. He leads us into suffering, into trial, into heartbreak, into the place where, humanly, there is nothing to get us through, and then His grace comes in. Thus, after the myrrh, comes the frankincense, the beauty of the Lord. And so He displays the riches of His grace through the Church in the fire.

Shall we not make it personal and say that when the Church is in the fire, the one thing that attracts attention is that there is Another in the fire, and that One is like unto the Son of Man.

That is our calling! It is a holy calling, a sacred calling, if you like, a costly calling, but it is a worthwhile calling. It is bringing God into His place and unveiling His glory. The Church is here for the glorifying of God. "He that overcometh, I will give to him to sit down with me in my throne, as I also overcame, and sat down with my Father in his throne." "If we suffer, we shall also reign with him."

The Church an Intercessory Instrument

Now we must also see that the Church is here to be an intercessory instrument for the Holy Ghost, for two purposes. We have the Book of Esther very much in mind here, and merely to mention that will explain to you what we mean.

In the first place, we have the intercessory instrument, as represented by Esther, for the purpose of preserving the life of God's people, and preserving the testimony to that

11

life of the Lord's people. Oh, that is a big calling and vocation! Here is this satanic scheme, as illustrated in Haman, who is bent on blotting out the people of God as the instrument of the testimony of God. Though at that time they were a poor, decadent instrument, they were nevertheless the people of God; and Esther comes into relationship with the throne in order to have that foul plan of the enemy reversed and destroyed, that the testimony of life may be maintained.

That is the Church's vocation, and that is what God means to secure—a company who will be to Him an instrument in this day to save His testimony in a decadent spiritual age and day; and many of the Lord's people are failing, are in captivity, are weakened, are robbed of their place, of their witness, and of their power by the evil one because of their own idolatry, and because they have been guilty of dividing God's rights and are not giving Him His whole place.

Idolatry is not merely the falling down and worshipping of gods of wood and stone. It is anything in all the universe which detracts from God. If a young man takes, to the smallest degree, the place of God in a young woman's life, then that is idolatry, and it is the same the other way round. Husband or wife, parent or child, business or home, or anything that comes in to take God's place is an idol. We can be idolaters with our time, with our money, with our affections.

If God's place is interfered with by any other consideration, that is idolatry. It was idolatry which brought about this spiritual condition amongst the people of God in Esther's day—and it always does. God would bring back

12

His people into such a relationship with Himself that they shall truly be His right representative on the earth.

To do that, He must get into relationship with Himself those who will become an intercessory instrument, like Esther, in order to save the testimony of the life of the Lord's people. He calls us for that, and we must take this thing upon our hearts as a tremendous burden, that is, the state of the Lord's people must become a heartache, a heartbreak.

The spiritual condition of those who are the Lord's people must ever be a tremendous burden upon the heart of the instrument that God would have for saving the situation, and in order to save that situation He must put that burden upon some hearts. Esther took it on her heart. She took her people before the throne, and to such an extent that she took her life in her hands, saying: "If I perish, I perish." She gave herself to this business without any personal interest or consideration whatever.

In this matter it was life or death.

Oh, that God could find today a company of men and women like that, so burdened, so weighed down, and so distressed by the spiritual condition of His own people and by the fact that the world is not having registered upon it the testimony of God through His own people! Oh, for such an instrument! Would that the Holy Spirit would light upon us and turn us into at least a part of that instrument for today! This instrument is to be God's instrument, by the Holy Ghost, of bringing about the overthrow of Satan. Oh, wonderful work! "God. . .shall bruise Satan under your feet shortly."

Within the decadent Church, Laodicea today, the Lord would have overcomers through whom He will bring about

13

the undoing and the overthrow of Satan. It is solemn and terrific business, but it is the Lord's decision, not ours. He has chosen to do it, and, having chosen, He is well able to do it, and if the Holy Ghost constitutes the instrument, it will be done.

The Exaltation of the Lord Jesus

I want to put in here a little about the Church's appreciation of the exaltation of Christ, as we have it typically in the Book of Esther. Here is Mordecai sitting in the background, at the gate, unrecognized, unacknowledged and despised. Nevertheless, he is watching and bringing the information to Esther, giving her the urge and telling her how to do things. He is laying a great responsibility upon her.

Then Esther, inspired by Mordecai, goes into this solemn and tremendous business through deep preparation, and the thing is done. But what is the issue? The greatest issue of all is, not only that the Lord's people are saved and Haman is overthrown, but that Mordecai is exalted to the throne.

That, in type, is the greatest thing, and the greatest thing that will ever happen in this universe will not merely be the salvation of the Lord's people, though that will be an inseparable part of the rest, and it will not only be the overthrow of Satan, but it will be the exalting of Jesus Christ to the Throne. The whole Church rejoices in the appreciation of that! You notice in this Book how the whole land rejoices in the appreciation of Mordecai's exaltation to the throne.

They had a special feast, the feast of Purim. When we look at that feast of Purim we find that the people of God are called together to rejoice in the wonderful character of

14

the work of God by Christ, in virtue of which they, the Lord's people themselves, are set free from the power of the enemy and from the presence of evil, and they walk in the fullness and in the joy of the Lord Jesus Himself.

That is Mordecai translated into the realm of Jesus Christ—the feast of Purim being the Church coming into its rejoicing in the exaltation of Christ. That is the main end in view.

But does it appeal to our hearts? Does it so appeal to our hearts that we say: "Yes, that Jesus Christ shall be exalted high over all is more than my salvation, more than my glorifying or having riches of the Kingdom, and more than the overthrow of the devil." Is it the thing that stirs and warms our hearts? Do we walk in the light of that great prospect and anticipation?

This brings us back to the practical outworking. What about the instrument which is going to bring that about? If He is to be exalted, then we have to enter into this matter which, in a sense, seems to be a matter of life and death. I dare not stay with that longer, nor with the other thing in this Book of Esther, which is a very blessed thing, namely, the anticipating of the full display of the glory of God in Christ. There is a prophecy in this Book, for the full display of the glory of God in Christ is seen here and there is an anticipation of it, but I do want, in closing, to touch upon:

The Holy Spirit and the Coming Again of the Lord Jesus

I am not going to speak along the line of prophecy or the signs of the times so much, but I want you to see the connection of all these things. I want you to recognize that,

15

when we speak of the Holy Spirit and the coming again of the Lord Jesus Christ, the Holy Spirit's work is one work, whether it be by the Cross, in that Christ, "through the eternal Spirit, offered himself without blemish unto God," or whether it be in constituting the Church for the testimony of God as the instrument for the overthrow of Satan, or whether it be the coming again of the Lord. There are not three works. It is all one work.

The Cross is always related to the coming again, and the Church is always related to the coming again. When the Lord Jesus sits down to take the Jewish Passover and translates it into the Lord's Table, what is He doing?

Why, He speaks of His Blood shed and His Body given, and Paul says: "As often as ye eat this bread, and drink the cup, ye do proclaim the Lord's death till he come."

He is saying, in effect, that that Passover is eaten with loins girded, sandals on the feet, and the staff in hand, ready to take a journey, the end of which is the Glory. The Cross is the beginning of a journey, and the beginning of a journey which is conducted by the Holy Spirit. The Holy Spirit begins at the Cross, and His eye is on the goal, the Divine Glory, the coming of the Lord, all the time.

This overcomes all the problems of the questioners which even existed in the days of the Apostles, for we read that some men were saying then: "Where is the promise of his coming? For since the fathers fell asleep, all things continue as they were from the beginning of the creation."

How much more ground, in that realm and on that plane, men have for talking in that way today! It seemed that even Paul was expecting the Lord in his lifetime, but two thousand years have passed.

What is the explanation?

It is that there is no time with the Holy Spirit, for He lives in eternity. The Holy Spirit has brought the two ends together in His work, and whenever you come on the Cross you have the witness of the Spirit, and whenever you come on the Advent, whether two thousand years ago or today, the thing is still alive, and it is the very life of the thing by the Holy Spirit that is here in the Book.

It is just as much alive after two thousand years as it was then.

The explanation is that the Holy Spirit has this as an abidingly living thing in His mind and intention. It is never dead with Him. Is it not remarkable? We may argue and question, and we have all done it. I turned right away from the "Second Coming" because in my childhood I heard people say day after day: 'The Lord may come tonight I''; at last I became so scared—but He never came.

So I said: "Well, now, they have been talking about this for centuries, and here are people living in this thing and it has made them so happy. They rejoice in it—but they die, having said that they would live to see the Lord come." So I turned away from the whole thing, but I missed the secret of it.

Why is it that you cannot sing a hymn about the Lord's coming when you are amongst the Lord's people without the Holy Spirit making the thing become marvelously alive? In spite of their reasoning and their arguments, and in spite of the mystery of the postponement, people sing the hymn, and if the Holy Ghost is in them, they are all alive.

It is the Spirit's witness to the thing which is always in His mind. The end of the Cross is the Advent. Let no one

17

ever say that you are always speaking on the Cross and therefore strumming on one string! You cannot isolate the Cross! With the Cross you have everything that is involved in it. The coming of Christ is on the ground of the Cross. The Cross demands His coming, for it is the consummation of all its content. So at the Cross the Church has its birth, the beginning of its pilgrimage, the end of which looms immediately upon the horizon—the Rapture!

A Hebrew Idyll

You remember that beautiful romance in the Old Testament—the seeking of Rebekah. We read first of Abraham and his servant, of the vow of the servant, and his going to a far country to find a bride for Isaac.

The servant sets out, taking with him the treasures of Abraham's house, and, arriving at his destination and putting God to the test, the seal of God comes upon his quest and he discovers the bride. Then all kinds of things set to work to try and cause delay and to keep the bride back.

Her friends want to detain and entertain the servant rather than respond to what he is after. So today we want to keep, to entertain, to have the Holy Spirit, but He is here for a purpose. The bride's friends tried to entertain the servant, to be nice to him and to hold back the thing for which he had come, but Eliezer would have none of it. He said: "Look here, I am not going to stay here. I want to know if you are going to accede to the thing for which I have come."

In spite of all their maneuvering, he came to the point and said: "Now about the business!" And they had to put the question straight to Rebekah: "Wilt thou go with this man?". Without any hesitation she said: "I will go."

Then were brought out the treasures of his master's house, and, adorning her, he led her away.

Now, the Holy Spirit has come on behalf of the Lord. He has come here to get the Bride for Christ. He has come with the riches of His grace to adorn that Bride and to speak of the glories of the Bridegroom and of His inheritance. But the Holy Spirit is not going to be entertained or detained. He has come on business and is saying: "Are you coming with Me?" His business, by a covenant with God, is that He will do His work thoroughly and present the issue clearly.

So the Holy Spirit is here to get us started on a journey, the end of which is to find the Lord Jesus coming out to meet us, just as Isaac went out from the house and on the way, doubtless anticipating, expecting, scanning the horizon and eagerly waiting.

The rapture is the issue of the Cross in the Church, for all these things are one. It is not possible to accept the Lord Jesus in relation to the Cross without seeing that it is going to issue in the rapture and His coming again. I want you to notice that the thing is all one.

Primarily, the Glory of God

It is the testimony of God in the earth. This involves the very spiritual life of God's people; then, behind that, the— overthrow of Satan; and finally, as through all that, the exaltation of Jesus Christ.

These are the things which are all at stake, so to speak, and which are in view. Are they not immense and tremendous things? The glory of God in the universe, the exaltation of Jesus Christ, the testimony of God on the earth, the spiritual life of God's people, and the overthrow of Satan.

19

What more tremendous things could you think of? These are the things which are before us, in a sense, committed to us, entrusted to us, to which we are called. Do they not give an adequate motive for the Cross? Do they not make the Cross worthwhile? Do they not constitute a sufficient basis of appeal for identification with Christ? Surely they do! Surely this is a ground good enough to call for the 'presenting of our bodies a living sacrifice, holy, acceptable to God'?

What greater appeal could there be to our hearts for letting God have us altogether? That, then, gives the strength of the motive for an uttermost surrender, but that also presents to us:

The Urgency and Necessity for a Life in the Fullness of the Spirit

All that is only going to be realized by the energy and power of the Holy Ghost, so we must seek that, being emptied of all else by the Cross, we shall be filled with the Holy Ghost. The Church must begin to pray for that incoming fullness of the Spirit to restore its testimony, to save its life, to constitute it God's instrument for His glory and the exaltation of Christ. It requires the Holy Ghost to do that, but He is not going to do it apart. He is going to do it by the Church, and that is His instrument.

Oh, we must pray that in this day of decadence God will yet again fill an instrument with His Spirit and make it His effective instrument at this time.

It is true that we are in the last of those Church ages, the Laodicean age; and what are the characteristics of that age?

Well, mediocrity—neither one thing nor the other,

neither hot nor cold; nothing outstanding or conspicuous on the spiritual side. It is a very ordinary level, yes, a compromise, but worse than that—self-satisfaction, complacency, lack of vision, and a feeling that all is well. "I am rich and increased with goods, and have need of nothing." It is all right.

Plenty of good work is being done, there is plenty of enterprise, plenty of organization, plenty of machinery, and plenty of people being busy. What have you got to grumble about? Oh, but there are other eyes, and you note what is said: "Saith the Amen."

It is a significant introduction. What is the meaning of that "Amen"? "Saith the Verily", which means: "Saith the One who is positive." 'You are negative, and you are not in oneness with Me in spirit in this age of complacency and contentment amongst those who call themselves My people.'

I am speaking in a very broad way about this.

That is true, but worse still, there is awful blindness to the condition by reason of this compromise. 'Thou knowest not that thou art blind.' If you talk to many Christian people about spiritual matters they do not know what you are talking about. If you talk about spiritual needs, they gape at you and really do not know what it is you are getting at.

I have talked to many ministers and multitudes of Christian workers, and when I have used the phrase: 'spiritual things', I discovered that they thought I was talking about mysticism and metaphysics. Those may be extreme cases, and there are different levels of that, but we do not have to come out to a very wide circle to discover that there is an awful blindness to spiritual matters and to spiritual needs amongst the people of God. The tragedy is that they do not know that they are "wretched, and miserable, and poor, and blind, and naked," and that is the trouble. It is the condition of the age.

One characteristic of the whole thing, and the explanation, is that things have got big. When they had to fight for their very existence their spiritual condition was different, but when they became successful and big they lost their spiritual power; and that is the position of many Christians, and of many a thing which once had a testimony for God.

When it succeeded on an extensive scale it discovered, or recognized, that it no longer had to fight for its life, and thus, losing its fighting force, it lost its vision and its testimony. It is a good thing to be kept in a place where you have to fight for your life, if it means drawing upon God for spiritual power. God save us from ever getting to the place where we feel it is no longer necessary to fight!

But this is the spirit of the Laodicean age. What is the appeal that is made here? "What the Spirit saith." And what is the Spirit saying in the midst? "Him that overcometh." Overcometh what? This awful state of things, this tragic spiritual weakness, this decline, this blindness, this indifference! The Spirit says, in effect: 'In the midst of this, I want some to rise up and throw this thing off, and get to God in desperation to save the situation.' Will that have our response? The Spirit saith: "To him that overcometh."

Do we respond? Have we an ear to hear what the Spirit saith? Is all this falling merely upon our brains as special teaching, doctrine, and ideas? Oh, *God forbid!*

Believe me, this is not something that has been got up for an address. It has been wrung out almost like blood, and

22

the assaults of the enemy in relation to it have been almost unspeakable. It has been withstood up to the last moment. The enemy has tried to stop it, is to hinder these words and to get us out of it altogether.

There has been awful conflict, day and night. Surely, if that is true, you are not going to regard it as a mere discourse? Surely the Spirit is saying something? What is He saying?

God wants that company of those who may be called overcomers, who, in the power of the Holy Ghost, take upon themselves the burden of the Lord's interests in the universe, to see that He gets His rights to bring about the overthrow of the enemy, to save the spiritual life of many of His people and to maintain His testimony in the earth. Shall we consecrate ourselves to that?

May the Holy Spirit aid us!

The Lord's Testimony and the World Need

The Lord's Testimony and the World Need

1

The World Need: "Life."

Romans 1:1-6

In this matter of the world need; everything can be gathered up in one word, "life." It does not matter where we look we find that that *is* the need.

We have witness borne to that fact in all directions, and we can gather those up into some specific forms of expression.

We begin with the widest range. There is *the witness to the fact in the realm of the ungodly*. Upon that we need not dwell very much, but it is quite patent that the world outside of Christ is showing in a new way, with a new strength, its desire for life, its need of life. It has its own ideas of how that need is going to be met, and its quest for life takes its own peculiar forms, the forms peculiar to the world's own blindness, darkness and ignorance. Nevertheless it is manifest that the world is seeking life. We do not mean by that that it is seeking its life in God. We do not mean by that that it is seeking what we understand by life, Divine life, spiritual life, eternal life, but it is seeking what it would call "life." Life is the thing which it desires.

Passing from that more outward realm, the general mass of ungodly men and women, to inward circles, we have *the witness to this fact* which is clearly borne, (perhaps, again, largely in ignorance) *by what we may call*

3

the nominal Church. As to how far the nominal and secular "Church" is alive to the real nature of its need we may not be able to judge, but it is giving very real evidence of its consciousness of a need, and by the means it employs and the methods it adopts it is showing that life is the thing that it is after.

The very fact that it is entering so strongly into competition with the world along the line of pleasures, and amusements, and entertainments, and many other forms of occupation, is, on the one hand, a proof that it is conscious of the lack of something to satisfy, and, on the other hand, it reveals that only what it would call "life" will justify its existence. Although perhaps unconscious of the full implications of its ways, it is displaying the fact that what is needed is life, and that only life will satisfy. It would say that to be without these things which it adopts is to be dead, and we in that realm—a very superficial realm—hear people speak very often of "a live religious community" because it has many of these activities.

They say : That is a very live Church! and when you ask: What do you mean by being alive? What are the characteristics of this life? the reply is: Oh, it has this, and it has that, it has a dramatic society and a good concert program, and many other things. That is what is meant by being alive.

So its quest is for life; mistakenly, blindly, nevertheless it is all a disclosure of the fact that only life can justify its existence, and only life will meet the need.

Then, moving perhaps a little more inward, *we have the witness of those many doubtful and mixed religious movements,* with their tremendous sweep, things about which we may well have serious questions, to which we could never give our full heart confidence. We see them as religious movements, as Christian movements, with a
4

Gospel in part, in smaller or greater degree, sweeping the earth, and carrying multitudes with them, drawing crowds after them. We ask: What is the secret of the success of these things?

It does not require a very thoroughgoing investigation to disclose that there are serious doubts as to the soundness of their position, of their doctrine. There are serious lacks in some, and there are serious preponderances in others. What is the secret of their sweeping success, and that so many are caught up and carried on by them?

The answer is that these things have a semblance of life, they are the offset against a state of religious spiritual death. They are in contrast with what is merely traditional and historic in Christianity, which has become moribund. It is that which is called "life" about them which draws so many after them, which gives to them their success. And in that realm of these successful(?) Christian movements, when you take the long spiritual, Divine view about success, there is a witness to the fact that, after all, it is life that is needed, that the world in every part needs life.

There is a still more inward sphere where we have *the witness of the spiritually hungry of the Lord's children.* We would not overestimate this; we would not be caught in imagining that things are better in this direction than they are, for you can really only prove that people are spiritually hungry by what they are prepared to sacrifice in order to get their hunger satisfied, and what they are prepared to suffer and endure; But nevertheless, though we might even have to sift this company, there is undoubtedly a hunger amongst the Lord's own children all over the world which is showing itself, which is not difficult to discover.

In almost every place there are those who are altogether disappointed with what there is available of spiritual life

5

and food, and the question which is being asked in all directions is: Where shall we get food? The tremendous increase and development of the Convention movement amongst the Lord's own people is one sidelight upon this fact; the fact that if any servant or servants of God really have something of spiritual food to give they will always find those who are ready for it, and there is always an open door for such ministry.

This, with so many other symptoms, and indications, is a witness to the fact that there is a need, a deep, strong need for life, for what is living, in every realm. That is the general situation as to the world need. It is all gathered up into that word—LIFE.

What do we mean by Life?

But we must analyze and define the word. If we were to ask any of these people what they mean by "life," I think we should discover, whether they used the actual words or not, that what they think of, what their hearts are after, can be expressed mainly in three words:

(1) REALITY. If you asked again: What do you mean by reality? You would be led to understand that what is meant, and what is desired, is a living experience as over against a theory; a doctrine, a creed, a form; that which comes into the inner being as a living reality. Probably the word ''experience'' itself would be used by more than would use any other word, and they mean ''reality.'' Life for them means that which is real, as over against that which is only theoretical, mystical, abstract, a matter of words.

(2) POWER. The second thing which would arise in an inquiry as to what is meant by "life" would be "power." We use the word "dynamic" a good deal. It is life, not merely as something active as over against the inactive,

6

but life which is in the direction of power; being able for this or for that, whatever it may be; being put into a position of ability by having the resource of energy, vitality, effectiveness. It is all gathered up into the word "power."

(3) FULNESS. Thirdly, in the definition of "life" we should undoubtedly be led to understand that what is meant is "fulness." Another word which might be used is "satisfaction," but seeing that man is not easily satisfied, it would require a very great fulness to arrive at real satisfaction. So that "fulness" is a feature of "life."

This sums up the world need—life, which means reality, something which comes within the compass if living experience; which means power, dynamic, force, ability, resource to accomplish, to achieve, to arrive, to be effective, as over against being weak, defeated, failing, never reaching a goal—a sense that you have come into a realm where your deepest need is met, and that you need not seek in any other realm for the answer to that need. That is the world need.

We are concerned with the world need, and the Lord's Testimony, so that we may proceed to see in the Lord's Testimony the answer to the world need. We have touched the world at every point, and the Lord's Testimony, therefore, touches the world at every point. We are not going to dwell with the first realm mentioned, the world of the ungodly; and we are not going to be occupied very much with the second realm, that of the nominal and secular Church; we may be more immediately concerned with the other two, certainly with the fourth, the spiritual hunger of the Lord's people, but we may incidentally touch that realm of doubtful and mixed Christian activity.

The Lords Testimony—the Answer:

"Resurrection."

The Lord's Testimony is the answer to the need at every point, and just as all the need is summed up in the one word "life," so all the answer, as represented by the Lord's Testimony, is summed up in the one word "resurrection."

A very superficial reading of the New Testament will make it perfectly clear that "resurrection" is the key word to New Testament Christianity. If you have not gone through the book of the Acts, for instance, marking the occurrences of the word "resurrection," and noting their connection, you have missed one of the most profitable, helpful and important studies of that book. It is the keyword to the Christianity of the New Testament.

"Resurrection" has also to be defined, just as we have defined "life," and we look to the New Testament to define its own terms. "Resurrection," as defined by the New Testament, means also four things:

Firstly, it means an *entirely new position for man*. Let us give full weight and force to every word; *an entirely new* position for man. "Resurrection," then, means that there is nothing of the old left, that all is new. It means that man is in a position which he has never occupied before, and that in that position there is none of that obtaining which has obtained before. One of the most important things for all the Lord's people to know is that resurrection in union with Christ does mean that everything as to position must be entirely, utterly new.

Secondly, resurrection means that the *basic message of Christianity is the Cross*, because there can be nothing new in this way until all that is old is put away. In order to

8

secure that all is new the Lord very definitely cuts in between the new and the old; and the Cross, therefore, is basic to resurrection, because resurrection has no meaning only in the realm where death has taken place. It is futile, it is foolish, to talk about resurrection with Christ without recognizing that it presupposes death with Christ, and that the resurrection of the Lord Jesus, for any spiritual value in us, demands that the death of the Lord Jesus shall also have had a spiritual effect *in* us.

The Testimony of the Lord is in resurrection, which means an entirely new position for man, and unto that an *utter* winding up of the old position, with all that is related to it.

Thirdly, resurrection means, on the positive side, *an entirely new power in man*. This power is not *of* man, not in any form, of any kind. Life and work in resurrection union with Christ is on the basis of the power which comes from God alone, and not one bit of it from man. It is here that there has been such sad failure in apprehension, that here man can do nothing, man is a minus quantity, man can provide no ground of power for the accomplishment of what lies in the realm of the resurrection of the Lord Jesus.

Everything in that realm is of that nature, that no human power can achieve it either in life or in service. Is it not strange that, although that is made so clear, and although that might be generally accepted as a fact, the whole history of the Church and the history of the majority of Christians contradicts that, that the Church and multitudes of believers have sought both to live as Christians and to do the Lord's work by energies of their own.

Look at the enormous amount of human energy which is poured into Christian activity and counted upon for the

9

accomplishment of Christian ends. Almost entirely what is called "organized Christianity" is upon the basis of man projecting and developing plans, programs, schemes, enterprises, purposes; and drawing in all the human resources of mind and brain, of will, of material, of interest, of enthusiasm, to accomplish those ends, and at the end of these many centuries we find something which, with the enormous development, falls far short of a few short years at the commencement of the Christian era in its power of accomplishment.

See the power of accomplishment in those first years. See how things went down before the Lord's Testimony at the beginning. See how every force which opposed it had to yield. See how even mighty empires, in putting forth all their resource to quench that Testimony, were themselves quenched, while the Testimony went on. And see today the ability of world forces to resist the Testimony, to stand against it, to hold it up! (Perhaps we are wrong in saying the Testimony; we should say organized Christianity.)

What is the meaning? The answer is to be found here, that in resurrection union with Christ the power is altogether other than that of man. It is an entirely new power, to which man has got to yield, and not that which man has got to take hold of and use or try to use. It is an entirely new power, all of God.

Fourthly, an *entirely new knowledge* is bound up with resurrection. Here is what is called "revelation." On resurrection ground there is, for those who are truly there in a living, spiritual way, a new knowledge which is of the character of Divine revelation by the Holy Spirit. To put that in other words, it is a direct teaching of the Holy Spirit to the heart of the believer of that which relates to the

Lord Jesus. That, as differing entirely from accepting a Christian history, a Christian tradition, a Christian story, a Christian doctrine, a Christian creed, something which has become commonly accepted as being the interpretation of Christianity thhrough the centuries, but that which comes directly to the believer as the work of the Holy Spirit in revealing Christ to the heart; revelation, not apart from the Word, the Scriptures, but through the Scriptures; not just grasping the letter of the Scriptures and knowing what is in the Bible as you might know what is in any other book (although you might regard the Bible as different and superior to all other books); but as a shining through the Scriptures, so that the spiritual content is disclosed, not all at once, but progressively, very largely through experience.

It makes necessary the trials and adversities and difficulties, situations of perplexity; paving the way for a disclosure of Christ to meet that particular need. A living, active, practical unveiling of Christ to the heart by the Holy Spirit, an opening up of the great realm of eternal, spiritual reality, as gathered up in the Person of Christ. Resurrection means an inward knowledge after that kind.

We may add one other thing. Resurrection means an *entirely new fulness.* That is, resurrection means the limitless; moving in the realm which has no bounds. A living, spiritual experience brings that consciousness upon you, so that it matters not how long you may have gone on with the Lord, and how much the Lord may have taught you, how full may be your apprehension of the Lord, you are very conscious that you are only yet at the beginning of things, and it matters not how long you go on, you will always remain there, that you are only at the beginning of things. You have come out into the limitless, and there is infinitely more to be known than all that you have known and do know. But the heart is at rest, satisfied in Christ.

Resurrection brings that consciousness, that you have come into fulness, but that fulness is so much beyond you that you know quite well that you can go on for ever. It is a very blessed thing to have ministry in that realm. The question of too many in ministry is: Shall I be able to last out? I shall soon exhaust all the texts in the Bible, and what is going to happen then? *Never.*

It seems that multitudes of preachers have exhausted all the texts in the Bible, and have gone outside for their texts! Resurrection is what is needed. It brings into this realm of a new position, a new power, a new energy, a new fulness, through the Cross. That is the Testimony of the Lord for the world need.

Gathering all that up, and putting it into other words, it means this: The need which is supplied in the Lord's Testimony is, firstly—

An Experimental Knowledge of the Meaning of the Cross.

That is a far more challenging statement than may dawn upon us at the moment. We look into every realm where we see spiritual death, or, as we have put it, the need for life, which means that there is death more or less, and we ask, in every one of those directions where there is death: What is the cause of the death? What will be the way of life?

We find that the cause of death is the fact that either there has been ignorance of or rejection of that meaning of the Cross which has an inward application. In many realms that meaning of the Cross is not known. It is an altogether new revelation. All that is known about the

Cross is that objective work, grand and glorious, but only a part of what Christ has done *for* us by His Cross; and there is little or no knowledge of that vast realm of that other important, essential aspect of the Cross, that what Christ has done for us has got to be made good *in* us. That is, if He died *for* us, the effect of His death has to be registered in us, and we have got to die with Him.

And Christ in death as us is not only the death of sin, but the death of the natural man. He may be a very good man according to the standards of this world, but in the death of Christ, with all his goodness he has died, as well as with all his badness.

That is accepted in, shall we say, an intermediate realm of believers as a doctrine, as a truth, but it goes no further. In another realm that is rejected, and what is called the subjective side of the Cross is refused. You will find in all those realms a lack of spiritual life. There may be much truth, much doctrine, what is called "light."

There may be a good tradition, and a history in the past which was mighty, but you will find there death now, a severe limitation of spiritual life, and you can trace it basically to this fact that the full meaning of the Cross in an experimental way does not obtain there. Therefore the need is for the Cross in its fulness to be brought again into this world, represented, expressed in the lives of the Lord's people. That means, secondly, that—

The Power of His Resurrection has to be made Manifest again in this World.

The thing which muffles the power of God, which neutralizes its expression, works against its exercise, obscures its manifestation, is un-crucified man. If you want to know the power of God nakedly active, all that numbing,

13

deadening, muffling, uncrucified natural man must be got out of the way.

If Paul was an example of the power of God working through a man, then Paul is a clear example of how that which is natural as a ground of strength and wisdom has been set on one side, for this man has been brought down to a very low place of utter dependence upon God for his very life, not only spiritually but physically. "We despaired even of life," he said. "We had the sentence of death in ourselves, that we should not trust in ourselves, but in God which raiseth the dead."

Then, thirdly—

A Holy Ghost living Revelation of Christ.

Not preaching and teaching about Christ, but a Holy Ghost revelation of Christ. These are the things which gather up what we have said.

Unto the meeting of this need there must be vessels. There must be individual vessels, and there must be collective vessels, though they be small. There must be ministries, in all of which these things are true, that the Cross has become a very real thing in the setting aside of what is of nature, of man, in which the power of His resurrection is *the* power which is being exercised, the power which is of God and not of man, in which there is a living apprehension of Christ by the revelation and illumination of the Holy Spirit.

The world need in every sphere is life. The answer of the New Testament is, Yes, but resurrection is the life that is needed. Resurrection means, first of aall, a place of death, so tha there can be resurrection. That is the Cross in its fulness. There must be the working of that Divine power which is all of God and not of ourselves. That must obtain

14

and reign in vessels. There must be not doctrine, not teaching as such, not what is called "light," but there must be revelation by the Holy Spirit through the Word, so that there is a growing apprehension in a living way of the fulness of Christ.

This is resurrection, and this must be expressed, exhibited, maintained in vessels, individual and collective, and in ministries.

Now that is a general survey of the position. There is a great deal more gathered up into that than we have time to mention, but, that being the need, we see the direction in which prayer is needed. We are brought back to seek the Lord with real purpose of heart that, as to ourselves and as to His Testimony in this earth in the nations, He will move to bring these things into a place of reality again, the real meaning of the Cross, where man does let go, and entirely resigns from the work of the Lord in a right way; that is, when what is of man ceases and gives place to what is of God.

But where that is done through a definite experience of the Cross initially and continually the Lord will do a new thing. In a word, the Lord would have crucified men and women, crucified companies of His children, thoroughly crucified instruments, living in the power of God, which is the power of resurrection, living under an open heaven, with the Holy Ghost revealingChrist to the heart. This is the direction for prayer, that He will raise up a ministry after this sort.

2

The Vessel of the Testimony

II Cor. 4:1-7.

More than once we have heard it said that what the world needs today is another Paul. But two things have to be said in answer to that statement. One is that another Paul, or even Paul himself, would hardly get a hearing in the Christian world of today. He would be found to be running too severely counter to the Christianity of our time that it would do with him what Judaism did with the Lord Jesus, and with Paul, at the beginning.

The other thing, which seems somewhat to contradict that is this, that it is very necessary and important to remember that Paul was a representative of the Church, or corporate vessel of the Lord's Testimony for the dispensation, and that the Lord never intended to repeat Paul personally, and to have an individual or personal Paul in every generation of this dispensation.

But what the Lord did intend was that the whole of the Church should be in this dispensation what Paul was. Paul was brought in as a type, a representative, an embodiment of the whole Church for the dispensation, and that which was embodied by His servant Paul was to be the very constitution of the Church. Those features of Paul's spiritual life were to be the constituents of the Church throughout the dispensation, so that we should be nearer the mark if we said that what is needed today is not another Paul but **THE CHURCH ACCORDING TO PAUL**, as spiritually constituted.

It is not the individual or the personal Paul, but it is what came in through and with Paul spiritually, as constituting the Church, the whole Body.

A Chosen Vessel

That is the foundation of our present consideration. We are dealing with the vessel of the Testimony, and we know that right at the outset of Paul's spiritual life that very word is attached to him. In the very first hours of his relationship to Christ in a saving way the words concerning him were: "A chosen vessel unto me." We find that in the full unfolding of his spiritual life he does become a representative vessel, that is, a vessel to which the Church is to be conformed so far as the spiritual elements are concerned.

We are not forgetting that the Church is to take its pattern from Christ; that Christ is the Pattern of the Church, and that the Church takes its character from Christ and is to be conformed to Christ. But Christ has become in a peculiar way revealed to and in and through His servant Paul for practical purposes here in relation to the Church.

It only needs to be said that not in a definite and systematic way was the Church revealed through Christ, but Christ revealed in that definite and systematic way the truth of the Church to and through His servant Paul. It is not the Church of Paul, but the Church of Christ; but the revelation of Christ has come through Paul.

We must remember that no revelation is of value only in so far as it is wrought into the very experience of the person to whom it is given; so that it is Paul's spiritual history and experience which gives value to the revelation, and in that sense the truth has become of practical value because wrought in a man.

When we consider this chosen vessel, this representative vessel, there are quite a few things which are related.

The previous Vessel supplanted

We begin by saying that he, representatively, was the vessel which supplanted the other vessel. Perhaps the best way of explaining that is to turn to the Scripture itself, and compare two passages.

We look at a familiar passage in Jeremiah 18, where we are shown the potter's house, the potter's wheel, and the potter's vessel. Verses 3-4, 6:

> "Then I went down to the potter's house, and, behold, he wrought a work on the wheels. And the vessel that he made of clay was marred in the hand of the potter: so he made it again another vessel, as seemed good to the potter to make it.
> . .O house of Israel, cannot I do with you as this potter? saith the Lord. Behold, as the clay is in the potter's hand, so are ye in mine hand, O house of Israel."

Now note, verses 7-10:

> "At what instant I shall speak concerning a nation, and concerning a kingdom, to pluck up, and to pull down, and to destroy it; If that nation, against whom I have pronounced, turn from their evil, I will repent of the evil that I thought to do unto them. And at what instant I shall speak concerning a nation, and concerning a kingdom, to build and to plant it; If it do evil in my sight, that it obey not my voice, then I will repent of the good, wherewith I said I would benefit them."

Now turn to the letter to the Romans, chapter 9, and verses 21 - 25:

> "Hath not the potter power over the clay, to make out of the same lump one vessel for honor, and one for dishonor? But what if God (though willing to show forth His wrath, and to make known His power) endured with much long-suffering vessels of wrath, fitted for destruction (and cast them not at once away)? And what if thus He purposed to make known the riches of His glory bestowed upon vessels of mercy, which He had before prepared for glory? And such are we, whom He has called not only from among the Jews, but from among the Gentiles, as He saith also in Hosea, 'I will call them my people which were not my people, and her beloved which was not beloved' " (Conybeare).

The implications are perfectly clear from the context. Israel was a nation concerning whom God purposed good. That nation did evil, and the Lord repented Him of the good, and He plucked up that nation. When did He pluck up that nation? Changing the metaphor, it was the day when He cursed the fig tree, and the Jewish nation, which did evil in His sight although He had purposed good for it, was set aside.

That was the first vessel, and it was marred in the hand of the Potter. The Potter proceeds to make another vessel as is good to Him, to take its place, which supplants it, and which will fulfil the purpose which He had in His heart which the other vessel has failed to fulfil. The vessel which supplants the vessel that was is the Church, and Paul is a type of that as the chosen vessel. The whole history of Paul is a clear unveiling of the fact that God has brought in another vessel, which puts Judaism out of the way.

20

Is not that the import of the life of Paul, that Judaism is put away? And was not his supreme conflict with Judaism, the vessel that was still seeking to push itself into the place of God's purpose, but which God had repudiated? The Lord made another vessel, the Church, to be brought into its place. Paul was the very type and spiritually the embodiment of that, so that Paul becomes, as the representative, the vessel which supplants the other vessel.

That carries with it a very definite and wide significance for the Church. It means that in God's thought the Church is a vessel which spiritually fulfils all that purpose which was represented by Israel, but which Israel failed to fulfil. That is a very wide sphere of meditation, as to why Israel was constituted, the purposes of Israel. Those purposes are many and varied, and very wonderful; but Israel failed.

God brings in a new vessel to fulfil those purposes spiritually, to take up all the spiritual things which lay behind what was typical in Israel. We only have to read the letter to the Hebrews (in the writing of which we verily believe Paul had some influence, and a very definite influence) to see that fact established, that in the Church there are spiritually all those things which lay behind the religious life of Israel.

We leave that for the moment with this closing remark, that the Church comes in and is represented by Paul as something which is in the place of a merely external religious system, even though that system may have been in vital relationship with God, even although that may have been brought about by God. Immediately that thing fails to be a spiritual force in the world it ceases to be God's instrument, God's vessel. And the same will have to be said of Christianity, any part of Christianity which goes the same way. Immediately it ceases to be a spiritual force in the world it ceases to be God's instrument. So we draw our first conclusion from this, namely, that the Church is called in to be a spiritual force, and not merely an organized religious system. That is the vessel which comes in with Paul, and is bound up in his person.

A New Cruse

The second thing, which is closely akin to it, is that Paul very clearly represents the new cruse, a newness of the vessel. We are now thinking of the clean and clear cut which is seen in the life of the Apostle between what had been as his life religiously, and that which came in by his new relationship to the Lord Jesus. Things were undoubtedly absolutely new. We do not mean by that that they were just fresh. There is all the difference between freshness and newness. You can make an old thing look fresh, but that is not the sense in which we are thinking of this new vessel. It is not fresh, it is new. It is something which never had been before. It means that there was an entire and final end to one history.

That history of the Apostle Paul before the Damascus Road experience was closed fully and finally. The end came to that history, and an entirely new history began there. The two are divided by three years of solitude in Arabia, and then the beginning of something which was so utterly different from all that had been. There was no carrying over from the past.

It would be well for you to read again thoughtfully these letters of Paul; in order to be confirmed in that one thing, of how completely the past history was closed for him, and how utterly different and new all was from the time when he came to see who Jesus of Nazareth was, and all that was bound up with Him.

Now come back to our point, which is Paul as representative of the vessel of the testimony, the embodiment of all the spiritual features and principles of the Church according to the mind of the heavenly Lord, and in this second thing we find the Church defined as something which is utterly new, carrying over nothing from the old life. It is, in its constitution, in all its members, in all its methods, in all its means, in all that it is and all that it has, something absolutely new. It brings nothing over from the old creation, from the old life; that is, there has been a history brought finally to an end where the Church is concerned.

To put that more simply it means this, that the Body of Christ, the Church which is His Body, is composed of a company of people who have a clean cut between an old history and a new, and who do not bring over into their new realm, their new life, their new service, anything of the old creation, not even religiously.

That has been the snare of the enemy with so many, that while it is admitted that you do not bring over your old sinful ways or old sinful life, you do bring over something religiously. Now Paul is an outstanding example of the fact that that is not so. He will tell us that, so far as his religious life was concerned, it was of the white-heat kind, passionate, intense; "more exceeding zealous," he said. He came to see that it was all wrong, and it was all governed by other forces than the Holy Ghost. You may take it that any life governed by any otherforce than the Holy Ghost is a deceived life. It does not matter, though we may be intensely, and passionately, and utterly devoted to the Lord's interests, if we are putting the strength of our own natural life behind that passion we may be the most deceived of all people.

I never had any doubt, but I am more convinced today than ever I was, that the ground of deception is a strong natural will projected into religious things, and the stronger the natural will projected into spiritual things the deeper the deception.

In the case of Saul of Tarsus you have a terrific will projected into the realm of religion, and he has to confess in the end: "I verily thought that I ought to do many things contrary to the name of Jesus." He did what he thought he ought, and found that he was under deception, it was working in exactly the opposite way to which he thought it was working. There is a terrific danger of projecting any part of our natural life into the things of God.

The church, in the mind of the Lord, is a thing which is new, out from heaven, all its energies and spiritual resource are of the Holy Ghost. You cannot have that until you have definitely closed the old creation history.

This is something for us to lay hold of, if we cannot understand it completely. If it seems somewhat beyond us, nevertheless to lay hold of, as simply as we can. The necessity that the Lord has a vessel which is new, that is, which has its old history of the natural life closed, and is now something altogether under the control, and government, and direction of the Holy Spirit, is something for which to pray, that the Lord shall get a people like that.

That is what we mean when we say that Paul was brought in by the Lord to be a representative of the Church, and the embodiment of the principles of the true Body of Christ. What is needed through this dispensation is that what is revealed through the Apostle Paul should be the nature of the Church: no carrying forward of old creation elements.

Divinely Apprehended

The third thing in this vessel of the testimony was a definite, Divine act of apprehending. Paul spoke of himself as having been apprehended of Christ Jesus. That is how he explained his experience on that road, that he was suddenly, out from heaven, apprehended. He was laid under arrest. It was as though, to speak in our more up-to-date language, the Lord said suddenly: I have got you! I have been on your track for a long time, but now I have got you!

And Paul knew that he was apprehended. But it was a sovereign act, an act from heaven. Our present thought in connection with this apprehending is that he represents the Church in that. The Church is not something which man can make. It is not something constituted by man. It is not something that we can set up, that we can bring about. It is not something which we can organise, and get people to join. We cannot make adherents to the Church.

The Church which is called "the Church" today is very largely made up of those who have come under some sort of human influence, yielding to which they have "joined the Church"; and the trouble after that is to get rid of them, you wish most of them had never joined. When you get on to that level that is bound to be the trouble.

The point is this, that the Church is a Divinely constituted thing, a thing which is the expression of the Divine Sovereignty. All that we can do is preach Christ. The Holy Ghost has to do the rest, and any member not added by the Holy Ghost to Christ will be a weakness to His Body. Apprehended of Christ Jesus! You are very safe when you are on that ground.

The Vessel Liberated

Once more, in this representation of the vessel we see the vessel liberated. Of course, our special means of seeing how completely this was so is Paul's own letter to the Galatians, the key word of which is "liberty," "our liberty in Christ." We know by now what the difficulty was.

Those Judaisers still regarded Judaism as the Church, with its ritual, its form, its system, its order which they desired to impose upon every convert, and cause every believer to observe in the rigid letter of the law. Paul, in his own experience, by his own Divine revelation, stood utterly and absolutely against that whole thing, having seen that Christ is no longer a set of laws and regulations, external rites and forms; but Christ has fulfilled all that in His own Person, and now makes good spiritually to His own the value of that. He is the Altar; God and man meet in Him. He is the Sacrifice; sin is dealt with in Him. He is the Priest; the one Mediator between God and man. He is the very Tabernacle itself, and all gathering together in worship is not now to some temple, to some specific building, of necessity, but anywhere so long as He is the Center; He constitutes the Church.

The Church does not constitute itself by a membership roll and a special building, a place of assembly; it is being together with Christ in the midst which is an expression of the Church. He is the Church by His presence in and with His own. And so you go over the whole system and you find that it has ceased to be some external thing, and it has become purely a spiritual relationship to Christ in a living way.

But the Judaisers said, No! except ye be circumcised you cannot be saved! This and that must be observed as the law! And so the battle raged, and Paul fought through to victory for the liberty of believers from all the law. We have not to fight today that battle with Judaism, but a similar situation has arisen as Christianity has become very largely a system of external forms, rites, orders, largely man-governed, regulated and controlled; and the life has very largely gone out of the whole thing, it is a matter of bondage and spiritual death.

Paul stands as a vessel absolutely liberated from all that sort of thing, and so he is a representation of the Church, whose liberty is of that character that Christ is Everything, and knowing Christ in a living way you have everything. You are not under any kind of external law, and you never need fear that you will break moral laws if you are in a living relationship with the Lord Jesus. The vessel is liberated. "Our liberty in Christ," Paul calls it—

The Vocation of the Vessel

This can be summed up in one word from II Cor 4:6. Paul said: "We have this treasure in earthen vessels. . ." What treasure? The shining forth of the knowledge of the glory of God in the face of Jesus Christ! What is the vocation of the vessel? What is the work, the ministry, of the Church? Unto what are we called as parts of that? For the shining forth of the knowledge of the glory of God in the face of Jesus Christ. That is a great calling, but it is a great searching. We can test Churchmanship by that statement (if we may use that word). We say that we belong to the Church, and we are members of the Church. Well, what about the shining forth of the knowledge of the glory of God in the face of Jesus Christ? That is the purpose of the Church. That is the object of the vessel. Nothing can substitute that, but a very great deal can veil it. We would like to add one word more to this, that in the case of Paul,

27

not only was that true, but there is a marvelous manifestation of God in that vessel, especially in the direction of resurrection life.

It seems that this is one of the primary aspects of the revelation of God in Christ. If you look for the traces of the knowledge of the glory of God in the New Testament you will find that the outstanding trace of that glory of God is the power of His resurrection. Take Paul as an illustration again, and read the whole catalogue of his sufferings, of what he went through, and see him in his brokenness, weakness, feebleness; "in deaths oft," he says, despairing of life, with the sentence of death in him; and yet, what achievement! What ministry! What a tremendous accomplishment! What a range! What a depth! What a fulness! What an endurance! For he is mightier today than he has ever been. How do you explain it? You do not explain it by Paul's physical strength. No!

You do not explain it on any human ground. Though much has been said about his intellect, about his persistence, his wonderful will, and all these things; Paul would repudiate the whole thing, and he does. Here he says: "We have this treasure in vessels of fragile clay, that the exceeding greatness of the power might be of God, and not of ourselves." That is quite definitely saying: I am but a vessel of fragile clay, and if there is any accomplishment, if there is any endurance, if there is any effectiveness, it is to be set down to the power—the exceeding greatness of the power—of God and not of myself! It is God in this vessel, in the power of resurrection life.

Returning to our original thought, we see that Paul is a type of the church as God means it to be in all its members, that there shall be that there which can never be accounted for on human grounds, the power of God in resurrection.

Do you feel like a vessel of fragile clay? What do you follow that up with? Do you say, Well then, I am no good, I can serve no purpose, it is no use expecting anything from me, I have not got what is necessary to be of any use to the Lord! Is that what you are saying, because you feel a vessel of fragile clay? Paul was that, *but* (a mighty "but") you see what is possible through vessels of fragile clay: The exceeding greatness of His power!

The church as we know it today is all the time trying to be something other than a vessel of fragile clay; it does not want the world to look upon it as such. It wants to be something very imposing, which can stand up to the world on its own ground, meet it in its own terms. Yes, it has taken on the very habit, or it has developed the very habit, of trying to impress the world with its *own* resources. But in the New Testament it was a vessel of fragile clay. The comparison between the effectiveness today and the effectiveness then is a very sad comparison.

Now we have to sum up all this in a word of application. We have seen what the vessel of the testimony is, and we must set ourselves more than ever earnestly to pray that the Lord will have a vessel after this kind; that we individually may be such vessels; that companies of the Lord's people here and there may be constituted such vessels; that the Lord may have a vessel, represented by individuals and groups in this earth according to this pattern of his servant Paul, in whom He has given the revelation of His own mind in a living, experimental way as to what the Church, the vessel of the Testimony, should be.

It is that which comes in in a spiritual way, as over against a merely historical and traditional way; that which marks the end of the history of nature, and the beginning of the history of the Holy Spirit in man; that which is

29

sovereignly raised up by the Lord Himself, and not brought about by any activities of man by way of constituting it; that which is absolutely free in Christ, and to whom Christ is Everything, He fulfilling all the need of man as typically represented in the Old Testament—ritual, prophet, priest and king, altar and mercy seat, sacrifice and temple.

He being all that, and in Him the knowledge of the glory of God going forth through vessels of fragile clay in the power of His resurrection. Now you see that is a high thing. Can it be? Is it possible? Is it any use praying the Lord to have something like that? If it is true that that is the Lord's will, if that is the Lord's revelation, we shall be wrong in abandoning anything that the Lord has revealed as His will, though it seem impossible, though its recovery be exceedingly hard, nevertheless it is possible. It is possible in the individual. It is possible in you; it is possible in me, that in some real measure these things shall be true. And if it is possible in individuals, then what is the company but the aggregate of the individuals? Therefore the Lord can do this work. We must pray the Lord to bring about something like this in the earth; not a new sect, a new denomination, a new organization, but His own children living in fellowship with Him on this ground. Let us pray for that very definitely.

3

The Need—God-given Vision

Proverbs 29:18; 1 Sam. 3:1; Zech. 4:1-2,
Acts 26:16-19; Rom. 1:1-3.

Were I asked what I considered to be a need which
embraces the greatest number of vital issues amongst the
Lord's people, I should sum it up in one word, "vision,"
vision God-given.

If you reflect for a few moments you will see that the
Bible is almost entirely a matter of vision, that the whole
of the New Testament Christianity is a matter of vision,
that all Christian life and service which is that in truth is a
matter of vision.

Vision, of course, has two parts. It means something
seen, and it also means a capacity for seeing; something
presented to be seen, and the power of seeing that which
is presented. That is vision. There may be a vision in the
first sense which is not seen, a presentation not discerned.
It would very difficult indeed to estimate the value and the
importance of vision Divinely given.

In the New Testament another word is used for vision.
It is the word "revelation." That is a very comprehensive
word. No matter at what point we touch the New
Testament Christian life we touch vision or revelation.

The Initiation of the Spiritual Life

The initiation, or the initiatory stage, of the Christian
life in the New Testament is seen to be a matter of revelation
or vision. It is a presentation to the heart and a heart

31

apprehension of the Lord Jesus, and unless that is the nature of the beginning of the Christian life there is something essential and vital lacking.

Any Christian life which is simply a matter of giving a mental assent to certain propositions of Christian truth, and the writing down of the name, for instance, upon a slip of paper, saying that you become a Christian, lacks something which is essential to make that Christian life a mighty force.

In the New Testament, the beginnings of the Christian life are a revelation of Christ to the heart, and a heart apprehension of Him. It is a matter of inward spiritual vision. It may be of a very elementary character; it may be very imperfect so far as the fulness of Christ is concerned; but it is sufficient for its immediate purpose, and it is tremendously real to those who have it; to those who are able to say in any form of words: I have come to see the Lord Jesus as my Savior! When that can be said in reality it represents vision, if it is the vision of the heart. When you touch the beginnings of Christian life in the New Testament you are touching vision.

The Continuance of the Spiritual Life

When you touch the continuance of Christian life in the New Testament you are touching vision. The continuance of Christian life is the development, the increase, the progress, which means the greater fulnesses of Christ; and whenever you touch some fuller meaning of Christ in the New Testament, whenever you come to some progress, some movement, some advance, some development, some increase, you will always find it is by fresh vision or revelation. It is a further unveiling, a fuller revelation. It is a new heart apprehension of something presented, and something seen by the enablement of the Holy Spirit. It is so different from merely an intellectual grasp of Christian doctrine, which may fall altogether short of that dynamic power of enlarging the spiritual life.

True progress as we find it in the New Testament is on the basis of a fresh revelation, a fuller revelation, a new vision. So that the true, living believer marks his or her progress by being able to say, as at the beginning, I have come to see the Lord in a new way, in a fuller way; and that with the eyes of the heart being enlightened.

The Consummation of the Spiritual Life

What is true of the initiation and the continuation is true of the consummation of the spiritual life.

If you touch the consummation of the spiritual life in the New Testament you find it has to do with an unveiling of Jesus Christ. What is the consummation of the spiritual life? It is His appearing, and with His appearing there is closely and inseparably linked the completing of our spiritual progress. "Behold what manner of love the Father hath bestowed upon us, that we should be called the children of God." That is the initiation.

"It doth not yet appear what we shall be, *but* when he shall be manifested we also shall be manifested with him . . .*we shall be like him for we shall see him* as he is." That is the consummation of the spiritual life.

We shall be like Him because we shall *see* Him. There is a marvelous changing power in seeing the Lord from the beginning to the end.

Vision Needed for Service

The same thing holds good in service. Touch service in the New Testament, and you find that is bound up inseparably with vision. If the Apostle Paul is an inclusive representation of the true spiritual service, it is patent that the basis of it all with him was vision.

He says: "I was not disobedient unto the heavenly vision." He was constituted a minister and a witness because the Lord appeared unto him. He referred to that in his letter to the Galatians, in words very familiar to us: "It pleased God. . .to *reveal* his Son in me, *that I might preach him* among the nations." Service is bound up with vision.

Vision Emancipates

How important is vision, then, if it really is the background, the foundation, the basis of life and service in relation to the Lord Jesus. Vision has a wonderful power amongst the Lord's people. One of the effects of true vision, God-given vision, is to emancipate them from all that is less than the Lord, and that is no small effect.

It is an emancipating power. This is where vision is needed so badly to-day. The Lord's people are so cramped, so small, so narrow, so bound, so shut in, hedged in, so parochial in their spiritual horizon. They are so limited by the common traditional acceptances, by "as it was in the beginning, is now and ever shall be" so far as a system is concerned. That is something which has become static, fixed.

Paul himself moved in a very rigid and fixed realm, the realm of "Thou shalt," and "Thou shalt not," which had almost countless points of application in the sphere of a very rigid system of religious life, which mainly held him down to this earth.

Then he had the vision of the Lord, and in the day in which he received his God-given vision he was emancipated from this earth, emancipated from everything earth-binding even in a religious way.

He was emancipated from all that which had so rigidly and firmly, and with such terrific power, bound him all his previous life. It is—and we have often referred to it—one of the miracles of the New Testament how a rabid Pharisee, such a deeply dyed Jew as was Saul of Tarsus, should be stripped of the whole of that tyranny and bondage of Judaism, and come right out into a clear place where he said such a thing as this: "For in Christ Jesus neither circumcision availeth anything, nor uncircumcision, but a new creation."

Think of a man like Saul of Tarsus saying that, with all the history behind him, the birth, the upbringing, and the training. It is not easy to get rid of a thing which is in your blood, and has been in your blood for countless generations. It is you to be that; you can never think of anything else. It is no passive thing, but an active, energetic thing in your very being to take that course. That was Judaism.

All that tremendous vehemence of Saul of Tarsus as he was, more zealous than the rest; "I advanced. . .beyond many of mine own age . . .being more exceedingly zealous . . ." he said—all that was in the man's blood. And then you find that man out of it, repudiating it and turning upon it, ready to fight it, with a new force and a new power to lay it low. What has done that? Vision! Not just a mystical vision, but something more than the psychical.

It is the miracle of a revelation of Jesus Christ, and nothing other than that will do it. This kind of vision emancipates from all that is less than the Lord, even though it be of a religious order.

Vision Unifies

Then again, vision, true, God-given vision, is a wonderful unifying and consolidating power. The passage we have taken from the book of Proverbs touches that. The Authorized Version reads: "Where there is no vision, the people perish," but the word "perish," while it is very good, does not really indicate what is there in the Hebrew.

The Revised Version is a little better perhaps, but it only just seems to touch it: "Where there is no vision, the people cast off restraint." More literally it is this: Where there is no vision, the people disintegrate; if you like, go to pieces, fall apart, lose their cohesiveness, lose their solidity. That is very true. You have only to look to the days of Samuel. "In those days there was no frequent vision," and what were those days? Tragic days, terrible days!

One of the tragic fruits of those days was that people said, "Make us a king like unto the nations," by which request they repudiated the theocracy, the Kingship of God, and wanted a man in the place of God. That is always disastrous. Up till that time God had been their King, their Lord; He had been on the Throne, but now they have lost their vision and put a man in His place, and what tragedy it was. The people went to pieces in those days. The Philistines got the upper hand, the Ark went into captivity, everything was marked by weakness, disintegration, the people fell to pieces, there was no vision.

There is a pathetic lack of that cohesion amongst the Lord's people to-day. Why all this disintegration, these fragments, these scattered parts ? Why is there all this division amongst the Lord's people? Why? Because man's interpretations have taken the place of the Holy Spirit's revelation. Is that the truth? Oh, yes, that is true! When

36

the Holy Spirit is in His place, and the people are being illumined and taught by Him there are no two minds; there is one mind, one vision, a wonderful integration.

This is a tremendous need today, that there should be a new revelation by the Holy Spirit to the heart of God's people,so that they come into that revelation of Christ which the Holy Spirit gives, and with revelation they become one people, dominated by one vision. That is how it was at the beginning.

You say: You are putting forth a counsel of perfection, something for which we dare not hope in these days. Well, I do dare to hope for it; not as embracing all the Lord's people, but I believe a far greater measure of this is possible than now exists. We are called to prayer that the Lord will give a vision to His ministering instruments in this day which will bring His people into a new revelation of Himself, and thus bind them together, not as an organization, nor as a multitude of people who are accepting a certain interpretation, but bind them together by spiritual ties, because they have come to see the Lord in a new way.

And all that we are asking for is that there shall be such a ministration of Christ by revelation of the Holy Spirit in this earth, that all that is less than Christ will go, and people will be bound to the Lord Himself. And if they are bound to Him, then there will be oneness, the falling apart will cease.

Vision Sustains

Then again, what a sustaining power vision is. Take the Apostle Paul again as an example. What was it that kept him going? If ever a man (speaking naturally) ought to have given up, it was he. I can conceive of Paul having resigned at quite a few places. If you or I had been the

37

pastor of the Church at Corinth, I think we should have resigned very quickly. Perhaps at some of the other places too we should have chosen a roving pastorate (if that is not a contradiction of term), because we could not endure it.

But Paul stuck to it to the end; even when they gave him up he did not give them up. And how much he suffered, how much there was to make him break down, but he went through until he could say: "I have finished my course, I have kept the faith." I can hear an echo even of the Master's words in that, in another sense: "No man taketh it from me, I lay it down of myself." It is a continuing unto the end by the power of God. But what was it that kept him going through? It was his vision of the Lord. It was the heavenly vision. It is a great sustaining power, this unveiling of Christ.

The Nature of the Vision

To say that it is a vision of Christ that we need may not get us very far, although we may see the need of it and the value of it.

Paul says here that by the prophets concerning His Son revelation has been given in the Scriptures. But what we want to see, what we need to see, is that in the New Testament we have a gathering up in a spiritual way of the deeper meaning of the visions of the prophets. In this word at the commencement of the Roman letter, where the Apostle says that we have received that which was promised through the prophets concerning His Son, we have at least the suggestion that what is in the New Testament is the spiritual value of what the prophets saw, of what is in the vision of the prophets.

We can only stay to indicate what we mean, and illustrate it in one or two instances. We have said that in
38

the New Testament we have in a spiritual way, for our own apprehension of Christ, that which was behind the vision of the prophets in truth and in principle. Let us take perhaps four illustrations from the prophetic vision.

The Vision of Christ as Sovereign Head of the Church

We turn to the prophet Isaiah, in chapter 6 of his prophecies, and read that which is very familiar: "In the year that king Uzziah died I saw the Lord, sitting upon a throne, high and lifted up, and his train filled the temple." The Gospel concerning His Son, promised through the prophets in the Scriptures. What is the Gospel in that? That is vision! What is our New Testament value of that? The New Testament is full of the Lord high and lifted up, sitting upon a Throne, and the New Testament is full of His train filling the Temple. What is that in other terms?

It is the absolute Sovereignty of Jesus Christ as Head of His Church. ". . . raised him from the dead, and made him to sit at his right hand in the heavenlies ("sitting upon a throne"), far above all rule, and authority, and power, and dominion . . . ("high and lifted up") and gave him to be head over all things to the church, which is his body, the fulness of him that filleth all in all ("his train filled the temple")."

It is a revelation of Christ in His Sovereign Headship over all things to the Church which is His Body, which is to be the fulness of Him. Get a vision of that.

Get a revelation of that to your heart by the Holy Spirit, and see its emancipating power and its sustaining power. And that is for present revelation to the heart. That is the thing which the Lord has been seeking to reveal to our hearts more and more for a long time.

The point is this, that, inasmuch as that is the side of

39

vision presented, you and I have to seek the Lord for spiritual capacity to see it.

And that leads us to that other fragment in the same letter, from which we have just quoted: "That he would grant unto you a spirit of wisdom and revelation in the knowledge of him, the eyes of your hearts being enlightened. . ." "The eyes of your hearts being enlightened"! That is the other side of vision.

Will you pray this for yourself? Will you pray this for all God's people? When the Lord's people get a new spiritual Holy Ghost revelation of the Sovereign Headship of Christ, and begin to hold fast the Head, they let go of everything that is local, and personal, and different, and scattered on the earth. That is the place to which to come for unity. We cannot be at variance with one another as the Lord's children if Christ is absolute Sovereign Head in our lives. When the Lord Jesus gets the complete mastery as Head in our lives, then all independence of action, and life, and all self-will, self-direction, self-seeking, self-glory and self-vindication, will go. These are the things which set us apart from one another.

You pass from Isaiah, and as you do so you remember that you have the results of such a vision seen in this man Isaiah. Such a vision immediately has the effect of humiliating him to the dust. Oh, yes, we lose all our pride, all our importance when once we see the Lord in glory. "Woe is *me*. . ." That is humiliation! Then, after humiliation, there is consecration: "Lo, this hath touched thy lips; and thine iniquity is taken away, and thy sin purged." And, "after humiliation and conse-cration, there comes vocation: ". . .who will go for us?" "Then I said, Here am I; send me."

A life suitable to the Lord's purposes in service is altogether the result of a revelation of the absolute

40

Sovereign Lordship and Headship of Jesus Christ. It comes out of that. So it was in the New Testament. Go to the book of the Acts and you will see that the service which flowed out there flowed out from the exaltation of Christ which they had seen.

The Vision of Christ in Universal Dominion

Passing, then, from Isaiah, and Ephesians, and Colossians, we move to Daniel. We have to be fragmentary. We cannot go right through Daniel's visions, but, summing up the visions of Daniel, what is the main result?

Is it not the course of this world's history moving toward Christ as its consummation? The empires pass like a pageant before the spiritual eyes of this prophet. In swift succession by this vision he sees these mighty world empires, each one going down before its successor.

And then at the end he sees a stone, cut without hands, break into the history of this world, and a Kingdom set up, the end of which is not seen and never will be seen; and the dominion, and the authority given to the people of the Most High, and Him coming to reign Whose right it is to reign; the consummation of the history of this world. The pageantry of empires all moving toward Christ.

That is a great thing to apprehend spiritually, but the spiritual value of that is caught up immediately in the letter to the Colossians as well as in other places in the New Testament, and them it is made perfectly clear that God's predestined purpose for this world is that Christ shall at the end be All and in all, absolutely pre-eminent universally, and that, although it may seem that other powers are controlling this world's history, there are mighty forces coming in and swaying it, and seeming to touch its destiny.

As Daniel saw these forces at work, as he saw, for

41

instance, the conquests of Alexander the Great throughout this world, no doubt he wondered what the end of this was to be. This man had captured and conquered everything, subdued everything, and he had no more worlds to conquer, he had absolute dominion. And then Daniel saw Alexander the Great smashed with a blow, cut off before he reached middle life, and another power coming in. And Daniel looked on!

What will the end of this be? He sees the end in the hands of the Son of Man. You look out on the world to-day, and you might well say, looking at it naturally: Well, what will happen next? Things are going from bad to worse! Look at the state of things!

Look at that awful thing which has its home in Russia, and what it is able to do; the millions of its own children within its own borders done to death on the slightest pretext of allegiance to God! You see that and other things in this world, and you say: What will the end be?

Well, the end will be Jesus on the throne of universal dominion; nothing can hinder that! Get that into your heart, and see what a power that vision will have. Vision has mighty power. Where there is no vision the people will certainly go to pieces. You would go to pieces if you were left a prey to these world conditions, and if they were all that you could see; men's hearts truly failing them for fear; but it makes all the difference when you have vision.

Colossians I settles it once and for all. "In him were all thing created. . . all things have been created through him, and unto him; and he is before all things, and in him all things hold together," and He is destined by the eternal counsels of God ultimately to have pre-eminence in all things. The first chapter of the letter to the Colossians is the spiritual summing up of the visions of Daniel.

42

The Vision of the Church which is His Body

Pass swiftly from Daniel to Ezekiel, and amongst many visions of God which Ezekiel had we just select one, with which we are very familiar, from chapter 40, the vision of the temple which never has been yet, the temple which is for the end.

The vision there is of an angel with a measuring rod— a reed—going in and measuring the court, measuring the temple, putting down precisely to a detail the measurement of everything related to that temple; the walls, their height, their length, their breadth; every passage, every corridor, every chamber, every vessel; all put down in its exact dimensions.

Then it is precisely stated what these things are for; what this chamber is for, and what that chamber is for. Everything is described, in its nature, its dimensions, and its purpose. And then out from the temple the river, from beneath the altar, issuing, gaining volume, depth, width, strength as it goes on and on. The trees on either side, bearing fruit continually, with leaves never fading. You say: What is the Gospel of that? Well, again you look to the letter to the Ephesians, and you have the whole thing quite clearly and precisely described and explained for you.

This temple has its counterpart spiritually in this dispensation in the Church which is His Body; and here in this temple we have Christ presented as the Church, and the measurements of Christ into which His people are to come, so that every one has to function, as Paul says in that letter "in due measure" (Ephes.4:16).

That is your measure in Christ. Do not fall short of it, and do not try to exceed it. And then coming up to our measure when we are together; Paul says, "Till we all attain unto the unity of the faith. . .unto a full-grown man, unto

43

the measure of the stature of the fullness of Christ."

Not only have we a degree, but we have a place in which to function in Christ, for there are in this Temple the places of ministry, and every one has his appointed place in ministry, and every joint is to function, every member to fulfil his office: "For as the body is one, and hath many members . . ." (I. Cor 12:12) ". . . and all the members have not the same office" (Rom. 12:4,) yet they all have an office; not all the same, but all having a ministry.

Then there are these chambers for rest for the servants of the Lord. The resting places! And you and I have come to rest in Christ. We are so familiar with this that it strikes no new note of wonder in our hearts, but the Gospel is there in it all, and has come by revelation through the prophets.

If only you and I had that vision, of the Church which is His Body, the wonderful heavenly order, that every one of us is given a measure "according to our measure," and that we have to be effective in that measure! Every one of us is given a place in Christ, and every one of us is given a ministry in Christ, and every one, because we have a place and a measure and a ministry, may know our own rest in Christ.

The spiritual revelation of the Church as the Body of Christ is a wonderful thing, and when we see the Church like that how we feel ashamed of ourselves that ever we thought of some institution down here on this earth being the Church.

In this heavenly revelation of what the Church is; all the saints in their place, respectively, coming up to their measure in Christ, fulfilling their ministry in Christ; that is the Church, the Temple, "a holy temple in the Lord."

Will you pray for that vision, that revelation? Will you

pray that the Lord's people everywhere may have that brought to them? It is something to pray about! That is a need today.

The Vision of the "Overcomer" Vessel

We close with just a word from Zechariah. Amongst the visions of Zechariah is that one from which we have already read in chapter 4. "And the angel . . .waked me, as a man that is wakened out of his sleep. And he said unto me, What seest thou? And I said, I have seen, and behold, a candlestick all of gold. . ."

A candlestick all of gold! What is that in New Testament revelation? It is an instrument here on this earth which is wholly of God for bearing the Testimony of Jesus; something wholly of God; not man-made, man-constituted, but something which God has produced, in which there is the flaming Testimony of Jesus by the oil of the Holy Spirit.

Who shall say that the Lord does not need that today? Who will say that the Lord's people do not need to come back to that, or to go on to that, be for Him a vessel, an instrument, which is wholly God-constituted, made up of those Divine elements of the pure gold in which the Testimony flames and burns, and does not go out, because the unceasing oil of the Spirit is flowing unhindered? It is not impossible! It is not beyond the Lord's will for now.

These are parts of the vision of the Lord Jesus. They are only aspects of Christ, are they not? This is what we mean by the revelation of Jesus Christ. You see Him Head of the Church, Sovereign Lord, so related to His Body that He is the Body and His Body is Himself spiritually.

And then all that that means of place and measure and ministry and enjoyment of the Lord. Then the Lord as here expressed in a vessel which is all of Himself, with His

Testimony livingly, flamingly in it.

Let this not be merely visionary. Ask the Lord to save you from the thing becoming visionary in that sense, but, oh, do pray that this which is Christ may become a living revelation in your heart. It is not something of the mind or of the imagination.

Beloved, this is real!

It can be put in colder language and terser terms, but this is the thing which has become the passion of some of our hearts; this is the thing which has emancipated some of us; this is the thing which is sustaining some of us; this is the thing which is constituting the ministry of some of us; and so we can say this is the thing which is holding some of us together, whereas nothing else would hold us together. It is the Holy Spirit's enablement of us to apprehend Christ.

We will close by asking the question of the angel: "What seest thou?" What is your vision? In the first place have you got a vision? Everything of life, and progress, and ministry springs out of vision, otherwise it counts for nothing. What seest thou? It is also important, when we have a vision, to be able to declare our vision. If you have a vision, can you state it? Can you declare it? Is it locked up in you?

All this leads, then, for the future to very definite prayer. This is the direction for prayer—the Lord's Testimony in reality, a vessel for that Testimony, true spiritual vision, the revelation of Christ to the heart.

The Lord's people everywhere need vision.

Let us pray that their eyes may be opened, that we may be, as far as possible, given an eye-opening ministry, that it might be true of us: ". . . to whom I send thee, to open their eyes, that they may turn from darkness to light, and from the power of Satan unto God, that they may receive remission of sins and an inheritance among them that are sanctified by faith in me."

"Where there is no vision, the people perish. " "I was not disobedient unto the heavenly vision." Let us ask the Lord to give us the vision Himself.

Give me The Vision. Lord that I may see you! Lord that I may know you! Lord that I may know you!